Identity and Ethos

Sol Liptzin

Identity and Ethos

A Festschrift for Sol Liptzin on the Occasion of His 85th Birthday

edited by
Mark H. Gelber

PETER LANG
New York · Berne · Frankfurt am Main

Library of Congress Cataloging in Publication Data

Identity and Ethos.

Includes bibliographies.
1. Yiddish literature - History and criticism.
2. German literature - Jewish authors - History and criticism. 3. Jews in literature. 4. Hebrew literature, Modern - United States - History and criticism. 5. American literature - Jewish authors - History and criticism. 6. Bible in literature.
7. Liptzin, Solomon, 1901- . I. Liptzin, Solomon. II. Gelber, Mark H.
PJ5120.5.I34 1986 839'.09'09 86-7191
ISBN 0-8204-0328-8

CIP-Kurztitelaufnahme der Deutschen Bibliothek

Identity and Ethos: A Festschr. for Sol Liptzin on the Occasion of His 85. Birthday / ed. by Mark H. Gelber. - New York; Berne; Frankfurt am Main: Lang, 1986.
ISBN 0-8204-0328-8

NE: Liptzin, Sol: Festschrift; Gelber, Mark H. [Hrsg.]

Printed by Lang Druck, Inc., Liebefeld/Berne (Switzerland)

Foreword

The essays collected in this *Festschrift* have been written by colleagues, friends, students, and admirers of Sol Liptzin, to be presented to him on the occasion of his 85th birthday. The essays are concerned with topics within the domains of literary and cultural study pursued and enriched by Sol Liptzin himself: (I) Yiddish literature, (II) German-Jewish studies and German literature proper, (III) English-German literary relations, (IV) Jews and Jewish literature in America, (V) Biblical themes in world literature and Jewish cultural history. My hope is that this modest testimony to Sol Liptzin's work will represent some of the range and coherence of his scholarly efforts. The partial, selected bibliography of his publications included in this volume indicates, in a complementary way, the scope and energy of his engaging and lively mind.

Sol Liptzin was born on July 27, 1901 in Satanov, Russia, and came to New York at the age of nine. He was educated at the College of the City of New York (B.A. 1921) and at Columbia University (M.A. 1922, Ph.D. 1924). From 1923 until 1963, he was a member of the faculty of C.C.N.Y., serving as Professor of Comparative Literature (1933-1963) and chairing the Department of Germanic and Slavic Languages (1942-1958). He has been Visiting Professor at Northwestern University, the University of California, Los Angeles, Yeshiva University, and Bar-Ilan University. He immigrated to Israel and taught as Fulbright Lecturer at Tel Aviv University and Rothschild Lecturer at the Technion (Haifa), before becoming Professor and Dean of the Faculty of the Humanities at the American College in Jerusalem (1968-1974). Today, he continues his scholarly pursuits as professor emeritus at his home in Jerusalem.

On behalf of those who care for Sol Liptzin, I wish to thank him for all he has given us over the years and for being the very special, warm, and generous person he is. May he and his wife Anna be well and enjoy many more years of happiness together, and may we be near them to wish them well, when they arrive at the Biblical age of 120!

I would like to thank collectively all of those who enthusiastically supported the idea of this *Festschrift* from its inception, especially the scholars, whose participation contributed directly to its realization, and the many former students of Sol Liptzin, whose warm outpouring of gratitude and support testifies to his durable pedagogical impact at the City College of New York for over four decades. Special thanks are due to Professors Harry Zohn, Jeffrey Sammons, Noam Flinker, and Donald Daviau for their advice and encouragement, and to Sol Liptzin's daughters, Karen Sitton and Yelva Lynfield, for their attentive, familial concern, which helped insure publication on time. Also, I am sincerely grateful to Suzi Ganot for her devoted secretarial help and to Ben-Gurion University, which supported this project in diverse ways, too numerous to detail here. Finally, I wish to thank my wife Jody for her assistance at every stage of this project.

Mark H. Gelber

Contents

Sol Liptzin – Bibliography (Selected): 1920-1986

1920
"My Shield," (pseudonym O.S.) *City College Mercury*, LXI, No. 5 (1920), 2.

1921
"Lafcadio Hearn," *City College Mercury*, LXII, No. 1 (1921), 7-8.

"Ernest Dowson," *City College Mercury*, LXII, No. 3 (1921), 8-9.

1924
Shelley in Germany (New York: Columbia University Press, 1924).

1926
The Weavers in German Literature (Göttingen: Vandenhoeck & Ruprecht, 1926).

"Gottfried Kinkel and Hermann Semmig," *The Germanic Review*, I, No. 2 (1926), 120-124.

"Chamisso as a Social Poet," *Philological Quarterly*, V, No. 3 (1926), 235-241.

1927
"The Lyric of Nascent Modern Realism," *The Germanic Review*, II, No. 4 (1927), 298-311.

1928
Lyric Pioneers of Modern Germany (New York: Columbia University Press, 1928).

Heine (Richmond, Va.: Johnson Publishing Co., 1928).

1929
From Novalis to Nietzsche (New York: Prentice-Hall, 1929).

Review. Gunther Keil, *Max Kretzer. A Study in German Naturalism* in *The Journal of English and Germanic Philology*, XXVIII, No. 3 (1929), 459-460.

1930
"Richard Beer-Hofmann," *Monatshefte für deutschen Unterricht*, XXII, No. 4 (1930), 103-109; 133-140.

Review. F.A.H. Leuchs, *The Early German Theatre in New York* in *The Journal of English and Germanic Philology*, XXIX, No. 2 (1930), 313-314.

Review. J. A. Hess, *Heine's Views on German Traits of Character* in *Monatshefte für deutschen Unterricht*, XXII, No. 1 (1930), 28.

1931

"The Genesis of Schnitzler's 'Der Einsame Weg,' " *The Journal of English and Germanic Philology*, XXX, No. 3 (1931), 392-404.

"The Genesis of Schnitzler's 'Das Weite Land,' " *Publications of the Modern Language Association*, XLVI, No. 3 (1931), 860-866.

"The Genesis of Schnitzler's 'Professor Bernhardi,' " *Philological Quarterly*, X, No. 4 (1931), 348-355.

1932

Arthur Schnitzler (New York: Prentice-Hall, 1932).

"The Call of Death and the Lure of Love," *The German Quarterly*, V, No. 1 (1932), 21-36.

"Arthur Schnitzler," *Books Abroad*, VI, No. 1 (1932), 16-17.

Review. Deutsche Literatur in Entwicklungsreihen, Bd. IV and Bd. VI in *Modern Language Notes*, XLVII, No. 3 (1932), 179-181.

Review. Arthur Schnitzler, *Der blinde Geronimo und sein Bruder* in *Monatshefte für deutschen Unterricht*, XXIV, No. 5 (1932), 166.

1936

Historical Survey of German Literature (New York: Prentice-Hall, 1936).

Richard Beer-Hofmann (New York: Bloch Publishing Co., 1936).

From Novalis to Nietzsche (New York: Prentice-Hall, [Second Printing Revised], 1936).

1937

Review. Dorothy Lasker-Schlitt, *Grillparzer's Attitude toward the Jews* in *The German Quarterly*, X, No. 3 (1937), 155-156.

"The Eternal Road – Not our Road," *Ramah*, I (1937), 33-35.

1938

Review. Hans B. Bussmann, *Hundert Meister der deutschen Sprache* in *The German Quarterly*, XI, No. 1 (1938), 54.

"The Apocalyptic Novels of Thomas Mann and Jakob Wassermann," *Ramah*, I, No. 1 (1938), 19-22.

1939

"Early History of the A.A.T.G. (1926-1931)," *The German Quarterly*, XII, No. 1 (1939), 20-30.

"Jewish Writers in German Literature," *Zukunft*, XLIV, No. 4 (1939), 20-30.

"Weltanschauung of Contemporary Germany," *Zukunft*, XLIV (1939), 459-462.

1940

"Reviewing a Review," *Monatshefte für deutschen Unterricht*, XXXVII, No. 6 (1940), 296-297.

1941

Richard Beer-Hofmann, "Lullaby for Miriam," (Translated by Sol Liptzin) *Poet-Lore*, XLVII, No. 4 (1941), 290.

"Young Vienna," *Poet-Lore*, XLVII, No. 4 (1941), 337-346.

Review. Franz Werfel, *Embezzled Heaven* in *Jewish Digest*, I, No. 4 (1941), 92-94.

Review. Alex Bein, *Theodor Herzl* in *Jewish Digest*, I, No. 7 (1941), 86-87.

Review. S. Posener, *Adolphe Cremieux, A Biography* in *Jewish Digest*, I, No. 8 (1941), 91-92.

"Richard Beer-Hofmann and the Jewish Renascence," *Jewish Digest*, I, No. 9 (1941), 41-45.

Review. A. A. Roback, *The Story of Yiddish Literature* in *The Modern Language Journal*, XXV, No. 8 (1941), 666-667.

1942

"A Comparison of Three Translations," *Yidishe Shprakh*, Vol. II, No. 1 (1942), 1-15.

Review. Isacque Graeber and Stewart, H. Britt (Eds.), *Jews in a Gentile World – The Problem of Anti-Semitism* in *Survey Graphic*, XXXI, No. 5 (1942), 260-261.

1943

"Edwin Carl Roedder at Seventy," *Monatshefte für deutschen Unterricht*, XXXV, No. 3/4 (1943), 97-100.

"Attitudes towards Heine's Jewishness in England and America," *Yivo Bleter*, XXII, No. 2 (1943), 163-177.

"Salons," *The Universal Jewish Encyclopedia*, IX, 329.

"Young Vienna," *Dictionary of World Literature* (Philosophical Library Inc.), 632-633.

"Heinrich Heine, 'Blackguard' and 'Apostate.' A Study of the Earliest English Attitude Towards Him," *PMLA*, LVIII, No. 1 (1943), 170-180.

"Heinrich Heine and the Early Victorians," *Monatshefte für deutschen Unterricht*, XXXV, No. 7 (1943), 353-364.

"Heinrich Heine, Hellenist and Cultural Pessimist. A Late Victorian Legend," *Philological Quarterly*, XXII, No. 3 (1943), 267-277.

Yivo's Way (New York: Yiddish Scientific Institute, 1943).

1944

Germany's Stepchildren (Philadelphia: Jewish Publication Society of America, 1944).

"Heine, the Continuator of Goethe. A Mid-Victorian Legend," *Journal of English and Germanic Philology*, XLIII, No. 3 (1944), 317-325.

"Heine, the Bard of Democracy: A Contemporary English Legend," *The German Quarterly*, XVII, No. 2 (1944), 55-66.

Review. Stanton Lawrence Wormley, *Heine in England* in *The Journal of English and Germanic Philology*, XLIII, No. 3 (1944), 369-371.

Review. Heinrich Heine, *Buch der Lieder* in *Monatshefte für deutschen Unterricht*, XXXVI, No. 6 (1944), 318.

"Is Yiddish the Language of the Uneducated Jew?" *Yidishe Shprakh*, IV, Nos. 3-6 (1944), 120-122.

1945

Yivo in America (New York: Yiddish Scientific Institute, 1945).

"Ben Hecht und Waldo Frank – Flaming Wrath and Olympian Detachment," *Yivo Bleter*, XXV (1945), 111-119.

Review. Heinrich Heine, *Germany. A Winter's Tale* in *Jewish Social Studies*, VII, No. 2 (1945), 177-179.

"Neo-Assimilation," *Yivo Bleter*, XXVI, No. 2 (1945), 321-323.

"The Contemporary Jew: A Legend," *The Jewish Post* (Winnipeg), Vol. XXI, No. 7 (Feb. 15, 1945), 2, 6.

1946

"Richard Beer-Hofmann – A Biographical Essay," in Richard Beer-Hofmann, *Jacob's Dream* (Philadelphia: Jewish Publication Society of America, 1946), 1-26.

"German Literature," in J. T. Shipley (Ed.), *Encyclopedia of Literature* I (New York: Philosophical Library), 330-358.

"International Themes in Peretz's *Self Sacrifice*," *Yivo Bleter*, XXVIII, No. 1 (1946), 153-156.

Peretz (New York: Yivo, 1947).

Columbia Dictionary of Modern European Literature (New York: Columbia Univ. Press, 1947). Articles on:
"Hermann Bahr," "Richard Beer-Hofmann," "Mendele Mokher Sforim," "Yitzak Leibush Peretz," "Felix Salten," "Arthur Schnitzler," "Sholem Aleikhem."

Review. Heinrich Heine, *Jüdisches Manifest* (Ed. Hugo Bieber) in *Jewish Social Studies*, IX, No. 2 (1947), 181-182.

"Yiddish: A Living Language," *The City College Alumnus*, XLII, No. 10 (1947), 8-10.

Review: S. Niger, *Short Story Writers and Novelists* in *Jewish Social Studies*, IX, No. 3 (1947), 265-266.

1948

Review. Otto Oberholzer, *Richard Beer-Hofmann, Werk und Weltbild des Dichters* in *Modern Language Notes*, XLIII, No. 5 (1948), 359-360.

"Introduction" in M. W. Grafstein (Ed.), *Sholem Aleichem Panorama*, in *Jewish Observer* (1948), 12-13.

"Sholom Aleichem Scans America," in *Sholom Aleichem Panorama, ibid.*, 30-31.

"Attitudes toward Heine's Jewishness in England and America," *Yivo Annual of Jewish Social Science*, II (1948), 69-80.

1950

Review. Guido Kisch, *The Jews in Medieval Germany* in *Jewish Horizon* (1950), 17.

Eliakum Zunser, Poet of His People (New York: Behrmann House, 1950).

Review. Mark Wischnitzer, *To Dwell in Safety* in *Jewish Frontier*, XVII, No. 7 (1950), 26.

"Goethe and Beer-Hofmann," *PMLA*, LXV (1950), 641-644.

Review. A. J. Heschel, *The Earth Is the Lord's* in *Jewish Social Studies*, XII, No. 4 (1950), 415-6.

1951

"*Daniel Deronda* (on the 75th Anniversary of its Publication)," *Jewish Book Annual,* (1951-52), 43-46.

1952

"Abraham Mapu, Dreamer of Zion," *Jewish Book Annual*, XI (1952-53), 172-175.

"Jewish Culture and its Books," *Jewish Horizon* (1952), 9.

1953

Review. Y. L. Cahen, *Studies in Jewish Folklore* in *Jewish Bookland* (1953), 7.

Review. Maurice Samuel, *Level Sunlight* in *Jewish Bookland* (1953), 1.

Eliakum Zunser (Tel Aviv: Tversky, 1953).

1954

Review. Oskar Seidlin (Ed.), *Correspondence between Arthur Schnitzler and Otto Brahm* in *Graduate School Record* (Ohio State University), VII (1954), 7-8.

Review. The L.M. Stein Book in *Jewish Bookland* (1954), 4.

"After Three Hundred Years. The Literary Legend of the Jew – and the Reality," *Jewish Book Annual*, XII (1954), 3-16.

The English Legend of Heinrich Heine (New York: Bloch Pub. Co., 1954).

1955

"A Call for Decision," *Congress Weekly* (March 14, 1955), 5-9.

Review. Uriel Weinreich (Ed.), *The Field of Yiddish* in *Congress Weekly* (April 4, 1955), 14-15.

Review. The Jewish People, Past and Present. Vol. IV: 300 Years of Jewish Life in the United States, in *Congress Weekly* (May 2, 1955), 14-15.

"Folk Playwright – The Drama of Goldfaden," *Menorah Journal*, XLIII, No. 1/2 (1955), 50-65.

Review. M. M. Kaplan, *A New Zionism* in *Jewish Bookland* (1955), 106.

"A *Ba'al T'shuva* Comes Home," *Jerusalem Post* (Sept. 16, 1955), 8.

"Thomas Wolfe and the Jews," *Davar* (Oct. 28, 155), 5.

"Poetess of Jewish Heroism," *Congress Weekly* (Nov. 14, 1955), 4-8.

"City of the Young," *Congress Weekly* (Dec. 5, 1955), 9-11.

"Heinrich Heine's Homecoming," *Jewish Book Annual*, XIII (1955-56), 55-57.

1956

"Origin y Desarrollo del idioma Yidish," *Tribuna Israelita* (Mexico City), (1956), 26-27.

"The World of Bergelson," *Congress Weekly* (May 7, 1956), 7-8.

"Emma Lazarus," *Davar* (August 3, 1956), 5.

"Ludwig Lewisohn and his Doubts about America," *Davar* (August 24, 1956), 5.

Review. Justine Wise Polier and James Wise (Eds.), *The Personal Letters of Stephen Wise* in *Jewish Bookland* (1956), 1.

1957

"David Pinski, Nestor of Yiddish Literature," *Jewish Book Annual*, XV (1957), 84-87.

1958

"A Revaluation of Abraham Goldfaden," *Congress Weekly* (Dec. 8, 1958), 10-12.

Encyclopedia Hebraica, IX: "Hermann Bahr," "David Bergelson," "Richard Beer-Hofmann," "Berl Broder," "Hermann Broch," "Bertold Brecht," "Clemens Brentano," "Aron Bernstein."

Review. Philip Friedman, *Their Brother's Keeper* in *Historia Judaica*, XX (1958), 141f.

1959

"Introduction," in Rachmil Bryks, *A Cat in the Ghetto* (New York: Bloch Pub. Co., 1959), 7-9.

"Sholom Aleichem's Jews Laughed," *Congress Bi-Weekly* (March 16, 1959), 4-7.

"Pinski: Last of the Yiddish Masters," *Congress Bi-Weekly* (Nov. 30, 1959), 10-12.

Review. Hannah Arendt, *Rahel Varnhagen* in *Historia Judaica*, XXI (1959), 58-59.

Review. E. M. Butler, *Heinrich Heine* in *Journal of English and Germanic Philology*, LVIII, No. 1 (1958), 171-173.

1960

"Yiddish Drama, A Century's Survey," *Jewish Book Annual*, XVIII (1960), 12-19.

"S.S. Frug, Poet of Sorrow and Hope," *Congress Bi-Weekly* (April 4, 1960), 9-11.

"Herzl's Literary Apprenticeship," *Congress Bi-Weekly* (Dec. 19, 1960), 15f.

Review: Armin Arnold, *Heine in England and America* in *The German Quarterly* XXXIII, No. 3 (1960), 395-396.

1961

"The Yiddish Press, A Century's Survey," *Jewish Book Annual*, XIX (1961), 60-66.

Review. Henry M. Rosenwald, *The Age of Romanticism* in *The German Quarterly*, XXXIV, No. 1 (1961), 89-90.

1962

"Mendele Mocher Sforim," *Jewish Affairs* (Johannesburg), (July), 30-35.

Review. Edgar Rosenberg, *From Shylock to Svengali* in *Revue des Études Juives* (January, 1962), 228-230.

Review: Wolfgang Mauser, *Karl Hillebrand* in *The German Quarterly*, XXXV, No. 2 (1962), 241-243.

1963

The Flowering of Yiddish Literature (New York: T. Yoseloff, 1963).

"Yiddish Fiction. A Century's Survey," *Jewish Book Annual*, XXI (1963), 41-48.

Encyclopedia Hebraica XVI: "Max Weinreich," "Jacob Wassermann," "Franz Werfel."

1964

"American Judaism in the Year 2060," in William Berkowitz (Ed.), *Ten Vital Jewish Issues* (New York: T. Yoseloff, 1964), 189-216.

"The Writer and His Heritage," *Hadassah Magazine*, XLVI, No. 1 (1964), 8, 32-34.

"Poet in Quest of Holiness," *Congress Bi-Weekly* (Dec. 21, 1964), 15-17.

1966

The Jew in American Literature (New York: Bloch Publishing Co., 1966).

"Americans in Israel, A Problem of Adjustment," *Hadassah Magazine*, XLVI, No. 5 (1966), 10-11, 26-28.

"Richard Beer-Hofmann," *Ha'aretz* (July 8, 1966), 33.

"The Yiddish Novel of Young America," *Chicago Jewish Forum*, XXV (1966), 9-14.

1967

"Richard Beer-Hofmann," in Josef Fraenkel (Ed.), *The Jews of Austria* (London: Vallentine, Mitchell, 1967), 213-219.

Encyclopedia Hebraica XIV: "Heinrich Heine," "Peretz Hirshbein," "M. L. Halpern."

1968

"Der Nister," *Zionist Record* (Johannesburg), (Sept. 20, 1968), 82-84.

"Pioneer Yiddish Writers of South Africa," *Jewish Affairs* (Sept.), 53-61, (October), 28-32.

Encyclopedia Hebraica XIX: "Yehoash," "Wilhelm Jordan."

1969
"Itzig Manger – An Appreciation," *Jewish Affairs* (March), 34-39.

Encyclopedia Hebraica XII: "I. M. Dick."

Encyclopedia Hebraica XIII: "Carl Hauptmann," "Arno Holz," "E. T. A. Hoffmann," "Hoffmann von Fallersleben," "Hugo von Hofmannsthal."

1970
The Maturing of Yiddish Literature (New York: Jonathan David, 1970).

1971
"Heinrich Heine – After 150 Years," *Judaism*, XX, No. 3 (1971), 351-355.

"Yehoash – A Centenary Tribute," *Jewish Affairs* (January), 33-36.

Encyclopedia Hebraica XX: "Abraham Cahan."

1972
A History of Yiddish Literature (New York: Jonathan David, 1972).

"Yiddish Today," *Jewish Spectator*, XXXVII, No. 1 (1972), 19-22.

"The Contrite Heart," *Dor le Dor*, II (1972), 5-8.

1973
"Yivo," *Encyclopedia Judaica Yearbook* (1973), 360-361.

Encyclopedia Hebraica XXIII: "Nachman Maisel," "Mattithyahu Mieses," "Shlomo Michoels," "Yitzkhak Manger," "Mani-Leib."

Encyclopedia Hebraica XXIV: "Moshe Nadir," "Arno Nadel."

"Beer-Hofmann and von Hofmannsthal," *Jewish Spectator*, XXXVIII, No. 6 (1973), 29-30.

1974
"Yiddish in Israel," *The Jewish Quarterly* (London), XX, Vol. 1, 59f.

"Ossip Mandelstam," *Jewish Spectator*, XXXIX, No. 4 (1974), 71-72.

Encyclopedia Hebraica XXV: "S. Niger."

1975
"Richard Beer-Hofmann and J.V. Widmann," *Modern Austrian Literature*, VIII, No. 3/4 (1975), 74-80.

"Jerusalem, A Yiddish Center," *Yiddish*, II, No. 1 (1975), 43-49.

1976
"Introduction," in S. Sheharyah, *Collected Essays* (Jerusalem: Undzer Veg, 1976), VII-XII.

"Lilith's Comeback," *Jewish Spectator*, XLI, No. 3 (1976), 43-45.

1977

"After Three Hundred Years," in Philip Goodman (Ed.), *Essays on Jewish Booklore* (New York: Ktav Publishing House, 1977), 53-66.

Encyclopedia Hebraica XXVIII: "Arnold Zweig," "Eliakum Zunser."

Review: Lothar Kahn, *Insight and Action. The Life and Work of Lion Feuchtwanger* in *Judaism*, Vol. 26, No. 1 (1977), 124-126.

1978

Einführung in die jiddische Literatur, with Helmut Dinse (Sammlung Metzler, Band 165), (Stuttgart: Metzler Verlag, 1978).

"Lafcadio Hearn, Hugo von Hofmannsthal, and Stefan Zweig," in Alfred Rosa (Ed.), *The Old Country and the New. Essays in Honor of Charles Angoff* (New Jersey: Fairleigh Dickenson University Press, 1978), 186-191.

1979

"Introduction," in Yitzhak Kahn, *Portraits of Yiddish Writers* (New York), V-VIII.

"Georg Brandes and Richard Beer-Hofmann," *Modern Austrian Literature*, XII, No. 1 (1979), 19-29.

"Jabotinsky's Samson," *Dor le Dor*, VI (1979), 74-80.

1980

"Arthur Schnitzler," *Jewish Book Annual*, XXXVIII (1980), 141-145.

1981

"Schnitzler's Sleepless Jews," *Jerusalem Post Magazine* (Oct. 16, 1981), 11.

1982

"Erinnerungen an Stefan Zweig," *Bulletin des Leo Baeck Instituts*, 63 (1982), 13-18.

"Yiddish Literature in South Africa," in Nathan Berger (Ed.), *Chapters From South African History* (Johannesburg), 113-129.

1983

"Introduction," in Sheva Glas-Wiener, *Children of the Ghetto* (Fitzroy, Australia: Globe Press, 1983), I-II.

1984

Review. E. N. Elstun, *Richard Beer-Hofmann* in *Jerusalem Post Magazine* (July 20, 1984), 16.

Review. Ruth Melnikoff, *The Mark of Cain* in *Jewish Affairs* (April), 79-81.

Review. D. E. Wolpe, *A Vort in Zein Tzeit (A Word in its Time)* in *Jewish Affairs* (Dec.), 72-73.

1985

Biblical Themes in World Literature (New York: Ktav Publishing House, 1985).

A History of Yiddish Literature (Middle Village, N.Y.: Jonathan David, 1985), [second reprinting].

"Yehuda Elberg," *Dorem Afrike* (January, 1985), 11-12.

Review. Sholom Aleichem, *Why do Jews Need a Land of Their Own?* in *Ariel*, LXI (1985), 90-92.

Review. Mordecai Tsanin, *Gzar Hadin (The Verdict)* in *Jerusalem Post Magazine* (September 20, 1985), 12.

Review. Abraham Lis, *Shmuesn Biktav (Conversations in Writing)* in *Jerusalem Post Magazine* (October 25, 1985), 18.

Review. Tomoo Ishida (Ed.), *Studies in the Period of David and Solomon and other Essays* in *Dor le Dor*, XIV (1985), 51-54.

Review. B.W. Anderson (Ed.), *Creation in the Old Testament* in *Dor le Dor*, XIV (1985), 115-118.

"Theodicy in the Bible," *Dor le Dor*, XIV (1985), 174-178.

1986

Review. D.A. Knight and G.M. Tucker (Eds.), *The Hebrew Bible and its Modern Interpreters* in *Dor le Dor*, XIV (1986), 192-194.

Review. P.W. Tax and R.H. Lawson (Eds.), *Arthur Schnitzler and his Age: Intellectual and Artistic Currents* in *The German Quarterly*, LIX, No. 2 (1986), 326-328.

On Yiddish, in Yiddish and for Yiddish: 500 Years of Yiddish Scholarship

Dovid Katz

For roughly five hundred years, Yiddish has attracted far more than sober scholarly interest and popular study. It has persistently drawn an almost obsessive angle-oriented and ax-grinding scrutiny from highly diverse groups of investigators, each of which was driven by its own peculiar ulterior motive. Indeed, an account of the history of literature *on* Yiddish will have to delve deeply into the sociolinguistic phenomena of love and hate of the language, both of which have been (and continue to be) rather intense. To the modern Yiddish linguist, virtually everything written about the language is of value at least as "corpus," that is to say, as a primary source providing data for analysis that might not otherwise be available, even from contemporary Yiddish documents *per se*. Still, the gist of much of the earlier literature on Yiddish often strikes modern Yiddish scholars as quaint or embarrassing. To the historian of Yiddish literature, however, these sources represent an important and understudied chapter in the history of that literature. Only in the early twentieth century, when societal, literary, and political forces converged in certain segments of East European Jewry to elevate the social and linguistic roles of the language to quasi-official national language status, did there develop an extensive scientific literature written in the language itself, rather than in Latin, German, and (to a much lesser extent) Hebrew. Only in the twentieth century do the two literatures – the literature *on* Yiddish and the literature *in* Yiddish – merge by way of the rise of a new literature on *and* in Yiddish.

While Yiddish glosses and wordlists may well go back much further, the first known thinkers on the subject of Yiddish are Christian Semitists of the sixteenth and seventeenth centuries, whose researches into Hebrew, Aramaic, Syriac, and other Semitic languages, in the spirit and traditions of European Humanism, led to a serious interest in Yiddish. To some, Yiddish represented a sideline to

Hebrew studies or a bridge to Hebrew. To others, the language seemed an exotic curiosity combining elements of Germanic, in a unique and distinct form, with elements and a writing system emanating from the ancient Near East. The oldest known monument of this type, which does have strong Christian overtones, is Johann Boeschenstain's *Elementale introductorium in hebreas literas teutonice & hebraice legendas*, an elementary handbook on Hebrew and Yiddish published in Augsburg in May, 1514. Boeschenstain (1472-1540), a pupil of the luminous pioneer of Hebraic studies among Christian German scholars, Johann Reuchlin (1455-1533), achieved a certain immortality in the history of Yiddish language studies, when, some four years later, he posted an advertisement on the door of a Regensburg inn offering to teach Yiddish in six days and for a most reasonable fee. Infinitely more sophisticated was Johann Buxtorf's (1564-1629) elaborate chapter on the Yiddish language, appended to his famed *Thesaurus grammaticus linguae sanctae hebraeae* (Basel, 1609). The chapter comprises a mini-bibliography of contemporary Yiddish literature (spanning religious works, secular romances, and translations from the Hebrew), the Yiddish alphabet and its spelling conventions, and a discussion of the fusion character of Yiddish morphology. Among the examples cited are analytic verb *tfíle ton* ('pray'), synthetic verb *gegánvet* ('stole'), and abstract noun *ázeskayt* ('insolence'). Although he did not get very far as a Yiddish dialectologist, Buxtorf did take note of certain lexical differences between Western and Eastern Yiddish. His chapter on Yiddish became the basis for comments on Yiddish in the works of later Christian Hebraists, including Sennert's *Rabbinismus* (Wittenberg, 1666), and Pfeiffer's *Critica sacra* (Dresden, 1680). Buxtorf's traditional crown in Yiddish Studies as the "father of Yiddish grammar" has been shaken recently by the spectacular discovery by Hermann Süss of Fürstenfeldbruck, West Germany, of a previously unknown section on Yiddish contained in Johann Meelführer's *Grammaticae hebraeae compendiosa institutio* (Ansbach, 1607). The possibility of a hitherto lost prior source upon which both Buxtorf and Meelführer may have drawn remains a question open to future research by historians of the literature on Yiddish.

A second body of literature on Yiddish was produced by Christian authors of "teach yourself Yiddish" handbooks of many descriptions. Written in German for a popular audience, rather than in Latin for a scholarly clientele, these works catered to a diverse Christian audience. The most prominent group of customers seems to have consisted of businessmen in need of a working knowledge of the language for their interaction with Jewish colleagues and customers. The earliest book of this type now known is Paul Helicz's *Elemental / oder lesebüchlen* (Hundesfeld, 1543). It concentrates on aspects of Yiddish most important to the businessman – the numeric system of the Jewish alphabet, names of coins and currency, and parts of the calendrical cycle. It concludes with the Lord's prayer (an old favorite language-teaching text) in Yiddish and a formal letter of debt – an early sixteenth century Yiddish I.O.U. A noteworthy eighteenth century sample of this literature is Eberhard Carl Friedrich Oppenheimer's *Hodegus ebraeo-rabbinicus*, which is, despite its bombastic title, a popular businessman's handbook of Yiddish, with the usual apparatus of letters, numbers, and dates. A special feature of this little book is its list of place names and of Jewish and Christian personal names, a sort of shortcut to "business Yiddish" sparing the learner the need to master the whole of the language. Not all of this "business literature" is of the general handbook genre. Some of its products are highly specialized. Suffice it here to mention the Yiddish section of the *Vol-eingerichtete Buchdruckerey* (Nurnberg, 1733), a manual for multilingual typesetters and printers, and Wolf Ehrenfried von Reizenstein's *Vollkommene Pferde-Kenner* (Uffenheim, 1764), a horsedealers' manual comprising an invaluable section on the special variety of Yiddish employed by Jewish members of the trade. A similar variety was found by Florence Guggenheim-Grünberg of Geneva in the Swiss villages of Endingen and Lengnau in the 1950s, in what is one of the century's most splendid discoveries in the field of Yiddish dialectology. The finest practical manual of Yiddish and the culmination of the business-oriented interest in Yiddish is Carl Wilhelm Friedrich's *Unterricht in der Judensprache und Schrift* (Prenzlau, 1784). Far too talented a linguist to content himself with the basics of the language, Friedrich provided an outstanding description of the now-lost Yiddish of East Prussia and proposed the first known classification of Yiddish dialects. He is considered the father of Yiddish dialectology.

Another major branch of premodern Yiddish scholarship is the literature on the language produced by missionaries and teachers of missionaries. Their precise motivations still need to be studied in detail, but they do comprise the notion that the Jews' language is an excellent medium for reaching their hearts and minds, and the idea that the successful missionary needs to become intimate with the daily language of his target group. The founding figure of this school was archmissionary Elias Schadeus, whose *Mysterium* (Strassburg, 1592) comprises an important chapter on Yiddish which includes fascinating, if scanty, remarks on phonology, lexicography, and morphology. Besides describing fusion morphology, Schadeus notes Yiddish specificities within the Germanic component of the language, e.g. the special Yiddish mechanism for diminutivization. The missionary school reached its zenith in 1729 when Johann Heinrich Callenberg (1694-1760) established the first known university course in Yiddish at Halle. Just as Friedrich produced a great work of linguistic description vastly transcending the initial motives of his book, so did one of Callenberg's star pupils. He is Wilhelm Christian Justus Chrysander (1718-1788) whose *Jüdisch-Teutsche Grammatick* (Leipzig and Wolfenbüttel, 1750) and *Unterricht vom Nutzen des Juden-Teutschen* (Wolfenbüttel, 1750), both written in a concise and relatively modern style, contain a huge amount of invaluable data. His approach is that of a linguist, not that of the author of handbooks, and his interest is therefore directed to the linguistically most interesting parts of Yiddish, rather than to the apparently most practical. In addition to an excellent description of the fusion machinery of Yiddish, Chrysander takes note of the specificities within each component of the language, e.g. *gevínen* ('give birth'), *méme* (Western Yiddish – 'mother'), and *náyert* ('only') from *within* the Germanic component. Chrysander's most quoted line is that Jews boast that one can travel the world with Yiddish.

The eighteenth century produced dozens of anti-Semitic works on the Yiddish language. The intentions were to make fun of Yiddish, while at the same time sensationalizing it by 'exposing' supposed Jewish 'secrets' and satisfying the most lowly obsessions of a readership seeking to discover Jewish views of Christians and Christianity. One of the earliest, and lowliest, of these authors is a certain "J.W." whose *Jüdischer Sprach-Meister* appeared around 1714. It "teaches" Yiddish by way of a bilingual book-length dialogue, in (Western) Yiddish and German on facing pages, between *Joune* (modern Yiddish *Yoyne* = Jonah), a simple Jew, and his corrupt rabbi, *Rebbe Jtzick* (modern Yiddish *Itsik* from *Yitskhok* = Isaac). It is replete with samples of early eighteenth century Yiddish slang, including sexual terminology. Most of the authors in this group, like "J.W.," hid behind pseudonyms, and most seem to have been apostate Jews. The works of "Christoph Gustav Christian" (1727), "Philoglottus" (Freiberg, 1733), and "Bibliophilus" (Frankfurt and Leipzig, 1742) contain a rich selection of eighteenth century spoken Western Yiddish, and, despite their evil motives, they provide the modern linguist with a vast corpus unobtainable from any other known sources. One curious "hybrid" book, combining the traditions of sixteenth and seventeenth century Hebrew and Aramaic grammars, written in Latin and containing sections on Yiddish, on the one hand, with the base nature of eighteenth century "exposés of Yiddish," on the other, is Franciscus Haselbauer's *Fundamenta grammatica duarum praecipuarum linguarum orientalium, scilicet: Hebraicae et Chaldaicae* (Prague, 1742). The physical composition of this volume, like its content and its Latin text, are reminiscent of earlier generations of true Christian humanists who studied Yiddish alongside Hebrew and Aramaic. But the anti-Semitic spirit of eighteenth century works is evident from the author's claim, at the beginning of his Yiddish section, that "any Christian who is present cannot understand what they are talking about, and is consequently more liable to vilification and fraud." The last major anti-Semitic writer on Yiddish was Itzig Feitel Stern (an obvious pseudonym whose identity is now being debated by scholars). His German-letter early nineteenth century works were renditions of plays and narratives, written in a Southern Western Yiddish dialect. Stern produced a two volume dictionary and grammar of Yiddish, *Lexicon der jüdischen Geschäfts- und Umgangs-Sprache* (Munich, 1833).

Probably more voluminous than any of these is the criminological research into Yiddish as a by-product of inquiries into Rotwelsch, the secret German underworld language. The classic work is the *Liber vagatorum* (c. 1510 and numerous subsequent editions), the famed book of false beggars and vagabonds which concludes with a vocabulary containing a number of derivatives from the Yiddish. Its best known edition was published in Wittemberg in 1528, and features Martin Luther's assertion that the underworld language emanates from the Jews. Indeed, a good part, but by no means all, of the *Gaunersprache*-literature has anti-Semitic overtones. Much of this most esoteric branch of literature on Yiddish was sponsored by local German police departments for practical reasons. Thus, for example, the second edition of von Train's *Chochemer Loschen. Wörterbuch der Gauner und Diebs – vulgo Jenischen Sprache* (Regensburg, 1832) contains a note on the title page explaining that the first edition went wholly to the Bavarian *Gendarmerie.* Ernst Rabben, police chief in Hamm (Westphalia), goes out of his way to distinguish between Yiddish and the Yiddish component in Rotwelsch in the introduction to his *Die Gaunersprache* (Hamm, 1906). This branch of Yiddish language studies also produced a great scholar who transcended by light years his original motives of research – German police chief and criminologist Friedrich Christian Benedict Avé-Lallemant (1809-1892), whose magnum opus, *Das deutsche Gaunerthum* (Leipzig, 1858-1862), in four massive volumes, contained what was up until that time the most comprehensive treatment of Yiddish. Although replete with amateurish philological shortcomings, Avé-Lallemant nevertheless compiled a vast amount of material on Yiddish, its literature, and the philological literature on the language. He came to acquire a profound respect for the language and had no problem in distinguishing it from the Yiddish component in Rotwelsch. Indeed, he was the first scholar to argue that the history of Yiddish begins with the settlement of Jews on Germanic speaking territory, a view no contemporaneous Jewish scholar would have dared to take.

Jewish scholarly interest in Yiddish before the nineteenth century concentrated upon practical lexicography in a colorful array of forms and genres. The earliest manuscript glosses and lists of glosses to classical Hebrew and Aramaic texts probably date back to the thirteenth century in a continuous tradition later codified in the *taytsh* literature. This comprised a set Yiddish rendition for each lexical item or sentence unit in the original, a formula which gave rise to a number of classical works of older Yiddish lexicography, such as Moyshe ben Yisokher Shertl's *Beéyr Móyshe* (Prague, 1605). Other genres include the Bible concordance (e.g. Reb Anshel's *Mirkéves hamíshne* [Cracow, 1534]); the Hebrew-Yiddish thesaurus arranged by semantic categories (e.g. the *Khínekh kótn,* [Prague, 1640]); and such multilingual dictionaries as Elye Bokher's *Shmóys dvórim* (Isny, 1542), offering Yiddish-Hebrew-Latin-German; Mordkhe Shmuel Yankev ben Yekusiel's *Díber tóv* (Cracow, 1590), giving Hebrew-Yiddish-Italian, and Nosn-Note Hanover's *Sófe brúre* (Prague, 1660) with Hebrew-Yiddish-Italian-Latin (to which Yankev ben Zeeyv added French in the Amsterdam, 1701, edition, after Hanover's death). More specialized works are limited to specific components of the Yiddish vocabulary. These include the dictionary of internationalisms in the *Khánekh landar* (Amsterdam, 1713), and of Semitic component vocabulary in Khayem ben Menakhem Mansh's *Máre haksáv* (c. 1717), a fascinating manual on and in Yiddish.

Yet, little is known of Jewish scholarly attention to the structure, history, or dialectology of Yiddish in previous centuries. The most linguistically sophisticated comments were provided by the luminous Hebrew and Aramaic grammarian, Elijah Levita (1468/9-1549), who alone amongst Ashkenazim attained the philological heights characteristic of Golden Age Spanish Jewry. Besides his prolific philological output, Levita, known in Yiddish as Elye Bokher, was of course the leading Yiddish poet of the sixteenth century, best known for his *Bovo d'Antona* (Isny, 1541) in *ottava rima.* It was in one of his Hebrew philological classics, however, that his enduring status as the father of Yiddish etymology was established. In his *Tishbi* (Isny, 1541), he proposed etymologies for such everyday Yiddish words as *katóves* ('fooling around, kidding'), and *mékn* ('erase') that remain classic, even if disputed. His scanty comments on dialectology and phonology remain indispensable.

It was not until the nineteenth century that the three schools of Yiddish linguistic scholarship which we know in our time truly came into being. It has been known that the first two – Yiddish as part of Hebraic Studies and Yiddish as part of Germanic Studies – have their roots in the early and late nineteenth century respectively. It is the just rediscovered "missing link" that changes the chronology of the rise of the third (and most successful) branch of Yiddish linguistic scholarship – Yiddish as part of Yiddish Studies, a field of scientific literature in and of itself rather than a satellite of another discipline. When Leopold Zunz (1794-1886) cofounded the *Verein für Cultur und Wissenschaft der Juden* in 1819, thereby initiating the Science of Judaism movement, Yiddish could not very well have been accorded a position on the agenda. Conditioned by the late eighteenth century German-Jewish Enlightenment, Zunz and his colleagues disparaged the Yiddish language, which they regarded with shame and contempt. Nevertheless, as scientists trained in university methodology, they could barely ignore a language and literature of such vast magnitude, and leaving aside their ideologically biased conclusions, they made a number of permanent contributions to Yiddish philology and literary history. Zunz's classification of the several components in Yiddish, with reference to their functions within the language, while inevitably flawed, has nonetheless remained the point of departure on the subject to this day. It is contained in the section on Yiddish in his *Die gottesdienstlichen Vorträge der Juden* (Berlin, 1832). The bibliographic spadework for the historian of Yiddish literature was brilliantly executed by Zunz's follower, the father of modern Jewish bibliography, Moritz Steinschneider (1816-1907).

In the arena of general linguistics, the nineteenth century gave rise to the comparative method by which the genetic interrelationships between related languages and language varieties could be determined with an exactness never before possible. The comparative method enables the skilled practitioner to reconstruct phases of language going back much further than the earliest surviving documents. By its inherent nature, it placed new emphasis on the importance of living, and therefore empirically real, language varieties as the raw material for reconstruction. Thus, it dealt a mortal blow to pre-nineteenth century linguistics, a schoolmasterly and normative discipline seeking to distinguish the "correct" from the "corrupt" on extralinguistic, socially and nationally motivated grounds. As it happens, the greatest part of this work was carried out in Germany by such masters as Franz Bopp (1791-1867), Jacob Grimm (1785-1863), and August Schleicher (1821-1868).

It was two Jews who, inspired by the comparative studies in the field of Germanic languages, brought Yiddish into the orbit of Germanics. They were Lazar Saineanu (1859-1934), a great Rumanian philologist whose four-volume Rumanian dictionary has been through nearly a hundred editions, and Alfred Landau (1850-1935), a native of Brody, Galicia, who settled in Vienna in his teens and, after giving up his law practice, spent the rest of his life in Vienna working on the history, lexicography, and dialectology of Yiddish. Most of his life's work was transferred upon his death to Vilna, where it perished at the hands of the Nazis. Saineanu, in his 1889 monograph *Studiu dialectologic asupra graiului evreo-german*, demonstrated that Yiddish could in no way derive from some general (modern) German, as its detractors had long insisted. Rather than deviating from modern German, both Yiddish (or, more exactly, the Germanic component in Yiddish) and modern German derive from the period designated as Middle High German. Landau's 1896 study on the Yiddish diminutive went a stage further by demonstrating the need to study Yiddish dialect phenomena in terms of medieval German dialect phenomena, rather than in terms of the standardized variant of Middle High German epic poetry. Partly in consequence of these efforts, doctoral theses in Yiddish philology became popular in some German universities. The most influential of these was probably Jacob Gerzon's 1902 Heidelberg dissertation, which systematically compared the phonology of a selected Yiddish dialect with medieval German. But unlike Saineanu and Landau, Gerzon and a number of those who were to follow did not know Yiddish first hand. Their distance from the language, its speakers, and its culture, was often exacerbated by an overdependence on classical Middle High German that could at its worst be intellectually crippling by precluding the discovery, systematization, and explanation of the internal creativity inherent in the history of Yiddish. They often had little inclination, moreover, to study the Semitic, Slavic, and other non-Germanic parts of Yiddish, as well as the vital interrelationships between Yiddish and the other two Jewish languages – Hebrew and Aramaic – with which it constituted the unique internal Jewish trilingualism characteristic of Ashkenazic Jewry. Still, the *germanistn* (Germanists), as they are called in Yiddish scholarly circles, did much to bring the science of Yiddish into the orbit of European linguistics.

Yiddish scholarship could only be liberated by scholars hailing from Eastern Europe, where a linguistically thriving Yiddish speaking civilization was in the midst of cultural renaissance, and was producing a major world literature. Part of that renaissance entailed the conscious elevation of Yiddish from vernacular status to national language status. Putting one and one together, the *a priori* child of linguistic scholarship and living Yiddish culture would be a literature that would, in the first place, be written *in* Yiddish, viewing Yiddish Studies as a discipline in its own right, a planet with its own satellites (phonology, dialectology, folklore, literary history, etc.), and would in the second, be founded upon the highest achievements of European linguistics. Needless to say, this approach would be infinitely distant from the field's stepchild status in areas of business vocabulary, horsedealers' manuals, and criminology. There is, moreover, an interesting metascientific issue here. Unlike the physical sciences, where the passion for discovery need not be coupled with a positive attitude toward the object of research, no science of a language can be adequate if the object language is, put quite simply, disliked by the investigator. All natural languages have their innermost stores of what might be called conscious and unconscious stores of collective human genius, and while a neutral view may be adequate, a positive view is invaluable. While the term *yidishistn* (Yiddishists, supporters of Yiddish) is most often thought of in a cultural-political context, where it may be opposed to *hebreistn* (Hebraists, supporters of Hebrew), it has another, somewhat less known meaning in Yiddish scholarly circles. Here it refers to Yiddish linguists dedicated to the field of Yiddish *per se* and is opposed to *germanistn* (scholars of German who have an interest in Yiddish). Be that as it may, historical forces dictated that the Yiddishists in the scholarly sense would *ipso facto* be Yiddishists in the popular sense.

The modern literature *in, on,* and *for* Yiddish can be traced to the floor of the celebrated Tshernovits (Chernowitz) Language Conference of 1908, organized by Nathan Birnbaum (1864-1937) and attended by a number of giants of Yiddish literature, the most luminous of whom was Yitskhok-Leybush Peretz (1852-1915). At the end of the morning session on the third day of the Conference, Tuesday, September 1, 1908, a relatively unknown twenty-three year old named Matisyohu Mieses (1885-1945) delivered the first linguistic paper describing Yiddish as a unique linguistic structure and delving into the history and sociology of the language from this perspective. The first paper of its kind in Yiddish, it presaged the rise of twentieth century Yiddish scientific literature, which is as massive in volume as it is inspiring in quality. Mieses's paper, despite its shortcomings, touched on numerous issues of history, dialectology, sociology, and linguistic theory, especially the debunking of the "pure" vs. "hybrid" dichotomy in language classification. For its time, it was no less than brilliant. Contemporary press reports recount that some listeners, upset at some of Mieses's views on the then heated national language issue, broke into fistfights with his supporters. The best known report on the Mieses confrontation tells of a distraught Hebraist (in the political-cultural sense), who burst into tears upon hearing Mieses's barrage of scientific evidence on the age, structure, and societal role of Yiddish, and of two girls who looked at him and broke into tears as well. On the tumultuous floor of the Tshernovits Conference was born, or almost born, a new science of Yiddish, combining progress in linguistic theory of the west with the Jewish cultural renaissance in Eastern Europe.

The simple reason why Mieses's pioneering paper failed to establish a new branch of Yiddish literature is that it was not published soon after the Conference, as Peretz had recommended it be. It was not published until 1931 when it was included in the reconstructed proceedings of the Conference published in Vilna by the Yivo. It remained for Ber Borokhov (1881-1917) to write the declaration of independence for Yiddish Studies. Although better remembered for his philosophical treatises on Zionism and socialism, Borokhov devoted a huge portion of the last decade of his short life to an odyssey through the great Western European libraries in search of the building blocks of the history of Yiddish language and literature. The results were astounding. The first major academic volume in and on Yiddish linguistics and literary history was Sh. Niger's *Pinkes* (Vilna, 1913). It begins with Borokhov's *Di úfgabn fun der yidisher filológye (The Aims of Yiddish Philology),* a farsighted essay on the urgent tasks of Yiddish philology, including the need for authoritative dictionaries and grammars, a history of the language, and the establishment of a central scientific academy dedicated to Yiddish language and literature. On the structure of Yiddish, Borokhov introduced the concept of synchronic unity in the face of historical diversity, pointing out that once indrawn elements become part of the system of Yiddish, "they cease to be German, Hebrew and Slavic. They shed their erstwhile guise and assume a new one: they become Yiddish." The underlying notion here is that of language as a synchronic structure functioning as a system at any given point of time, to be conceptually disentangled from diachrony, the historical evolution of language on the axis of time. Here are, of course, the classic Saussurian dichotomy (synchrony vs. diachrony), and the classic Saussurian basis of modern linguistics (structuralism in its broad sense), both of which led to the rise of twentieth century general linguistics, largely thanks to the posthumous publication of Ferdinand de Saussure's *Cours de linguistique générale* (Lausanne, 1916). Borokhov, putting these ideas forward a few years beforehand, correctly gauged the conceptual pathways of twentieth century linguistic theory. He called for the establishment of Yiddish philology both academically (research, teaching, publishing) and as a national Jewish science, whose goal would be to codify, preserve, and enhance Yiddish language and literature.

Soon after Borokhov's untimely death, a great many of his dreams were fulfilled to the letter. A number of highly talented young Yiddish scholars dedicated to Yiddishism in the double Borokhovian sense, began to explore both the historical treasure-houses of older Yiddish language and literature, as well as the theoretical issues of Yiddish grammar, dialectology, metrics, and more. Among the most prominent of these are Solomon A. Birnbaum (born 1891), Zelik-Hirsh Kalmanovitsh (1881/5-1944), Zalmen Reyzen (1887- c. 1940), Nokhem Shtif (1879-1933), and Max Weinreich (1894-1969), most of whom wrote largely or entirely in Yiddish. Reyzen and Weinreich settled in Vilna in the early nineteen twenties, and it was there that the headquarters of the Yiddish Scientific Institute (known as Yivo from its Yiddish acronym for *Yídisher vísnshaftlekher institút*) was established in 1925 by Shtif, Weinreich, Reyzen, and others, fulfilling Borokhov's dream of a Yiddish academy. In his inspired paper which was the direct impetus to the organization of the Yivo, Shtif put forward the notion that the science of Yiddish has a contribution to make to general science, a prediction that has long since been recognized as reality by leaders in the field of general linguistics. Most of modern Yiddish scholarship in interbellum Eastern Europe was brutally destroyed along with the bulk of East European Jewry during the Holocaust. Parallel scientific institutions in the Soviet Union were arbitrarily and cruelly closed by Stalin's regime. Despite these catastrophic climaxes to the feverish and prolific output of dozens upon dozens of top quality works in Yiddish in the field of Yiddish linguistics in the interwar period, the field of Yiddish continues to thrive and grow today. More than any other single event, its survival may be attributed to the coinciding of the Fifth International Congress of Linguists in Brussels with Hitler's invasion of Poland. Weinreich attended that conference, where he read a paper on the history of Yiddish, and thus was able to escape to America where he, and his prodigious son, Uriel Weinreich (1926-1967), established Yiddish linguistics in the west in the finest traditions of the East European Borokhovian paradigm.

For a number of decades now, Yiddish linguists have lamented the "loss" of the missing link in the modern history of the science of Yiddish. That link is a crucial study of Yiddish, written in the late 1880s in German and therefore akin to the work of the *germanistn*, but conceived in the spirit of developing a science of Yiddish centered upon the language itself and approaching its object with love and respect in the spirit of the later *yidishístn*. It is to the author of that study, Philipp Mansch (1838-1890), that Borokhov dedicated his *Ufgabn*: "gehéylikt dem líkhtikn zikórn funem fórsher fun yídish, dem éydeln farérer fun dem yídishn folk un shprakh, dem frítsaytik geshtórbenem un úmgerekht fargésenem Dr. Filip Mansh in Lemberg." Mansch, a Lemberg attorney who played a leading role in its organized Jewish community and edited its newspaper, *Der Israelit*, published his study in serial form in that paper from 1888 until his death in 1890. Mansch's study was without doubt the most profound descriptive study of Yiddish until that time, and it was the first grammar in any language of a dialect of Eastern Yiddish, which is tantamount geographically to the temporal concept of *modern* Yiddish. All previous studies of Yiddish had dealt with one or more varieties of Western Yiddish, which survived only in vestigial form past the eighteenth century, in consequence of the linguistic acculturation of its speakers to German and other languages in Central and Western Europe. By contrast Eastern Yiddish blossomed and strengthened in leaps and bounds – demographically, literarily, and politically – that were scarcely conceivable. Mansch's study was thus the first future-oriented monograph on Yiddish. In it, he deals with broad philosophical issues including the status of fusion languages and national languages, as well as with fine points of the phonology, morphology, and grammar of his native Galician Yiddish. His comments on the interrelationships between Yiddish and German dialects are the weakest part of his study, but even here he never failed to make highly original suggestions, some of which will undoubtedly prove fertile to further research. Suffice it here to say that the range of topics which Mansch included in the monograph – among them the role of Yiddish in Jewish history, the nature of Jewish languages in general, and the genetic ties between languages – have been and continue to be counted as the prime research targets of modern Jewish language science. If Borokhov is the father of modern Yiddish linguistics, it is fair enough to consider Mansch its grandfather.

In his 1923 Marburg University dissertation, Max Weinreich noted that the issues of *Der Israelit* containing Mansch's study had become so rare that he could not gain access to more than a small part of the study. By the 1970s, Yiddish linguists were going so far as to reconstruct what Mansch probably said about this or that point based on the early twentieth century descriptions of the study. A full typescript of the study was rediscovered in late 1984 by Christopher Hutton, among Max Weinreich's archives held by the Yivo in New York. Christopher Hutton, a doctoral candidate in Yiddish Linguistics at the University of Oxford, where the subject is taught in the Borokhovian tradition, thus achieved the breakthrough which will enable the history of Yiddish Studies to be compiled and written in its entirety. In its twentieth century phase, it is a magnificent branch of modern Yiddish literature.

Kabbalistic Ideas in the Women's Yiddish Prayer Book, *Tkheenes*

Zelda Kahan Newman

Few today are familiar with the *Tkheenes*, the Yiddish prayer book for women. Yet, for centuries the Jewish women of Ashkenaz prayed not from the traditional prayer book written in Hebrew, but from the *Tkheenes*, written in Yiddish, the language they could understand. For centuries in Ashkenaz, every Jewish household had a Bible and a prayer book, written in Hebrew for the man of the household, and a corresponding *Tseno-Ureno* and collection of *Tkheenes* written in Yiddish for the woman of the household. (The Yiddish form is derived from the Hebrew word "HiTKHaNaN" – to beg, to supplicate, – *tkheene* in the singular and *tkheenes* in the plural.)

Almost as soon as printed books became available, prayers for women in Yiddish appeared. The first complete translation of a Hebrew prayer book into Yiddish appeared in 1544.[1] Subsequent collections of prayers included not only translations of the communal prayers said by men, but also private prayers addressing such particularly feminine concerns as child bearing and rearing. The typical *tkheene*-collection had two types of prayers: one, a parallel, Yiddish version of a Hebrew prayer said in the synagogue – e.g., "olenu leshabeakh laadon hakol" – ("let us praise the Lord of all"); and, a second to be said at home, e.g., "mode ani... shehekhezarta bi nishmasi" ("I thank you God... for having returned my soul..."). This second type included prayers to be said before and after candle lighting, during pregnancy, and when giving birth.

Although some of the prayers were written by men, a good many of them were written by women. In the middle of the sixteenth century, Rivke, daughter of Meir Tiktiner, compiled prayers and prayer-poems in Yiddish.[2] Another author was Gele, daughter of Moshe son of Avrohom.[3] The best known author was Sara bas Tovim, of whom we know that her father's name was Mordekhay, and that her paternal grandfather was rabbi in Satanov.[4]

Meant as they were for private prayer, the *tkheenes* touched on the everyday concerns of the worshipper. They are therefore a treasure-house of information of an anthropological nature. Anything of concern to women made its way into the *tkheenes*: the dangers to itinerant Jews, the cruelty of local or state authorities, the mistreatment of women by their husbands, the struggle to feed and clothe the family.

Furthermore, the *tkheenes* provide evidence of dialectal variation and historical change. Unlike the Hebrew prayers which resisted syntactic change from one century to the next, the syntactic structures of the Yiddish prayers changed as the living language changed. To be sure, archaic forms were preserved long after they had gone out of daily use, but evidence of current usage inevitably finds its way into the text.

More than fifty years ago, the Reform rabbi and scholar Solomon Freehof noted the considerable influence of the Kabbalah on the *tkheenes*. However, quite probably because of his unconcealed disdain for the "fantastic superstitions" of the Kabbalah, he furnished only one example of a Kabbalistic idea in a prayer and wrote: "It is not necessary to cite any more single *Tehinnoth*, for almost every one of them betrays distinct Cabalistic ideas and phraseology."[5] It is these "distinct Cabalistic ideas" that we will examine here. From the whole cloth of the *tkheenes* we will separate individual strands to see precisely which Kabbalistic notions were woven in.

Although the grammatical forms in the *tkheenes* changed over time, the content achieved a remarkable degree of stability. As Freehof noted, "whether the *tehinna* is published in the eighteenth century in the older Juedisch-Deutsch, or... in Rodelheim, 1843, or... in New York [in the twentieth century], the contents are virtually the same."[6] The text we use here is called the *Shas Thkeena*. It was printed in Vilna sometime in the last two decades of the nineteenth century, and then reprinted by the Hebrew Publishing Company of New York, without any date of publication.[7]

The *tkheenes* abound in references to otherworldly figures and forces. Satan is a personalized creature whose evil influence must be thwarted. Evil angels and spirits must also be warded off:

(1) ven der sotn vet kumen un vet kholile onraytsen tsu beyzn, bet ikh hashem yisborakh zol alts mevatel zayn un ale di reyd zolen zayn botel umevutol kekheres hanishbor... (p. 27)

(when Satan will come and will, God forbid, entice to evil, I beg (you) God, let everything be annulled; and may all he says be annulled like shattered porcelain...)

(2) farshtop dem sotn zayn mol un zayne oyeren er zol oyf mir nit mekatreg zayn .. (p. 19)

(stuff up Satan's mouth and ears so that he will not prosecute me...)

(3) mayne likht zolen hel un loyter brenen tsu fartrayben di beyze rukhos un mazikim dos zey zolen avek fliyen far di likht... (p. 27)

(may my candles burn clear and bright to banish the evil spirits and harmful forces who will flee from the light...)

(4) un es zol tsu raysen ...ale mashkhisim vos makhen atsivishn sheyd tsivishn unz un tsivishn dir... (p. 70)

(and may all the destroyers who make a division between us and you be ripped apart...)

Not all the otherworldly forces are evil, however. Among the positive forces are the angels who are bearers of prayer, the spirits of righteous historical figures, and the souls of loved ones who have died. Each of these are asked in the *tkheenes* to intercede on behalf of the worshipper:

(5) un du zolst mir shiken di malokhim vos zey zaynen gezetst iber di tfiles fun di yisroel... (p. 6)

(and please send me the angels who are appointed over the prayers of Israel...)

(6) liber got loz mikh genisen dem zkhus fun muter khane... (p. 22)

(dear God allow me to enjoy the merit of mother Hannah...)

(7) un du helige un reyne neshome vos ikh tu hayntigen tog beten fun daynt vegen. dos glaykhen zolstu fun maynet vegen oykh tfile ton un beten hakodosh borukh hu. du zolst fun maynet vegen zayn a guter melits tsu derhoyben mayn mazel un dem mazel fun mayn man un mayne kinder... (p. 93)

(and you holy and pure soul for whom I pray today. The same may you do for me and also pray to God on my behalf. May you be a good interceder to increase my fortune and the fortune of my husband and my children...)

Whereas the Kabbalistic references in the *tkheenes* are manifold and clear, such references in the Hebrew prayer book are few and oblique. If we seek Kabbalistic references in the typical Ashkenazic prayer book for weekday and Sabbath services, we look in vain. To be sure, angels are indirectly mentioned in the Kedusha prayer: "nekadesh es shimkho boolam keshem shemakdishim oso bishmey morom..." ("let us sanctify your name in the world just as they sanctify it in the heavens above..."). Those who sanctify God's name in the heavens above are, of course, angels. They are referred to here, but only tangentially. In this prayer the worshippers are concerned with their own sanctification of God, and not with dwelling on the heavenly spirits. Furthermore, there is no indication here that angels intervene in any way in human affairs. In this oblique reference then, angels are neither a threat to, nor interceders for, the worshippers.

There are references to Satan and angels in the High Holy Day service, but once again, they are indirect and hidden. In the prayer "ovinu malkenu" we find:

> ovinu malkenu kale kol tsar umastin meyolenu... (p. 46)
> (Our father, our king, destroy every enemy and hateful being of ours...)
>
> ovinu malkenu sesom piyos mastinenu umekatregenu... (ibid.)
> (Our father, our king, shut the mouths of those who hate us and persecute us...)[8]

In the first of these two requests, Satan is not directly referred to, but the root S-T-N is placed in the verbal form maSTiN, where it refers in a general way to forces or beings that are hateful. Similarly, in the second request, the root S-T-N refers not to Satan but to "those who hate us" (mastineneu). These may be otherworldly forces, but they may also be human enemies.

There is one outright reference to Satan and angel-interceders in the High Holy Day services. It can be found in a prayer said only by the cantor:

> vesigar basoton leval yastineni... (p. 171)
> (and shout at Satan so that he not persecute me...)
>
> shekol hamalokhim shehem poaley sefilos yoviyu sifilosi lifney kisey kevodekho veyofitsu oso lefonekho... (ibid.)

(that all the angels who deal with prayers should bring my prayer before your throne of honor and spread it before you...)

Here is a prayer very reminiscent of what we find in the *tkheenes.* But only the cantor says it. What is more, in some congregations it is customary for the cantor to lower his voice when he reaches this part of the prayer so that he whispers the whole phrase in a barely audible voice.[9] The feeling clearly is that angels are not to be spoken of openly.

The dearth of Kabbalistic references found in the Hebrew prayer book should not be attributed to the fact that this particular prayer book was non-Kabbalistic in origin. Hebrew prayer books composed by known Kabbalists are not much different. Consider the *Beys Yakov,* a prayer book written by Jacob of Emden (1691-1776), a man of many seeming contradictions. Although he questioned the historical authenticity of the *Zohar*, he nevertheless espoused many Kabbalistic ideas. His *Beys Yakov* is said to combine "grammatical comments and Kabbalistic commentary."[10] The key word here is "commentary," for although Kabbalistic explanations abound in this prayer book, the Kabbalistic references are not part of the prayer text itself. For example, according to Emden, each of the four cups of wine drunk at the Passover Seder is meant to annul a different otherworldly force. Before the blessing to be said on the first cup of wine, Emden appends, in small letters, the following prayer:

hareni rotse lekadesh al hayayin ulekayem mitsvas kos rishon mearba kosos shehu keneged os yud shel havaye borukh hu shehu kodesh hanikro khokhmo veshehu keneged ruakh shtus levatel oso... (p. 231)

(I hereby wish to sanctify the wine and observe the mitsvo of the first of the four cups [of wine] which represents the letter yud of God's name, blessed be he, which represents the holiness that is called knowledge, and which is opposed to the spirit of foolishness to annul it...)

And before the blessing on the second cup of wine we find:

hareni rotse lekayem mitsvas kos sheni mearba kosos shehu keneged os hey rishona shel havaye borukh hu hi bino trin reyin delo misparshin, veshehu keneged ruakh znus levatel oso... (p. 249)

(I hereby wish to fulfill the mitsvo of the second cup of wine which represents the first letter hey of God's name blessed be he, which is wisdom and these are two friends that do not part, and is opposed to the force of adultery to annul it...)

Before the third cup of wine we find the following:

hareni rotse lekayem mitsvas kos shlishi mearba kosos shehu keneged os vav shehu tiferes veshehu keneged ruakh hamido roo levatl oso... (p. 251)

(I hereby wish to fulfill the mitsvo of the third cup (of the four cups) which represents the letter vav, which is glory, and which is opposed to the force of bad trait[11] to annul it...

And finally, before the blessing on the fourth cup we find:

hareni rotse lekayem mitsvas kos reviiy mearba kosos shehu keneged os hey akhrono shebashem shehu keneged ruakh hatuma levatel oso... (p. 253)

(I hereby wish to fulfill the mitsvo of the fourth (of the four cups) of wine which represents the last letter hey in the name [of God] which is opposed to the force of nonpurity to annul it...)

Each of these four pre-sanctification prayers is written in very small, close print. The print size is crucial. It indicates an acknowledgment that whereas the blessing on the wine is obligatory, the preparatory prayer (and its Kabbalistic grounding) is voluntary and can be omitted.

The *tkheenes* espouse the Kabbalistic view of the efficacy of prayer. In this view "...the divine light which flowed into primordial space... unfolded in various stages and appeared under a variety of aspects... . Since... the divine scheme of things involved the creation of finite beings and forms, each with its own alloted place in the ideal hierarchy, it was necessary that these isolated lights should be caught and preserved in special "bowls" created – or rather emanated – for this particular purpose. The vessels which corresponded to the three highest Sefiroth accordingly gave shelter to their light, but when the turn of the lower six came, the light broke forth all at once and its impact proved too much for the vessels which were broken and shattered."[12] This breaking of the vessels in which divine lights were scattered is a reversible process. "The historical process and its innermost soul, the religious act of the Jew, prepare the way for the final restitution of all the scattered and exiled lights and sparks. The Jew who is in close contact with the divine life through the Torah, the fulfillment of the commandments, and through prayer, has it in his power to accelerate or to hinder this process."[13] In the Kabbalistic view, then, the Jew is put in this world so that by his actions he can right not the wrongs of his immediate environment or of his society, but the imbalance of the cosmos. Each good deed and proper intention of prayer help reunite the scattered names of God. Thus, whereas in the Hebrew prayer book, the daily prayers are seen as a replacement for the Temple offerings, in the *tkheenes* they are seen as a means of restoring the cosmic balance:

(8) zol zayn glaykh az ikh volt gevust tsu... metsaref zayn ale di kavones un tserufey sheymos di helige vos geyen oys der tfile fun shakhris oder minkhe oder mariv... (p. 11)

(may it be exactly as though I knew how to join together all the intentions and holy name combinations which go out of the morning prayer or late morning or afternoon or evening prayer...)

The Kabbalistic doctrine of four basic worlds also finds its place here. In this doctrine there is a "series of worlds from above to below forming one basic vector along which creation passes from its primeval point to its finalization in the material world."[14] The four worlds are called "olam ha-azilut" (the world of emanation – the ten Sefirot), "olam ha-beriah" (the world of creation - the throne and the chariot), "olam ha-yezirah" (the world of formation – sometimes called the world of the angels centered around Metatron), and "olam ha-asiyyah" (the world of making – which sometimes includes both the whole system of the spheres and the terrestrial world, and sometimes the terrestrial world only)."[15] This conception, together with the worshipper's anxious attempt to commune directly with God, gives rise to the following passage:

(9) dos alts iz olam asiye un iber dem iz olam habriye un iber dem iz olam hoatsilus un ale di olomos tsu anander zaynen gor kleyn kegen dayn kise hakoved un der kise hakoved hot gor kayn erekh nit kegen dayn sheynhayt un akhperkayt un forkhtsum un shtarkayt... (p. 10)

(all this is the world of making and above this is the world of creation and above this is the world of emanation and all the worlds together are entirely trivial compared with [lit. against] your chair of glory and the chair of glory has altogether no value compared with [lit. against] your beauty and reverence and awe and strength...)

The Hebrew prayer book and the *tkheenes* tell us different things about death and the soul of the deceased. In the Hebrew prayer book there are two prayers for the well-being of the deceased's soul: "yizkor" (may he remember), and "el mole rakhamim" (God full of mercy). In the first, God is asked to remember the soul of the deceased and bind it up in the bundle of life along with the souls of righteous men and women:

> yizkor elohim es nishmas... tehey nafsho tserura bitsror hakhayim im nishmas avrohom yitskhok veyakov sore rivke rokhel veleyo veim sheor tsadikim vetsidkoniyos shebegan eden...
>
> (may God remember the soul of... may his soul be bound up in the bundle of life together with the souls of Abraham, Isaac, and Jacob, Sara, Rebecca, Rachel, and Leah, and with the souls of other righteous men and women who are in paradise...)

In the second, God is asked to find a proper rest (or peace) for the soul of the deceased:

> el mole rakhamim shokhen bamromim hamtse menukho nekhono takhas kanfey hashkhino bemaalos kedoshim utehorim kezohar horokiya mazhirim es nishmas... lokhen baal horakhamim yastireyhu beseser kenofov leolomim veyitsror bitsror hakhayim es nishmoso hashem hu nakhaloso veyonuakh al mishkovo...
>
> (God, full of pity, who dwells in the heavens, find a proper peace beneath the wings of the shekhina, in the heights of the holy and the pure like the glow of the heavens illuminate the soul of... Therefore may the master of pity hide him in the secret of his wing forever and bind his soul in the bundle of life. God is his legacy and may he rest in his resting place...)

There is no doubt that Kabbalistic notions have crept into these prayers. The "tsror hakhayim," for example, is "sometimes synonymous with the celestial paradise and sometimes taken to refer to one of the Sefirot themselves, to which the soul returns to partake of the life of the Godhead."[16] Nevertheless, the Hebrew prayer book does not tell us what happens if the soul of the deceased cannot rest in peace.

In the *tkheenes*, however, the fate of such a soul is spelled out in a tone of near despair:

> (10) di zind makhen nokh dem toyt ayn ayzerne vand un ayn tsoym far di neshomo zey farshtelen ir vag un zi ken nit aroyf geyn tsu ir ruhe (p. 85)

(after death the sins make an iron wall and a blockade for the soul; they disguise her path so she cannot go up to her resting place...)

Sometimes souls that did not atone for their sins before their death are forced to undergo a punishment known as "khibut hakever" (the beating of a body in its grave). At other times, in order to purify itself, the soul must undergo transmigration. The worshipper asks, therefore, that she and her loved ones be spared these indignities:

(11) un zolst (im) (ir) matsil zayn fun khibut hakever un fun verim un modin... (p. 92)

(may you save [him] [her] from the beating of a body in its grave and from worms and maggots...)

(12) ikh zol nit badarfen vider megulgel vern oyf der zindiger velt... (p. 24)

(may I not need to transmigrate in the sinful world...)

It is possible that what we have hitherto described as a difference between the Kabbalistic Yiddish prayer book for women and the non-Kabbalistic Hebrew prayer book for men is, in reality, a difference between private prayer and communal prayer. For most of the years that Ashkenaz existed, women typically prayed in the privacy of their homes, while men typically prayed communally. Both men and women had access to Kabbalistic prayers. Women could find them in their *tkheenes*, while men could find them in appended, optional prayers, like those found in the *Beys Yakov*, or exceptionally, in the prayer recited by the cantor alone on the High Holy days.[17]

Freehof asserts that "the two greatest sources from which Cabalistic influence came upon the prayer literature of Israel are the two Cabalistic prayerbooks, the *Shaare Zion* of Nathan Hanover, (first published in Prague, 1662) and the Shaar Hashamayim of Issaiah Horowitz, (first published in Amsterdam, 1717)."[18] It may well be that Hebrew prayer books with Kabbalistic overtones first appeared in Ashkenaz after the publication of these two books. But there is no reason to suppose that the same is true of Yiddish prayer books. In fact, there is every reason to believe the opposite. Yiddish prayer books and individual prayers in Yiddish are probably as old as Ashkenaz itself, and Kabbalistic notions appear in these Yiddish texts a full century before the publication of the two Hebrew prayer books mentioned above.

The first historical evidence we have of Yiddish prayers is found in the eulogy of the Kabbalist Rabbi Eliezer of Worms for his wife Dulce who was murdered in the Crusade of 1196. Rabbi Eliezer says of his wife: "meshoreres zmiros utfilo umedaberes takhanunim."[19] ("She sang songs and prayers and spoke supplications"). We have here the Hebrew root TaKHaNaN – the root shared by the word "tkheenes." This word is uniformly used in Ashkenaz for private supplication, usually in the vernacular. Although there is no extant text that can be attributed to Rabbi Eliezer's wife, it would seem that she composed prayers in the (Yiddish) vernacular and recited them aloud in the synagogue. There is another early reference to Yiddish prayers. We know of one Guta (or Gite), daughter of Reb Nosn, who died in 1308, and of whom it is said: "shehoyso mispaleles lanoshim bisfiloso hoadino."[20] ("She used to pray for the women with her gentle prayer.")

It is likely that both Rabbi Eliezer's wife and Guta/Gite, daughter of Reb Nosn served as "firzogerin" (literally, first chanter) in the women's section of the synagogue. A "firzogerin" stood in the front of the women's section and translated the Hebrew prayer into Yiddish for the other women who had come to pray. Sometimes the "firzogerin" translated more or less exactly; at other times she translated freely and added her own interpretation.

These two references point to the antiquity of Yiddish prayers. Although we can only guess at the content of these prayers, we do know what women wrote about a few hundred years later. In the middle of the sixteenth century, Rivke of Tiktiner wrote her "simkhes toyre liyd" – poem for (the holiday of) "simkhes toyre." In that poem, (which made its way into the *Shas Tkheena*), we find (a not unexpected) frequent mention of Satan and angels. When she translates the sixth commandment – thou shalt not commit adultery –, Rivke Tiktiner adds: "dos alts tut nor der sotn farfirin." (p. 148, "This Satan does just to mislead you.") Similarly, when she presents us with a debate between God and the angels over who should rightfully receive the Torah, she tells us that God spoke to: "sar yisroel der zelbiger iz mikhoel" (p. 149, "the minister of Israel none other than Michael.") Thus, she not only inserts a debate between God and the angels; she even knows the name of the angel who intercedes for Israel – this, a full century before the publication of Nosn Hanover's *Shaare Zion.*

We must, accordingly, revise Freehof's hypothesis on the origin of the Kabbalistic notions in the *tkheenes*. The Kabbalistic elements known to the folk made their appearance in Yiddish prayers before the publication of Kabbalistic Hebrew prayer books. However, the resurgence of interest in Kabbalah in the wake of the Lurianic movement and the publication of Kabbalistic Hebrew prayer books strengthened this trend and transformed it from a minor one into a major influence.

Notes

1 The author, Yosef Yakir (or bar Yakar), who published his book in the small town of Ichenhausen, admits in the introduction that he had before him older manuscripts and that he relied on them for his book. See Yisroel Tsinberg, *Geshikhte fun der Literatur bay Yidn* (Vilna: Tomor Publishing Co., 1933), Vol. 6, p. 113.

2 Tsinberg, pp. 274, 320. Rivke Tiktiner also authored a compilation of aggadic and musar literature entitled *Meynekes Rivke*. For more on authors of *tkheenes* see *Encyclopedia Judaica* (Jerusalem: Keter Publishing House Ltd., 1971), Vol. 11, p. 358.

3 Tsinberg, p. 274.

4 *Encyclopedia Judaica,* and Tsinberg, pp. 286-290. For a full list of women authors see S. Niger, *Bleter Geshikhte fun der Yidishe Literatur* (New York: Congress for Jewish Culture, 1959), p. 88 ff.

5 Solomon Freehof, "Devotional Literature in the Vernacular," *Yearbook of Central Conference of American Rabbis* (1923), pp. 3-42.

6 Freehof, p. 16

7 All the page references here are to the New York reprint.

8 This is a standard prayer that can be found in all Ashkenazic prayer books. The prayer book used here is the *Makhzor Raba*, printed by the Eshkol Publishing Company in Jerusalem.

9 I myself observed this in a khassidic (Transylvanian) congregation. I am quite sure this is deliberate, for the cantor repeated this practice year after year.

10 *Encyclopedia Judaica*, Vol. 6, p. 274.

[11] This *mido roo* is an expression for the evil which, according to some Kabbalists, inheres in the Godhead Scholem quotes from the *Sefer Habohit.*" ... we learn that the Holy One Blessed be He has a trait whose name is evil... ." See G. Scholem, *Pirker Yesod Behavant Hakabala Usmaleha* (Jerusalem: Mosad Boyalik Press, 1977), p. 194 ff.

[12] Gershom Scholem, *Major Trends in Jewish Mysticism* (New York: Schocken Books, Inc., 1954), pp. 265-66.

[13] Scholem, p. 119.

[14] Gershom Scholem, *Kabbalah* (Jerusalem: Keter Publishing House, 1974), p. 116.

[15] Scholem, *Kabbalah*, p. 119.

[16] Scholem, *Kabbalah*, p. 159.

[17] The Rabbinic misgivings about mystical contemplation are well known (see *Khagiga,* 14b). But since Kabbalistic ideas were so rooted among the folk, an apparent compromise was to reserve Kabbalistic prayer for the individual. From what Scholem says it would appear that at one time Kabbalistic Hebrew prayer books were more common than they are now. (Scholem, *Kabbalah,* p. 194).

[18] Freehof, p. 41.

[19] Tsinberg, p. 33.

[20] Tsinberg, p. 33, footnote 71.

Naphtali Herz Imber as a Yiddish Poet

Jacob Kabakoff

Naphtali Herz Imber (1856-1909) often characterized himself as the Jewish "national poet." On numerous occasions he would sign his literary contributions in Hebrew, Yiddish, and English as "Baal Hatikvah," never allowing his readers to forget that he was the author of the Jewish national anthem.

Imber's life and career have served as the subject of many articles and appreciations. Several of these were occasioned by the controversy surrounding the adoption of "Hatikvah" as an official anthem. The controversy flared up again as recently as March, 1984, when it was unsuccessfully sought to have the Israeli Knesset enact into law a bill to give the anthem formal recognition.

Because of his bohemian way of life and his non-conformism, Imber became a favorite subject for memoirists, and various writers and Zionist leaders have recorded their impressions of him.[1] The Yiddish press often devoted space to his career and featured discussions about his anthem and its melody.

It was perhaps this concentration on Imber as the author of "Hatikvah" that led to the neglect of other aspects of his trilingual writing. While attention has been paid to his Hebrew output,[2] his writings in both English and Yiddish remain uncollected.

Imber's Yiddish contributions are scattered in various American Yiddish periodicals and newspapers. On occasion, he would publish Yiddish versions side by side with his Hebrew poems. An original Yiddish poem, "Tsu di Yapanezer" ("To the Japanese"), was included by him in his third *Barkai* collection of Hebrew poems, while a Yiddish translation accompanied one of his Hebrew poems, "Arba Koses" ("Four Cups"), in his brochure *Leha-Ivriyah.* In all, I have located some two dozen Yiddish poems from Imber's pen, and they deserve to be collected together with the poet's occasional Yiddish prose pieces.

Imber's Yiddish writings saw publication during his American period which began in 1891. This period was one of wandering for the poet who often referred to himself as a "rolling stone." During this time he devoted himself mainly to literary work in English. He was the author of two English books as well as several brochures, the editor of a journal devoted to mysticism and kabbalistic science, and the contributor of articles to magazines and publications throughout the country. He did not completely neglect his Hebrew muse, however, publishing an occasional Hebrew poem in the press. The most important of his Hebrew writings in book form, published while he lived in America, were: *Barkai He-Hadash* (Zloczow: 1900), *Barkai Ha-Shelishi* (New York: 1904), and his translation of Edgar Fitzgerald's version of the *Rubaiyat of Omar Khayyam* entitled *Ha-Kos* (New York: 1905).

Actually, Imber began to publish in Yiddish even before his arrival in America. That Yiddish was his mother tongue is clear from the letters which he sent home from the various places to which he travelled. Several of these letters were deposited by his brother Shemaryahu in the Jewish National and University Library in Jerusalem. In a letter that the poet addressed to his mother from London in 1887, he indicated that he had become a contributor to the Yiddish weekly *Hashulamis*, which was edited by Jehiel Brill. In his Yiddish letter, which bears no date, he wrote:

> Dear Mother:
>
> I am, thank God, in good health. Do not think that my situation is a sad one. The devil is not as black as they paint him. I earn more than my needs. I am paid 5 gulden weekly by "Hashulamis" for my articles. For Rosh Hashanah I received 35 gulden for 2 articles... .

It was in London that Imber was befriended by Israel Zangwill, at whose instance he began to write in the weekly *Jewish Standard*. It was here that he published his series of articles later reprinted under the title *Topics of To-Day in the Talmud* (London: 1889) and his autobiographical chapters, "Leaves from My Palestine and Other Diaries." (1898-90) From London Imber emigrated to America in 1891 and lived at first in New York. He often visited Philadelphia, where Judge Mayer Sulzberger became his patron. Here he published various articles in the weekly *Jewish Exponent* (1891-92).

In 1893 Imber settled in Boston, where he contributed to the local *Jewish Chronicle* on such subjects as hypnotism and astrology and where he established connections with theosophist and spiritualist circles and lectured before Church groups on Jewish mysticism. In a letter to his mother from Boston he told of his activities at this time and wrote: "I am misunderstood...for the Orthodox I am a non-believer and for the Reform I am religious." It was in Boston that Imber launched his journal *Uriel*, "a monthly magazine devoted to Cabbalist Science." However, only one issue of the magazine, dated August 9, 1893 and written entirely by its editor, appeared. Imber's wanderings took him as far as California, and his English publications turn up in Indianapolis, Los Angeles, and elsewhere. At the beginning of the century he returned to New York, where he became a familiar figure on the Lower East Side and published also in Yiddish.

Among the Yiddish publications to which Imber contributed were *Der Yudishe Puk* (New York: 1895) and *Der Yidisher Odler* (Boston: 1901). A number of his poems are signed: "Naphtali Herz Imber, der ferfaser fun Hatikve" (Naphtali Herz Imber, author of Hatikvah). Most of Imber's Yiddish poems, however, were printed in *Minikes Monat Blat un Yontev Bleter,* during 1901-06. During 1902-03 he contributed also to Kasriel Tsvi Sarasohn's *Yidishes Tageblat,* as well as his weekly *Yudishe Gazetn,* which reprinted material from the previous week's *Tageblat.*

The chief motifs which find expression in Imber's Yiddish poems are those of lament for Jewish suffering and of hope for reestablishment in the Land of Israel. In his poems devoted to the Jewish holidays the poet often reiterated the line from his anthem "Hatikvah": *od lo ovdo tikvosenu* (our hope is still not lost). Two of his poems were devoted to America. Interestingly enough, Imber did not share the deep pessimism of other immigrant Hebrew and Yiddish poets regarding the new land. On the contrary, he extolled its spirit of freedom and saw in it a basis for his own hope to witness the reconstitution of Jewish freedom in Jerusalem. A few of his poems have a satiric edge. While Imber's poetic output in Yiddish is mainly of historical-cultural interest, it offers a number of variations on his themes of hope and national restoration and places him within the bilingual tradition of many leading Hebrew writers. It should be noted that a number of Imber's Hebrew poems, some of which are still uncollected, were also published in American Yiddish periodicals which were hospitable to his writings.

Imber's earliest Yiddish verses to be published in America were in the form of a poetic greeting to the weekly humoristic journal *Yudisher Puk.* To its first issue (October 20, 1895), he contributed "A Lakhediger Grus tsum Lachedign Puk" ("A Funny Greeting to the Funny Puck"), in which he declared that it was better for Jews to laugh than to mourn and sigh. At the same time, he stressed the theme of revenge for Jewish suffering, a theme to which he was to return, particularly after the Kishinev pogrom.

The poet's preoccupation with talmudic legends was evidenced in his Hebrew poetry as well as his English collections, *Treasures of Ancient Jerusalem* (Los Angeles: 1898) and *Treasures of Two Worlds* (Los Angeles: 1910). The rabbinic account of the defiant act of the last high priest, who cast the Temple keys heavenward when the Romans burnt the sanctuary, served as the basis for one of his Hebrew poems. It also was the subject of his Yiddish poem, "Der Letster Koyn Godl" ("The Last High Priest"), which he contributed to *Der Yidisher Odler* (August 15, 1901).

Imber began his participation in Khonen Yankev Minikes's publications with his poem "Zekher Liytsias Mitsrayim" ("In Remembrance of the Departure from Egypt"), published in the Passover *Yontev Bleter* of April, 1901. The poem was touted by the editor as being from the pen of "the great Jewish poet Naphtali Herz Imber." Recalling the Passover experience, the poet exhorted his readers to act in the spirit of the festival and strike out for freedom, rather than continue to suffer while awaiting the coming of the Messiah. He wrote:

> Gedenk un yetsias Mitsrayim,
> Gedenk di lektsyon,
> Gey tsurik kayn Yerusholayim,
> Dort vest du zayn a natsyon.
>
> (Remember the exodus from Egypt,
> Remember the lesson.
> Return to Jerusalem,
> Where you will be a nation.)

A short holiday piece in the same journal (February, 1902) was devoted to "Khamishoser Bishvat oder der Nay-Yor fun di Boymer" ("The Fifteenth of Shevat or the New Year of the Trees"). The poet commented on the symbolism of the holiday and included two stanzas of verse in which he compared man to a tree. Like the tree, man can renew himself and a people can be reborn:

Unzer lebn iz a troym,
Mir zind geglikhn tsu a boym.
Dokh unzere gedankn tsien,
Obvol mir zaynen troymer.
Mir veln vider blien,
Gleikh vi dize boymer.

(Our life is a dream,
We are like a tree,
Still our thoughts spread forth,
For we are dreamers.
We shall bloom again,
Like these trees.)

Another early poem, published in Minikes's journal in July, 1902, was in the form of a greeting to the publisher. Imber had words of praise for Minikes's efforts to edify the public and wished him success in his endeavors. In the same issue we find a Hebrew poem by Imber accompanied by his Yiddish translation. The poem, "Dray Idn" ("Three Jews"), draws a parallel between the tallit and the Jewish flag and asserts that as long as there are three Jews who hold fast to the flag, they will yet inherit their ancestral land:

Zo lang nokh dray idn
Haltn di fon in der hant,
Zo lang hofn mir nokh in fridn
Tsu hobn unzer land.

(So long as three Jews still
Hold the flag in their hand,
So long do we still hope in peace
To have our land.)

The August, 1902 issue of the *Yontev Bleter* contains three contributions from Imber's pen. His poem "Tishe Bov" ("The Ninth of Av") evokes the images of Jeremiah, the prophet of the destruction, and Mother Rachel, who implores God in behalf of her people. In addition to a short prose piece, "Shabes Nakhmu" ("Sabbath of Consolation"), that emphasized the need to look to the future and to derive hope from the Zionist vision, he published under the same title a poem in Hebrew together with his Yiddish translation. Here he enlarged on the comforting message of Isaiah and assured his people that their exile would soon be ended.

In September, 1902, Imber reprinted in Minikes's journal his Hebrew poem "Ha-Shofar" ("The Ram's Horn"), which had previously seen publication in *Ha-Meliz*, together with his Yiddish translation. Here the poet dwelled on the historic role of the ram's horn as a call to awakening and heroism:

Der antisemit, di vilde brie,
Macht zikh tsum kampf berayt;
Blozt idn a "true,"
Feraynigt aykh tsum shtrayt.

Blozt shoyfer tsu proklamirn
Dos heylige menshnrekht;
Nokh tsien unz tsu firn,
Tsu befrayn di knekht.

(The anti-Semite, the wild creature,
Prepares himself for battle;
Blow, Jews, a "teruah,"
Unite for the strife.

Blow the shofar to proclaim
The sacred human right,
To lead us to Zion,
To free the slaves.)

To Minikes's Sukkot issue of October, 1902, Imber contributed two items: his poem "A Gut Kvitl" ("A Good Message") and two prose pieces – "Di Royte Idlekh" ("The Red Jews") and "Shabes Breyshis" ("Sabbath of Genesis"). The poem is set in a Sukkah where, after taking leave of the special guests, the celebrant receives a favorable telegram informing him that he held a winning lottery ticket. "The Red Jews" discusses the background of the Yemenite Jews who returned to Palestine and were contributing to the upbuilding of the country. It is noteworthy that Imber again gave a laudatory portrayal of "The Red Jews" in an English sketch, which appeared in the Chicago *Reform Advocate* (February 22, 1908) as part of his notable series entitled "Imber's Picture Gallery." This work is a source of valuable background material on the poet's life and views. The second prose piece, "Sabbath of Genesis," offers some reflections on the seasonal changes in nature.

In December, 1902, the Hanuḳkah issue of Minikes's journal carried the Hebrew text and music of "Hatikvah." The republishing of the poem was occasioned by the following letter by Imber in which he announced the 25th anniversary of the composing of his anthem:

> Honored friend Kh.Y. Minikes, editor of the "Minikes Monat un Yontev Bleter":
>
> On the occasion of the anniversary of the "Hatikvo" I am sending you the "Hatikvo" with the original music as a present for your hundreds and thousands of readers, and for you in recognition of your efforts to renew the Jewish spirit, as well as Jewish literature and art, in America and Canada.

Appearing on the same page of Minikes's journal was a poem entitled "Khanike Fest der Makabeyer" ("The Hanukkah Festival of the Maccabees"), in which the poet has Mattathias cry out "Barkai" when he issues the call to revolt. The poet concludes with the hope that a modern Maccabee might arise to lead his people back to their homeland. The term "Barkai" is a recurring one in Imber's poetry. It appears in the titles of three of his poetry collections and was employed by the poet as a symbol of the dawning of a new rebirth. "Barkai" is the morning star whose appearance was announced by a watchman in Temple days, signalling the time for the daily morning sacrifice.

An announcement by the editor regarding the 25th anniversary of "Hatikvah" informed his readers that a special fund had been set up for Imber, who was said to be very ill and in need, and urged them to send their contributions care of Judge Mayer Sulzberger in Philadelphia. It was this announcement which called forth an attack upon Imber in the press.

Previously, Akiva Fleishman of New York had written to *Ha-Meliz* of Imber's illness and of the poet's desire to issue a third collection of his Hebrew poetry. In the issue of June 12, 1902, the editor of *Ha-Meliz* appealed for funds in Imber's behalf. On December 2, 1902, there appeared in this publication a letter by Imber in which he reported that a committee, consisting of Dr. Richard Gottheil, Zvi Hirsch Masliansky, Rabbi Bernard Levinthal, and Dr. David Blaustein, had been formed to commemorate the 25th anniversary of "Hatikvah." He added that if Zionists in other countries would follow suit, he would be able to issue his third *Barkai* collection of Hebrew poetry and to collect his scattered writings.

Imber published an indignant reply to his critics in the *Yudishes Tageblat* (December 7, 1902) entitled "A Poet Protestirt" ("A Poet Protests"). He stated that he had never begged and that he was not asking for charity. He indicated that as the author of the Jewish national anthem which had received such wide acceptance, he was entitled to public support. Moreover, he stated that his request had received the backing of the press. Imber denied the allegation that he had composed his anthem in a wine-cellar. He maintained that he had written it in Jassy, Rumania, in the home of Baron Waldberg. He further requested that the newspapers support his cause and that the Zionists repay the debt owed him.

In a poem entitled "Der Seder," which appeared in Minikes's Passover issue in 1905, Imber expressed the hope that the day might soon come when Jews would no longer need the reminder of the "morer and kharoyses":

Dokh kumen vird di tsayt
Fun der tsukunftign Peysekh fest,
Ven der yud vird aynladn
Di felker zich tsu gest.

Der tish vird zein gedekt,
Gefilt mit vayn di koyses,
Nur esn vird men nisht mer
Den morer un kharoyses.

(Yet will come the time
Of the future Passover Feast,
When the Jew will invite
The nations to be their guests.

The table will be set,
The glasses filled with wine,
But no more will we eat
The maror and haroset.)

Imber's holiday poem entitled "Di Idishe Yomim Toyvim" ("The Jewish Holidays") was printed in Minikes's *Yor-Bukh* for 1904-05. Here he characterized Passover, Shavuot, Sukkot, and Hanukkah as representing the people's fundamental ideals of freedom, education, the capacity to suffer, and courage. In the *Yomim Noyroim und Sukes Blat* for 1906 there appeared his poem "Di Ershte Slikhes"[3] ("The First Seliḥot"), in which he recalled the practice of the "shamash," who summoned the worshippers to the early morning penitential prayers. His poem concluded on a nationalistic note:

Gib unz vider unzer land,
Lomir shoyn hern dos vort "solakhti"!

(Give us our land again,
Let us hear already the word "Forgiven!")

Imber's poem "Tsu Amerike" ("To America") appeared in Minikes's *Yor-Bukh* for 1906. Extolling America's freedom, he indicated that it had served to strengthen his own resolve to live in freedom in the Jewish homeland. The poem is given here, followed by Joseph Leftwich's translation:[4]

Ikh shayde fun dir,
Du land der frayhayt.
Kayn Yerushalayim fur ikh,
Mayn heylike trayhayt.

Unter dayn odlers fligl,
Hob ikh ruik gelebt;
Ober tomed hobn mayne gedankn,
Nokh Yerushalayim geshtrebt.

Ikh hob bay dir gelernt,
Vi azoy tsu zayn tray;
Dayn lektsya iz mir heylik,
Dos heyst: "mentsh, zay fray".

Dort, oyf dem barg Moriye,
Als vekhter vel ikh shteyn;
Biz ale tsiens fonen,
Veln oyf dem har hazeysim veyn.

Ikh vel aykh mer nit zen,
Mayne libe brider;
Nor filn vet ir mayn vey,
Baym zingen mayne lider.

(I leave you now,
Land of liberty.
To Jerusalem I take
my fidelity.

Beneath your eagle wings
I lived at peace,
But my desire for Jerusalem
Will never cease.

You have taught me one thing
That a man must be,
I shall always remember it
"A man must be free."

There on Mount Moriah
On guard I shall stand,
Till from the Mount of Olives
Zion's flags wave over the land.

Farewell, my brothers,
I shall not see you again,
But when you sing my songs
You will feel my pain.)

As indicated, Imber also contributed several poems to Kasriel Tsvi Sarasohn's periodicals. In honor of the fifth convention of the Federation of American Zionists held in Boston, he published in the *Tageblat* (May 23, 1902) his rousing verses entitled "Hura fir Tsien" ("Hurrah for Zion"). A holiday poem in honor of Shavuot (*Yidishe Gazetn*, June 13, 1902) was entitled "Unzer Konstitutsyon" ("Our Constitution") and extolled the Torah which made the Jews a nation.

Begrist idn,
Mit fridn,
Unzer sheyne konstitutsyon.
Unzer skhoyre,
Di heylike Torah,
Hot unz gemakht a natsyon!

(Greet, Jews,
In peace,
Our lovely constitution
Our commodity,
The holy Torah,
Has made us a nation!)

Of greater importance is Imber's poem "Tsum Fertn Zhulay" ("On the Fourth of July"), published in the *Tageblat* (July 1, 1902), in which the poet compared American and Jewish freedom.[5] He lauded America for upholding Jewish rights and in his concluding stanza prophesied:

Mir veln nokh derlebn
Unzer land vird zurik gegebn.
Dan Karmel vayn vet flisn,
Harmatn veln shisn.
Un mir veln oykh beshraybn
Yisroels Fertn Zhulay.

(We shall yet live to see
Our land restored to us.
Then Carmel wine will flow,
The cannons will boom.
And we, too, shall write of
Israel's Fourth of July.)

Imber's "Shabes Nakhmu Gedankn" ("Sabbath Nahamu Thoughts"), which appeared in the *Tageblat* (August 15, 1902), depicts the prophet of old who spoke his words of comfort atop the Mount of Olives. The poet looks forward to the day when the victorious Song of Deborah will again be heard in the homeland.

A memorable poem of Imber's, published in the *Tageblat* (August 27, 1902) in the original Hebrew together with a Yiddish version, was "Mayn Shvue" ("My Oath"). When Imber's bones were transferred to Jerusalem in 1953, the opening prophetic stanza of his poem saw fulfillment. Imber wrote:

Ikh beshver aykh shvester un brider,
Bay dem, ver dos lebn vebt,
Di vos hobn gehert mayne lider,
Ven ikh hob oyf der erd gelebt.
Ven Got, der arkhitekt eyner,

Vet aykh fun goles aroystsien,
Klaybt tsuzamen mayne beyner
Fun a fremd land nokh tsien.

(I adjure you sisters and brothers
By Him who weaves life,
You who have heard my poems
When I lived on earth.
When God, the supreme architect,
Will take you out of exile,
Gather my bones together
From a foreign land to Zion.)

Here, as in many other poems, Imber assumed the stance of a national poet and spokesman of his people, who never abandoned his faith that his message would live on after him.

Often Imber could strike a satiric and even sardonic note, as is evidenced by the familiar essays which he contributed to the English-Jewish press. In this vein his poem, "Varten oyf a Brif" ("Waiting for a Letter"), published in the *Tageblat* (June 29, 1902), describes the impatience of a man who awaits his mail, hoping to hear from a rich uncle or a lover. When a letter finally arrives, all it brings is a gas bill for two months.

Imber's moving poem, "Mayn Gebet tsum Shnyder" ("My Prayer to the Tailor"), appeared in the *Tageblat* on August 3, 1902. This was a rendering of his Hebrew poem *Tefillah le-Tofer* which the poet had also translated into English for the *Tageblat* (December 25, 1904). Both the Hebrew and English versions were reprinted in the poet's third *Barkai* collection. Comparing God to a Master Tailor, Imber besought him in the last stanza of his halting translation as follows:

Great Tailor, Thy praises I sing.
See my body is bent,
My old coat to Thee, I bring,
By Thee to be mend.
To old age is due,
From tooth of time torn,
From old age outworn,
From its symetric shorn,
Please make from it anew.

During 1902 Imber contributed two additional poems on holiday themes to Sarasohn's newspapers. In the *Gazetn* (October 1, 1902) there appeared the poem "Rosh Hashone oder a Gut Kvitl" ("Rosh Hashanah or a Good Judgment"), in which the poet's prayer for a new "kvitl" from the heavenly court includes not only a request for material well-being, but also the age-old hope that the Jews write a new chapter in Jewish history:

Shik unz a nay gut kvitl,
Freylikh zoln zayn di berikhte.
Shrayb un a nay kapitl
In der idisher velt-geshikhte.

(Send us a new, good judgment,
Joyous be the reports.
Write a new chapter
In Jewish world-history.)

Imber's "Khanike Lid" ("Hanukkah Song"), published in the *Tageblat* (December 8, 1902), utilized the symbol of the festival lights to recall the Maccabean spirit and to aspire to a revival of the national spirit in modern times:

Fun shteyn un tsementn
Makht men monumentn
Far heldn mit gever.
Mir yuden andresh zenen.
Mir tuen likhtlekh breyngn,
Un mit gezang anerkenen
Di heldn, di Makabeyer.

(Of stone and cement
They make monuments
For heroes with weapons.
We Jews are different.
We have candles brought,
And with song acknowledge
The heroes, the Maccabees.)

In his Hebrew poetry composed in Palestine during his sojourn there during the 1880s, Imber had sung a paean of praise to the early pioneers of Rishon le-Zion, Gedera, and Rosh Pinah. In America he followed the Jewish agricultural efforts and periodically spent time in such settlements as Woodbine, Rosenhayn, and Carmel in New

Jersey.[6] He was moved to pen a poem in praise of agricultural work, entitled "A Gezang tsum Feld Arbayter" ("A Song to the Farmer"), which appeared in the *Tageblat* (March 11, 1903). He extolled the virtues of pastoral life and expressed his own yearning to be part of it:

O gliklikher boyer,
O gliklikher held!
Vayt, vayt fun velts troyer
Ferlebst du in feld!
Nor un groys midn
Bliet oyf dayn gesheft.
Tsu dem volt ikh flien
Mit dir zikh beheft!

(O happy farmer,
O happy hero!
Far, far from the world's sorrow.
You abide in the field!
With but little effort
Your enterprise blooms.
To this would I flee
And join with you!)

Imber's eventful life served regularly as good copy for the trilingual American Jewish press which reported on the state of his health and his activities. Yet an article by Tashrak (Yisroel Yosef Zevin) that appeared in the *Tageblat* (March 4, 1903) spoke of Imber as "Der Fargesener Dikhter" ("The Forgotten Poet"). Tashrak invoked the pathetic figure of the poet at a Zionist meeting on a blistery winter evening. All sing "Hatikvah," but the forlorn and sick poet is bereft of hope.

When Kasriel Tsvi Sarasohn died, Imber penned a Hebrew elegy entitled "Kinah al Mot Sarasohn" ("An Elegy on Sarasohn's Death"), which appeared in the *Gazetn* (January 20, 1905). Imber had occasion to eulogize another prominent figure, the Yiddish dramatist Yankev Gordin, in a Hebrew poem which he published in the *Varheit* (June 13, 1909). When Imber himself died, the Hebrew-Yiddish writer Getsl Selikovitch published a Hebrew elegy on him in the *Gazetn* (October 11, 1909), in which the poet's name appeared in the form of an acrostic. The first stanza reads:

Naphtali! Azavtani, akh sefatekha lo ne'elmu.
Po'olekha be-shire tsiyon od yera'u al banenu:
Tashir be-kivrekha, hegyonotekha lo yitamu –
Le-yesha amkha – "od lo avdah tikvatenu".

(Naphtali! You forsook me, but your lips
are not silenced.
Your Zionist songs will still be cherished by
our children.
You sing in your grave, your thoughts shall
not perish –
For your people's salvation – "Our hope is
not yet lost.")

Among Imber's recurring themes was that of protest against Jewish suffering and persecution. He was particularly outraged by the Kishinev pogrom of 1903, and he devoted several poems to the tragic events in Russia. In 1904 he published his Hebrew poetry collection *Barkai Ha-Shelishi O Goel Ha-Dam (The Third Barkai or the Blood Avenger)*, in which he poured out his wrath. He dedicated his volume to the Mikado, because of the role which Japan played in combatting Russia. He excoriated the Russians as "savages," "Greeks," and "Edomites," and expressed satisfaction over their anticipated defeat at the hands of the Japanese. In addition to English translations of two of his militant poems ("To Ivan the Terrible" and "On to War"), he included his original Yiddish poem "Tsu di Yapanezer," in which he looked forward to Japan's victory over the Russians. He maintained that such a victory would be just retribution for the Czarist tyranny which had been responsible for the spilling of so much Jewish blood in Kishinev and Hommel. He proclaimed:

Geyt mutig Yapanezer!
Tsubrekht di finstere makht!
Geyt mutik Yapanezer!
Got firt far aykh di shlakht.

(Go courageously, Japanese!
Smash the dark power!
Go courageously, Japanese!
God leads you into battle.)

Imber also published a Yiddish version side by side with his Hebrew poem "Arba Koses" ("Four Cups") in his miniature brochure, *Leha-Ivriyah* (*To the Hebrew Language* [Phila.: 1909]). The four quartrains describe four cups: the cup of poison, the cup of sorrow, the cup of consolation and the cup of hope. Regarding the cup of hope, he wrote:

Trink fun dem bekher fun hofn,
Trink, der "Tikvo" vayn iz gut.
Dayn land vet zayn ofn
Shtreb dokh, mayn folk, mit mut.

(Drink the cup of hope,
The "Tikvah" wine is good,
Your land will yet be free –
Yearn, my people, courageously.)

When Imber died on Simhat Torah, October 9, 1909, the Yiddish press gave considerable space to his life-story and his funeral. Even prior to his death, the poet Avrohom Mikhl Sharkansky devoted a long poem to Imber, in which he praised him for his many years of devotion as a poet of "hope and pain," and commiserated with him in his loneliness and sorrow as a Jewish writer. He concluded with the verses:

Oremer Naftali Herts!
Sforim mer – heyst merer shmerts.
In ek velt klingt op dayn shir
Un es felt kheyune dir.

Host gezungn hoykh un zis,
Hofenungn, tsiens gris,
Un kayner eyner denkt un dir,
Krigst nor shteyner far dayn shir.

Oremer veyner, zeh nit veyn,
Fun di shteyner vert eyn shteyn.
Un dayn monument vert gants,
Vos farblendet durkh varn glants.

(Poor Naphtali Herz!
The more books – the more pain.
Your song is heard everywhere,
But you lack means of support,
You sang loudly and sweetly,
Of hopes and Zion's greetings,
And no one gives you a thought.

You receive only stones for your song.
Poor bewailer, do not weep.
The stones will be merged into one.
Your monument will then be complete.
And dazzle with true brilliance.)

Sharkansky also translated "Hatikvah" into Yiddish.[7]

Following Imber's death, Morris Rosenfeld published a long memorial poem in the *Forverts* (October 16, 1909), entitled "Tsvey Bekher" ("Two Goblets"). He described two golden goblets which God had ordained to be filled to the brim – "one goblet full of Erets Yisroel wine,/the other with the Jew's bitter pain." Imber had first drunk from the *golus* goblet and had bemoaned his people's sad fate. Then he refreshed himself from the second goblet and joyfully sang "Hatikvah." Rosenfeld wrote:

Er hot derlebt zayn umes yungster dor
Zol singn im di "Hofenung" in khor;
Er hot gezen vi der fertsagter, oremer id
Shtralt oyf mit tayneg fun Hatikvo lid.
Dokh im aleyn, on hofenung un on glik
Hot shtil der elent tsugemakht zayn blik
Gants vayt fun dort, vuhin er hot geshtrebt,
Fun dort vu zayn kholem hot geshvebt...

(He lived to see his people's youth
Sing his "Hatikvo" in chorus;
He saw how the despondent, sad Jew
Beamed with pleasure at his song of hope.
But he himself, without hope or luck
In loneliness quietly shut his eyes,
Quite distant from his place of yearning,
From the land where hovered his dream...)

Abraham Cahan published a necrology in the *Forverts* (October 9, 1909), which presented an evaluation of Imber as a misunderstood, tragic figure who possessed a poetic soul. The newspaper also carried in translation an extract from Israel Zangwill's *Children of the Ghetto*, in which Imber was said to be represented by the character Melchitsedek Pinchas. Morris Winchevsky, in a caustic article which he wrote for *Di Tsukunft* (November 1909), criticized those who had praised the poet after his death, but failed to pay him any attention while he was alive. He wrote:

Un tsentoyzent menshen hobn im melave geven, im aroysbeglaytendik fun der velt, vu er is far file geven a dorn in oyg, a flek oyf der mishpokhe, zogar a shter tsu der kdushe fun zein "Hatikvo" alayn.

Un aroysbeglayt hobn zey im mit prakht un glants, bekhatsotsroys vekol shoyfer, mit muzik un groys koved, in karates un tsufus.

Es is gut tsu zayn geshtorbn!

(Ten thousand people came to his funeral and escorted him out of the world, where for many he was a mote in the eye, a stain on the family honor, even an obstacle to the holiness of "Hatikvoh" itself.

They accompanied him with pomp and ceremony, with the blaring of trumpets, with music and great honor, in carriages and on foot.

It is good to be dead!)

The Yiddish memoir literature on Imber is extensive. Among the writers and personalities who included the poet in their published memoirs in book form were: Abraham Cahan, Gershom Bader, Mordecai Danzis, Zvi Hirsch Masliansky, Roza Shomer Bachelis, and Celia Adler. Imber also served as the protagonist in two short sketches based on events in his life by Joseph Opatoshu.[8]

Notes

1 For a survey of this memoir literature see my article, "N.H. Imber in the Eyes of His Contemporaries" (Hebrew), *Hadoar*, November 9, 16, 23, 1979.

2 On the occasion of the 50th anniversary of "Hatikvah," a committee published *Mivhar Kitve Naphtali Herz Imber* (Tel Aviv: 1929). His collected poems were published under the title, *Kol Shire Naphtali Herz Imber* (Tel Aviv: 1950), with an introduction by Dov Sadan and a biography by Shemaryahu Imber.

3 The poem was reprinted in *Yidishe Kultur* (November, 1956), on the occasion of the 100th anniversary of Imber's birth.

4 The poem appeared in Joseph Leftwich (Ed.), *The Golden Peacock: An Anthology of Yiddish Poetry* (Cambridge, Mass.: 1939), p. 800. It was included by Nachman Mayzel in his Yiddish anthology, *Amerike in Yidishn Vort* (New York: 1955), p. 57. An additional translation, by Moshe Kalmus, appeared in *Pioneer Woman* (October-November, 1977), p. 17.

5 Imber also published a Hebrew patriotic poem with the English subtitle, "A Jewish Salutation to the American Eagle," in the *Hebrew Standard* (New York, December 1, 1905). It extolled the American Eagle for spreading its pro-

tective wings over the Jews, and appeared on the occasion of the celebration of the 250th anniversary of the settlement of the Jews in the United States.

[6] See his article, "A Unique Jewish Colony – A Word to the Baron de Hirsch Fund," *Hebrew Standard* (June 8, 1906).

[7] In *Der Lider Magazin* (New York) No. 19, (1908). Another translation by Berele Chagy, the well known cantor, is found in the collection, Janot S. Roskin (Ed.), *Juedische Volkslieder* (Berlin: 1916), Samml. II, op. 12, Heft I, p. 15. Getzel Kressel published in *Haymish* (Tel Aviv), No. 47 (April, 1960), p. 8, the unpublished translation of "Hatikvah" by Zvi Ha-Kohen Shereshevsky, which can be found at the Genazim Institute, Tel-Aviv.

[8] The sketches appeared under the title, "Der Kenig fun di Shnorers" ("King of the Schnorrers") in *Der Tog* (January 5, 1929) and were reprinted in *Poylishe Idn* (June, 1927), pp. 17-18.

The Yiddish Theatre as a Species of Folk Art: Lateiner's *The Jewish Heart* (1908)

Dinnah Pladott

The Folk Roots of the Yiddish Theatre

Historians concur in tracing the development of the Yiddish theatre as an offshoot of the 19th century Haskala movement,[1] the Jewish Enlightenment. Although spearheaded by intellectuals, the Haskala aimed at reaching, modernizing, and uplifting the masses of Jews in Eastern Europe. Yet, while the Haskala was challenging traditional Jewish customs and practices in the name of secular ideas, a religious movement, Chassidism, was challenging the Jewish community from its religious flank. The Chassidic movement celebrated the common, unlearned man's mystical experience in preference to the Talmudic scholar's rarefied learning. It glorified spontaneous song and dance as personal expressions of trust and faith in the Divine principle; it legitimized and honored the humor, lyrics, and lore of the common people, all produced in the Yiddish vernacular. Above all, its emphasis was on the intuitive, emotional experience of the heart, rather than on the rational, analytic expressions of the mind. My intention in this paper is to discuss the manner in which the developing Yiddish theatre drew on these specific folk sources, creating a new and effective form of communal cultural activity.

The Jewish dramatists were neither free nor willing to pursue in their plays the desire for mere self-expression. They felt duty-bound to write not merely in the language easily understood by their people, in all senses of this concept, but to evoke folks yearnings in the folk idiom with rhythm and anecdote, drawing on folk themes, situations, and legends, which had one thing in common: "Jewish joys and Jewish sorrows, whether of the individual or of the people as a whole."[2] Jewish theatre practitioners, from the playwright Perez Hirshbein (1881-1948) to director Jacob Mestel (1884-1952), recognized and reasserted the fact that folk tradition, folk sentiments, and folk culture, whose values and significance were underscored by the Chassidic movement, were the core of the Yiddish play. The Jewish audiences may have demanded so-called "formula plays."[3] But formula plays were essentially the plays of the common folk.

Consequently, I suggest that in utilizing simple and uncomplicated theatrical forms, such as the melodrama, or the much-maligned *shund* mode, which relies heavily on crude and vulgar theatrical effects, insulting repartees, and puns, the Yiddish theatre was not "pandering to the masses," as critics often charged.[4] On the contrary, it was actually fulfilling its artistic mission: to carry on an intense dialogue with its community. In this dialogue, the Yiddish playwright played a dual role. On the one hand, he came to enlighten his audiences, in the best Haskala tradition. In plays translating ideas, situations, and characters from Jewish as well as non-Jewish plays into the immediate actuality of Jewish existence, he lay bare to critical view ignorant customs, superstitions, prejudices, and traditional abuse. On the other hand, the playwright had to have an acute perception of his community's spiritual needs and yearnings at the moment, expressing even in the most popular and entertaining plays the essence of the tragic and comic aspects of Jewish existence. Furthermore, the folkloristic elements which figured prominently in the performances – jokes, jests, folktales, and folksongs – were in turn incorporated very often into Jewish popular culture, as heightened moments of the plays were recited, sung, and danced by the people who viewed a performance, or by traveling actors and comics.[5]

Two members of The Prague Semiotic Circle, Bogatyrev and Jakobson, describe this dialogue as the process in which the folk theatre, as a species of folk creation, is shaped by the constant interaction of the artist and the community. "Let us assume," say Bogatyrev and Jakobson, "that a member of the community has composed something original. Should this oral work, created by the individual, be unacceptable to the community for one reason or another, should the other members of the community not appropriate it, it will be condemned to extinction."[6] This statement is tantamount to saying that in the folk theatre, the focus is on the receiver, rather than on the sender of the act of communication.[7] In the folk theatre, the act of communication between artist and audience must be successfully consummated if the work is to have any impact. The folk creator cannot choose to insist on far-reaching aesthetic innovation in the face of uncomprehending viewers, with the expectation or hope that some future audiences will demonstrate a greater responsiveness. To apply Jakobson's well-known terms, the highly innovative, aesthetically developed work emphasizes the "poetic function" of language, whereas the folk theatre subordinates the "poetic function" to both "phatic" and "conative" functions, and possibly also to the "referential" function.[8] The "conative" function of language, which concerns influencing and moving the audience, is here intertwined with the "phatic" function, which aims at keeping open both physical and psychological channels of communication. Hence, the folk playwright, who aims at reaching and affecting his audience, and is supremely concerned with eliciting a fruitful response from his viewers, needs to maintain a continuous contact between himself and the audience. He therefore goes to great lengths in order to insure that his code and his context are clear and persuasive at all times, so as to communicate successfully and appeal to the spectators' sensibilities and perceptions.

The Yiddish theatre illustrates Bogatyrev and Jakobson's thesis. Whether the playwright focused on enlightening the Jewish community about secular culture or on revitalizing the community's own Jewish roots, the Yiddish theatre turns out to have been in all its stages supremely sensitive to the specific communal needs.

Popular Theatrical Forms: Aesthetic Inferiority or Archetypal Thrust?

How could a theatre whose plays were as frequently inferior, crude, and vulgar as its critics claimed, function in such a sensitive and productive manner to satisfy the emotional and spiritual needs of its community? The question boggles the mind, unless we conclude that historians miss the point when they disparage the artistic quality of various plays, or types of plays, produced in the earlier stages of the Jewish theatre.[9] First, in condemning the utter responsiveness of the playwrights to the demands of their audiences, they criticize the Yiddish theatre for the dialogue which was, in effect, its greatest virtue. Second, the unsophisticated and apparently simple forms proved to be so effective in the dialogue between artist and audiences because they were able to convey directly and, so to speak, subliminally complex truths of the human spirit by virtue of their very simplicity. The melodrama, the farce, the tear-jerker, and the side-splitting slap-stick comedy – these "unrealistic" and extravagantly theatrical forms – are, in the final analysis, closely related to fairy tales and folk tales. The folk and fairy tales can be traced back not to any individual author, but to the anonymous, communal authorship of popular oral literature, the literature of the "unlettered people."[10] As Eliade observes, the world which these popular forms depict "is simple and clear [with] a total absence of the problematical." (p. 199) But although the tales often represent an unbounded optimism (the inevitable "happy end"), argues Eliade, their "content proper" nevertheless "refers to a terrifyingly serious reality: initiation, that is, passing, by way of a symbolic death and resurrection, from ignorance and immaturity to the spiritual age of the adult." (p. 201) The same thing may be observed about the popular theatre forms; the world they depict is "simple and clear" because it is rendered in a sharp chiaroscuro, but it is not Edenic. Even when the conflict and its outcome are humorous, the clash of good and evil is at their core, with issues of life and death hanging in the balance. If we group the comic popular forms used in the Jewish theatre with the "optimistic" fairy tale, and the tragic forms with the more somber folk tales, the analogy is clear.[11]

It seems to me that folk drama and theatre constitute, like myth and the folk tale, a form of communal and tribal cultural activity, whose fascination and effect reside in the reflection and enactment of an internal, rather than external, drama. Beneath the layer of ethnic and particularly Jewish details, the plots and action of Yiddish plays manifest for the spectators the conflicts and unravellings of psychic contradictions, repressed desires, wish-fulfillments, emotional crises, anxieties, and stages of spiritual development.[12] Furthermore, as the example of the Yiddish theatre will demonstrate, the unconscious fears and desires may pertain to the group and its journey of self-realization, rather than to the merely individual quest of any of its individual members. As a case study, illustrating (though by no means "proving") this contention, I undertake the analysis of a play often ridiculed and criticized for being artistically and aesthetically inferior.

By taking as an illustrative example a most popular play (in both senses of the words – "beloved of the masses" and "unsophisticated"), I want to test my hypothesis that even such a specimen has the potential to encode and represent what we have come to see as archetypal themes and concerns. Lateiner's *The Jewish Heart* (1908) is among those plays critics dismiss as "old operas and melodrama," "domestic drama," or "melodrama."[13] Yet, a close look at this "formulaic tear jerker" may throw a fresh light on the play's ability to function effectively in the dialogue between playwright and spectators. It may also throw into relief the fact that the very simplicity of the artistic form, its foundation of heightened contrasts and exaggerated distortions, constitutes a potential merit rather than a flaw.

The unfolding of the action in *The Jewish Heart* is simple. Yankev (Jacob), a poor Jewish orphan who is studying art in Rumania, wins a prize for a painting entitled "The Sinful Mother." This prize is won despite the bitter competition of his main rival, a Christian art student named Victor Popeska. Victor's jealousy at his failure is expressed in violently anti-Semitic remarks, although his mother, Madame Popeska, attempts to calm him down. Act I culminates in Yankev's surprising discovery that Madame Popeska is the mother who has abandoned him and his father (now dead) when he was still in the cradle. Moreover, Madame Popeska has run off with a Christian lover, and has born him Christian sons, so that Victor is in fact Yankev's brother.

Yankev is in love with the Jewish girl Dina. Act II centers around his need to get a parental signature in order to obtain a marriage license (in line with a new edict controlling Jewish affairs). His appeal to Madame Popeska at first meets with an emotional, positive response; mother and son, reunited, embrace. Victor, who comes in at that moment, is horrified both by the sight and by the news that he has a Jewish half-brother. The thought of a public acknowledgment of the facts is unbearable to Victor; he threatens Yankev with a gun.

Madame Popeska, torn between the two loyalties, finally refuses her signature. The curtain of Act II falls on Yankev's declaration to the weeping mother: "we remain strangers."

In Act III, Yankev and Dina decide that their only alternative is to leave Rumania and emigrate to America, where they will be free to marry without Madame Popeska's signature. However, Yankev has become ill since the confrontation with his mother and brother. Madame Popeska now comes to this sickbed. She calls upon his own love for Dina in order to elicit from him an understanding for her desertion of him and his father. She had been matched with her Jewish husband without love as a girl of fifteen and had fallen in love with her Christian lover three years later: "I sacrificed everything for him, for the emotions of my first love bewitched me, enchanted me. I acted without thinking, without considering. When I grew older, the first enchantment passed."[14] However, Madame Popeska explains that by that time she has already two Christian babies, whom she could not desert. Torn between her love for her Jewish and Christian children, she remained where she was, not knowing "who to sacrifice, and to whom." Happy for the chance which brought her together with her grown son, she now begs Yankev to pass judgment and to pronounce a sentence on "this sinful woman [...], your sinful mother." The intensely emotional scene reaches its peak in a blatant appeal to Yankev's "Jewish heart": "Demand the hardest sacrifice from me, and I will do it gladly, only let me be your mama. You are a Jewish child with a Jewish heart – have mercy on your unhappy mother and forgive her, forgive her."

At this moment Victor enters, and Madame Popeska hides. Victor has come to persuade Yankev to leave Rumania, and a confrontation ensues between the two brothers. Victor is full of bitter scorn and hatred for Jankev. He denies all traces of fraternal kinship with his Jewish sibling and insists that "Madame Popeska, my mother, ceased to be yours the moment she entered the Christian faith." Informed that Madame Popeska, whom Victor calls "my Christian mother," has just a few minutes before knelt before "her Jewish child" and exchanged loving maternal kisses with him, Victor exclaims: "Jew! Two of us is one too many for this earth." He pulls out a revolver, a struggle ensues, and Victor himself is accidentally shot to death. Madame Popeska, rushing out with Dina, takes the blame upon herself in order to save Yankev, and the police take her away.

Act IV enacts the wedding ceremony of Yankev and Dina; the wedding canopy is installed on stage. Madame Popeska is present in the custody of the police. At the end of the marriage ceremony, the Rabbi, at Madame Popeska's request, prays for the soul of Jankev's father, the dead Jewish husband she had abandoned in her youth. At the end of the prayer, Madame Popeska dies. Jankev sings a refrain from the song he had sung in Act I: "always remember your mother's song." The final curtain falls.

In discussing this "popular drama," Sandrow denounces the manner in which such plays "operate by pushing certain buttons calculated to bring on tears or laughter." (p. 122) Like many critics who condemn similar popular formats, she overlooks the fact that the topics she mentions – "sweethearts' love, lost innocence, a mother's love [...] guilt and the mother-child relationship" – are also in ample evidence in Shakespeare's plays. However, Sandrow does see that this sample of the "tear-jerker" is also a vehicle responding to the Jewish community's spiritual needs, satisfying the thirst for a reaffirmation and validation of Jewish identity and values:

> The main story, as opposed to the comic subplots, deals explicitly with Jewish identity. [...] Jankev insists throughout on pride in his Jewishness [...]. Besides, Yankev is essentially a good man, and always dealt honorably with his art school rival, whereas Viktor is essentially "heartless." This is Yankev's real victory over his tormentor – this and the winning away of his mother's heart – since the actual killing is not his responsibility. Yankev is further rewarded for his Jewishness by getting revenge on Madame Popeska for having deserted him; even better, it is revenge without guilt. In the course of such scenes, the audience vicariously gets its own back at all the Rumanians and Poles who insulted them and discriminated against them, both personally and as a group. Safe, together, and in a theatre on another continent, the audience watch (sic) a Jew conquer a Christian nobleman in a ritual of vindication. (Sandrow, p. 122)

The emphasis on the centrality of "the Jewish heart" is clearly rooted in the Chassidic celebration of the simple, unlearned man's intuitive goodness. Besides this glorification of popular and ethnic values, the melodrama also manifests a variety of themes and predicaments which modern psychology has made easily recognizable. These are revealed at different strata of the play with the aid of Freudian and Jungian analyses that complement one another. Once more, these analyses "prove" nothing more than the fact that even this simplest and least sophisticated melodrama is capable of encoding – and transmitting to its audiences in a symbolic manner – contents of a complex spiritual and psychological nature.

A Freudian View

To begin with, Freud's ideas illuminate the predicament of each of the three protagonists: Madame Popeska represents the most clear example of the vicissitudes resulting from a repressed sense of guilt. Repressed guilt and self-recrimination constitute a constant pressure on the conscious mind. This pressure may be expressed in neurotic symptoms, in physical illness, or in dreams of anxiety and punishment.[15] This agonizing can only be alleviated when the internalized condemnation of the self by the conscience, or Super-Ego, is modified or divested of its torturing power.[16] Madame Popeska's story illustrates each stage in turn. At first, she is able to abandon her husband and infant because she is able to repress completely her knowledge of the guilty nature of the act, justifying her actions in the name of love, the love "only an eighteen-year old loves for the first time in her life." However, the "forgotten," repressed materials do not remain submerged.[17] As she tells Yankev, "with time I recalled more and more strongly my own dear ones whom I left behind me in my Jewish home." The agony which is truly excruciating is further described as the predicament of the need to choose between two loyalties: "how often a burning longing came over me, and like a madwoman I wanted to run out into the world, run out and find my child, whom I left behind in the cradle. But by then I was already the mother of my two Christian children, [...] And this mother's heart was torn in two." Yet this inner conflict between two loyalties merely mirrors the initial opposing tendencies: loyalty to the unloved Jewish husband conflicting with loyalty to the Christian lover and loyalty to the beloved Jewish baby conflicting with the loyalty to one's own self. Translated into Freudian terms, the adult Ego needs to resolve the conflict between the demands of the exacting Super-Ego and the claims of the Id.[18]

The Jewish Heart demonstrates that the unresolved inner conflict cannot remain repressed and forgotten indefinitely. The claims of the dead husband and the lost (absent) son must be consciously recognized. This is the symbolic meaning of Popeska's request for a prayer to be said for the soul of her dead husband – not a mere recognition that the world of the dead and the world of the living constitute two facets of the same entity, but a reestablishing of contact between her and the repressed memory of the wrong she has inflicted. The process of "the return of the repressed" is even more clearly expressed in the "fortuitous" meeting with the long-lost son. The meeting provides Madame Popeska with the opportunity of achieving the necessary resolution between the conflicting claims by acknowledging her relationship to both Jewish and Christian sons. When this reconciliation is prevented by the opposition of Viktor, the only avenue left open is the expiation of guilt through a call for mercy and forgiveness and through self-inflicted punishment. Madame Popeska assumes responsibility for the killing of Viktor. The circle of error, guilt, penance, expiation, and absolution has been completed, and the newly wedded couple, Dina and Yankev, set out on a new beginning.

Equally interesting is the story of the two brothers, a central motif in many fairytales, both as an example of sibling rivalry and as an illustration of various stages of psychological development.[19] On the one hand, we have Yankev, whose story typifies the tale of the deserted or abandoned child. Bettelheim points out that both cruel desertions and slight "abandonments" may similarly evoke the situation wherein the deserted child responds with a feeling of unbounded anger against the offending parent, an anger which he in turn strives vainly to bring under control and to bottle up. However, the punishment of the errant parent is necessary if this bottled-up anger is to be brought to a positive resolution.[20] The fact that the play begins with Jankev's winning a prize for a painting titled "The Sinful Mother" is ample proof that Jankev indeed desires revenge. However, in this play we are confronted with two brothers, one of whom has been abandoned, while the other has enjoyed parental love and care. The ensuing confrontation between the two, instead of emphasizing the desire by the abandoned one to punish the guilty mother, throws into relief Yankev's willingness to let his "Jewish heart" dictate mercy and forgiveness. It is Viktor who adamantly refuses the claims of any emotions except jealousy, hatred, and possessiveness. The encounter between the two has all the markings of sibling rivalry. As Bettelheim observes: "this mis-miserable passion has only incidentally to do with the child's actual brothers and sisters. The real source of it is the child's feelings about his parents. When a child's older brother or sister is more competent then he, [...] fearing that in comparison to them he cannot win his parents' love and esteem is what inflames sibling rivalry."[21] The play, which begins with the bitter rivalry and jealousy expressed by Viktor against his competitor in the attempt to get the first prize, progressively manifests the underlying reasons for that rivalry. In Act I, Yankev wins first prize for the painting, "The Sinful Mother." The situation prefigures, or constitutes a *mise en abyme* of, the subsequent contest for the actual *sinful mother's* total love:

> Jew, be very carful how you speak. [says Viktor to Yankev when he comes to his home in Act III] I forbid you to repeat that expression "our mother." My mother cannot also be your mother.
>
> Yankev: I beg your pardon a thousand times for having been born to the same woman as you. Believe me, if she had asked me, I would have told her it was better for me never to be born than to have you as a brother.
>
> Viktor: Jew, who gives you the right to call me brother? [...] And I insist to you that Madame Popeska, my mother, ceased to be yours in the moment when she entered the Christian faith.
>
> Yankev: Brother Esau, my mother never entered the Christian faith. The proof is that now after twenty years there beats in my mother's breast a warm Jewish heart. [...] Your Christian mother is now at that very moment in my Jewish house. Just a few minutes ago she knelt here before me and was overjoyed to hear the word "mother" from me, her Jewish child.
>
> Viktor: Take back your damned lie. Madame Popeska would never sink so low.
>
> Yankev: And her Jewish son pressed her to his Jewish heart and called her mother, for she is and she remains my Jewish mother." (Sandrow, pp. 120-121).

Yankev refers explicitly to the Biblical sibling rivalry between Jacob and Esau, an analogy his name already alludes to. However, the moral struggle which follows recalls the more lethal sibling rivalry between Cain and Abel. In the Cain-Abel story, the son who has initially received the divine parent's approbation pays for it with his life. Yankev recoils at the thought of taking on Cain's role, exclaiming: "Beast, do you want me to cause a murder?" Yet, the struggle culminates in his becoming victorious without incurring the actual guilt of fratricide. He has indeed become Viktor, the beloved of his mother, and replaces his brother, symbolically as well in actuality.

A Jungian View

The light thrown on the action of the play by Jungian insights is equally fascinating. The two brothers, Yankev and Viktor, although they are not actual twins, illustrate Neumann's comment that "the twin-brother motif in mythology [...] expresses the mutual affinity of opposites."[22] This is the opposition of the self with its "shadow brother" or "shadow sister."[23] However, as Neumann writes, "consciousness of the bond between the male opponents is the beginning of masculine consciousness." The action of *The Jewish Heart* revolves to a great extent around the fact that such mutual recognition does not take place. As the above-quoted confrontation scene demonstrates, Viktor repeatedly applies a single epithet whenever he addresses Yankev: "Jew." This is not merely an anti-Semitic symptom. Viktor clearly considers Yankev to be a representative of "the inferior personality component,"[24] and adamantly refuses to admit his kinship to that "shadow brother." The fact that Yankev calls Viktor "heartless beast" and "my enemy" is no coincidence, either. These epithets sum up the crux of the struggle between two principles, for which "Jew" and "Christian" are merely convenient tokens. Yankev is subjectivity incarnate, guided by the principles of forgiveness and mercy, i.e., the realm of the heart. Viktor, on the other hand, is completely identified with the antipodean system, where external attributes take precedence over internal qualities. He repeatedly refers to his mother as "Madame Popeska," emphasizing her social role as a member of "the Popeska family [which] is one of the most aristocratic and noblest in Rumania." He is outraged at the thought that the social standing of this aristocratic institution will be devalued by the intrusion of "the Jew," once more considering Jankev's civic standing, not his individual person. For Viktor, feelings are continuously translated into the terms of business dealings and "calm" shrewdness. When he comes to Yankev's house, he explains: "I come to you as one businessman to another [...] I come to make you a proposition." This proposition, it turns out, is "the means whereby you [Yankev], who destroyed our happiness, can make good that misfortune which you brought upon our house." The magnitude of that "misfortune," Viktor believes, is in direct proportion to the aristocratic and noble standing of the family in the community which is now besmirched.

However, the *shadow* need not be truly evil; it may be simply the unconscious, repressed brother of the consciously accepted self and the outer-directed mask, or *persona.*[25] Whereas one's "inner personality," the soul, or Anima, in the case of the male hero, is concerned with "the relations to the subject," its antipodean complement, "the outer face, the *persona* is exclusively concerned with the relations to objects."[26] The *persona*-ridden Viktor, obsessed by his external appearance in the world as the scion of "nobility" and "aristocracy," repudiates his Jewish "shadow brother" and insists on cold compensation in the form of a business transaction. Relentlessly "heartless," he cannot recognize and reinstate the forgotten inner-directed, subject-oriented soul or Anima. Furthermore, his failure is thrown into relief by Yankev's success. Unlike Viktor, Yankev intuitively senses that *the shadow* has a potential "positive value and a luciferian [sic] light-bringing quality."[27] The fruitful encounter with the *shadow brother or sister* may provide the individual "with opportunities to increase consciousness."[28] In other words, "the more shadow the ego can integrate, the more vital, substantial, and strong it becomes."[29] And indeed, as the confrontation with Viktor progresses, Yankev increasingly absorbs from him the ability to be "calm," that is, ironic, cool-headed and immovable, without losing the precious relationship to the heart. It is therefore Yankev who is able to surmount the opposition of seemingly irreconcilable differences and to recognize the fraternal bonds which exist between them: "Once again, I beg your pardon a thousand times. Unfortunately, we are, against our will, two brothers, And if you have read the Bible, you have found there two such unsuited brothers as we are: Jacob and Esau." This is the psychological reason why, at the end, Yankev is not merely the victor in the encounter, but is really transformed into Viktor, symbolically as well as in his attributes as the noble hero. He has integrated the most productive aspects of *the shadow* into his ego, allowing the merely destructive and hateful aspects to be permanently "killed" and buried. As a result, his own ego has been amplified and strengthened. The story of these two brothers consequently operates, like the stories of myth and folktales, to dramatize not a particular story of individual – and highly individuated – people, but a legendary tale of representative and symbolic figures. It is not a clinical history of a particular family, but a drama which its audiences could perceive as having a universal and timeless import.

The symbolically charged confrontation between the two brothers gains an added dimension when we consider the role played by the mother, Madame Popeska. In the transpersonal analysis of Jung, the struggle with the parental figures reflects not a personal, but an archetypal situation – archetypal in the sense that the archetypes are associated by Jung with "identical psychic structures common to all men," which "correspond to the concept of "the pattern of behavior" in biology."[30] This confrontation is a crucial stage in the process whereby the libido is developed and transformed. By confronting the "terrible" and destructive aspect of the parent, the protagonist at the same time "liberates the fruitful and bountiful aspect."[31] Male as well as female must overcome the parental model in order to make possible an integration of conscious and unconscious, intellect and feeling, sexual and non-sexual love, self and soul.[32]

The mother, according to Jung, "corresponds to the collective unconscious." She is the incarnation of the feminine aspect of identity, as well as the image of the soul.[33] In coming to terms with the mother, one gains access to the soul, that metaphysical entity defined by Jung as "the inner personality [which] is the way one behaves in relation to one's inner psychic processes; it is the inner attitude, the characteristic face, that is turned toward the unconscious."[34] As we have already seen, the soul, or Anima in the case of the male hero, is completely antithetical to the outer-directed, object-oriented *persona*.

In the beginning of the play, Yankev – who has grown up in the absence of a mother, and who in addition knows himself to have been abandoned by his mother – has no real sense of an "inner personality." His recriminating painting, "The Sinful Mother," expresses his reliance on external data, on the outer, visible circumstances of his case. This "objective" attitude changes after Yankev challenges his newly found mother, demanding her required signature. This is not merely a demand for a symbolic blessing for the marriage; it is first and foremost a demand for parental recognition of the long-lost son. When Madame Popeska, after several changes of mind, does acknowledge her love for her Jewish son, Yankev is free to react to the internal truth of the action. In fact, from the moment in which Madame Popeska appeals to his "Jewish heart," Yankev demonstrates the progressive integration of the various facets of identity. First, he draws on the regenerative unconscious riches of the Anima, or soul, and responds to the errant woman with compassion, pity, and love. Second, he successfully confronts his *shadow brother* and emerges enlightened and potent. This process clears the way for the fruitful union between him and Dina in a mature and positive expression of erotic love.

Viktor's relationship to Madame Popeska reveals once more the tortuous relationship with the mother archetype. "The mother imago," observes Jung, "represents the unconscious, and it is as much a vital necessity for the unconscious to be joined to the conscious as it is for the latter not to lose contact with the unconscious."[35] The individual who is alienated from the mother is not merely cut-off from the feminine aspect of himself, which is the emotional, intuitive aspect. He is also forever cut-off from the opportunity to delve into the dark depths of the soul, a step which is the necessary prerequisite for rebirth and regeneration. Thus, Viktor, in archetypal fashion, arrives at the point where his mother is seen as "the mother of all abomination [...], the receptacle of all that is wicked and unclean,"[36] by virtue of her relationship to Yankev. This could be the propitious moment to confront what he sees as the evil, tainting "Jewish" element which he, as his mother's son, has inherited. Then, and only then, could the evil element, newly conscious of its imperfection, be transformed and made perfect through rebirth. Viktor, as we have seen, allows no such recognition to take place. Far from acknowledging the "Jewish" element within himself, he strives to prove that his mother is "Christian," i.e., good and untainted. Moreover, he refuses to accept the fact that he shares the mother, "who is [also] the equivalent of "the world-soul," with his loathed and repudiated sibling.[37]

The Play as a Trans-personal Saga

The story of the two brothers, Yankev and Viktor, in which the hate-filled Viktor dies, transcends the boundaries of the personal, and even the Jewish, situation. It gives a vivid dramatic expression to Jung's increasing conviction that each human individual is by definition a fraternal sharer in the primordial, maternal *collective unconscious* as well as the maternal *world-soul*. The individual who, like Viktor, denies his fraternal bond to his *shadow brother*, in effect claims that this despised and detested *shadow brother* is shorn of his human *soul*. This position pierces through all racial hatreds. Thus, Jung comments on the tendency of Americans to represent "the inferior side of the personality, the *shadow*, [...] by a Negro or an Indian."[38] Yet, *The Jewish Heart* demonstrates that Viktor's position is untenable; psychologically as well as dramatically, the victim of the bitter fraternal hatred is the hate-filled brother himself.

The story of Viktor has further implications for the egalitarian *weltanschauung* of this and other Jewish plays, which often pit "the haves" against "the have nots." "Nothing endangers this connection [of conscious and unconscious] in a man more than a successful life," observes Jung, "it makes him forget his dependence on the unconscious."[39] Viktor, blessed from birth not only with maternal loving care, but with an aristocratic position, wealth, and rich prospects for the future, is indeed oblivious of his "dependence on the unconscious." The result of such a divorce from any access to the unconscious is in the first instance a "one-sided, rationalistic, warped mentality."[40] As we have seen, Viktor's "one-sided" and "warped" mentality is expressed in his excessive subjugation by the object-ridden *persona*. But this "over-valuation of objects as compared with the low-valuation of subjects" is detrimental to the individual himself, comments Jung.[41] Ostensibly injuring others, the *persona*-ridden individual himself is the prime loser, since he abdicates the "blissfulness" which results from the feeling of "a oneness of being, a relationship between conscious and unconscious in which, of course, the unconscious predominates."[42] Thus, the transpersonal analysis of Jung comes full circle and converges with the specifically Jewish and the universal human levels of the play. It underscores the lesson of this melodrama: hatred does not pay.

This analysis of *The Jewish Heart* illustrates the fact that the most "artistically primitive" of folk plays has the potential to make dramatically manifest complex and deeply seated truths of the human spirit. Moreover, the very absence of any overt psychological rendering of the characters makes the simple drama of Jewish life all the more pregnant with primordial images, situations, and meanings.[43] Hence its ability to sway and affect multitudinous audiences need not be necessarily attributed to its appeal to stock responses, but to its encoding of psychic contents in a "simple and uncomplicated" structure. It is the very simplicity of the structure which makes these covert primordial materials easily accessible even to the most unlettered of spectators.

In fact, the experience of Yiddish theatre audiences bears out the hypothesis that folk theatre, like folktales and fairytales, has the potential to make accessible truths of the greatest spiritual magnitude. Mukdoiny observed that the folk-religiosity of the Yiddish theatre stems from "the religious scene," with its broad humanity that transcends the national limits, and with its deep pathos, far-reaching mysticism, rich color, fiery excitement, inspiration, aspiration, and creativity. Furthermore, he asserted that this religious folk root indicates a desire by the folk for a universal and communal experience through theatrical means. The theatrical performance, in which the audience completely participates with the action enacted on stage, and in which a dialogue is instituted between the author via the production and the actors, and his spectators, became charged with significance. For secular Jews it took on a spiritual, regenerative, and transformative function, as meaningful as the religious ritual, from the holiness of Sabbath observance to the grand drama of Yom Kippur or the great pageantry of the High Holiday worship.[44]

It is small wonder then that the critic Stark Young suggested the folk nature of the Yiddish theatre as the reason for its continuous thriving in New York, while other national or ethnic theatres languished. Young concluded that the folk art of the Yiddish theatre contained a more complex, more universally human art, an art whose realism was that "of intense feeling with spiritual depth [realizing a] spiritual truth," as opposed to the mere "surface, naturalistic melodrama of the Sicilians."[45] In other words, the point of interest for Young was not whether the artistic forms used were more or less sophisticated; but, to what extent the same popular form – such as the melodrama – was made to realize deeply rooted truths of the human spirit (or psyche). These archetypal truths may turn out, eventually, to be not timeless and universal, as Jung believed, but grounded in Western (or European) culture and lore. Yet, the fact remains that the Yiddish folk theatre did manage to transmit within its "unsophisticated" and popular forms what we have come to consider as metaphysical notions of great magnitude. The unlettered spectators may have not been analytically conscious of the truths revealed in the theatrical performances. However, they did experience, by all reports, the transfiguration and emotional regeneration of a secular ritual.

Notes

[1] See Isaac Goldberg, *The Drama of Transition* (Cincinnati, Ohio: Stewart Kidd, 1922); B. Gorin, *The History of the Yiddish Theatre* (in Yiddish), 2nd ed., 2 vols. (New York: Max Maisel Library Publishers, 1923); Jacob Mestel, *Unzer Teater* (in Yiddish), (New York: Yiddisher Kultur Farband, 1943); David S. Lifson, *The Yiddish Theatre in America* (New York: Thomas Yosselof, 1965); Nahama Sandrow, *Vagabond Stars: A World History of Yiddish Theatre* (New York: Harper and Row, 1976).

[2] Lifson, p. 29. Cf., Sister Frances Jerome, *Cultural Values of American Ethnic Groups* (New York: Harper and Brothers, 1956), pp. 140-1.

[3] Lifson, p. 303. See also Mestel, pp. 24, 63-5, 87-112; or Samuel Niger, "Yiddish Culture," in B. Abramovitch *et al.* (Eds.), *The Jewish People: Past and Present* (New York: Central Yiddish Culture Organization [Jewish Encyclopedic Handbooks], 1946), p. 272.

[4] Sandrow, p. 111. See also Ludwig Lewisohn, *The Answer* (New York: Liverwright Publishing Corp., 1943), p. 287.

[5] Sandrow, pp. 56, 66.

[6] Petr Bogatyrev and Roman Jakobson, "Folklore as a Special Form of Creativity," in Peter Steiner, (Ed.), *The Prague School: Selected Writings 1926-1946* (Austin, Tex.: University of Texas Press, 1982), p. 35. See also Petr Bogatyrev, "Forms and Functions of Folk Theatre," in Ladislaw Matejka and Irwin Titunik (Eds.), *Semiotics of Art: The Prague School Contributions* (Cambridge, Mass.: M.I.T. Press, 1976), pp. 51-6.

[7] See Roman Jakobson, "Linguistics and Poetics," in Richard and Fernande de Georges (Eds.), *The Structuralists from Marx to Levi Strauss* (New York: Doubleday, Anchor, 1972), pp. 85-122. The terms Jakobson utilizes are "addresser" and "addressee."

[8] Jakobson, p. 95.

[9] Sandrow, pp. 91-131.

[10] Mircea Eliade, *Myth and Reality* (New York: Harper Colophon, 1963), p. 200.

[11] It comes as little surprise, therefore, that Jacob Gordin (1853-1909) provided in his plays inspiration for a number of Kafka stories, after the writer had seen the plays performed in Prague (see Sandrow, p. 160).

[12] See Victor Turner, *From Ritual to Theatre: The Human Seriousness of Play* (New York: Performing Arts Journal Publications, 1982) for a slightly different slant; see also Eliade, pp. 195-202; Joseph Campbell, "Bios and Mythos: Prolegomena to a Science of Mythology," in John Vickery (Ed.), *Myth and Literature* (Lincoln: University of Nebraska Press, 1966), pp. 15-23; cf., Geza Roheim, "Myth and Folktale," in Vickery, pp. 25-32.

Psychological readings of fairytales and folktales are found in C.G. Jung, *Symbols of Transformation* (Trans., R.F.C. Hull) Bollingen Series (Princeton: Princeton University Press, 1976); C.G. Jung, *Psychological Types* (Rev. and Trans. R.F.C. Hull) Bollingen Series (Princeton: Princeton University Press, 1977). Eric Neumann *The Origin and History of Consciousness*, Bollingen Series (Princeton: Princeton University Press, 1973); Eric Neumann, *The Great Mother: An Analysis of the Archetype.* Bollingen Series (Princeton: Princeton University Press, 1974); Eric Neumann, *Amor and Psyche: The Psychic Development of the Feminine.* Bollingen Series (Princeton: Princeton University Press, 1971); Marie Louise von Franz, *Interpretation of Fairytales: An Introduction to the Psychology of Fairy Tales* (Zurich, Switzerland: Spring, 1973); Marie Louise von Franz, *Problems of the Feminine in Fairytales* (Zurich, Switzerland: Spring, 1972); Marie Louise von Franz, *An Interpretation of Apuleius' Golden Ass: with the Tale of Amor and Psyche* (Irving, Tex.: Spring, 1980); Bruno Bettelheim, *The Use of Enchantment: The Meaning and Importance of Fairy Tales* (New York: Vintage, 1977).

[13] Lifson, p. 51; Sandrow, p. 114.

[14] Sandrow, p. 118.

[15] Sigmund Freud, *A General Introduction to Psychoanalysis* (Trans. and Ed., James Strachey), (New York: Norton, 1965), pp. 219, 221, 297-301, 401-4; Sigmund Freud, *The Ego and the Id* (Rev. Ed., James Strachey, Ed.), (New York: Norton, 1962), pp. 39-42.

[16] Freud, *The Ego*, pp. 27, 42.

[17] Freud, *A General Introduction*, p. 326.

[18] Freud, *The Ego*, p. 48.

[19] Bettelheim, pp. 75, 93, 95, 238.

[20] *Ibid.*, pp. 29-30.

[21] *Ibid.*, p. 238.

[22] Neumann, *The Origin*, p. 180; cf., Jung, *Symbols*, pp. 240, 386.

[23] Jung, *Symbols*, p. 259; see Neumann, *Amor and Psyche*, p. 73.

[24] Jung, *Symbols*, p. 183.

[25] *Ibid.*, p. 163.

[26] Jung, *Psychological Types*, pp. 456-67.

[27] Von Franz, *Interpretation*, p. 92.

[28] *Ibid.* Cf., Neumann, *Amor and Psyche*, pp. 73-91.

[29] Von Franz, *Apuleius' Golden Ass*, p. 114.

[30] Jung, *Symbols*, p. 158; cf., his discussion of typologies in *Psychological Types.*

[31] Neumann, *The Origin*, p. 163.

[32] *Ibid.*, pp. 195-209; c.f., Bettelheim, pp. 11, 91-95.

[33] Jung, *Symbols*, pp. 259, 388, 266ff.

[34] *Ibid.*, p. 467.

[35] *Ibid.*, p. 298.

[36] *Ibid.*, p. 214.

[37] *Ibid.*, pp. 234, 281.

[38] *Ibid.*, p. 183.

[39] *Ibid.*, p. 298.

[40] Jung, *Psychological Types*, p. 270.

[41] *Ibid.*, p. 249.

[42] *Ibid.*, p. 248.

[43] C.G. Jung, *The Spirit in Man, Art and Literature* (Trans., R.F.C. Hull) Bollingen Series (Princeton: Princeton University Press, 1972), p. 88.

[44] Alexander Mukdoiny, *Teater* (in Yiddish), (New York: Mukdoiny Jubilee Committee, 1927), p. 29.

[45] Stark Young, "After the Play," *New Republic*, XXIX (January 4, 1929), p. 157. See also Stark Young, *The Flower in Drama* (New York: Scribner, 1923); Stark Young, *Immortal Shadows* (New York: Scribner, 1948).

Sholem-Aleykhem's "Stantsye Baranovitsh"

Jonathan Boyarin

I.

Sholem-Aleykhem's works bridge the gulf between us and the world he evokes. That gulf, immeasurably deepened by the Holocaust, was already evidenced by the distinction between the Russian-speaking author, Sholem Rabinovitsh, and the Yiddish persona "Sholem-Aleykhem." One aspect of Rabinovitsh's enduring genius may be identified as the awareness of the break between the world in which live storytelling was commonplace and the world in which Rabinovitsh lived, and his consequent creation of unique artifices – such as the Sholem-Aleykhem persona[1] – to bridge the gap without denying it.

Walter Benjamin's essay on "The Storyteller"[2] may help a reader to appreciate Sholem Rabinovitsh's art. Perhaps central therein is Benjamin's observation that "[one] listening to a story is in the company of the storyteller." The auditor is thus linked to the characters, setting, and events of the story by the narrator. The narrator shares something of himself as he tells the story. A live storyteller may use rhetorical devices to place himself within his tale as much as do those who "write stories." His account of the world within the tale is not marred thereby. His presence as a sharer of meaning helps to make a story out of an unconnected series of events. Furthermore, it is a commonplace that "a story need not have happened to be true." For a story to be true, the storyteller must create confidence in the *intent* of his narration. For Benjamin, the ability to share this kind of truth is exceedingly rare at "the present time," which he dates from World War I.

A second characteristic of a story, according to Benjamin, is its longevity: "It preserves and concentrates its strength and is capable of releasing it even after a long time." For him, part of this economy is the freedom of the story from the burden of explicit social or psychological analysis. By this open-endedness stories invite reflection, retelling, and reinterpretation. They are irreducible, in the sense that their essence cannot be separated from their expression. They are also inexhaustible, receiving new energy each time they are told.

Benjamin contrasts these aspects of the story with what he calls "information," the predominant mode of communication in the present. Where the story is evocative, information is explicit. Where the story retains its power far from its place and time of origin, information rapidly loses its significance. Most important, whereas the story stands or falls on the basis of who tells it and how, the accuracy of information is defined as its independence from the judgment of the one who conveys it.

II.

Throughout his career, Rabinovitsh wrote for newspapers. His early feuilletons were surrounded by the kind of "information" that Benjamin deplores; they provided stuff for the mundane conversation of the passengers who appear in Sholem-Aleykhem's *Railroad Stories*. This volume contains, along with "Stantsye Baranovitsh,"[3] nineteen other stories written in 1902 and 1909. The framing device for all the stories is a railroad car full of Jews.

The frame narrator of the entire volume is a travelling salesman, a *komivoyazher*, who "explains" in an introductory note that he has decided to occupy his time on trains writing down the stories he hears there. In the brief preface to the volume, Rabinovitsh uses two devices to make his readers feel they know this narrator. First, he deflates the artistic pretensions of the Yiddish writer, the "Mr. Sholem-Aleykhem" to whom the Tevye stories are respectfully recounted:

> Vey-vey, vos me zet zikh on untervegns! A shod, vos ikh bin nit keyn shrayber. Dos heyst, az me vil tsurik, mist vos bin ikh nit keyn shrayber? Vos iz azelkhes, eygentlekh, a shrayber? Yeder mensh kon zayn a shrayber. Ubefrat nokh – of idish. "Zhargon" – oykh mir an eysek! Me nemt a pen un me shraybt.

[The things you see when you're travelling! It's a pity I'm not a writer. On the other hand, why should I say I'm no writer? After all, what's a writer? Anybody can be a writer. Especially in Yiddish. "Zhargon" – big deal! You pick up a pen and you write...]

The author thus creates a narrator who accords perfectly with the merchants from whom he is to hear most of the tales he records, by thinking of his stories as goods:

yeder geshikhte hob ikh gegebn an andern nomen, fayntshik, vi es geher tsu zayn – mayse soykher. Ikh vays nit, tsi vel ikh inem gesheft fardinen, tsi ikh vel brekhen ruk un lend. Halevy zol ikh khotsh aroys mit mayn keren.

[... I gave every story its own name, the way one is supposed to – like a salesman. I don't know whether I'll make money on the deal or lose my shirt. I hope I'll get out with my capital intact...]

The concerns of the narrator's travelling companions are stock market and grain prices and the social advancement and protection of their children. They are anything but fanatics, either of the religious or revolutionary type. They are "regular Jews."

III.

In addition to the immediate effect of simply reading or hearing "Stantsye Baranovitsh," we can reinforce our connection to the time the story was written by reviewing the relevant criticism. This helps us move beyond the most common American-Jewish response to Sholem-Aleykhem's genius: a somewhat bizarre nostalgia for the sentimental powerlessness of Jews in the Russian Empire, combined with admiration for verbal techniques seen as "quintessentially Yiddish," rather than distinctive to Rabinovitsh.

The only essay devoted solely to the *Railroad Stories*[4] argued that the author depicts therein a class trapped in self-delusion. Maks Erik, the eminent Soviet Yiddish critic, emphasized the immediate historical situation and the class character of the passengers in the train, and identified two main themes in the volume. The first was the hopelessness of the Russian Jewish petit-bourgeoisie in the aftermath of the failed revolution of 1905 and the repression attendant on it; the second was what he called the *idiotizm* of the petit-bourgeoisie as a result of their hopeless situation.

While praising Sholem-Aleykhem's art and humor along the way, Erik ultimately accused the author of the same narrow vision shared by his characters. He identified the absence of historical analysis in the stories with the "limitations" of Sholem-Aleykhem's world view: "Sholem-Aleykhem's humor is incapable of freeing itself from the nightmare of Tsarist Russia." Whether Erik actually believed this, or intended to satisfy the censors, is uncertain. The fact is that it is precisely the hapless autonomy of Sholem-Aleykhem's characters that is so striking. They are indeed buffeted by history, but not by the didactic concerns of their creator. For that reason, they continue to live long after the specific historical situation has disappeared.

After World War II, a new generation of critics attempted to understand the ability of the "comic writer" Sholem-Aleykhem to move those who had no living memory of the world he describes. The considerations elaborated in various essays by Walter Benjamin on the relations between language, history, and the sharing of personal experience are quite evident in this recent work. Ruth Wisse, for instance, has discussed the central theme of successful and failed communication in Sholem-Aleykhem's work.[5] The shared language of the Jews is celebrated but also shown as dangerous. It can create a false sense of insulation from the outside; it can be manipulated by unscrupulous people within the community. This ambiguity is evident in several titles within the *Railroad Stories*: "The Luckiest Man in Kodny" is so because he has managed to get a great doctor to see his deathly-ill son; three men discuss their sons' being "Taken" – into the gymnasium or into the army; and "The Miracle of Hoshane Rabe" is an averted disaster.

Dan Miron has analyzed Sholem Rabinovitsh's creation of the Sholem-Aleykhem persona as a versatile artistic device, bridging the social and geographical gap between author and reader, who meet via the Yiddish newspaper.[6] The term "Sholem-Aleykhem," as Miron notes, is used between two fellow Jews who are either strangers, or who have not seen each other for a long time, or who wish to express respect and welcome. In Yiddish, it is thus used to reduce distance. Here again, the author takes the technology of "information" – the newspaper – and creates a successful imitation of the storytelling situation. It is worth adding that he manages to personalize even the newspaper, breaking through the reification of the medium and fancifully reminding his readers that the link between them and himself is actually a human one:

Sholem-aleykhem!
Aleykhem-sholem!
Fun vanen fort men?
Fun varshe.
Vos iz ayer gesheft?
Ikh bin a idishe tsaytung.
Ma shmeykhem?
Idishe folkstsaytung.

(Sholem-aleykhem!
Aleykhem-sholem!
Where are you travelling from?
From Warsaw.
What do you do?
I am a Jewish newspaper.
What's your name?
Yidishe Folkstsaytung.)[7]

In this way, the reader is allowed to eavesdrop on the private affairs on the writer and his publisher, so to speak. "Sholem-Aleykhem" is here the writer on the train doing business, the mirror of the *Railroad Stories' komivoyazher*, whose persona is that of a business man trying his hand at writing. In this early quotation, we see the author in the process of establishing a common world with his readers through the semblance of dialogue.

In the pages David Roskies devotes to the *Railroad Stories*,[8] he notes that, along with increasing desperation, the allusive resources of Jewish language still seem to hold their own in this volume written in the first decade of the century. That was just before the Great War, from which, as Benjamin wrote, "men returned ... grown silent – not richer, but poorer in communicable experience."[9] Roskies corroborates the identification of that war with a collapse of communication, observing that it was not until the outbreak of World War I that one of Sholem-Aleykhem's characters was reduced to helpless silence. Roskies goes on to explain the significance of such a silence:

> These unredeemed moments are the very ones that etch themselves into the collective memory, for a silence beyond prayer is the ultimate dead end... such breakdowns do irreparable damage unless they are remembered. The act of remembering draws the broken links into a chain. ...[10]

Sholem Rabinovitsh's act of genius in "Stantsye Baranovitsh" was to create such an unredeemed moment in fiction. Today, the story serves us as a sort of prescient *kapore*, an artificial and controllable version of the actual historical disaster which affords us a sense of connection to that earlier time.

The train is, of course, representative both of the intimacy of the "shtetl" and of its dislocation. Likewise, it is both a new form of the classic storytelling situation – in which people's hands were busy and their minds were free – and a perversion of that situation, since on a train, the passengers are actually harnessed to technology, rather than being in control of it. The schedule of the train will, therefore, both provide time for the story-within-the-story to develop and ultimately cause its interruption. A brief summary of the plot will allow me to detail the written and "oral" rhetorical heightening of narrative which is necessary for the missing conclusion to have its full force.

Like many of the stories in the volume, the bulk of "Stantsye Baranovitsh" consists of a narrative recounted by one of the passengers in the third-class carriage. In this case, the encapsulated monologue is sparked by mention of Azev, a famous *agent-provocateur* who infiltrated the Social Revolutionary party around the time of the 1905 Revolution. The speaker announces that in his home town of Kaminke, in his own grandfather's time, there was a traitor who could have put Azev to shame. His name was Kivke, and he was an innkeeper. Once Kivke got into an argument with some peasants about theology, and the upshot of it was his being sentenced to run the gauntlet. The Jewish community was outraged, and led by the narrator's grandfather, Reb Nisl Shapiro, hit on a plan to save Kivke: They had him fake a heart attack in prison, staged a burial (bribing the proper authorities), and secretly got him across the border to Brody in the Austro-Hungarian Empire. They celebrated properly but soon a letter came from Kivke asking for money. The money was collected and sent, but requests for increasing amounts were repeated at various intervals over the next few years. The narrator's grandfather found it more and more difficult to collect the money requested, and when it was not forthcoming, Kivke replied by making explicit the threat of blackmail implied from the start. If the money did not come soon, he would have no choice other than to return to Kaminke (thus spelling disaster for the entire community) or commit suicide. Reb Nisl Shapiro thereupon wrote a letter to Kivke, in which he asserted that absolutely no more money would be sent. At that, Kivke wrote back that if the money was not sent, he would write to the governor explaining the whole story, and include Reb Nisl Shapiro's signed letter as evidence. At this point in the account of Reb Nisl Shapiro's troubles with Kivke, the train on which the story is being told reaches Baranovitsh, where the narrator has to change trains, and he departs.

The abrupt ending of even such a summary paragraph is a bit shocking. Throughout "Stantsye Baranovitsh," the author is successful (more, I would suggest, than in any of the other *Railroad Stories*) at playing off the train situation against the rhythm of the Kaminker Jew's monologue. He thus heightens the spiralling tension of the Jewish community held hostage from across the border with sardonic allusions to the dialectic of story and information.

Before the monologue begins, everyone in the car is talking about nothing in particular: "everybody was talking. All at once. As usual." The pace of these sentences already suggests the wheels of a train, rolling fast and jerky. No one, however, commands the crowd's attention. Everything about the cacophany suggests lack of control and lack of genuine dialogue:

> Ot redt men, dakht zikh, funem "urozhay," a geret of veyts un of hober, un ot iz men ariber (a smikhes haparshe!) of milkhome. Nisht gehalten zikh bay der milkhome keyn finf minut, tut men a shprung-ariber glaykh tsu der revolutsye. Fun der revolutsye git men zikh a vorf in der konstitutsye, un fun der konstitutsye falt men shoyn bemeyle arayn in di pogromen, mit di retsikhes, redeyfes un naye gzeyres of iden, miten traybenish fun di derfer, mitn loyfenish keyn amerike ... .
>
> [Here we are talking, one would think, of the harvest, chatting about wheat and oats, and then we switch (some connection!) to the war. We don't keep talking about the war five minutes before we jump over to the revolution. From the revolution we throw ourselves into the constitution,

and from the constitution we somehow fall into the pogroms, with the murder, harrassment, and new anti-Jewish proclamations, with the expulsion from the villages, with the race to America....]

The verbs "switch," "jump," "throw," "fall" suggest purposeless motion, lack of self-direction. The phonic association between "*revolutsye*" and "*konstitutsye*" implies the language of modernity controlling its users. From the references to the "expulsion" and the "race" – Erik's complaint notwithstanding – we sufficiently infer the historical helplessness of the Jews of Russia in 1909.

Relief only comes with the mention of Azev and the Kaminker Jew's cry: "A – zh – e – v!" To signal that a tale is about to be told "orally," the author has the *komivoyazher* explain that the Jew from Kaminke pronounces "z" as "zh," because he is missing teeth in front. The *komivoyazher* adds: "I immediately took a liking to this character. I liked his openness, his language, his calling us all cows. I enjoy, I envy that sort of person." This last passage is cited by Maks Erik in defense of his thesis about the "idiocy" of petit-bourgeois life as a theme in the *Railroad Stories*. In this crowd of potential competitors, the Kaminker's contempt for his audience perversely reinforces his charisma; Benjamin remarks that the main contribution of traders (read *komivoyazher*) as storytellers was "to refine the tricks with which the attention of the listener was captured."

In any case, everyone is eager to hear the story, and the Kaminker begins, making assurances that what he will relate is no "*bovemayse fun toyzent un eyn nakht*," no mere fantasy. Rather, he has heard it from his father, whose father in turn told it "countless times." Two more characteristics of stories – their repetition and their transmission from generation to generation – are thus cited. Furthermore, "the whole story was written down in an old chronicle, which was burned a long time ago." Such a reference, of course, adds mystery as well as authority; but it also prefigures the disruption of memory.

At the point in the Kaminker story where Reb Nisl Shapiro decides on his plan to rescue Kivke – but has not divulged it to the community – the Kaminker decides to pause for effect (and for a cigarette). Thus his monologue is broken, and the reader is drawn into the circle of listeners. At various points further along the Kaminker will pause with rhetorical comments such as: "Good, no? ... Take your time... These things are easier said than done."

The story continues with Kivke's feigned "death," parodying the enchantment customary in a fairy tale. The potency of the mention of death is underlined when the narrator describes it as "*aza min apopleksye* ["a sort of apoplexy"], *nit do gedakht.*" "*Nit do gedakht*" is one of several phrases employed in Yiddish to ensure that reference to evil does not bring it closer. Here, in addition to the obvious irony that even Kivke in distant Kaminke two generations earlier had suffered no apoplexy, the warning reinforces the sense of connection between the characters of the monologue and the audience in the train, and between all these and the Yiddish reader. (That the average Yiddish reader would hardly make such an analysis merely reinforces the point that the author's art focused on brilliant manipulation of an intimately shared idiom.)

At the exact midpoint of "Stantsye Baranovitsh," there is an "intermission"; the train pulls into a station, and the Kaminker checks with the stationmaster to find out how far they are from Baranovitsh. Aside from adding suspense again, this affords the chorus of passengers time to comment:

"Creative."

"Has what to say."

When the Kaminker returns, he relates the second letter from Kivke. The letters reveal the ornamental Hebrew which Rabinovitsh uses elsewhere in his characters' letters.[11] The first letter, announcing Kivke's safe arrival, begins with the words: "*Bokashti lehodiye, az ikh bin in Brod*" ("I beg to inform you that I am in Brod"); on receiving it, the community rejoices. The second begins identically, but continues "*Bokashti leshloyekh*" ("I beg you to send"). The contrast between the two captures in a nutshell the theme of blackmail from afar; language subverts as well as celebrates. Indeed, when this letter is ignored, it is followed by another, "without an 'I beg to inform you,' but with an 'I beg you to send,' all by itself," and ending with the first threat to return to Kaminke.

This perverse power of language goes hand-in-hand with the helplessness of the Jewish community. When the money is finally sent for Kivke to get married, traditional greetings go along with it, together with the wish that: "It will make him forget that there's a Kaminke in the world." Could anything be more of a sign of despair than this desire to be forgotten? The subsequent attempt at silence, a decision "not to respond at all" to Kivke's next letter, is consistent.

When Kivke repeats his threat of blackmail, Reb Nisl Shapiro decides to give language one more try, writing a letter to Kivke (and signing it). Even the proud Jew from Kaminke is forced to admit: "he should pardon me, it was his greatest foolishness" (incidentally suggesting that his references to his grandfather's wisdom were all made tongue in cheek). Signature is thus cited as the most dangerous form of language. The fact that the climax of the story hinges on writing adds another term to the play of oral and written elements in "Stantsye Baranovitsh."

The last moments of the monologue are Kivke's threatening reply, and Reb Nisl Shapiro's panic upon receiving it. The ensuing catastrophe is, however, far worse than anything the Kaminker Jew's narrative could have held on its own: The train pulls in at Baranovitsh, and the speaker interrupts himself: "Jews, we're stopping? Where are we?" A voice from the platform answers, as impersonal as the tolling of a bell:

"Stantsye Baranovitsh, Stantsye Baranovitsh." At this, the Kaminker jumps out, and asks everyone on the platform:

> Baranovitsh?
> Baranovitsh.
> It looks like the scene when we bless the New Moon:
> 'Sholem-Aleykhem?
> Sholem-Aleykhem.'

Here we have reached the sharpest of contrasts between the exchange of information and the communication of self. The fact that this is indeed Baranovitsh can only be requestioned and reconfirmed; the repetition of the formula of greeting, on the contrary, contains reaching, emotion, and personality, and the exchange is a new experience each time as different Jews repeat it. It also is the author's by-line.

This is not quite the end of "Stantsye Baranovitsh," however. There is still time for the passengers to demand the end of the tale, and for the Kaminker to respond impatiently, "What ending? It's just the beginning!" We readers are won over, but not so the *komivoyazher*, who has the last word:

"May the station at Baranovitsh burn to the ground!"

Notes

[1] Dan Miron, "Sholem-Aleykhem: Person, Persona, Presence," *The Uriel Weinreich Memorial Lecture I* (New York: YIVO Institute for Jewish Research, 1972).

[2] Walter Benjamin, *Illuminations* (New York: Schocken, 1969), pp. 83-109.

[3] Sholem-Aleykhem, *Ayznban-geshiktes (Ksovim fun a komivoyazher)* (New York: *Spetsyele morgn-frayhayt oysgabe*, 1937), pp. 41-59.

[4] Maks Erik, "Vegn Sholem-Aleykhem's 'ksovim fun a komivoyazher,' " *Afn visnshaftlekhn front*, 1935), 161-172.

[5] Ruth Wisse, "Sholem Aleichem and the Art of Communication," (Syracuse: The B.G. Rudolph Lectures in Judaic Studies, 1979).

[6] Miron, *ibid.*

[7] Sholem-Aleykhem, *Idishe shrayber* (New York: *Spetsyele morgn-frayhayt oysgabe*, 1937), pp. 41-59.

[8] David Roskies, *Against the Apocalypse: Responses to Catastrophe in Modern Jewish Culture* (Cambridge and London: Harvard University Press, 1984).

[9] Benjamin, p. 84.

[10] Roskies, p. 181.

[11] *Ibid.*

Sholem Asch, Joseph Leftwich, and Stefan Zweig's *Der begrabene Leuchter*

Mark H. Gelber

> Ich kann keinen anderen Sinn finden. Die Seele zermatert, das Geist gequält, die Augen ermüdet, die Nerve zerquält – ich weiss kein Sinn. Irgendeine Macht – nennen Sie sie Gott, Schicksal – irgendeine Macht will, daß wir noch dauern. How? Als Volk? Volk nicht! Als Rasse. Kein Rass. Als Religion? Keines ganz mehr. Sind eine Schicksalsgemeinschaft... Etwas Unzerstörbares.
>
> Stefan Zweig, "Jüdisch," in "Notizen America" (Stefan Zweig-*Nachlass*, London)

When Stefan Zweig published *Der begrabene Leuchter (The Buried Candelabrum)* as a separate volume in 1937, he dedicated this Jewish legend to his "friend Sholem Asch."[1] Despite the fact that Zweig mentioned Asch in passing in *Die Welt von gestern* (1942), their friendship has been glossed over or entirely neglected in the secondary literature, probably owing to the general relegation to minor importance of Jewish-related aspects in the major studies of Zweig. This approach was encouraged in part by Zweig himself, but also dictated in a sense by Friderike Zweig, his first wife, who dominated Zweig scholarship and set the prevailing tone for nearly thirty years after his death.[2] Her conception of Zweig as the modern cosmopolitan humanist *par excellence* prepared the way for the dissemination of a quasi-mythic image of him as the *grand europèen*, which is firmly established, despite repeated attempts over the years to supplement this view in different ways.[3] Zweig's very cordial relationship with Asch constitutes an important Jewish-related aspect of Zweig studies –

a truth which is thoroughly corroborated by the substantial and intensive correspondence between the two writers, beginning in 1929.[4] Furthermore, this friendship provides a suitable framework for a far-ranging consideration of Zweig's relationship to the world of Yiddish. It is precisely in this context that the translator, author, and journalist, Joseph Leftwich, a mutual friend of both Asch and Zweig, played a central role in mediating between Yiddish and German(Austrian)-Jewish sensibilities. *Der begrabene Leuchter* is a literary locus for Zweig's ongoing re-evaluation of his Jewish self during the mid-1930s, and the background of his relationships to Asch and Leftwich, as well as to Yiddish in a wider sense, sheds certain light on literary aspects of this text.

In 1930 Zweig's major tribute to Asch on the occasion of the latter's fiftieth birthday appeared as a front-page article in *Die literarische Welt* (Berlin). This essay not only testifies to Zweig's detailed familiarity with, and literary-critical enthusiasm for, Asch's writings; it also provides documentation for Zweig's own acquaintance with Yiddish language and literature. While contrasting Asch's difficult cultural breakthrough (from a remote *shtetl* existence to the chief representative of an entire people and its literature before the world) with his own career and the typical Western European artist's far easier cultural task, Zweig confessed that he had known virtually nothing about Yiddish before his encounter with Asch's work: "...wusste ich nicht einmal Deutliches weder von der Sprache...noch von der Literatur...obwohl selbst Jude, wusste ich lange nicht, dass es eine ernste und ernst zu nehmende jiddische Literatur gibt...."[5] In a more general sense, Zweig lamented the "tragic situation" of those writers whose natural readerships were perforce severely limited, and in this context he included Yiddish together with other similarly handicapped languages: Catalán, Bulgarian, Provençal.

This particular, self-cultivated image of Zweig as a latecomer to Yiddish, which can be documented further,[6] seems to contradict other evidence which suggests that Zweig probably enjoyed relative familiarity with certain aspects of Yiddish language and literature in German translation at a much earlier stage in his artistic career. This evidence is directly related to his association with the little known cultural-spiritual Zionist art movement, the "jungjüdische Bewegung," which flourished around the turn of the century.[7] This movement promoted Yiddish literature, chiefly by means of translation and publication in German and by stimulating linguistic research and literary criticism of Yiddish literature in German-Jewish and Zionist periodicals. The key figures in this movement were the Galician-born artist, Ephraim Moses Lilien, Zweig's close friend at the beginning of the century, and the Moravian-born cultural Zionist ideologue, Berthold Feiwel, who together with Martin Buber founded the Jüdischer Verlag in 1902 in order to realize their cultural Zionist and "jungjüdisch" objectives. Zweig's flirtation with the "jungjüdische Bewegung" is a separate chapter in its own right.[8] It suffices here to mention the plain fact that in the very same "jungjüdisch" publications which contained some of Zweig's earlist work there also appeared "serious" Yiddish literature translated into German. For example, the first rather sensational "jungjüdisch" collection, the *Jüdischer Almanach* (1902, 1904), edited by Feiwel and Lilien, contained poems by Zweig ("Spinoza," [1902, 1904] "Trugland" [1902]) and his early *Novelle* "Im Schnee" (1904) alongside works by Yiddish masters, such as Mendele Mokher-Sforim, Sholem-Aleykhem, Y.L. Peretz, and the young, aspiring Sholem Asch ("Die Stimme gestohlen"). It seems quite likely that the equally young and precocious beginner, Stefan Zweig, would not have failed to appreciate the literary significance of the Yiddish contributions in the *Almanach*, a volume which created almost frenetic excitement in the Jewish and non-Jewish press following its publication.

His full-length introduction to a collection of E.M. Lilien's work, published in 1903, indicates more specifically Zweig's familiarity with aspects of Yiddish literature, in addition to providing a clear demonstration of his readiness to utilize "jungjüdisch" racial and aesthetic categories. In this essay, thirty years before his sensitive appraisal of Asch's precarious cultural journey from East to West, Zweig depicted Lilien's somewhat similar achievement: his emergence "aus dem Dunkel eines östlichen Dorfes," and his realization of a synthesis of "modern-universeller meisterlicher Technik und jüdischrassigen nationalen Gehaltes."[9] In his discussion of Lilien's illustrations for Morris Rosenfeld's *Lieder des Ghetto*, translated from the

Yiddish by Feiwel, Zweig emphasized the "Blutverwandtschaft" of Lilien and Rosenfeld. Concerning "die leuchtende Hoffnung des Zionssternes," which figures in the work of both, Zweig wrote: "Und beiden leuchtet in stillster Seele das gleiche Licht seliger Hoffnung: der messianische Heimatstraum des verstossenen Volkes."[10] Zweig neglected to comment in this essay on Yiddish-related aspects of Rosenfeld's *Lieder*, possibly owing to the fact that Lilien's work, and not Rosenfeld's, was the primary object of interest. Likewise, Zweig made no mention of Feiwel in this context, who, in addition to translating Rosenfeld's *Lieder*, also wrote a critical introduction to *Lieder des Ghetto*, focusing on the very nature of the Yiddish language and its extensive literature. Here Feiwel went to great lengths to provide detailed, scholarly evidence and references to buttress the contention – at the time a rather controversial contention, which only later became widely accepted – that Yiddish was in every linguistic sense a fusion language, a "Weltsprache." It was neither a corruption or dialect of German, nor "Kauderwelsch" or "Jargon." As Feiwel summed it up tersely: "Es ist eine Sprache, so gut wie eine andere."[11] In his outline of the historical development of Yiddish literature contained in his introduction, he expatiated on Mendele Mokher-Sforim, Sholem-Aleykhem, Y.L. Peretz, and others, while claiming that Yiddish poetry reached its apex in the *Lieder* of Rosenfeld.

It is quite tempting intellectually, although simultaneously problematical in a scholarly sense, to link directly Zweig's formulations in his introduction to Lilien's work to some of his own Jewish-related works, written well after the turn of the century, and to *Der begrabene Leuchter* itself. His poetic description of "die leuchtende Hoffnung des Zionssternes," or, more specifically, his juxtaposition of hopeful illumination within the soul (in Lilien and Rosenfeld) and "der messianische Heimatsstraum des verstossenen Volkes" is literary language strikingly appropriate for a discussion of *Der begrabene Leuchter*, although it was written more than thirty years after Zweig penned the piece on Lilien. Still, more generally, Zweig's flirtation with the Jewish cultural ambience which produced the *Jüdischer Almanach, Lieder des Ghetto*, and many other books, journals, and newspapers certainly provided him with an intellectual framework for the subsequent creation of works like *Jeremias* (1917) and *Rachel rechtet mit Gott* (1924), but also for the composition of East European, Yiddish-speaking literary figures, who appear scattered in his fictive work, like the hapless Salomonssohn in *Untergang eines Herzens* (1927), Buchmendel, or Lämmel (Leopold) Kanitz-Kekesfalva in *Ungeduld des Herzens* (1938).

There are numerous correspondences between Zweig's early Jewish-related works and *Der begrabene Leuchter*. The *Novelle* "Im Schnee," written before his initial well-known encounter with Theodor Herzl and his association with the "jungjüdische Bewegung," contains specific references to the candelabrum, the menorah, which in time became an important symbol for him. Typical for Zweig, the Jewish-religious material and related scenes in the *Novelle* provide solid evidence of his ignorance or misunderstanding of Jewish rituals and traditional mores. To give but one example, Zweig describes here a Chanukah menorah ("Wahrzeichen und Symbol des heiligen Abends, der siebenarmige Leuchter"[13]) as having seven branches, whereas every Chanukah menorah invariably has eight branches for the eight days of the festival *and* an additional one for the "shamas[h]," the candle which will serve to kindle the others. More important, the depiction of the defenseless Jewish community in "Im Schnee" finds its exact parallel later in the initial description of the Jewish community in Rome in *Der begrabene Leuchter*; both communities are depicted in a virtually helpless state, paralyzed by any unexpected knock on the door. The seven-branched menorah described in "Im Schnee" reappears prominantly illustrated as an engraving on the original book cover of Zweig's Jewish-pacifist drama, *Jeremias*. Furthermore, although the legendary material concerning the destruction of the Jewish Temple and the fate of the Temple vessels, including the menorah, is never developed explicitly or incorporated into the text of the play, it is conceivable that Zweig became acquainted with this literature during his work on the prophets and the destruction of Jerusalem as preparation for writing *Jeremias*. This legendary material is extensive in itself and by no means unified; only sometimes is Jeremiah entrusted with the care of the sanctuary and the sacred utensils during the period of exile. Concerning the menorah, the motifs of concealment, exact duplication, secrecy, burial, and ultimate restoration in the Messianic age repeatedly come to the fore, and they all find their way into *Der begrabene Leuchter*.

Various avenues were easily accessible to Zweig, which would have led him to make even more serious engagement with Jewish sources, or with Hebrew and Yiddish, a real priority in his life; yet, he never was willing or able to make this type of life-commitment. Still, he never endeavored to separate himself entirely from the world of Jewish culture. Certainly, his friendships with Asch and (later) with Leftwich, the rise of Nazism, his subsequent exile in England, and his relationship with Lotte Altmann combined to intensify his inner search for a formula which might explain the mystery of Jewish existence to him, as well as his own particular Jewish destiny in the same intellectual-emotional framework.

In addition to Zweig's appreciation of Asch's human qualities and his stature as a writer, Asch came to symbolize for Zweig a unique "transcendent/non-trancendent" Jewish self, precisely at the time – that is, in the wake of Nazism – that such a symbol fulfilled an important psychological function in his own process of self-understanding. In other words, Asch had been successful in freeing himself from his East European, *shtetl* background, but he remained at the same time permanently and comfortably fixed in that milieu, owing to the fact that he continued to write in Yiddish and to represent Yiddish, the language of East European Jewry, before the world. In 1935, during their trip to the U.S., Asch took Zweig with him to visit the Yiddish cultural scene in New York. Zweig compared the café-world he witnessed with its counterparts in Warsaw and his native Vienna (Leopoldstadt):

> ...diesel/ben/ klugen, scharfen aber fahlen Gesichter unserer Nation, unheimlich gleich in ihren Formen und doch nie ganz fassbar und formulierbar... Alle diese Leute haben etwas Verstossenes, sie stehen ausserhalb der Weltliteratur in einem eigenen engen Kreis. Einzig Asch ist es gelungen, die Grenzen zu überstreiten.[14]

Whereas the duality of Zweig's German (Austrian)–Jewish existence had intrigued him intellectually to varying degrees before, after 1933 it became of paramount importance, an issue of life and death. Because Asch represented for him the comforting image of a unified Jewish personality, Zweig could feel relieved somewhat by the fact that he *and* Asch were on the same Nazi blacklist and that the works of both had been burned on the same Nazi pyre (see letter to Asch, May 19, 1933).

To be sure, Asch appreciated Zweig's literary accomplishments, his popularity, influence, and human goodness. As much as Zweig strove to promote Asch with his French and American publishers, so did Asch take commensurate steps in order to see Zweig's work published in Yiddish. Asch particularly encouraged Zweig when it came to Jewish-related writing. In a letter dated January 9, 1930, Asch called *Buchmendel* "ein kleines Meisterwerk von einem grossen menschlichen Werth," and he made arrangements to see it translated into Yiddish. In an undated message to Asch from 1936, Zweig noted that he had just completed a Jewish legend, as Asch had long wished of him. Correspondingly, Asch's enthusiastic response to *Der begrabene Leuchter* was expressed in a letter to Zweig on October 18, 1937 (original orthography):

> ...das Buch ken wirklich eine lieblich der jüdischen Kindern werden. ich möchte dich bitten, dass du mir schreibst wo du den Stof bekommen hast. ist es nur deiner Phantasie? Der Stof für sich ist schon herlich – und from – Jüdisch. ich habe das Buch sehr lieb gewonen.

In December of the same year, Asch wrote how he had sent a copy of *Der begrabene Leuchter* to be translated into Yiddish for publication in *Haynt* (Warsaw). That Asch himself confessed ignorance of the source material for Zweig's composition indicates a degree of complexity and depth of preparation, insofar as the Jewish material is concerned, which has not been appreciated in the secondary literature on Zweig.

Der begrabene Leuchter is composed of an amalgam of insufficiently congealed literary material derived from several distinct literary sources and related to various other projects contemplated by Zweig over the years – this, supplemented by material of his own invention. The sections of the legend dealing with the advent of the Vandals and the pillage of Rome, as well as a good part of the text set in Byzantium, are certainly related to one of his historical miniatures, "Die Eroberung von Byzanz," which came to be included in late editions of the popular *Sternstunden der Menschheit*. In the text of "Die Eroberung von Byzanz," Zweig related the fall and plundering of Byzantium to the earlier fall of Rome: "Manchmal spielt die Geschichte mit Zahlen. Denn genau tausend Jahre nachdem Rom von den Vandalen so denkwürdig geplündert worden, beginnt die Plünderung Byzanz' ...Nie wird die Menschheit zur Gänze wissen, ...wie viel bei den Plünderungen Roms, Alexandriens und Byzanz' der geistigen Welt verlorenging."[15] Zweig utilized secondary historical source material concerning the Vandals, while preparing to write his legend. For example, a book order slip from the British Museum Library for Ludwig Schmidt's standard work, *Geschichte der Wandalen*, may be found in the same notebook together with the original manuscript of *Der begrabene Leuchter* in the Zweig-*Nachlass* in London.[16]

More important, though, is the fact that the primary source work for this period, *The Vandal Wars* by Procopius of Caesaria (6th century A.D.), supplies a direct connection to the Jewish material used by Zweig, that is, to the legend of the "wandering" Temple vessels. In Book I, Chap. 5, Procopius narrates the plundering of Rome by the Vandals; in Book II, Chap. 9, he relates Belisar's successful campaign against the Vandals in North Africa, culminating in the triumphal procession in Byzantium. Textual correspondences between Zweig's legend and Procopius's account leave no doubt that Zweig knew this work intimately. Procopius links Belisar's capture and display of the fantastic spoils from Carthage to the earlier plundering of Rome by the Vandals through reference to the treasures of the Jews. In turn, he links the destruction and despoilment of Jerusalem by Titus to the later, similar fate of Rome at the hands of the Vandals:

> Geiserich hatte ja, wie schon in den früheren Büchern berichtet, den Kaiserpalast in Rom ausgeplündert. Schliesslich gehörte noch der Judenschatz dazu, den Titos, der Sohn des Vespasianos, nach der Einnahme Jerusalems mit anderen Beutestücken zusammen nach Rom gebracht hatte.[17]

Furthermore, Procopius incorporates a short literary digression into his account, which serves to explain Justinian's decision to send the Temple vessels to Jerusalem. According to Procopius, a Jew witnessing the victory parade and display (cf. Benjamin Marnefesch's presence in the arena in Byzantium during the very same procession) let it be known to an appropriate personality in the emperor's entourage that the vessels could only bring misfortune to Byzantium, since they were to blame for the fall of Rome and, in turn, the fall of Carthage. This Jew advised sending these particular spoils to Jerusalem. Upon hearing of this advice, the emperor immediately sent the vessels off to Christian churches in Jerusalem. Thus, the extent to which Zweig amplified and transformed imaginatively this literary account in *Der begrabene Leuchter* may be measured precisely. Although Procopius makes no specific mention of the menorah itself, Zweig was almost certainly referring to Procopius's account when he wrote to Ben Huebsch in the spring of 1936 that he would treat poetically the story of the wandering Temple vessels, which was totally unknown to the public: "die (der Allgemeinheit völlig unbekannte) Wanderung der Cultgeräte des Tempels, vor allem des Leuchters." (Zweig-Huebsch, April 29, 1936; Library of Congress, Washington, D.C., microfilm)

The idea to link the sack of Rome and the fate of the menorah may also have been reinforced by way of Zweig's familiarity with the writings of Emil Bernhard Cohn, a largely forgotten author, who perhaps influenced Zweig to choose the literary form of the legend for his work. In a letter dated February 27, 1926, Zweig thanked Cohn for sending him his *Legenden:* "sie scheinen mir etwas absolut Vollendetes im Sinne der Legende."[18] Although Cohn's legends, in truth quasi-artistic retellings in German of aggadic material from the Talmud, have no pertinent intertextual connection to Zweig's legend beside the generic one, other works by Cohn may have aided Zweig in a sense to contemplate bringing the Jewish material into the non-Jewish, general historical frame in *Der begrabene Leuchter*. Specifically, Cohn's *Die jüdische Geschichte*, which appeared in 1936 treats briefly the fall of Rome and the rise of the Vandals,[19] tending throughout to locate Jewish activity within the larger, primary context of world history. This tendency is identical to Zweig's literary strategy in the legend. Furthermore, Cohn's popular lexicon, *Das jüdische ABC* (1935),[20] may have served Zweig as a useful, if very rudimentary, reference tool, providing basic information about Jewish customs and traditional religious life.

Yet, by no means can Zweig's possible familiarity with Cohn's writings even begin to account for the incorporation of more esoteric or sophisticated Jewish-related material in *Der begrabene Leuchter.*[21] A careful consideration of the two very different, transliterated Hebrew epithets, which are utilized repeatedly in the text to characterize the major Jewish figures, underscores the creative complexity of Zweig's composition, as well as the limitations of source criticism in this particular case. The first epithet, "Kab ve Nake," is explained in the legend as part of a litany of praise: "...der Oberste der Gemeinde, der Älteste, der Weiseste... der grosse Deuter der Schrift, Rabbi Elieser, den sie Kab ve Nake, den Reinen und Klaren, nannten."[22] The second epithet, "Marnefesch," is correspondingly explained as follows: "Benjamin Marnefesch nannten sie ihn um seines zerschlagenen Armes willen, was besagen will: den Mann, den Gott bitter geprüft ...." (p. 137)

Whereas the correspondence between Stefan Zweig and Joseph Leftwich illuminates definitively how Zweig came to the epithet "Marnefesch," the corresponding background of "Kab ve Nake" remains a mystery.[23] On July 14, 1936, Zweig, continuing his work on *Der begrabene Leuchter* while on a visit in France, wrote to Leftwich and asked him to provide an appropriate Hebrew epithet that would mean "der Geprüfte" or "der Beschädigte." Although Leftwich's response is not available, Zweig's missive of July 19 makes it clear that Leftwich proferred the term. Zweig wrote:

> Mir und Joseph Roth scheint am richtigsten das Wort "Marnefesch." Aber kann ich es im Deutschen dann auch erklärend übersetzen mit dem dichterischen Worte "der Geprüfte" oder "der Geschlagene?" Und zweitens, wie nennt man einen solchen Menschen in einem solchen Falle? Sagt man dann "Benjamin Marnefesch" oder "Benjamin *el* Marnefesch?" Ich glaube das letztere.

These questions underline once more Zweig's basic dearth of knowledge and lack of familiarity with simple Hebrew or Jewish material – a lack which he never overcame. At the same time, he did indicate a genuine desire to avoid error, while providing the legend with a Jewish flavor by way of incorporating transliterated Hebraicisms, which are duly explained in the text. "Marnefesch" (literally "bitter soul") means neither "der Geprüfte" nor "der Geschlagene," but it certainly does convey the emotional state of one, like Zweig's Benjamin-figure, who has been sorely tried over the years. Zweig was to revert to this concept in *Die Welt von gestern*, which evidences in several places extreme sensitivity to Jewish suffering. One of his suggested working titles for his memoirs was, in fact, "geprüfte Generation," and in an undated letter to Leftwich, Zweig related his work on *Die Welt von gestern* to the Jewish predicament in medieval Spain during the time of the expulsions: "Hätte nicht auch ein Maranne die Geschichte seiner Heimat schreiben sollen – wie die Juden dort lebten, ehe sie vertrieben wurden?"

This questionable literary use of "Marnefesch" may be contrasted with the dubious translation of "Kab ve Nake" as "pure and clear." In fact, "Kab ve Nake" has no such meaning, or, at least, this meaning for the term cannot be found in standard Biblical, Talmudic, or modern Hebrew lexica. Actually, "Kab" is an ancient measure. "Kab ve Nake" derives from the Talmud, where it is used to characterize the Mishna of a certain Rabbi Elieser ben Jakob. His Mishna, although one of but few in number, was purported to be quite reliable, in that it did serve to clarify certain questions. As Jacob Levy, the distinguished lexicographer, explained: "die Mishna des R. Elieser ben Jakob füllt blos einen Kab aus (d.h. sie sind wenig), ist aber geläutert."[24] Perhaps Zweig's rendering of the term as "pure and clear" was a simple transference of qualities originally associated in his mind with the menorah itself, since the gold required for its manufacture had to be absolutely pure (Ex. 25:31-40). In any case, it is significant that, as in the Talmud, this epithet is used in Zweig's legend in connection with the character named Rabbi Elieser.

More problematical though is the fact that this term is rather esoteric, and no pat explanation exists which might explain how Zweig came to it. The standard modern Hebrew dictionary of Eliezer ben Yehuda indicates that Chaim N. Bialik employed the term "Kab ve Nake" in his well-known essay on the Jewish painter A.L. Pasternak. This essay was available to Zweig in German. It would have certainly interested him in light of his admiration for Tolstoy (whose portrait Pasternak painted) and because of Bialik's sophisticated treatment of the issue of Jewish-national art. Yet, it contains no transliterated Hebraicisms in the German translation.[25] It may very well be that Zweig had access to an unknown or inaccessible source, from which he borrowed or transformed material for *Der begrabene Leuchter*, and perhaps the identification of this source would shed some light on the literary origin of this usage of "Kab ve Nake."

Whether or not Leftwich may have also provided this epithet is unascertainable. However, from the time of Zweig's arrival in London in 1933, Leftwich served to facilitate and broaden Zweig's contact with various aspects of the Jewish cultural scene in London, some of which are relevant to a discussion of *Der begrabene Leuchter*. Leftwich introduced Zweig to several of his colleagues, talented Yiddish writers like Zalman Shneour, Leon Shalit, Yitzhak Manger, and Leo Koenig, whom Zweig came to appreciate sincerely after reading their work. With Leftwich's encouragement, Zweig attended performances of the Vilna Yiddish Theater in London, and he spoke at a public reception for the company at the Whitechapel Art Gallery in 1934. Leftwich subsequently wrote of Zweig's "frequent attendances at the performances" and his "considerable interest in Yiddish language and the kind of Jewish life associated with it."[26] To Leftwich he expressed his hope that the "coming generation will realize that Yiddish is the most effective means of keeping Jews together," and he confided his feeling that it was possibly a mistake to develop Hebrew in the *yishuv* in Palestine, instead of Yiddish. Zweig felt that he could have lectured in Yiddish, but never in Hebrew, at the "Jerusalem University."

The combination of Leftwich and Zweig, their collaborative efforts, reflect imaginative cooperation and creative ideas, only some of which were realized. For example, the idea of a film about Theodor Herzl, whom both men revered, is a fascinating topic discussed in their correspondence in early 1935.[27] Zweig opined that it would have to open with scenes from the Dreyfus trial, but he doubted that the emotional desperation and mass ferment, which characterized Herzl's funeral in 1904, could ever be conveyed on the screen. Also, the exciting plan to found an international Jewish cultural magazine crystallized around the same time, and one of the ostensible purposes of Zweig's trip to the U.S. in 1935 was to raise funds for this project. Leftwich translated a talk into English for Zweig, which he gave at the home of Mrs. Anthony de Rothschild to raise money for Jewish children, exiled or homeless in wake of the political upheaval in 1933. Zweig's sensitive concern for Jewish youth expressed in this piece is mirrored poignantly in *Der begrabene Leuchter.*[28] Leftwich translated into Yiddish a paper Zweig wrote for a symposium organized by "Dos Yiddishe Vort," subsequently published in English as "Whither Jewry?"[29] Zweig regularly recommended many worthy German-Jewish works to Leftwich for translation into English, like Soma Morgenstern's *Der Sohn des verlorenen Sohnes* and Fritz Heymann's *Chevalier de Geldern*, and he urged Leftwich (and Leo Koenig) to write a major history of Yiddish literature. Zweig also supported enthusiastically Leftwich's bulky Jewish anthologies, *Yisröel. The First Jewish Omnibus* (1933) and *The Golden Peacock* (1939), which approximated his ideal of international Jewish creativity and unity: "Während die anderen schwatzhaft und zänkerisch das 'Wesen' des Judentums durchdiscutieren – leeres Stroh – haben Sie [Leftwich] das schöpferische Judentum *dargestellt*. Ihre beiden Katalogen sind Denkmäler...."[30]

For his part, Leftwich succeeded in persuading Zweig to contribute articles to Yiddish and English-Jewish newspapers and magazines, and Zweig agreed to write introductions to Leftwich's own timely work, some of which had been stimulated by Zweig in the first place. Zweig's introduction to Leftwich's *What Will Happen to the Jews?* voices support for his friend's proposal to encourage *both* national and international Jewish emigration, since "the Jewish problem is today much greater than Palestine."[31] Although in Leftwich's mind this position was probably dictated by considerations of contemporary *Realpolitik*, Zweig saw this dual affirmation of national and international (or universal) tendencies as squarely traditional in view of the Jewish experience throughout the ages. Also, this stance reflected his long-standing view of Jewish nationalist/Zionist endeavors as positive to an extent, but never as the sole path for Jewry. Zweig had not changed his mind about this point even after the rise of Nazism.

The significance of the Jewish-nationalist/Zionist aspect of *Der begrabene Leuchter*, which is related to Leftwich's book and Zweig's engagement with the issue of Jewish survival during the 1930s, has been debated extensively in the secondary literature, and there appears to be no general consensus concerning the extent to which the legend affirms or refutes Zionist tenets.[32] What is clear, however, is that the reception history, precisely regarding the Jewish-nationalist/ Zionist aspect, is quite complicated; the text evoked from the start a wide range of responses in this regard, some of which are absolutely antithetical. Whereas Sol Liptzin considered *Der begrabene Leuchter* "as sad an affirmation of Judaism as ever penned in this century" – a reading supported by Harry Zohn, Steven Garrin, and others[33] – a good number of reviewers and critics responded over the years quite positively to the Jewish-nationalist/Zionist content. For example, the Zionist writer Max Brod conveyed his enthusiastic response to Zweig in a letter dated December 24, 1936:

> Soeben in tiefer Erschütterung Ihren "Begrabenen Leuchter" gelesen. Ihnen war es gegeben, mit dieser Legende unserem Volk ein messianisches Symbol zu neuem Leben zu erwecken – Ich bewundere sehr die Komposition Ihrer Erzählung....Dass wir als Zionisten besonders Seite 307 "kein Volk kann so leben ohne Heimstätt" etc. nahekam, brauche ich nicht zu betonen.[34]

In the same letter, Brod wrote of his plans to circulate the piece among some American Zionists, and he pledged to send it on to journals in Prague, ostensibly for reviewing. In contrast to this reading, Zweig had reported to Brod in May of the same year on his progress in writing this Jewish legend, which, he intimated, would bring little strengthening or comfort to those who needed fortification in difficult times.[35] Interestingly, the American-Jewish reception, according to Ben Huebsch's report to Zweig on December 21, 1937, was also positive:

> Although I cannot report a large sale for "The Buried Candelabrum" it is going along steadily and is producing the nicest echoes from all quarters, particularly, as you might surmise, amongst Jews. Rabbis use it as a subject for discourses, and the wife of Rabbi David de Sola Pool... told me that they were using the book effectively in their Sunday School, for reading aloud, and as prizes for the children.

This complexity of reception stems in part from the dual perspective subtlely interwoven into the text. Thus, regarding the menorah as a symbol, Margarita Pazi observed that it functions as a "Symbol des jüdischen Leids, allerdings auch des jüdischen Wesens und Überdauerns."[36] That is, the menorah is a sign for both Jewish suffering *and* at the same time for Jewish continuity and life. Perhaps the fact that Zweig decided eventually in favor of the title, *Der begrabene Leuchter*, instead of his original working title, "Der ewige Leuchter," (letter to Huebsch, April 29, 1936) is pertinent in this context. The "eternal menorah" suggests a certain confidence, optimism, and ultimate justification lacking in "Der begrabene Leuchter." The "leuchtende Hoffnung" of the Zionist dream, referred to in Zweig's introduction to E.M. Lilien's work, is buried at the end of this legend, but that dream is never totally extinguished. Alfred Wolf, writing in 1937, could term this work fundamentally optimistic, "wenn auch in ferner Zukunft."[37]

The dual perspective pertains as well to incorporation of concrete aspects of Palestinian geography in the legend. Although Benjamin Marnefesch ultimately arrives in the land of Israel after years of troubled wandering and a turbulent diaspora existence, thereby fulfilling a Zionist precept, he has come in truth to bury the menorah and to be buried himself, which is a traditional Jewish religious custom, guaranteeing proximity to Jerusalem. There the Messianic age would be proclaimed first and the dead would come to life. The Zionist potential of the narrative is thus never realized, or it is only realized in the protagonist's fantastic Messianic dream before his death, which, as in Jeremias' vision in the eighth *Bild* of Zweig's play, leads to the potential hallucinatory confusion of dream and reality. This vision is, in truth, a far cry from practical or political Zionist activity. Yet, real geographical landmarks are cited in the text, in Jaffa and Ramleh, and they do suggest a lively, contemporary acquaintance with the terrain between Jaffa and Jerusalem. Probably, Zweig knew Sholem Asch's accounts of his journeys to Palestine, in particular his travelogue "Von Jaffa nach Jerusalem," which describes the same road partially traversed by the aged Benjamin Marnefesch. This depiction is intertextually close to the final scenes in *Der begrabene Leuchter*. Asch's "I-persona" describes the "Wüst und Öde auf beiden Seiten des Weges," while sketching a poetically mysterious landscape, capable of metamorphosis and expectant of the Messiah: "Es scheint zuweilen, als wären die Felder eingeschlafen, als wären sie durch einen Zauberspruch in starren Stein verwandelt worden und harrten nur des Messias, der sie aus ihrem geheimnisvollen Schlafe erwecken soll...Nur da und dort eine Palme...."[38] This vision is interrupted as the first Jewish station is reached – Ramleh, which is the last geographical location mentioned in Zweig's legend.

Although there is no celebration of Jewish suffering and weakness in *Der begrabene Leuchter*, as one finds for example in the earlier *Jeremias*, there is a grudging, doubting acceptance of the possible meaningfulness of this condition in terms of Jewish existence. This aspect supplements the traditional, religious explanation of Jewish uniqueness and survival, offered faithfully by Rabbi Elieser in the first part of the legend. Yet, as Benjamin Marnefesch concedes in the end: "Kein Volk kann so leben ohne Heimstatt und Ziel, wandernd und ewig umgrenzt von Gefahr. Ein Licht müsste man ihnen entzünden, einen Weg ihnen weisen, sonst verzagt und verdorrt es, dies gejagte verlorene Volk." (pp. 189-190) The mass gathering of the Jews at Pera to receive Benjamin Marnefesch seems to parody to an extent the ideal of the Zionist Congress and its goal to transform Jewry in a radical way, but the narrative point of view, which identifies with the protagonist, makes clear the limitations of the character and his ultimate inefficacy in bringing about fundamental change in the social relationship between the Jews and their rulers. The narrative voice in the legend repeatedly identifies with the sorely tried protagonist or with the unjustly oppressed Jewish communities, engendering sympathy and understanding, as well as occasional moments of hope for a better future. Marnefesch exclaims: "Doch vielleicht – und mein Herz ist voll dieser Zuversicht – vielleicht wird sein Wille es wollen, dass unser Volk heimkehre zur Heimat." (p. 208)

The tendency of the protagonist, supported in a sense by the narrative voice, to search for and to derive meaning from examples of Jewish suffering is problematical in a Zionist context, since one of the central impulses of political Zionism aimed at terminating Jewish suffering by normalizing Jewish life on an international scale within the framework of the creation of a Jewish state. Political Zionism sought to distance itself from passive religious Messianism. *Der begrabene Leuchter*, given its medieval setting and accompanying, fictionally verisimilitudinous, religious literary idiom, could not convincingly convey any pertinent political Zionist message, except, perhaps, by way of a cogent illustration of the necessity for radical change in Jewish life; yet, this aspect is lacking in the legend. *Der begrabene*

Leuchter does accord with cultural-spiritual Zionist categories, in that it artistically reflects moments of Jewish life in the diaspora with sensitivity and without Jewish self-abnegation. Still, Marnefesch's persistence and willingness to accept the present, however difficult, exemplify a special Jewish mission in the world and reflect Zweig's own concept of Jewish uniqueness, which in a way is antithetical to any Zionist plea for normalcy. His concept of Jewry as a *Schicksalsgemeinschaft*, which he developed in the 1930s, is related to this literary formulation. Influenced by the work of Viktor Zuckerkandl (*Die Weltgemeinschaft der Juden*, 1936), which Zweig recommended highly to Leftwich, and possibly by Emil Bernhard Cohn's *Aufruf zum Judentum* (1934), as well as by his appreciation of the important role of Yiddish language and culture, Zweig became convinced that modern Jewry would continue to exist indefinitely, despite its having lost its religious foundations and without its having to embrace collectively political Zionism. Continued Jewish wandering (immigration), anti-Semitism, Yiddish culture, and recurrent cultural Zionist tendencies and expressions which encouraged Jewish creativity and unity would serve to keep this *Schicksalsgemeinschaft* in tact.

Furthermore, the primary, underlying Jewish goal, the "Aufstieg ins Geistige," as he defined it in *Die Welt von gestern*, stood to benefit from this condition. Until the end, he believed that Jewish suffering yielded a net gain on individual spirituality, the "seelische Superiorität der Besiegten." Taking this idea to its logical extreme, Zweig even perceived "spiritual improvement" in his associates, who had suffered in Nazi internment camps. In a letter to Felix Braun dated April 27, 1939, Zweig wrote:

> ...hier war ich mit Heinrich Eduard Jacob zusammen, der durch das furchtbare Jahr in Dachau und Buchenwald ganz anders geworden ist, viel ruhiger, viel bescheidener, viel sympathischer. Alle, die solche Prüfungen überstanden haben, zum Beispiel Auernheimer, haben ein Plus dazu gewonnen. Das ewige Flüchten ermüdet vielleicht mehr als das Gefangensein.[39]

The fatigue which Zweig felt already in 1939, despite whatever spiritual gain it may have signified in his own view of things, eventually paralyzed him and helped lead to his suicide. He wrote to Ben Huebsch on December 31, 1941, that is, less than two months before he killed himself: "It is better to make no plans at all, to avoid fear and hope, which Spinoza calls the most dangerous enemies of mankind." Zweig was reduced to this state by a series of psychological setbacks, and his Jewish perspective could by no means provide tangible succor. His menorah, as the legend describes it, was already buried.

Notes

1 The dedication reads simply: "meinem Freunde Schalom Asch." See Stefan Zweig, *Der begrabene Leuchter* (Vienna, Leipzig, Zürich: Herbert Reichner Verlag, 1937). *Der begrabene Leuchter* first appeared in the collection *Kaleidoskop* (Vienna, Leipzig, Zürich: Herbert Reichner Verlag, 1936), pp. 228-329.

2 See Mark H. Gelber, "Stefan Zweig und die Judenfrage von heute," in Gelber (Ed.), *Stefan Zweig – heute* (Bern: Verlag Peter Lang, 1986).

3 For example, Harry Zohn's repeated attempts to understand Zweig's cultural mediatorship as a Jewish characteristic would have to be considered in this context. See Zohn, "Stefan Zweigs kulturelles Mittlertum: ein jüdischer Charakterzug?" *Bulletin des Leo Baeck Instituts*, 63 (1982), pp. 19-31.

4 Asch's letters to Zweig are housed in the Zweig archive in the Reed Library, SUNY-Fredonia. I would like to thank Yvonne Wilensky and John Saulitis for their generous help during the time I worked in Fredonia. Zweig's letters to Asch are housed in Yale University's Beinecke Library (Asch Collection). I would like to thank Dr. Christa Sammons, curator of the German collection, for her helpful guidance during the time I worked in New Haven.

5 Stefan Zweig, "Geburtstagsgruss an Scholem Asch," *Die literarische Welt*, No. 43 (October 24, 1930), p. 1.

6 See, Donald Prater, *Stefan Zweig. Das Leben eines Ungeduldigen* (Trans., Annelie Hohenemser), (Münich: Carl Hanser Verlag, 1981), p. 269, *et passim.*

7 See Mark H. Gelber, "The *jungjüdische Bewegung:* An Unexplored Chapter in German-Jewish Literary and Cultural History," *Yearbook of the Leo Baeck Institute*, Vol. XXXI (1986).

8 See also Mark H. Gelber, "The Impact of Martin Buber on Stefan Zweig," *Modern Austrian Literature* Vol. 14, No. 3/4 (1981), 313-335; and Gelber, "Karl Emil Franzos, Achad Ha-am und Stefan Zweig," *Bulletin des Leo Baeck Instituts*, 63 (1982), pp. 37-49.

9 Stefan Zweig, "Einleitung," in E.M. Lilien, *Sein Werk* (Berlin, Leipzig: Schuster & Loeffler, 1903), pp. 10, 20.

10 *Ibid.*, p. 22.

11 Berthold Feiwel, "Einleitung" in Morris Rosenfeld, *Lieder des Ghetto* (Berlin: S. Cavalry & Co., 1902).

[12] During my research, I came across a reference to a separate book review of *Lieder des Ghetto* written by Zweig, ostensibly in 1903 in the *Allgemeine Zeitung* (Munich). However, I have not been able to locate this review.

[13] Stefan Zweig, "Im Schnee," in Berthold Feiwel and E.M. Lilien (Eds.), *Jüdischer Almanach* (Berlin: Jüdischer Verlag, 1904), p. 159.

[14] Stefan Zweig, *Tagebücher* (Frankfurt a. Main: S. Fischer, 1984), p. 374.

[15] Stefan Zweig, "Die Eroberung von Byzanz," in *Sternstunden der Menschheit* (Frankfurt a. Main: S. Fischer, 1964), pp. 46-47.

[16] I wish to thank Mr. Kurt L. Maschler, the executor of Zweig's literary estate, for his many kindnesses during the period I worked in London.

[17] Prokop von Caesarea, *Vandalenkrieg II* (Munich: Ernst Heimeran Verlag, 1971), p. 225. Several German editions of Procopius's works were available to Zweig – one in a popular series of works by ancient and medieval historians. See *Der Vandalenkrieg* (Trans., D. Coste), (Leipzig: Verlag der Dykschen Buchhandlung, n.d.); in series: Die Geschichtschreiber der deutschen Vorzeit.

[18] Original letter in the London-*Nachlass*. Cohn's legends were reprinted in 1933 by Verlag Siegfried Scholem (Berlin-Schöneberg). Charles Reznikoff translated these legends into English some years later. See Emil Bernhard Cohn, *Stories and Fantasies from the Jewish Past* (Philadelphia: Jewish Publication Society of America, 1951).

[19] Emil Bernhard Cohn, *Die jüdische Geschichte* (Berlin: Jüdische Buchvereinigung, 1936), pp. 56f.

[20] Emil Bernhard Cohn (Ed.), *Das jüdische ABC* (Berlin: Verlag Erwin Löwe, 1935).

[21] Harry Zohn cites a remark by "Dr. Zeitlin at Dropsie College" to the effect that a source for Zweig's legend may be some "medieval German book." See Zohn, "The Buried Candelabrum," *Jewish Affairs* (February, 1959), p. 35.

[22] Stefan Zweig, *Der begrabene Leuchter* in his *Legenden* (Frankfurt a. Main: S. Fischer, 1959), p. 94.

[23] Leftwich's correspondence with Zweig is housed in the Central Zionist Archives (Jerusalem).

[24] Jacob Levy, *Wörterbuch über die Talmudim und Midraschim*, Bd. 4 (Berlin, Vienna: Verlag Benjamin Harz, 1924), p. 233.

[25] See Chaim Nachman Bialik, "A.L. Pasternak," in *Essays* (Trans., Viktor Kellner), (Berlin: Jüdischer Verlag, 1925), pp. 191-214.

[26] Joseph Leftwich, "Stefan Zweig," (typescript), Central Zionist Archives, Jerusalem. In 1939, Leftwich and Zweig attended Maurice Schwartz's Yiddish Art Theater in London, as well.

[27] Cf. Joseph Leftwich, *Theodor Herzl. The Man and the Legend* (London: Robert Anscombe & Co., n.d.). In this book, Leftwich mentioned Stefan Zweig in connection with Zionism: Zweig "for a time seemed inclined to throw [himself] into this Jewish work [Zionism]." (p. 11)

[28] See the early scene, in which Benjamin, the seven-year old child, is awakened in the night: "...es war ein Kind, erst sieben Jahre alt, aber ein jüdi-

sches Kind in der Fremde und gewohnt darum aufzuschrecken, wenn ein Unvermutetes kam....Noch hatte er die Schrift nicht gelernt, jedoch dieses eine wusste er schon: Furcht zu haben vor allem und jedem auf Erden." (*Der begrabene Leuchter*, p. 103). Cf. Zweig, "The Jewish Children in Germany," (Nov. 30, 1933[pamphlet]).

29 Stefan Zweig, "Whither Jewry?" in *World Jewry* (July 6, 1935), p. 211

30 Letter to Leftwich, August 29, 1939. See also Joseph Leftwich, "Did you know Stefan Zweig?" (typescript), p. 23 (Zweig-*Nachlass*, London). This manuscript is an early, longer version of Leftwich's "Stefan Zweig and the World of Yesterday," *Yearbook of the Leo Baeck Institute*, Vol. III (1958), pp. 81-100.

31 Stefan Zweig, "Forward," in Joseph Leftwich, *What Will Happen to the Jews?* (London: P.S. King & Son, Ltd., 1936), p. x. Cf. Zweig, "Yidn inem algemaynen politishn lebn," *Oyfn Shaydveg* (Paris: 1939), 103-105.

32 Several contemporary observers have tended to view the work as pro-Zionist. See Joseph P. Strelka, *Stefan Zweig, Freier Geist der Menschlichkeit* (Vienna: Österreichischer Bundesverlag, 1981), p. 112; and Klara Carmely, "The Ideal of Eternal Homelessness: Stefan Zweig and Judaism," in Marion B. Sonnenfeld (Ed.), *The World of Yesterday's Humanist Today* (Albany: SUNY Press, 1983), pp. 111-117.

33 Sol Liptzin, *Germany's Stepchildren* (Philadelphia: Jewish Publication Society of America, 1944), p. 218. Cf. Harry Zohn, "Stefan Zweigs kulturelles Mittlertum: ein jüdischer Charakterzug?" *ibid.*, p. 28; and Steven H. Garrin, "Stefan Zweig's Judaism," *Modern Austrian Literature*, Vol. 14, No. 3/4 (1981), p. 280.

34 Original in Stefan Zweig archive, Fredonia.

35 Quoted in Margarita Pazi, "Stefan Zweig: Europäer und Jude," *Modern Austrian Literature*, Vol. 14, No. 3/4 (1981), p. 298.

36 *Ibid.*

37 Alfred Wolf, *Jüdische Elemente im Werke Stefan Zweigs*, (typescript), (June: 1937), Stefan Zweig archive, Fredonia.

38 Sholem Asch, "Von Jaffa nach Jerusalem," in *Im Lande der Vaeter* (Berlin: Jüdischer Verlag, n.d.), p. 22.

39 Xeroxed copy in Zweig-*Nachlass*, London. Cf. Prater, p. 259; and Donald G. Daviau and Jorun B. Johns (Eds.), *The Correspondence of Stefan Zweig with Raoul Auernheimer* (Columbia, S.C.: Camden House, 1983).

The Unpublished Letters of Richard Beer-Hofmann to Hermann Bahr (with the unpublished letters between Beer-Hofmann and Theodor Herzl)*

Jeffrey B. Berlin

> "Es gibt ein Gedicht von Beer-Hofmann 'Schlaflied für Mirjam', so wunderbar weich und wiegend, für mich das schönste, das seit 'Über allen Gipfeln' den Deutschen geschenkt worden ist."
>
> Hermann Bahr[1]

It is firmly established that the so-called "Jung-Wien" group consisted of, among some other figures, Hermann Bahr (1863-1934), Richard Beer-Hofmann (1866-1945), Hugo von Hofmannsthal (1874-1929) and Arthur Schnitzler (1862-1931). Bahr, often referred to as the leader of the group[2] (even though they did not recognize themselves as part of a literary "school"),[3] once observed:

> Als ich ankam, hatte dieses junge Wien eben die Feuertaufe bestanden. Es galt den Spöttern jahrelang als eine meiner Erfindungen; der 'Herr aus Linz',[4] der sich zum 'Herrn von Wien' aufgeworfen, diese Wendung verlock-

* The original Richard Beer-Hofmann letters to Hermann Bahr are in the Österreichische Nationalbibliothek (Vienna). The original Bahr letters to Beer-Hofmann are in the Yale University Collection of German Literature at the Beinecke Rare Book and Manuscript Library (New Haven). A few original Anna Bahr-Mildenburg and H. Bahr letters to Beer-Hofmann are in the Houghton Library Reading Room at Harvard University (Cambridge). The original Theodor Herzl/Beer-Hofmann letters are in The Central Zionist Archives (Jerusalem), with an additional two Herzl cards at Harvard University. I sincerely thank all of these depositories for many courtesies extended to me. I also thank Mrs. Miriam Beer-Hofmann Lens for her many kindnesses and permission to publish her father's letters, as well as Dr. Alex Bein (Jerusalem) and The Central Zionist Archives for permission to publish Herzl's letters. The original orthography has been retained in all cases, and any editorial emendation has been so noted by square brackets. The punctuation has not been altered.

te Feuilletonisten. Sie tut mir zu viel Ehre: nicht ich war es, der 'Jungösterreich', 'Jungwien' Pate stand, sondern Henrik Ibsen.[5] Ihn hatte der neue Direktor des Burgtheaters, Burckhard, im April 1891 zur Aufführung der 'Kronprätendenten' geladen....[...] Aus den Händen Ibsens übernahm ich es.[6]

In this connection, a statement Beer-Hofmann made to Werner Vordtriede in February, 1943 is revealing: "Hätte ich nicht durch reinen Zufall in einem einzigen Sommer den Hugo Hofmannsthal, Schnitzler und Bahr kennengelernt, wäre ich vielleicht nie zum Schreiben gekommen."[7] While the relationship between Beer-Hofmann, Schnitzler, and Hofmannsthal, and between Bahr, Schnitzler, and Hofmannsthal has been studied, to date no attention has been paid to the Beer-Hofmann/Bahr friendship.[8]

The present edition offers eleven previously unpublished letters and one telegram from Beer-Hofmann to Bahr. In addition, the unpublished letters and cards between Beer-Hofmann and Theodor Herzl (1860-1904), which clarify an additional topic discussed here, are also presented. While most of the Beer-Hofmann communications to Bahr are casual in nature, five in particular are especially distinct, namely: the letters of March 29, 1900 about Beer-Hofmann's *Der Tod Georgs*; November 3, 1903 about Bahr's *Dialog vom Tragischen*; July 12, 1904 about Herzl's death; August 9, 1904 about Bahr's *Dialog vom Marsyas*; and June 12, 1919 about Bahr's *Die Rotte Korahs.* Bahr and Beer-Hofmann, who met in the fall of 1890,[9] probably in the now-famous Café Griensteidl that was near the old Hofburgtheater in Vienna, shared many experiences, and the present letters document several of these. Nevertheless, some of Beer-Hofmann's letters or cards to Bahr are probably lost, because the first available Beer-Hofmann letter to Bahr is dated March 29, 1900, while that of Bahr to Beer-Hofmann is dated, it seems, April 2, 1894. In addition, there are several times as many Bahr letters and cards as Beer-Hofmann ones available.[10] Indeed, the extant Beer-Hofmann letters, as well as some notations from Beer-Hofmann's unpublished *Daten* and other sources, are designed to present additional aspects of the life-style, interests, and daily activities of Richard Beer-Hofmann and of his friendship with Hermann Bahr (and, tangentially, with Theodor Herzl).[11]

In a note of July, 1894[12] Bahr asked Beer-Hofmann if he could borrow a copy of Dante's *La Vita Nuova*, a work that was meaningful to Beer-Hofmann and which he later found appropriate to quote as a preface and elsewhere in his *Paula. Ein Fragment.*[13] In 1894, however, Beer-Hofmann probably could not yet relate to the essence of *La Vita Nuova*, but a year later he recorded in *Daten*: "Donnerstag, den fünften Dezember [1895], Abends [8 P.M.], sehe ich zum erstenmal Paula. 'Incipit vita nova.' "[14] Just as a new life began for Dante when he first saw Beatrice, so too did a new life begin when Beer-Hofmann saw Paula Lissy (1879-1939), whom he married on May 14, 1898. To be sure, Bahr's note documents that Beer-Hofmann had a copy of this work by Dante, which he and Bahr most likely discussed. Bahr, of course, referred to *La Vita Nuova* only a few months later in his well-known essay *Décadence.*[15]

The other extant Bahr cards and letters to Beer-Hofmann reveal many aspects of their lasting friendship, but we may observe that the Bahr side of the exchange usually is not extremely detailed. Nevertheless, his cards and letters do provide much information about his various travels and activities, and they certainly reveal a cordial friendship. Since this latter issue concerns us, a brief synopsis of some of Bahr's more significant observations expressed in his cards and letters to Beer-Hofmann will help further introduce and familiarize us with the general tone and nature of these exchanges; additional references to other Bahr cards and letters to Beer-Hofmann are recorded in the notes. Thus, Bahr comments to Beer-Hofmann that he was in Munich to honor Ibsen (5/25/94);[16] requests Beer-Hofmann's advice (2/20/95); wishes to borrow books, such as Brandes' *Moderne Geister* (undated card – postmark 11/5/95); wants to discuss Beer-Hofmann's works (9/21/96); notes his nervousness, even about riding an American bicycle (4/2/94? and 6/22/96); speaks of his negative moods (6/22/96); seeks information about the background of Karl Gustav Vollmoeller's *Catherina, Gräfin von Armagnac und ihre beiden Liebhaber* [S. Fischer, 1903] (7/15/03); raises philosophical issues[17] (2/10/04); observes that Max Reinhardt (1873-1943) has accepted his latest work (8/5/04); comments about his own and Paula's heart problems (8/5/[04] and 1/24/05); speaks about a secret relationship with a woman (1/24/05); praises Beer-Hofmann's work (2/28/05); agonizes over money problems (9/11/05); inquires if Beer-Hofmann has received his new novel, most probably *Drut* [S. Fischer, 1909] as well as his *Tagebuch* [Paul Cassirer, 1909] (6/18/09) – the period covered in the *Tagebuch* is 1905 to 1908, and examination of it reveals that Beer-Hofmann is not mentioned; expresses appreciation of Beer-Hofmann's immediate assistance at a crucial time (7/4/20). Finally, after Bahr's death there was a brief exchange between Beer-Hofmann and Anna Bahr-Mildenburg (see note 58), who wished copies of her late husband's letters; as her still unpublished letter of March 17, 1936, now housed in the Beer-Hofmann *Nachlass* collection at the Houghton Library Reading Room at Harvard University reveals, Beer-Hofmann complied with her wishes.

Hermann Bahr, "der Mann von Übermorgen," "der grosse Überwinder," the "Verwandlungskünstler," the "Seismograph seiner Epoche," to cite some of the descriptions used to characterize his life and work, remains an important, if neglected, figure of the "Griensteidl-Kreis" and of other movements (if we may so express it) of which he was a part.[18] On the other hand, Beer-Hofmann's impact was different. As Erich Kahler said of Beer-Hofmann's writings:

> Sie haben den Juden, sie haben der Welt den einzigartigen Sinn und die historische Rolle Israels vor Augen gestellt, und sie haben den Juden vor allem in ihrer furchtbaren Not einen unschätzbaren Trost und eine aufrichtende Lehre gegeben: die erhabene Legitimierung, und damit die Selbstübersteigung ihrer Leiden. Sie haben den Juden die richtige Haltung gezeigt: die Haltung der Würde, des Stolzes, der inneren Entrücktheit. Den Stolz der weisen Demut, die alle Demütigungen zerspellt, den Stolz der Überschau über die Zeiten und Welten und Erfahrungen, den Stolz der seelischen Unberührbarkeitskraft dieser inneren Erfahrungen. Endlich den Stolz eines Volkes, das von altersher die Idee der Gerechtigkeit und der Vollkommenheit über alles andere gestellt hat. Und auch er selbst, der Mann Beer-Hofmann, hat diese Lehre der Haltung und des Stolzes gegeben, und es tat wohl, das Judentum einmal in der Gestalt eines fürstlichen Menschen repräsentiert zu sehen.[19]

1. [Handwritten original] Aussee 29. III 1900

Lieber Bahr! Ich danke Ihnen dass Sie daran dachten mir die Zeitung zu senden.[20] Ich freue mich auch, dass Sie – wo die Versuchung persönlich zu werden so nahe war – es vermochten sachlich zu bleiben. In Vielem, gewiss in mehr, als Sie vermuten, bin ich Ihrer Ansicht.
In drei Tagen bin ich wieder in Wien;[21] vielleicht erfolgt dann Ihr so oft und prunkvoll angekündigter Besuch.
Ich grüsse Sie herzlich.

Richard Beer-Hofmann

2. [Handwritten original] Rodaun 3/XI 03

Lieber Bahr!
Ich danke Ihnen für den "Dialog".[22] Ich habe ihn in der "Rundschau" nur flüchtig (Hugo[23] ist der Besitzer) lesen können, und erst jetzt habe ich mich mit Ruhe daran gefreut. Von den andern Aufsätzen war mir nur "Der böse Goethe"[24] bekannt. Selbstverständlich – das heisst, selbstverständlich für Jemanden der mich kennt – musste mich "das unrettbare Ich", und was sie darin von Euripides und seiner Art die Unsicherheit des "Ich" zu betonen, sagen, am tiefsten berühren. Hoffentlich sehe ich Sie bald in Rodaun.

Herzlichst Ihr
Richard

3. [Handwritten original] Aussee 12./VII. 04

Lieber Hermann! Ich hab Sie nicht drum beneidet, dass Sie zu Herzls Begräbnis haben gehen müssen.[25] Mich hat die Nachricht in Salzburg getroffen. Ich habe erst jetzt bemerkt wie starke Sympathieen zwischen ihm und mir all diese Jahre latent waren.[26] So oft wir uns – immer in langen Zwischenräumen – trafen, in Wien, in Ischl, Aussee-

zuletzt am Abend des Hagenbundes[27] drehte sich das Gespräch darum – warum wir eigentlich miteinander nicht *mehr* verkehrten. Ich erklärte ihm immer von neuem wie sehr – abgesehen von unsern so gründlich verschiedenen künstlerischen Anschauungen – wie sehr der Ton seiner Rede der überlegen, oder auf die Schulter klopfend war, es mir unmöglich mache oft mit ihm beisammen zu sein. Er erklärte lächelnd sich bessern zu wollen, schickte mir Tags darauf zwei Bände seiner Feuilletons,[28] und wollte dass ich – zwei Tage später – mit meiner Frau bei ihm speisen sollte. Ich sagte ihm ab, geärgert durch das gerade erschienene Hagenbundfeuilleton das mir begreiflich machte, wie unmöglich wir uns künstlerisch verständigen könnten, auch deshalb weil ein mir unbekannter französischer Bildhauer auch dabei sein sollte, zuletzt auch vielleicht ein wenig beeinflusst durch Hugos[29] Eifer, der mir zu beweisen versuchte was für gesellschaftliche Pflichten ich mir (zu meinen vielen andern!) da auf den Hals lade, wie schon ohnehin alle möglichen Leute zu mir kämen etc.
Zwar schrie ich sofort "Namen nennen!" zwang Hugo zu feierlichem Wiederruf, gab ihm das "alle mögliche" zurück aber schliesslich gieng ich nicht, und fühle jetzt – kindisch – fast Reue, als hätte diese eine Zusammenkunft irgendetwas Wichtiges bedeuten können.
Der N. Fr. Pr.[30] habe ich nicht condolirt. *Sie* müssten es als College, Arthur[31] als – wenn auch sparsamer – Mitarbeiter; mir war es widerwärtig ohne Zwang mich in die Gesellschaft der genant werden wollenden zu begeben.[32] Ich habe seiner Frau und der Mutter condolirt. Burkhardt[33] sprach ich einmal, er dürfte schon in St. Gilgen sein. Vielleicht können Sie doch um 15. herum auf ein paar Stunden zu uns hieher kommen? Ich möchte mich sehr freuen. Geht es aber durchaus nicht dann teilen Sie es doch so ein, dass wir uns *nach* Bayreuth hier oder in Salzburg – lieber hier – sehen können. Ich, Paula, und Mirjam grüssen Sie von Herzen.[34]

Ihr
Richard

4. [Handwritten original] Aussee 1/VIII 04

Lieber Hermann! Aus Ihrem Salzburger Brief[35] hab ich entnommen:

I. Dass Sie *nur* meinetwegen über Salzburg wollen

II. Dass Sie *nachts* in Salzburg ankommen, und *nachts* nach Wien fahren müssen

III. Dass All das nur wegen *eines* Tages geschieht.

Schön wär es gewesen wenn wir doch zwei Tage hätten in Salzburg sein können. Zwischen Mirabell, Hellbrunn, Pferdeschwemme und Hohensalzburg[36] und irgend einer Spazierfahrt am Abend zwischen Feldern und Gehöften hätten sich ein paar Stunden wol gefunden, wo ich gerne mein Stück (das noch unfertige – heu!)[37] Ihnen vorgelesen, und Sie mühelos zugehört hätten. So hätte das Stück den Tag gefüllt und für Salzburg, und uns Beide wäre nichts übrig geblieben. Ein Unrecht gegen alle Drei. Ich will jetzt recht fleissig sein, vielleicht giebt sich dann Ende des Monates, irgend eine Gelegenheit uns noch vor Wien zu sehen. Arthur kommt Ende August nach Ischl.[38] Hugo hat sich heute Vormittag bei mir gemeldet. Die drei schon vernunftbegabten von uns Paula, Mirjam und ich grüssen Sie von Herzen, die andern zwei[39] liegen jetzt faul und verfressen im Gras.

Ihr
Richard

5. [Handwritten original] Aussee 9.VIII.04[40]

Lieber Hermann!

Ihren lieben Brief hab ich erhalten.[41] Hätt ich gewusst dass Sie *jedenfalls* in Salzburg sind, wäre ich ja gekommen. Sind Sie nicht wieder überarbeitet? Seit Griechenland ein Stück und einen Dialog[42] – *ganz fertig* – Sie begreifen mein Staunen – machen. Den "Marsyas"[43] habe ich heute zum zweiten mal, und mit vieler Freude gelesen. Die Momente, an die er anknüpft, haben mich an jene Zeit – jetzt finde ich sie schön – erinnert, in der mir der Plan zur "Ariadne" im Kopf herumgieng.[44] Flöte und Leier waren mir damals wichtige Symbole für Dionysos und Orpheus, die sich auf Naxos treffen sollten. Orpheus ein untergehender, Dionysos ein aufgehender Gott, der seiner noch nicht sicher ist, und für den Ariadne und ihr Schicksal – ihr Tod und das Aufflammen ihrer Krone am Abendhimmel – eine Bekräftigung seiner Sendung ist. Dort – auf Naxos – sollten die Mänaden Orpheus zerreissen, und in den jubelnden Zug des Dionysos hätte das Klagen der Leyer tönen müssen, die zusammen mit dem singenden Haupt des Orpheus den Bergbach hinab, auf's Meer hinaus – nach Lesbos trieb, für Dionysos eine beklemmende Ahnung, dass auch Götter sterben. Damals wusste ich Einiges von diesen Dingen. Dass bei Theophrast die Zubereitung des Flötenrohres beschrieben war: wie das Rohr nur selten wuchs, in einem kleinen Bezirk, und nur bei den Überschwemmungen des Cephissus, die alle neun Jahre wiederkehrten, und wie auch die Zeit nicht gleichgiltig war zu der man es schnitt. Die Flöte des Marsyas aber, hatte ein ähnliches Schicksal wie die Leyer des Orpheus. Sie schwamm den Mäander hinab, über's Meer, zu den Sikyoniern. Aber alle diese Dinge waren Ihnen diesmal nur Anlaufslinie. Und dass Sie diese wählten, erscheint mir wie ein schönes dankbares Grüssen, hinüber zu jenen Gegenden, die Sie in diesem Frühjahr gesehen haben. Je weiter ich im "Marsyas" las, desto mehr war es mir, als wendeten Sie Sich im Reden, einem von uns zu: Dem Arthur, oft dem Hugo, und, manchmal vielleicht auch, – ich denke an das "espressivo"[45] – mir.

So Vieles – mehr als ich jetzt Ihnen darüber schreiben kann – wäre darüber zu sagen, und ich hoffe, es wird auch im Herbst, – peripathetisch, unter den Bäumen unseres Gartens in Rodaun – gesagt werden. Wegen des "espressivo" aber: "Léonard est un expressif" sagt Seailles[46] von ihm; ich habe das schöne Buch – das Sie ja auch kennen, mit.

Mit Ihnen – leider zu sehr mit Ihnen – bin ich bei Allem was Sie auf den letzten zwei Seiten (des Bürstenabzuges) sagen. Leider – weil ich nur zu sehr empfinde, wie leicht solche Dinge, gerade *mir*, Beruhigung geben, wenn ich an meine Trägheit denke. "Düngt Euch mit Aufregung, ja! Dann aber steht der Bauer und harrt bis die Erde will!"[47] Das klingt meinen Ohren nur zu lieblich! Aber Bauer und Erde sind hier eins, und wenn er zulange harren muss, taugt am Ende die Erde nicht viel. So ist es mir erlaubt, Ihnen, in einem versteckten Winkel meines Ichs zuzustimmen. Aber laut muss ich mich, vor mir selbst, dagegen wehren – aus hygienischen Gründen – sonst könnte ich mich ja mit Ihrem Spruch "beruhigt auf eine Faulbett legen."

Das Citat: "L'ordinare è opra signorile, l'oprare è atto servile,"[48] kannte ich nicht; es ist wunderschön! "Servile" lass ich, gelten, denn die Conception ist unser Herr. Aber "l'oprare" *muss* nicht "atto servile" bleiben – ich glaube es darf es gar nicht. Wer im "oprare" nicht getrieben wird von der Sehnsucht nach dem verlornen Paradiese der ersten Conception der taugt nicht viel. Und die Qual und Spannung, das Ringen – und "nicht lassen, denn Du mich segnest" vermag auch im "oprare", signorile Gefühle zu geben.

Da Sie nun einmal von diesen Dingen laut gesprochen haben, darf ich ja auch vielleicht – ganz leise – Ihnen – sagen, dass in diesen vielen Jahren – wo ich für Andere – manchmal auch für mich – der Faule war, ein wenig von dem Stolze gehalten wurde, dass mein Arbeiten nie blos "atto servile" gewesen ist. Immer habe ich versucht (was immer ich von mir aussage – es gilt von meinen Intentionen, nicht vom Gelingen) im Arbeiten, etwas von den verlorenen Schaudern der ersten Empfängnis wiederzufinden. Aber wenn man auch diese nie wiederfindet – sie sind einzig und unwiederbringlich – wie Alles – andere, nicht geringere Schauder werden und geschenkt, wenn – nach allen Qualen der Ohnmacht und der Selbstverachtung endlich widerspenstige Massen zu glühen und zu fliessen beginnen. Und auch diese Schauer sind "herrlich" – "signorile".

Wie es Leonardo beim "oprare" gegangen ist, erzählt Bandello[49] – ich finde die Stelle bei Séailles. Er arbeitet an dem Abendmal. Und manchen Tag erscheint er ganz früh am Morgen, läuft das Gerüst hinauf, isst nichts, und bleibt – bis er herunter muss weil es Nacht ist. Ein andermal rührt er 3 - 4 Tage nicht an sein Werk. Er kommt nur und bleibt ein bis zwei Stunden mit gekreuzten Armen vor seiner Arbeit stehen. Und einmal sieht man ihn – in den Hundstagen um Mittag, von der Citadelle (wo er an seinem Pferd arbeitet) durch die leeren Strassen der Stadt laufen – quer durch – den nächsten Weg, nicht den schattigsten. Er springt aufs Gerüst, setzt ein paar Pinselstriche hin – ein oder zwei – sagt der Bericht, und lauft wieder nach Hause. Hier haben Sie es: Die guten gesegneten Tage, wo erst die Nacht uns – wie seelig verspielte Kinder – wider unsern Willen zur Ruhe bringt; die bösen Tage, wo uns widert an unser Werk zu rühren – aber davorstehen müssen wir, und hinstarren, und mit erbarmungslosen Augen unsere Schwäche erkennen, und den Abgrund der zwischen *den* Wesen klafft, die wir einmal, wundervoll bewegt in Licht und Luft mit geschlossnen Augen sahen – und jenem Roth und Blau und Grün das wir auf den Malter hinstrichen. Und endlich jene dritten Tage! Wir waren mit Gleichgültigem beschäftigt, dachten nicht an das Werk – oder glaubten – besser gesagt – nicht daran zu denken (als könnten wir das). Aber plötzlich fühlten wir den Funken in uns fallen und geschüttelt vor Angst, er könnte erlöschen ehe er gezündet, stürmen wir hin.

Sie sehen, lieber Hermann, Sie haben von Sich in diesem "Marsyas" gesprochen, und ich habe von mir darin gelesen. Wie grosse Egoisten, vermögen wir Künstler nichts Anderes, als von uns zu reden. Aber was uns von Jenen scheidet, ist, dass ein Gott unsern Zungen den Zauber gegeben hat: Wieviel wir auch von *uns* reden, andere hören nur von *sich* darinnen.

So hab ich mir aus Ihrem "Marsyas" ein wenig Muth für mich herausgelesen. Ich kann ihn gut brauchen; denn für mich sind jetzt Tage wo ich mit verschränkten Armen und bösen Augen vor der bemalten Wand stehe.

Vielen Dank also für den "Marsyas". Schreiben Sie bald; Mirjam kennt Ihre Schrift schon, und ruft es mir zu meinem Fenster hinauf, wenn die Post kommt, und ein Brief von Ihnen darunter ist.[50]

Ich grüsse Sie von Herzen.

Richard

6. [Handwritten original] [Postmark 5.II.05]

Lieber Hermann! Ich fahre jetzt nach München wo sie nächste Woche den Charolais[51] geben. Maria-Theresia – Biedermeier nicht – aber vielleicht Kaiser Josef das auch steif ist. Beim Antiqu-Händler Fischer (I Führichgasse) glaub ich – *zweite* Gasse links unter Kärntnerstr. wenn man von der Oper kommt – war vor kurzem ein kleiner sehr hübscher Eck-Glasschrank Kaiser Josef zu haben. Wenn's nicht eilt so [illegible, probably "suche ich"] nach meiner Rückkehr etwas Passendes.[52]

Herzlichst

Richard

7. [Handwritten original]

Grand Hotel Des Bains
Lido-Venise
6/IX.05

Lieber Hermann!
Arthur hat mir Ende Juli die Übersendung des Stückes[53] angezeigt, so dass ich meinen musste, es läge in meiner Wohnung (als Buchpaquet verkleidet) und Auftrag gab alles danach zu durchsuchen. In Wahrheit aber wurde es erst am 23/Aug. (von Reichenau glaub' ich) an mich abgeschickt und ich habe es erst seit drei Tagen hier. Ich möchte es nun doch sehr gerne lesen – lassen Sie es mir also – (wenn es geht) noch ein paar Tage.[54]
Die Salzburger Grüsse hat Vanjung[55] überbracht. Mein Sommer war nicht sehr schön, und bessert sich erst hier, wo Meer und Venedig doch sehr nachhelfen. Ich möchte bis Ende des Monates hierbleiben. Ist es ausgeschlossen, dass sich – so beim Herumkramen – irgendwo ein paar vergessene Urlaubstage finden, die Sie für den Lido, und für Venedig – und für uns benützen? Paula und ich wären sehr froh. Wir Beide grüssen Sie von Herzen.

Ihr
Richard

8. [Handwritten original]

Wien 10./VIII. 07

Lieber Bahr! Vielen Dank für Ihre lieben Wünsche[56] – ich nehme sie, als gutes Omen, nach vielen bösen Tagen und Nächten; mein Vater[57] ist am eilften Juli gestorben.
Wir waren bis 3. Aug. in Maria-Schutz [am Semmering], weil wir schon früher dort Wohnung genommen hatten, seither sind wir wieder in Wien – müde, und froh zu Hause zu sein. Nach 18. Aug. will ich mit Paula und den Kindern nach Villach – für ein paar Tage an einen Kärntnersee, dann nach Südtirol, wahrscheinlich an den Gardasee. Sind Sie um diese Zeit noch im Süden? Wir beide grüssen Sie herzlich, danken der Mildenburg[58] für Ihre freundlichem Grüsse, die wir erwiedern, und würden uns freuen Sie bald, hier – oder noch schöner, irgendwo, da unten zu sehen.[59]

Ihr
Richard Beer-Hofmann

9. [Handwritten original] Weissenbach a. Attersee 8./VII. 14

Lieber Bahr, so oft ich an der alten Linzer Ansicht, die bei mir hieng, vorübergieng, sagte sie mir, dass sie eigentlich zu Ihnen gehöre. Um diesem unleidlichen Zustand eine Ende zu machen, habe ich sie Ihnen gesandt, und für Ihre Frau die "Gedenkrede auf Mozart"[60] (v. Jahre 1906) beigelegt. Von mir und meiner Frau, Ihnen Beiden herzlichen Grüsse! Ihr

Richard

10. [Handwritten original] Wien 12.VI.19

Lieber Hermann! Spät erst danke ich Ihnen für Ihre lieben Glückwünsche.[61] Da Sie Sich nun einmal auch noch um die Kritiken gekümmert haben (was ich Ihrem "Tagebuch"[62] entnehme) schicke ich Ihnen ein paar Besprechungen, die – weil sie in Mittag- oder Abendblättern standen – Ihnen wol kaum zu Gesicht gekommen sind. Ausserdem noch das Buch von Travers Herford[63] über die Pharisäer, das Sie in mancherlei Hinsicht interessiren dürfte.

"Die Rotte Korah"[64] habe ich gestern zu lesen begonnen, habe sie aber nach dem III. Kapitel bei Seite gelegt, da das Buch gerade *mich* zu Bejahendem und Verneinendem so stark anregt, dass ich möglichste Sammlung und Ruhe brauche um ihm gerecht zu werden.[65] So geht es nun mit aufs Land. Das heisst, wenn Ober-Oesterreich es gestattet. Wenn – so hoffe ich in den ersten Julitagen in Ischl (Grazerstrasse 52, Kupferschmiedvilla, Telephon unter *Villa* Kupferschmied), zu sein, und freue mich Sie dann in Salzburg aufsuchen zu können. Dass es Ihnen – Gott sei Dank – gut geht, freut mich von Herzen; die Nachricht, dass Sie schon wieder auf dem Gaisberg (oder gar Untersberg?) waren, ist auf Umwegen bis zu mir gedrungen.

Herzliche Grüsse von uns Allen, Ihnen und Ihrer lieben Frau, und auf baldiges Wiedersehen!

Ihr
Richard

11. [Handwritten original] Wien 4.II.20

Lieber Hermann!
Mit Salzburg ist es nichts. Die Herren haben zwar mir und Paula Bewilligung erteilt, für die Kinder hätte ich aber "von Fall zu Fall" einreichen sollen. Da ich ja wirklich bereit war, mich um die Festspiele[66] zu kümmern, fand ich die Art der Salzburger Herren doch zu wenig freundlich. Wir haben es uns also notdürftig mit 2 Eisenöfchen eingerichtet und hoffen bis zum Frühjahr so auszuhalten. Mirjam hatte Masern, Paula ist stark erkältet – auch sonst Sorgen und wenig Frohes. Gott bessere es! Herzliche Grüsse und gute Wünsche Ihnen und Ihrer lieben Frau! Ihr

Richard

12. [Telegram] 24.12.1920

wuensche[67] herzlich das beste richard beerhofmann

APPENDIX I: Richard Beer-Hofmann and Theodor Herzl

Beer-Hofmann and Herzl were acquaintances for many years. There exist two Beer-Hofmann letters to Herzl and three Herzl cards and three letters to Beer-Hofmann. These unpublished documents help clarify some aspects of their friendship. Herzl's letter about Beer-Hofmann's narrative works *Das Kind* and *Camelias* (R. B-H., *Novellen* [Berlin: Freund und Jäckel, 1893]) is significant:

[Handwritten original] Aussee 14/9.94

Lieber Doctor!
Nach Wien ist mir Ihr Buch nachgekommen. Ich danke Ihnen sehr für das Vergnügen und die Anregung die ich darin fand. Ich will mir nicht erlauben, Ihnen zu sagen, dass Sie Talent haben. Das wissen Sie noch besser als ich. Ebensowenig möchte ich Sie mit kritischen Bemerkungen behelligen.
Aber dass ich von jetzt ab alles lesen werde, was Sie schreiben, ist klar. Wenn Sie mir's nicht schenken, werde ich's mir kaufen. Sie haben seit dem 10 September einen lebenslänglichen Leser
an Ihrem ganz ergebenen
Th. Herzl
Es ist Unsinn, das in diesem Brief zu schreiben: ich weiss Ihre Adresse nicht genau. Hoffentlich kommt es doch an. Aber es erklärt, warum ich mich kürzer fasste, als es in einem der Ankunft sicheren Brief geschehen wäre.

Even more significant are the exchanges on March 13, 1896. At this time Herzl wrote to Beer-Hofmann:

[Handwritten original] Neue Freie Presse
Redaktion: Wien
Kolowratring, Fichtegasse Nr.11

Mein lieber Doctor!
Ist es wahr, dass Sie ein Anhänger der in meiner Broschüre [*Der Judenstaat, Versuch einer modernen Lösung der Judenfrage* (Leipzig,

Vienna: M. Breitensteins Verlagsbuchhandlung, 1896)] ausgesprochenen Ideen sind?
Es würde mich stolz machen, wenn ich Leute wie Sie begeistert hätte. Wollen Sie nicht ein bißchen plaudern kommen? Uebermorgen Sonntag treffen Sie mich vor elf Uhr V.M. sicher zu Hause.
Mit herzlichem Gruss

Ihr aufrichtig ergebener
Herzl

Beer-Hofmann responded the same day:

[Handwritten original] 13.III.96

Verehrter Herr Doctor!
Dafür, dass Sie so lieb waren mir Ihre Brochure zu senden, danke ich Ihnen herzlich. Ich habe nicht erst darauf gewartet, um sie zu lesen. Mehr noch als Alles, was *in* Ihrem Buche, war mir das sympathisch, was dahinter stand. Endlich wieder ein Mensch der sein Judentum, nicht wie eine Last oder ein Unglück resignirt trägt, sondern stolz ist, mit, der legitime Erbe uralter vornehmer Cultur zu sein
Ich freue mich Sie Sonntag zu sehen.
Ihr herzlichst ergebener
Beer-Hofmann

In his diaries Herzl includes only one notation about Beer-Hofmann, namely that of April 9, 1896, observing that Beer-Hofmann had suggested the development of a "great medical school" in Palestine for all Asians that would help improve sanitation in the Orient. The other written exchanges were brief. On February 18, 1901 Herzl penned on his calling card (located in the Beer-Hofmann *Nachlass* at Harvard University): "[Dr. Theodor Herzl] dankt herzlich für die Uebersendung von Georgs Tod, der schleunigst gelesen werden soll." And on June 19, 1902 Beer-Hofmann wrote to Herzl from Rodaun:

[Handwritten original]

Sehr verehrter Herr Doktor!
Ich weiss, wie innig Ihr Verhältniss zu Ihrem Vater war, und habe in diesen Tagen mit aufrichtiger Teilnahme daran gedacht, wie viel Schweres Sie jetzt zu tragen haben.
Ich grüsse Sie herzlich.
Richard Beer-Hofmann

Herzl answered:

[Handwritten original]

Sehr geehrter Herr Dr,
herzlichen Dank für Ihre theilnehmenden Worte
Ihr ergebener
Herzl
Alt Aussee 22.VI.902

There are two additional undated notes. In one Herzl suggests they meet so they may continue to converse. In the other (located in the Beer-Hofmann *Nachlass* at Harvard University) Herzl writes: "[Dr. Theodor Herzl] nimmt herzlich Theil an Ihrem Schmerz, den er kennt."

Notes

1 Quoted in: Herbert Steiner (Ed.), *Richard Beer-Hofmann. Besprechungen seiner Werke* (Zürich: Buchdruckerei Berichthaus, 1939), 22.

2 Oskar Walzel is succinct: "Hermann Bahr nahm sich erfolgreich dieser neuen Wiener Richtung an, sorgte dafür, dass sie der weiten Welt bekannt werde, verfocht sie als Kritiker und dichtete in ihrem Sinn. Noch hatte Österreich niemals einen Organisator der Literatur besessen, der wie Bahr die Mauern einriss....

Er zeigte, wie anders die Wiener sind als die Deutschen des Nordens. Und er forderte mit Erfolg, dass der Deutsche des Nordens dieses künstlerische Wienertum begreife." Quoted in: Peter de Mendelssohn, *S. Fischer und sein Verlag* (Frankfurt am Main: S. Fischer Verlag, 1970), 191-192.

[3] To Olga Schnitzler (1882-1970), Beer-Hofmann once stated: " 'Man fragt mich hier immer wieder um das Wesen der Wiener Schule. ... Ich weiss nichts von einer Wiener Schule, ich weiss nur von einigen Menschen, die ich gern hatte, die mich interessiert haben, und so hat mich auch das interessiert, was sie produziert haben. Von einer 'Schule' war nicht die Rede'." In: Olga Schnitzler, *Spiegelbild der Freundschaft* (Salzburg: Residenz Verlag, 1962), 131-132.

[4] Bahr was born in Linz (Oberösterreich). In his important early work *Die demolirte Literatur* (Wien: Verlag von A. Bauer, 1897) the Austrian satirist, essayist, and dramatist Karl Kraus referred to Bahr as "der Herr aus Linz," which became one of many terms used to characterize Bahr.

[5] Years earlier, in October of 1888 Bahr had met Ibsen in Munich. Bahr's inscription in the copy of his *Die grosse Sünde: Ein bürgerliches Trauerspiel* (Zürich: Verlagsmagazin J. Schabelitz, 1889) that he sent to Ibsen read: "Dem Grossmeister des modernen Dramas Henrik Ibsen in ehrfürchtiger Liebe. Paris im Frühling 1889" (in: *Henrik Ibsen. Brev 1845-1905. II. Kommentarene*, ed. Øyvind Anker [Oslo: Universitetsforlaget, 1981], 104). This inscription summarizes well the attitude of the "Jung-Wien" writers toward Ibsen. See, for example, Jeffrey B. Berlin, "Die Beziehungen zwischen Ibsen und Schnitzler," *Text & Kontext* 10.2. *Zeitschrift für germanistische Literaturforschung in Skandinavien*. (München: Wilhelm Fink Verlag, 1982), 383-398. For more on "Jung-Wien", see, for example, Sol Liptzin, "Young Vienna," *Poet Lore*, 47, iv (1941), 337-346; or, Gotthard Wunberg (Hrsg.), *Das Junge Wien. Österreichische Literatur- und Kunstkritik*. 2 vols. (Tübingen: Max Niemayer Verlag, 1976); and, Bernhard Zeller (Hrsg.), *Jugend in Wien. Literatur um 1900* (München: Kösel Verlag GmbH, 1974).

[6] Hermann Bahr, *Selbstbildnis* (Berlin: S. Fischer Verlag, 1923), 277.

[7] In: Werner Vordtriede, "Gespräche mit Beer-Hofmann," *Die neue Rundschau*, 63, No. 1 (1952), 131. Beer-Hofmann added: "Aber in jenem Kreise war man überzeugt, ich würde schreiben, und zwar etwas Gutes." In *Daten* Beer-Hofmann records: "Im Frühsommer [1891] habe ich zu schreiben begonnen."

[8] Eugene Weber, "The Correspondence of Arthur Schnitzler and Richard Beer-Hofmann," *Modern Austrian Literature*, 6, No. 3/4 (1973), 40-51; Eugene Weber (Hrsg.), *Hugo von Hofmannsthal/Richard Beer-Hofmann. Briefwechsel* (Frankfurt am Main: S. Fischer Verlag, 1972); Donald G. Daviau (Ed.), *The Letters of Arthur Schnitzler to Hermann Bahr* (Chapel Hill: University of North Carolina Press, 1978); Gotthart Wunberg, "Hofmannsthal and Hermann Bahr," in his *Der frühe Hofmannsthal. Schizophrenie als dichterische Struktur* (Stuttgart: W. Kohlhammer Verlag, 1965), 125-132; and, Wolf Wucherpfennig, "Das Junge Wien und seine Väter. Bahr und der junge Hofmannsthal im gesellschaftlichen Zusammenhang," *Hofmannsthal Forschungen*, Bd. 7 (Hrsg. Wolfgang Mauser), (Freiburg i. Br.: Hugo von Hofmannsthal Gesellschaft, 1983), 145-180.

[9] Beer-Hofmann did not keep a diary, but in 1911 began compiling *Daten* (which was made available to me by Mrs. Miriam Beer-Hofmann Lens). In it we find: "[I met] ... im Herbst [1890], in Wien, Arthur Schnitzler [Beer-Hofmann met Schnitzler on October 8, 1890, as Schnitzler's own diary records], Hugo Hofmannsthal ... später Hermann Bahr."

[10] The Yale University Collection of German Literature has the following original Bahr to Beer-Hofmann documents: 34 letters; 30 postcards; 5 telegrams; 2 calling cards (with notes); 1 unsigned postcard; 1 card from Rosa Bahr; 1 card from Anna Bahr-Mildenburg. The Beer-Hofmann *Nachlass* collection at Harvard University has the following original Bahr to Beer-Hofmann documents: 1 postcard; 1 greeting card; 1 letter and 1 card from Anna Bahr-Mildenburg; 1 unsigned card.

[11] *Daten* provides no details about Bahr. After noting that he was in Salzburg from September 26 to October 18, 1916 (Beer-Hofmann began *Der junge David* on September 19, 1916) Beer-Hofmann's only remark about Bahr is: "Mit Hermann Bahr täglich, von 8 bis 10 Uhr morgens (Caffee Tommaselli und Spaziergang) beisammen." Not all of the Bahr diaries are published (cf. note 50). Within his writings, very brief remarks or references to Beer-Hofmann may occasionally be found; these remarks add nothing of major importance for this study. Cf., for example, Joseph Gregor (Hrsg.), *Meister und Meisterbriefe um Hermann Bahr. Aus seinen Entwürfen, Tagebüchern und seinem Briefwechsel* (Wien: H. Bauer Verlag, 1947), 184. For additional aspects about Beer-Hofmann see the richly informative study by Esther N. Elstun, *Richard Beer-Hofmann. His Life and Work* (University Park and London: The Pennsylvania State University Press, 1983). See also: *The Correspondence of Stefan Zweig with Raoul Auernheimer*, edited with an introduction and notes by Donald G. Daviau and Jorun B. Johns, *and with Richard Beer-Hofmann* [*and with Sol Liptzin*], edited with commentary and notes by Jeffrey B. Berlin (Columbia, South Carolina: Camden House, 1983).

[12] This card is undated, but bears the postmark July 2, 1894.

[13] See Richard Beer-Hofmann, *Paula, Ein Fragment*, in his *Gesammelte Werke* (Frankfurt am Main: S. Fischer Verlag, 1963), pp. 677, 79, and 770.

[14] In *Paula* (p. 770) Beer-Hofmann's translation of "Incipit vita nova" is "Hier hebet an das neue Leben!"

[15] Hermann Bahr, "Décadence," *Die Zeit* (Wien), Bd. 1, Nr. 6 (10 Nov. 1894), 87-89. Now in: Hermann Bahr, *Zur Überwindung des Naturalismus. Theoretische Schriften 1887-1904* (Hrsg., Gotthart Wunberg), (Stuttgart: W. Kohlhammer Verlag, 1968), 167-172.

[16] On this date Ibsen was in Christiania (Oslo), Norway. Around this time Bahr reviewed Ibsen's *The Wild Duck*. See Caph [=Bahr], "Excellenz Hjalmar," *Die Zeit*, Nr. 4 (1894), 56.

[17] This "Preisfrage," as Bahr termed it in this letter to Beer-Hofmann, was also raised with Redlich. To Redlich, on January 29, 1904, Bahr had written: "Hauptsächlich lese ich Mauthners Sprachkritik.... Da habe ich mich in das The-

ma 'Ist Denken und Sprechen identisch? Oder gibt es ein Denken ohne Sprache'? verbissen." In: Fritz Fellner (Hrsg.), *Dichter und Gelehrter. Hermann Bahr und Josef Redlich in ihren Briefen 1896-1934* (Salzburg: Verlag Wolfgang Neugebauer, 1980), 24.

18 For further information see, Donald G. Daviau, *Der Mann von Übermorgen. Hermann Bahr 1863-1934* (Wien: Österreichischer Bundesverlag, 1984).

19 Erich Kahler, "Richard Beer-Hofmann," *Die neue Rundschau*, 2 (1946), 237.

20 Hermann Bahr, "Der Tod Georgs," *Neues Wiener Tagblatt*, Nr. 81 (24 März 1900), pp. 1-3. This review is now available in *Das Junge Wien*, Bd. II, pp. 1036-1040.

21 Before his return on March 12, 1900 to Vienna Beer-Hofmann had been traveling in Italy.

22 Hermann Bahr, "Dialog vom Tragischen," *Neue Rundschau*, 14 (1903), 716-736. In this essay Bahr expounds on his point of view that the "Ich" is not distinguishable from the "continuity of life," which is in itself important. The "unrettbare Ich" is dependent upon the reception of the elements of life. As Bahr says, "da werden wir erkennen, dass das Element unseres Lebens nicht die Wahrheit ist, sondern die Illusion." Hermann Bahr, "Das unrettbare Ich," in his *Zur Überwindung des Naturalismus*, 192.

23 Hugo von Hofmannsthal. Cf. Hofmannsthal's remarks to Bahr about the "Dialog vom Tragischen." In: Hugo von Hofmannsthal, *Briefe 1900-1909* (Wien: Bermann-Fischer Verlag, 1937), 128-129.

24 Hermann Bahr, "Der böse Goethe," *Neues Wiener Tagblatt*, Nr. 199 (22 Juli 1903), 1-2. In this essay Bahr quotes some of Goethe's contemporaries and observes that Goethe was often depicted not as a Olympian, shining figure, but as a torn, moody, depressed, bitter, disinterested individual with whom it was difficult, if not painful, to associate. Beer-Hofmann's interest in Goethe never subsided.

25 Theodor Herzl. Cf. Hermann Bahr, "Herzls Tat," in: *Zeitgenossen über Herzl* (Hrsg., Dr. T. Nussenblatt), (Brünn: Jüdischer Buch- und Kunstverlag, 1929), 20-21.
Bahr's depressed mood at the time is characterized well in Hofmannsthal's letter of August 8, 1904 to Schnitzler. However, Schnitzler's answer of August 9, 1904 to Hofmannsthal relates that Bahr was now recovered, but added that Bahr had been depressed because of Herzl's death: "Seelische Depressionen wirken auf seinen phys. Zustand am heftigsten: so war er nach dem Tod Herzls kränker als seit lang...." In: *Hugo von Hofmannsthal/Arthur Schnitzler Briefwechsel* (Hrsg., Therese Nickl and Heinrich Schnitzler), (Frankfurt am Main: S. Fischer Verlag, 1964), 194.

26 See Appendix I, which follows the Beer-Hofmann letters to Bahr, for more on the Beer-Hofmann/Herzl relationship.

27 The "Hagenbund," originally the younger, more revolutionary members of the *Künstlerhausgenossenschaft*, who met at the café *Zum Blauen Freihaus*

in the Gumpendorferstrasse, later withdrew from the *Künstlerhausgenossenschaft* on November 29, 1900. The included Rudolf Bacher, Adolf Böhm, Josef Engelhart, Johann Viktor Krämer, Friedrich König, Ernst Nowak, Alfred Roller, and Ernst Stöhr. They were referred to as the "Hagenbund" (or "Hagengesellschaft"), so named after the proprietor of the café.

28 Theodor Herzl, *Feuilletons* (Wien: Wiener Verlag, 1904), 2 vols. In March, 1904, as the handwritten inscription date on the volume shows, Herzl gave Beer-Hofmann a copy, signing it: "Meinem Freunde dem Juden Richard Beer-Hofmann. Theodor Herzl."

29 Hugo von Hofmannsthal.

30 The Viennese *Neue Freie Presse* carried an extensive front-page obituary. Herzl had been the Paris correspondent (1891-1895) of the *Neue Freie Presse* and then its feuilleton editor from 1895 to his death in 1904.

31 Arthur Schnitzler, whose diary notation of July 4, 1904 records: "Nm. Kunde von Theodor Herzls Tod, der mich sehr erschütterte." Quoted in: Arthur Schnitzler, *Briefe. 1875-1912* (Hrsg., Therese Nickl and Heinrich Schnitzler), (Frankfurt am Main: S. Fischer Verlag, 1981), 899.

32 In *Die Welt von gestern* Stefan Zweig vividly recalled the events: "... nur zum Friedhof mehr konnte ich ihn begleiten. Ein sonderbarer Tag war es, ein Tag im Juli, unvergesslich jedem, der ihn miterlebte. Denn plötzlich kamen auf allen Bahnhöfen der Stadt, mit jedem Zug, bei Tag und Nacht, aus allen Reichen und Ländern, Menschen gefahren, westliche, östliche, russische, türkische Juden, aus allen Provinzen und kleinen Städten stürmten sie plötzlich herbei, den Schreck der Nachricht noch im Gesicht; niemals spürte man deutlicher, was früher das Gestreite und Gerede unsichtbar gemacht, dass es der Führer einer grossen Bewegung war, der hier zu Grabe getragen wurde. Es war ein endloser Zug. Mit einemmal merkte Wien, dass hier nicht nur ein Schriftsteller oder mittlerer Dichter gestorben war, sondern einer jener Gestalter von Ideen, wie sie in einem Land, in einem Volk nur in ungeheueren Intervallen sich sieghaft erheben. Am Friedhof entstand ein Tumult; zu viele strömten plötzlich zu seinem Sarge, weinend, heulend, schreiend in einer wild explodierenden Verzweiflung, es wurde ein Toben, ein Wüten fast; alle Ordnung war zerbrochen durch eine Art elementarer und ekstatischer Trauer, wie ich sie niemals vordem und nachher bei einem Begräbnis gesehen." Stefan Zweig, *Die Welt von gestern. Erinnerungen eines Europäers* (Frankfurt am Main: Fischer Bücherei, 1970), 87-88.

33 Max Eugen Burckhard (1854-1912). Lawyer, writer, and critic. Director of the Viennese *Burgtheater* from 1890 to 1898.

34 Paula Beer-Hofmann and their daughter Mirjam Beer-Hofmann.
On July 17, 1904 Bahr responded to Beer-Hofmann, noting that he had, happily, seen Herzl seven days before he died. Bahr recollected how he felt about his parents' death (his father died in 1898, his mother in 1902) and added that one realizes how one truly felt about someone only after that person's death.

35 Bahr began his Salzburg letter of July 24, 1904 to Beer-Hofmann by noting his annoyance that Beer-Hofmann had sent Hofmannsthal but not him a

photograph of both Paula and the children. However, he continued by expressing pleasure at having heard from Schnitzler about Beer-Hofmann's work, presumably *Der Graf von Charolais*, which Bahr later reviewed. See Bahr, "Der Graf von Charolais," *Neues Wiener Tagblatt* (16 Mai 1905).

36 Mirabell, castle in Salzburg; Hellbrunn, castle located in a large park in Salzburg; Pferdeschwemme, baroque fountain, originally a spot for washing horses; Hohensalzburg, the fabulous castle on the "Mönchsberg" in Salzburg.

37 heu = abbreviation for the Archimedean "heureka." In his *Daten* Beer-Hofmann records: "Ende Mai [1904] nach Budapest (Hôtel Bristol), wo Reinhardt gastiert. Schliesse mit ihm Vertrag ab über 'Charolais' an dem einiges im IV. und V. Akt noch nicht fertig ist. Anfang September beendet."
Writing from Salzburg at the Grand Hotel de L'Europe on July 30, 1904, Bahr responded to Beer-Hofmann that he would be very pleased to listen to Beer-Hofmann's work, but only if he (Bahr) would not disturb Beer-Hofmann.

38 Bad Ischl. Austrian spa.

39 Refers to Beer-Hofmann's son, Gabriel Beer-Hofmann (1901-1971), and other daughter, Naëmah Beer-Hofmann (1898-1971).

40 After reading the galley proofs of Bahr's *Dialog vom Marsyas*, Beer-Hofmann wrote this letter to him. A draft of the letter, dated summer, 1904, which – content-wise – is similar to that offered here, was published by Miriam Beer-Hofmann Lens (in: Richard Beer-Hofmann, "Über Hermann Bahrs 'Dialog vom Marsyas'," mitgeteilt von M. B-H L., *Für Rudolf Hirsch. Zum siebzigsten Geburtstag am 22. Dezember 1975*, Redaktion: J. Hellmut Freund [Frankfurt am Main: S. Fischer Verlag, 1975], 335-337). The letter presented here may now be exactly dated and represents that which Beer-Hofmann actually mailed to Bahr. Bahr also sent galley proofs to Schnitzler, as Schnitzler's diary notation of August 7, 1904 demonstrates: " 'Den Marsyas (Correctur, von Bahr geschickt) zu Ende gelesen, und anschliessend daran Notizen geschrieben, eine graphische Erklärung den Unterschied zwischen Künstler und Literaten betreffend, gefunden, die mich sehr beruhigte'." Quoted in: *The Letters of Arthur Schnitzler to Hermann Bahr*, 143-144. Even after the appearance of the *Dialog vom Marsyas* Bahr apparently was still concerned about it, evidenced by Bahr's September 27, 1904 letter to Redlich (in: *Hermann Bahr und Josef Redlich in ihren Briefen*, 34).

41 Most likely Beer-Hofmann is referring to Bahr's letter of August 5 (1904, year added by Beer-Hofmann). In this letter Bahr, who describes himself as being in an almost unbearable condition, says that he would have liked to have read an (unnamed) work that Beer-Hofmann supposedly decided not to write. Bahr sympathized with Beer-Hofmann's decision. Bahr also complained that his heart and aorta were giving him trouble.

42 Hermann Bahr, *Unter sich: Ein Arme-Leut' Stück* (Wien: Wiener Verlag, 1904). Bahr's "Dialog vom Tragischen" (see letter 2, note 22). Bahr referred here to the book version: see Hermann Bahr, *Dialog vom Tragischen: Essays* (Berlin: S. Fischer Verlag, 1904).

43 The book version appeared the next year. See Hermann Bahr, *Dialog vom Marsyas: Ein Gespräch über Kunst* (Berlin: Bard, Marquardt & Co., 1905).

44 Cf. Richard Beer-Hofmann, "Aufzeichnungen zu 'Ariadne auf Kreta' und 'Ariadne auf Naxos'," mitgeteilt von Eugene Weber, *Hofmannsthal Blätter*, 13/14 (1975), 3-14.

45 Beer-Hofmann's daughter states: "Das 'expressivo', auf das sich Beer-Hofmann bezieht, hatte Bahr definiert als 'die Aufregung des Darstellers, [die] den Wert der Darstellung übertreffen soll'." In: Miriam B-H Lens, "Über Hermann Bahrs 'Dialog von Marsyas,' " 335.

46 The author of a number of books, Gabriel Séailles (1852-1922) published two works about Leonardo de Vinci: *Léonard da Vinci. L'artiste & le savant. Essai de biographie psychologique* (Paris: Perrin et Cie, 1892) and *Léonard da Vinci, biographie critique* (Paris: H. Laurens, 1903).

47 See: *Dialog vom Marsyas* (p. 65) where this is discussed.

48 Bahr provides the following clarification in his *Dialog vom Marsyas:* " 'Willst du den Wert einer Zeit', sagte der Meister, 'an der Zahl ihrer Werke messen? Ist dir, wer verschwendet, mehr als wer sich bewahrt? Was bleibt, was das nächste Geschlecht brauchen, wovon es leben kann, nur dieses wird gelten. Grosse Zeiten sparen für die Erben. Die fortwirkende Kraft, die sie hinterlassen, ist es allein, wodurch uns Zeiten und Männer gross sind. Denkt an den grössten, denkt an Leonardo! Wie wenig hat er ausgeführt! Habt ihr nie nachgedacht, warum? Wir haben einen Brief des Fra Petrus Nuvolaria an Isabellen von Este, worin er bitter über Leonardo klagt, vom dem, was immer er versprechen und wie hoch er es beteuern möge, nichts fertig zu bekommen sei; 'es scheint', sagt der Karmeliter, 'er lebt nur in den Tag hinein, zum Malen hat er keine Geduld, er zieht die Geometrie vor'. Glaubt ihr, wirklich? Und der grösste Mensch, den wir noch kaum erraten und eine höhere Menschheit erst erkennen wird, wäre faul gewesen? Aber in der Tat: er hat das meiste nicht ausgeführt. Warum? Darüber sagt er selbst einmal das geheimnisvolle Wort: l'ordinare è opra signorile, l'oprare è atto servile [= Arranging things is the work of a master, executing them that of a servant]. Dies heisst: wenn er künstlerisch empfing, hat er sich als Herrn gefühlt, im Ausführen knechtisch'." In: Hermann Bahr, *Dialog vom Marsyas* (Leipzig: Insel Verlag, n.d.), 67-68.

49 Matteo Bandello (1485-1562), Italian writer, is best known for his novella, "Romeo and Juliet."

50 Bahr responded in a letter of August 16, 1904 to Beer-Hofmann. He conveyed that he was very much pleased with Beer-Hofmann's letter which, as Bahr says, had touched upon points of considerable interest to him. Bahr describes as one of his greatest artistic problems his inability to give adequate expression to his inspirations and visions. Bahr added that he hoped to discuss these topics with Beer-Hofmann in a personal conversation in the very near future. Bahr's letter of August 16, 1904, we may note, was copied by him into his still unpublished diary of 1904, as Anna Bahr-Mildenburg's unpublished letter of March 17, 1936 to Beer-Hofmann (in the Beer-Hofmann *Nachlass* at Harvard University) relates.

51 *Der Graf von Charolais* was being performed at the *Hoftheater* in Munich under the production of Ernst Ritter von Possart (1841-1921). Its première took place in Berlin at the *Neuen Theater* on December 23, 1904 and was produced by Max Reinhardt. Of *Der Graf von Charolais* Bahr wrote to Beer-Hofmann on February 28, 1905: "Ich war neulich anderthalb Tage in Berlin, hab den Charolais gesehen und muss Ihnen doch sagen, dass er von der Bühne sehr stark und stellenweise ...geradezu gross auf mich gewirkt hat."

52 Probably Bahr and Beer-Hofmann discussed this subject because the following comment is included in Bahr's letter of February 28, 1905 to Beer-Hofmann: "Ich habe Antiquitätenschmerzen, soll zwei Zimmer alt möblieren, hab manches im Kopf, aber nur Sie können mir helfen." On the reverse side of Beer-Hofmann's letter to Bahr, incidentally, Bahr made some notes about antiquarians.

53 Hermann Bahr, *Die Andere:* Schauspiel in 5 Akten (Berlin: S. Fischer Verlag, 1905). Regarding *Die Andere*, on July 30, 1905 Schnitzler had very critically written to Bahr. See: *The Letters of Arthur Schnitzler to Hermann Bahr*, 89.

54 On September 11, 1905 Bahr had written Beer-Hofmann that *Die Andere* was now published and that a copy was being sent to him. Bahr added that he was eager to know, as he says, "ob Ihnen das von mir sehr empfundene Ding etwas sein kann."

55 In his letter of August 21, 1905 Bahr expressed the hope that Leo Van-Jung (1866-1939), a musician, mathematician, and mutual friend, had conveyed his (Bahr's) Salzburg greetings. Beer-Hofmann had met Van-Jung in Pörtschach (probably at the Café Werzer) in 1890 and he, together with Arthur Schnitzler, had later served as a witness at Beer-Hofmann's wedding.

56 On August 2, 1907 Bahr, in Venice at the Lido Villa Trieste, wrote Beer-Hofmann how exceptionally lovely ("das Allerschönste") his vacation spot was and noted that Beer-Hofmann could compare it to act three of Bahr's comedy *Ringelspiel* (Berlin: S. Fischer Verlag, 1907). In the third act of Bahr's work we find a most pleasantly described beach scene. Excluding some intrigue, we witness children at play on the beach. There is good food and drink. The idea is conveyed that we should enjoy life because the meaning of life is that it has no meaning (cf. the conversation in *Ringelspiel* between Harald and the King, p. 119).

57 Beer-Hofmann's adopted father, Alois Hofmann (1830-1907), a "Fabrikant." Beer-Hofmann was the son of Hermann Beer (1835-1902), an affluent attorney, and Rosa Beer (née Steckerl [1843-1866]), who had died five days after her son's birth. Richard was then reared by his aunt and uncle, Bertha (1840-1891) and Alois Hofmann, who legally adopted him on April 9, 1884.

58 Anna Bahr-Mildenburg (1872-1947), Bahr's second wife, whom he married in Aigen/Salzburg on August 22, 1909, was a well-known Wagnerian opera singer (and the first "Frau Welt" in Hofmannsthal's *Das Salzburger grosse Welttheater* [1922]). In May of 1909 he had separated from Rosa Jokl, an actress at the Viennese *Deutsches Volkstheater*, whom he had married in 1895.

59 Bahr responded on August 14, 1907 to Beer-Hofmann's comments, expressing sorrow about Beer-Hofmann's "bad summer" ("bösen Sommer") and wishing him all the best ("das Schönste und Beste") for his vacation trip.

60 Richard Beer-Hofmann, *Gedenkrede auf Wolfgang Amadé Mozart* (Berlin: S. Fischer Verlag, 1906).

61 Bahr had sent Beer-Hofmann a telegram dated [Sunday] April 6, 1919, offering congratulations for the première of *Jaákobs Traum* that was performed at the *Burgtheater* the day before. A few days earlier, on March 31, 1919 Bahr had apologized to Beer-Hofmann because he would miss the première, but, as Bahr says, a "zunehmende Drehkrankheit," made it necessary to avoid "alles Menschengewürrl." In November/December, 1918 Beer-Hofmann sent Bahr a copy of *Jaákobs Traum*, and Bahr's letter of December 16, 1918 to Beer-Hofmann conveys his thanks for the book, as he says, "auf das ich mich heute noch stürzen will."

62 Hermann Bahr, *1918: Tagebuch* (Innsbruck, Wien, München: Verlagsanstalt Tyrolia, 1919). Redlich's comments of June 17, 1919 to Bahr are descriptive: "Nur zwei Worte herzinnigsten Dankes für das schöne Tagebuch '1918', das ich gestern empfing: diese Chronik des furchtbarsten Jahres der Ernte für Deutschland und Österreich! Welche Erinnerungen! Und *wie* sich dieses Jahr in Ihrem Geiste spiegelt!" In: *Hermann Bahr und Josef Redlich in ihren Briefen*, 370.

63 R[obert] Travers Herford, *Pharisaism, its Aim and its Method* (London: Williams & Norgate; New York: G.P. Putnam's Sons, 1912).

64 Bahr's March 31, 1919 letter to Beer-Hofmann notes that he was sending Beer-Hofmann a work that would appeal to him. Probably it was Bahr's novel *Die Rotte Korahs* (Berlin: S. Fischer Verlag, 1919), a work that both Redlich and Hofmannsthal in particular had discussed with him. Cf. *Hermann Bahr and Josef Redlich in ihren Briefen*, letter of October 29, 1917 (p. 275) and *Hugo von Hofmannsthal/Josef Redlich Briefwechsel* (Hrsg., Helga Fussgänger), (Frankfurt am Main: S. Fischer, 1971), letter of May 7, 1919 (p. 43).

65 Beer-Hofmann must have been especially interested in this work. Indeed, during the summer of 1894, while traveling in Italy, Beer-Hofmann had seen Sandro Botticelli's "Bestrafung der Rotte Korah." In fact, on October 9, 1894 in Rome, he even made notations about it. See: "Richard Beer-Hofmann in Italien. Unveröffentlichte Aufzeichnungen aus dem Jahre 1894," mitgeteilt von Eugene Weber, *Neue Zürcher Zeitung* (9./10. August 1975), Nr. 182, 39.

66 On the occassion of the first "Salzburger Festspiele" Hofmannsthal's *Jedermann*, directed by Max Reinhardt, was performed on August 22, 1920.

67 This was probably a Christmas or New Year's Greeting.

Adalbert Wogelein's Justice, Allegorical Justice, and Justice in Schnitzler's *Die Frau des Richters*[1]

Richard H. Lawson

Although the fact is too often overlooked, as if it were perhaps an embarrassment to the typical claim that Arthur Schnitzler had no or but little interest in political remedies for injustice, the fact is that Schnitzler wrote some trenchant political-social allegory. This is not surprising to readers familiar with his *Der Geist im Wort und der Geist in der Tat* and *Und einmal wird der Friede wiederkommen*. For example, "Legende" (1900) may be taken as a direct allegory of the plight of the Habsburg empire, or rather of its citizenry, of the impossibility of enlightened change in an ossified system. By this reckoning an absolutistic if benevolently ruled fictional principality, pervaded by religion, apparently in India, is the model of absolutistic and benevolent Catholic Habsburgia at the turn of the century.

Somewhat similarly in *Die dreifache Warnung* (1909), an absolutistic force – in this case, to be sure, more spiritual than political – defeats the efforts of an intrepid questioner and tester of the regime's fiat. In chapters three and four of *Die Hirtenflöte* (1909) the allegory is again, as in "Legende," more direct, more concrete, more susceptible to a denominator of political and social justice. In fact the political dimension is very much in the foreground, complicated by industrialization, exploitation, and strikes. Indeed, industrialization, coming comparatively late to the Habsburg realm and then largely confined to the German and Czech lands, experienced a boom in the 1890s, accompanied by widespread social unrest. The purport of the allegory in the relevant portion of *Die Hirtenflöte* is that, while genuine innovation might contain the potential for salvation, the regime, however doomed, is incapable of being other than resistant to change.

Die Frau des Richters (1924) may be similarly read as, among other things, a socio-political allegory of justice in Habsburg Austria in the years preceding 1918. Schnitzler, following his well-known habit of composition, had worked on the material of this long novella well before the year of publication, quite possibly around the time he was working on "Legende," *Die dreifache Warnung*, and *Die Hirtenflöte.*[2]

For whatever reason, perhaps because it doesn't fit the stereotype of an apolitical Schnitzler, perhaps because of its interwoven complexity – the "among other things" suggested in the paragraph above – *Die Frau des Richters* has been scanted by critics. With the exception of the interpretations by Dickerson and by Blackall and occasional perfunctory notice elsewhere, it has received virtually no attention in the critical literature.[3]

It appears, however, that the justice meted by the titular judge, Adalbert Wogelein, may be understood on three levels, none of them, even including the political, unfamiliar in Schnitzler's *oeuvres.* At one level it is a finely nuanced psychological novella; for Wogelein's dispensing of justice proves perilously susceptible to his own personal insecurity and psychological crisis. Second, as I have suggested, the novella seems to offer an allegory on the justice to be encountered in Habsburgia at, let us say, the turn of the century. And finally, extending from, perhaps containing the allegory, is a substantial thematic concern with the inherent relativism of justice. Such a thematic preoccupation need not surprise us any more than political allegory does – we have only to recall the *Aphorismen und Betrachtungen.* In short, then, *Die Frau des Richters* is an eminently and quintessentially Schnitzlerian work, despite the fact that critics, if they mention the novella at all, incline to view it as somehow different from Schnitzler's other writings.

Schnitzler was careful about putting significant titles on his works, and too soon I may be seen as joining those critics who quietly ignore the author's title in order to dwell on the villain of the story – a fascinating villain, "ein originaler Kopf," Tobias Klenk – or on existential futility as theme. But the novella is exceedingly rich in detail of Agnes, the wife of the judge.[4] Her defection from Adalbert is the catalyst that forces *us* – but probably not her once and occasional husband – to see that justice has to be imperfect. (Adalbert is scarcely more introspective juridically than personally.) One precaution here: Agnes is manifestly blind to social injustice; we should therefore not permit her to completely siphon our credence from Adalbert – and even granted that Adalbert emerges as a liar. Not only is *Die Frau des Richters* complex – if familiar – as to possible levels of interpretation; narrative reliability is often uncertain.

Further, the narrative point of view as focused on Adalbert is pentagonal. Agnes's narrative vision, despite her inability to discern social injustice, is probably the most telling, the richest in psychological insights, some stated, others situationally suggested. The four further narrative visions of Judge Adalbert Wogelein include those of the narrator, of Adalbert himself, of his returned boyhood friend, the infamous Tobias Klenk, and finally that of the young Karl Eberhard XVII, Duke of Sigmaringen, recently succeeded to power and giving every early indication of being an enlightened sovereign. If critics have faulted *Spiel im Morgengrauen* for the single break in its narrative point of view, we can imagine the distress that would be occasioned by *Die Frau des Richters* if this novella were accorded equally wide critical attention.

The story is discontinuous, consisting of five narratively unbridged chapters of widely varying lengths. The first three chapters run to seven or eight pages each; the fourth is approximately as long as the first three taken together, and the concluding chapter is a scant two pages, a devastatingly ironic epilogue, similar to the conclusion of *Spiel im Morgengrauen*. Five chapters, five narrative points of view – but if we are searching for structural symmetry rather than complexity, we should be advised that the five chapters are by no means individually concurrent with the five narrative visions of Adalbert's travails.

Judge Wogelein's justice, on the basis of samples that we witness, is characterized – as the justice of a Civil Code judge should be – by a firm reliance on the letter of the law. He does not venture to interpret law; rather he applies the law as a given to the particular cases that come before him. If none of his litigants or defendants is disposed to compare him to Solomon, he is not, on the other hand, supposed to be a Solomon. One feels that his justice, as well as his very execution of the judge's office, is a rigid – but professionally sanctioned – refuge for a complex, precariously balanced, petty, self-satisfied middle-class personality.

Certainly Adalbert's grip on things, above all on himself, is easily, even spectacularly loosened by the return of Tobias Klenk. Tobias's dominant role in the unlikely adult friendship – between an unsavory picaro with violent-revolutionary tendencies and the judicial pillar of ducal and bourgeois society – is authenticated by the revelation that Tobias was the dominant member of the childhood friendship as well.

The infelicitous effect of the vagabond on the judge is evidenced first in the tavern. With Tobias at his side and his cup always in reach, Adalbert loudly and recklessly denounces the justice of the social order of which he is a most reliable cog. His seditious if bibulous speechifying, already of concern to his more temperate bourgeois fellows, including his father-in-law, is most painful of all to his wife, when his imprudence is duly reported to her. For Agnes feels the smooth regularity of her comfortable – but as we later divine perhaps not deeply satisfying – middle-class domestic life to be threatened.

Indeed, so stirred up is Adalbert by his infectious reassociation with Tobias, with its drinking and its revolutionism, that the effect is soon felt in the marital bedroom. Agnes, well familiar with the stages of her husband's emotions under normal, pre-Tobias conditions, is thrown quite off balance when his behavior is not what she is accustomed to. Her disconcertion occurs initially at the end of the first chapter, to be repeated at the outset of the second chapter. In the first instance Adalbert returns home late from the tavern in a highly agitated state, giving loud vent, while he undresses, to his outrage at "das Unrecht, ... das rings in deutschen Landen Bürger und Bauer zu erleiden hätten."[5] Unprecedentedly, Agnes dares to contradict him, observing that as far as she can see, no one in the duchy is suffering unjustly. At her unwonted interruption Adalbert reaches new heights of agitation. But then, once in bed, he falls asleep far more quickly than Agnes expects or believes possible after such a passionate outburst.

Our inference that she is displeased at such brusque dismissal finds its confirmation the following evening after supper when Adalbert repeats his rejection more explicitly, even cruelly. Comfortably full, sitting in his easy chair, he draws Agnes to him. His disposition to kiss and caress her leads her to imagine she will have no difficulty tonight in keeping him home from seditious carousing. But suddenly he jumps up, smiling in apparent delight at her discomfiture, seizes his hat and cane and departs for the tavern. Upon his returning home, late and drunk and wrought up about socio-political injustice, Agnes, usually so uncontentious, reproaches him severely for his inappropriate seditiousness: "... er, ein richterlicher Beamter, ein Ehemann und vielleicht später einmal Familienvater,...." (391) After all, she continues, Adalbert has not been appointed "um die Übel auszurotten, an denen Deutschland kranken möge, von denen aber gerade in ihrem Herzogtum weniger zu verspüren sei als anderwärts;...." (392) And, the new Duke will perhaps make their duchy the happiest country in the entire Reich.

The usually tranquil Agnes, rejected, frustrated, and angry, is ripe for an affair, although at this moment she would possibly still deny it. We may even anticipate she will have an affair with the Duke. Thus, while the judge, under the outwardly improbable but psychologically unsurprising spell of Tobias, gravitates to the fantasy of ideal justice and revolution, the judge's wife, under the spell of marital disgust on the one hand and opportunity on the other, improbably but also understandably gravitates to a liaison with the Duke.

A process of dissolution is underway. As the marriage deteriorates, the rejections accumulate. At first it is Adalbert who rejects, Agnes who suffers. As her attention is drawn to the Duke, helped along by the fortuitous personal encounter when the Duke's carriage breaks down near the Wogelein home, it is next Agnes who rejects and Adalbert who suffers (and finds solace with the housemaid). Not merely his subservience to Tobias, then, but also his collapsed or collapsing marriage contribute to Adalbert's stress when he is called on, in the normal run of judicial business, to preside at the trial of his friend, charged with carrying a gun on the Duke's hunting preserve and resisting arrest.

If Adalbert has shown signs of being unequal to this dual stress, he is unnerved disastrously when the Duke appears as a courtroom visitor during Tobias's trial. We do not miss the irony that Adalbert, who speechifies in his cups in behalf of ideal justice, metes not merely pedestrian justice as usual but contaminates even that with what looks like personal revenge. We may venture the comparison: the justice that Adalbert delivers resembles the justice that Professor Bernhardi receives.

From the confusing testimony brought before Adalbert, from Tobias's clamorous accusations of governmental malfeasance (all underlain by an apparent personal indifference to self-incrimination), one may indeed wonder: where is truth? where is honesty? Probably Tobias is exactly right, when he declares that the gun he was carrying was just as honestly acquired as the hunting preserve of many a German princeling. Probably at this trial not even Solomon could render justice. Certainly Adalbert doesn't.

Complicating the difficulty, making the ambiguity of justice even more ambiguous – as we for the moment put ourselves in Tobias's shoes, or rather his gauche yellow high boots – is the fact that such ducal courts as the one presided over by Adalbert are not designed, almost certainly not meant to bring discrete justice to quarreling drunks, rancorous peasant spouses, or Tobias Klenk. The nature of this justice is circumscribed to the extent that its inherent beneficiary is circumscribed: the upper and middle classes.

In short, justice in the Duchy of Sigmaringen reflects with some accuracy the socio-political structure of the eighteenth century. It is therefore like justice in Schnitzler's late nineteenth-century Austria after the rout of liberalism. As head of state sits an absolute but rather benevolent monarch, whose administration, however, is run by members of the middle class. We may confidently assume that the fictional Duke Karl Eberhard XVII's drinking and hunting companions – "God's mercy on the peasants while the hunt is underway!" Adalbert exclaims at one point – belonged to the otherwise unemployed nobility. Emperor Franz Joseph's Austria offered precious little active role for the hereditary German-Austrian nobility, the principal exception being the foreign service.

The place name Sigmaringen locates us in southern German-speaking areas. As to the personal names in the novella, while they are indubitably German, they are not without an Austrian, or Bavarian-Austrian ring. That is probably convincing in the cases of the chief forest ranger's assistants, Kuno Waldhaber and Franz Rebler.[6] Quite likely the most convincing is the potential Austrianness of the name of the chief forest ranger himself, Franz Sever von Wolfenstein. It is not at all unusual for Schnitzler to bestow relevant names on his fictional characters, so that the suggestions above are not far fetched.[7]

Suggestive nomenclature is of course one thing; thoroughgoing identity is another. While *Die Frau des Richters* seems to be an allegory of Habsburg politics and justice, as well as an engrossingly complex psychological novella, we probably should not regard it as a *Schlüsselnovelle* – at least not to the extent that *Der Weg ins Freie* (1908) is a *Schlüsselroman*. In the novel Schnitzler's bourgeois liberal, Therese Golowski, goes to jail for *lèse-majesté*, whereas in the novella the vagabond Tobias Klenk is sentenced for more active if also more petty offenses against the regime. But mostly in the novel the liberals in the salon just engage in discussion; and justice and the downfall of Austria are among the topics they discuss. On the other hand, in the allegories, in "Legende," in *Die Hirtenflöte*, in *Die dreifache Warnung*, the striving for justice takes a more specifically active and revolutionary course. In all but *Die dreifache Warnung* this involves mass movements or, as in *Die Frau des Richters*, the strong, repeated suggestion of a mass movement. (Tobias is believed by Adalbert to be a member of a revolutionary conspiracy extending well beyond the boundaries of Sigmaringen.)

Characteristically, when the call for revolution and justice is encountered in Schnitzler's works, it contains an admixture of diffidence and irony. In *Die Frau des Richters* the irony implies an ultimate question: why revolt in pursuit of a fragile ideal justice if you are already living in a relatively benevolent, if fundamentally authoritarian, state? Such an intuitive observer as Agnes, after all, sees nothing amiss. Tobias's revolutionary fulminations aside – and whatever substance they may have, they are effectively contained – revolution is implicitly advocated here just as little as in, say, *Professor Bernhardi*: that is, not at all. Duke Karl Eberhard XVII is not such a bad ruler. Having been in his Paris days an associate of Diderot, upon assuming office he probably understands the complications of justice and morality.

Early on the Duke appears amenable to ideal justice. But in the longer run, when he becomes acquainted with his subjects, with complex and imperfect people – for example, Adalbert and Tobias, conceivably Agnes too – in the longer run, what is the point, why bother? The originally well-meaning – as far as we can judge, well-meaning – Duke is too much a *Menschenkenner* for his own good, for the good of his subjects, and for the good of justice. Why not – we are drawing inferences here – why not rather, after the model of his ancestors, forget justice and Diderot as well, and enjoy such pleasures as are, or become, available to a man of his station? For instance, the judge's wife?

Like many a Schnitzler woman, Agnes, however undiscerning her view of Sigmaringen society, sees the fundamentals of human relationships in a clear light. Especially is this true after the human landscape is even more powerfully illuminated for her by the return of Tobias Klenk, by the unhappy effect of Tobias on her husband, and by the advent of the new Duke. She comes to see Adalbert for the indifferent lover that he is. She sees him, when under pressure he reverts to type, for a coward, for a poseur, a liar. In throwing herself at the Duke – is she as well reverting to type? – she evokes and focuses the inherent – atavistic – lechery in the Duke, who now also reverts to type.

Agnes regards the arrival of the new Duke almost like the advent of a savior, even before she has met him. "Er ist da!" she exults, as though her savior were her Saviour.[8] When a *Märchen*-like fate[9] in the form of a ducal carriage accident allows her to meet him, she is infatuated to the point of speechlessness. She is prepared to have an affair, to be the first *Gartenmägdlein* of the new Duke, even while retaining – evidently at the Duke's behest, but we can't be sure – a nominal marital relationship with Adalbert.

With Agnes's defection to the Duke's bed and the subsequent birth of a son, who is brought up as a Wogelein, an ultimate level of imperfect but approximate justice is attained. Judge Adalbert Wogelein, having preached social revolutionism and social justice, continues to dispense individual, approximate legal justice, even as his wife *lives* individual revolutionism. Naturally, the justice she encounters remains approximate. Her two sons, one of them a bastard – the Duke, as planned before he met Agnes, marries a Princess of Württemberg – do not attain the social level of their parents or partial parents, the Wogeleins. Tobias Klenk, on a foreign gallows, receives his doubtlessly only approximate justice.

As we have seen, Adalbert Wogelein's justice, ever literal and pedestrian, cannot survive the emotional stress brought about by the return of Tobias Klenk, the disintegration of Adalbert's marriage, and the Duke's visit to his courtroom. His meager potential for a broader justice expires in a maze of self-justifying boasting and prevarication.

Allegorical justice similarly provides no grounds for an encouraging resolution: Austria in 1900 replicates Sigmaringen in the eighteenth century – or vice versa.

And justice in the simple, absolute, and ideal sense is necessarily made ambiguous and relativized by the complex and imperfect human medium. Whether this really amounts to a statement of futility, as Dickerson asserts...?[10] We are simply back to the human dimension, the personal.

Notes

1 This essay sprang from early research carried out in collaboration with Jeffrey B. Berlin, to whom I am indebted for many of my formulations.

2 The earliest dramatic sketches, at least those preserved, are from 1916, but the inspiration came from a work on the German petty princes that, according to notations in the *Nachlaß*, Schnitzler was reading around 1908. See Eric Blackall, "Tobias Klenk," in *Austriaca. Festschrift für Heinz Politzer* (Tübingen: Niemeyer, 1975), pp. 267-84, esp. p. 279. One internal detail that might suggest an early genesis is to be found in Judge Adalbert Wogelein's early derogation of the new Duke of Sigmaringen. (See *Die Frau des Richters* in Arthur Schnitzler, *Die Erzählenden Schriften*, Vol. 2 [Frankfurt am Main: Fischer, 1961], p. 393. [Subsequent references to this work will be enclosed in parentheses in my text.]) The Duke reportedly consorted with wenches of the worst sort in Paris and therefore probably contracted syphilis. The youthful Schnitzler led a checkered social life in Vienna, in which his greatest fear and deterrent was the much-mooted possibility of contracting syphilis. Another, somewhat more fragile clue to an early genesis may lie in Adalbert's grandiose boast to his wife Agnes about the impact of his promised acquittal of Tobias: "Aber es könnte wohl sein, daß mein Wort auch von hier aus ins Weite dränge und sich an meinem Spruch eine Fackel entzündete, die über ganz Deutschland leuchtete" (397). *Die Fackel*, the icono-

clastic journal of Schnitzler's contemporary, Karl Kraus, was founded in 1899 as an ethical forum against the spiritual corruption prevalent in Austria, most prominently, as Kraus saw it, in the press, but also in politics and justice as well as in the arts. Admittedly, the linguistic and rhetorical coincidence centering on "Fackel" could just as well be fortuitous.

[3] In addition to Blackall, "Tobias Klenk," note 2 above, see also Harold D. Dickerson, Jr., "Arthur Schnitzler's *Die Frau des Richters*: A Statement of Futility," *The German Quarterly*, 43 (1970), 223-36.

[4] The briefer and more casual critics of *Die Frau des Richters*, while observing the at least titular centrality of Agnes, typically fail to go much beyond that observation. See, for example: Josef Körner, "Arthur Schnitzlers Spätwerk," *Preußische Jahrbücher*, 108, No. 2 (May 1927), pp. 155-57; Richard Plaut (later Plant), *Arthur Schnitzler als Erzähler* (Diss. Basel, 1935), pp. 30, 72; and somewhat more recently, Michael Imboden, *Die surreale Komponente im erzählenden Werk Arthur Schnitzlers* (Bern: Herbert Lang, 1971), pp. 31, 33.

[5] P. 389. Comparisons drawn even earlier, in the third paragraph of the novella, seem to suggest an allegorical identity between Sigmaringen and Austria: "Obwohl sich's daher in dem kleinen Lande [Sigmaringen], ... behaglicher und ungefährdeter leben ließ als in manchem anderen deutschen Fürstentum, fehlte es auch hier nicht an Unzufriedenen und Aufmuckern, deren manche sich zuweilen kecker äußerten als ihre Gleichgesinnten in anderen Ländern ..." (383).

[6] It might even be suggested that Schnitzler is throwing out occupational puns as well as possible national identifiers.

[7] *Die Frau des Richters* appropriately lacks the Slavic and Hungarian personal names that characterize Schnitzler's Vienna scenes. The only mention of a Slavic name occurs when we are advised that Duke Karl Eberhard XVI, the father of Karl Eberhard XVII, is half Poniatowski, a noble Polish family (and a historical one). The Poniatowski reference may remind us of the prominent role of Polish nobility at the Habsburg court of Franz Joseph I.

[8] Compare Fräulein Else's cry of joy when her libido finds release in the reappearance of the *Filou*: "Er ist wieder da, er ist wieder da!"

[9] Schnitzler's other allegories, "Legende," *Die dreifache Warnung*, and (at least in part) *Die Hirtenflöte*, are couched in *Märchen*-like form, take place in a *Märchen*-like ambiance, and even bear titles suggestive of *Märchen*. Neither by form, by title, nor, on the whole, by ambiance does *Die Frau des Richters* evoke the traditional *Märchen*. (Although, perhaps significantly, it does bear comparison with Kurt Eisner's *Sozialmärchen*; cf. *Feste der Festlosen. Hausbuch weltlicher Predigtschwänke* [Dresden: Kaden, 1906].) But what *Die Frau des Richters* does contain is an unmistakable central *Märchen* motif, the *Märchen* motif *par excellence*: make a wish and it shall be granted you. Agnes's formal wish to be a ducal *Gartenmägdlein* is granted.

[10] In his title: "Arthur Schnitzler's *Die Frau des Richters*: A Statement of Futility," *The German Quarterly*, 43 (1970), 223-36. See also p. 235.

Neglected Nineteenth-Century German-Jewish Historical Fiction

Lothar Kahn

Nineteenth-century German-Jewish historical fiction bears an unmistakable kinship to *Ghettoliteratur.*[1] At times the boundary between the two genres is almost imperceptible. Only the reference to a particular historical figure enables the reader to situate the work specifically in the past. Generally, too, this type of historical fiction is placed outside of German-speaking lands, though this is not always so.

Whatever the period or place, medieval England or seventeenth-century Constantinople, the narrative is told against the backdrop of oppressed Jews. The authors are liberal, apologetic, and acculturated German Jews, who are intent upon proving the virtues of the Jewish people. They are eager to demonstrate to their fellow Germans that, given half a chance, Jews would be as bold, courageous, and moral as the Germans themselves. They want to demonstrate, too, that Jews are flesh and blood. The historical novelists gravitate towards those periods in which Jews could be soldiers and more nearly "normal," i.e. like the non-Jewish population. The novels were written at a time when scientific, scholarly study of Jewish history was still relatively undeveloped, and liberties with historical fact could easily escape notice. A favorite liberty is the invention of a fighter-hero and his assignment to a time that would tolerate his heroism.

Another distinguishing quality of German-Jewish historical fiction is its elaborate plotting and disregard for all verisimilitude. Some of the works are patterned after Walter Scott or Alexandre Dumas, except for the importance of the boudoir. If love exists at all, it is presented in the form of a gentile maiden enticing a young Jewish male away from the ancestral faith. Sometimes, too, a heroic Christian knight will obscure the moral vision of a chaste Jewish girl. Occasionally, both the young Jewish male and female will withstand wiles, threats, and other inducements to approach the baptismal font. One or two may die for their faith, but more of them will convince bishops and sultans of their Jewish steadfastness, morality, and courage, and be freed without having to undergo conversion.

In most instances, these historical works were written by rabbis who had a clearly didactic intent. In the rabbis' hands, such fiction could become a many-pronged pedagogic weapon. It could, first of all, militate against conversion, in their eyes the bane of nineteenth-century German Jewry. Secondly, it could teach moral principles that had guided earlier Jewries through even more perilous times. Thirdly, it could attempt to present the essence of Jewish history, although the rabbis, like other writers, took historical licence if it suited a broader objective. The personalized human history developed in a fictional work could translate into easily comprehensible terms some of the scholarly historical findings of an Isaac Marcus Jost (1793-1860), Leopold Zunz (1794-1886), or Heinrich Graetz (1817-1891), which would otherwise have been restricted to the most literate Jews. The fact bears repeating that the goal of historical fiction was not mainly to vivify the past, but to use it as a tool for instructing freely about the present.

Both historical and ghetto fiction evolved under the aegis of Romanticism, with its general historical outlook and its emphasis on discovering the "root-essence" of ethnic groups. Moreover, like the Romantics, the Jewish writers cultivated sentimentalism, nostalgia, and the virtues of chaste romance. Jewish family life, customs, and folkways are all enveloped in a warm, romantic glow. Just as Christian Romantics turned to medieval religiosity, (the fervor that went into the building of great cathedrals, and the dalliance with chivalry), so Jewish novelists often turned to the medieval era to depict the heroism needed to withstand Christian fanaticism.

***

Let us now look briefly at the themes and plots of several of these works, which are justly forgotten for their doubtful literary merit, but which can still tell us something about the needs of the Jewish psyche in this period. Eugene Rispart, writing as Dr. ISAAC ASCHER FRANCOLM (1788-1849), spent much of his short life as a religious teacher in his native Breslau. He leaned toward the Reform and the rabbinic authorities forbade him such practices as confirming girls – a ritual he had initiated. His *Die Kreuzfahrer und die Juden* (1843) ventured into the medieval England of Richard the Lion-Hearted. Here follows an abbreviated summary of the plot:

A Spanish Jew visits England to fetch the bride chosen for him long ago. He is enlightened, well-read, and courageous, which the Jews of England are not. He falls in love with Hadassah, the daughter of Benedict of York, though his bride, affianced to him at birth, was Malka, daughter of the court Jew Jossen. True love triumphs, partly because Malka has fallen in love with a Christian knight who rescued her from a hateful mob. The knight, it turns out, is none other than Richard the Lion-Hearted himself, whose identity she discovers only on the day of his coronation. Though the novel revolves around the motif of the beautiful Jewess, a victim of a royal infatuation,[2] it is thematically an attack on intellectual darkness, prejudice, economic exploitation of Jews, and, above all, Christian rationalization of criminal acts.

Religious and economic circumstances converge to bring about mob violence during the week of Richard's coronation. The author, Francolm, is modern in his realization that religious and psychological biases often conceal economic motives. His mightiest noblemen seek loans from Jewish financiers, invite exploitation, and are, indeed, exploited. When the time comes to repay the loans, the degree of Christian dissatisfaction with Jews suddenly mounts; a mob is quickly aroused and stands by to eliminate the "wealthy, usurious Jews."

Francolm's tone is bitter. For him, Christianity, the religion of love, knows neither love nor compassion. It punishes all who will not accept its monopoly on unprovable truths. Bishops and noblemen pretend to be the friends of Jews, but on the chosen days of "Christian vengeance," they conveniently absent themselves. Although sophisticated in terms of economic motivation, Francolm is more primitive in blaming the lower classes for the murderous onslaught on the Jews of York and elsewhere.

The historical figure of Benedict of York knows that a Jew must be prepared to flee at a moment's notice, that he must have a ready-made place of refuge, and ready cash in store. His theory is sound, but the application fails. Benedict does not recognize the moment of danger and is killed. Hadassah and her bold Spanish admirer escape to Iberia, for he, unlike the English Jews, has the determination and will to act. In this way, Francolm deplores the impact on the Jewish psyche of chronic fear, worry, and immobilization of the will.

***

In *Gabriel* (1869), inaccurately subtitled "Eine Geschichte der Juden von Prag," SALOMON KOHN (1825-1904) takes his reader into a nearer past, the Thirty Years War (1618-1648). The hero, Gabriel Suess, born near Köln, is grandson of the physician to the Margrave. Gabriel is visiting his cousin and fiancée Blumele when the news reaches him of his mother's impending death. He rushes to her side, only to hear her confession that her husband was not his father. Suddenly a "bastard," Gabriel is shunned by the community at Rosh Hashanah services, and even Blumele is silent about his shameful condition. In his confusion and revulsion, Gabriel denounces Judaism, converts to Christianity, and embarks on lengthy travels. On one of these he comes to the rescue of an embattled warrior, is told he has saved the life of a hero, and himself becomes a hero and warrior. In fact, we first encounter him – the story is told in many confusing flashbacks – as an outstanding general and feared swordsman, who vents his vindictive feelings against his father, the Jews, and especially Blumele.

He has learned that Blumele is in Prague and he arrives there posing as a Talmudic scholar. Received as such by the "shammes" of the Old Synagogue, he mystifies all by the wealth of his Talmudic knowledge and his flaunting of all Jewish law. He locates Blumele's house, visits her, and threatens her callously. If she will not be his within ten days, her captured husband will suffer dire consequences.

Before the tenth day arrives, Gabriel is summoned to fight for his emperor and slays the most feared soldier on the enemy side. He returns to Prague incognito and there meets the famed scholar Michael Glogau. The latter divines Suess's identity and reproaches him for his vindictive actions. Gabriel Suess, with his intelligence and wealth, could have become a mainstay of his oppressed people, succored it, and become its blessing and defender. Gabriel turns thoughtful; the suspicion dawns that he might have erred. After several hours of inner conflict, he decides to forgive Blumele and sees her reunited with her husband.

The structure of the story is awkward and confirms that Kohn, an experienced writer and journalist, was not a gifted novelist. Besides its involved structure, this novel suffers from the presence of too many stock characters, and the author also resorts too often to premonitions of doom and death to introduce his actions. Yet, he is imaginative and he vividly depicts both the customs and attitudes of Jews; he dwells at length on the kindness given to strangers on the Sabbath; the practice of guests displaying their Talmudic virtuosity after the Sabbath meal; the devotion to learning which, sometimes in excess, unhinges a mind; resignation in the face of flight and possible death; disinterest in the politics and dynastic struggles of the Christians. Only one question interests the Jewish community as a new ruler is crowned: what can or will he do to the Jews?

Physical courage again plays an important role. General Mar (Gabriel's Christian title and name) is an example of the bravery that once was and could again be a Jew's. Kohn is no friend of excessive mental activity or asceticism. He regrets that the fencing masters of Prague are not permitted to teach their art to Jews, the very people most in need of self-defense. The author does not condone, of course, the hate-filled soul of his hero or his recourse to alien ways. Changes, yes! Physical activity, yes! But, Kohn insisted on both within the framework of Jewish morality.

***

MORITZ WASSERMANN (1811-1892), who wrote *Judah Touro: Eine biographische Romanze* (1871),[3] derived much of his information about Touro from a brother in America. Like other rabbinic novelists, Wassermann was eager to show his Jews as ethically motivated persons, open and fair with gentiles, and not preferential in their treatment of fellow Jews. Wassermann's approach was intensely apologetic. He appears to have had before his mind's eye an imaginary anti-Semite, whom he wished to enlighten on the admirable qualities of Jews. Like other apologists, Wassermann was a liberal, sympathizing with weak and oppressed groups, be they Blacks, Jews, or servants. He is an inveterate foe of privilege by birth; he is friendly to the U.S. as the *promised* land of liberty and equality for all. His spiritual closeness to the U.S. occasionally causes him to be unfair to England, and as a German author, he is traditionally unkind to France.

Wassermann lauds Touro's bravery as his ship is under attack by pirates and the young American Jew acquits himself with honor and dignity. While recognizing anti-Semitism as an ever-present evil, the author does not let his Touro despair. Through him, Wassermann denounces the role of Christian theologians in fomenting Jew-hatred; he attacks scapegoating, stereotyping, indeed all prejudice resulting from specific Christian miseducation.

A major theme is intermarriage, which Touro repudiates without ever offending Christian sensibilities. Though Touro falls in love with Christian women in isolated Louisiana, where there are few Jewish women, he decides against a union outside the faith.

Wassermann repeats the belief that local custom, however widespread, must never triumph over morality. Towards the end of his life, Touro concludes that it is "better to be a fool in the eyes of man all my life than be an offender in the eyes of God for only one second." Though Touro in the wilderness had long before ceased to be an observant Jew, he never forgot the religious admonition "not to let the mocking of man deter one from the fulfillment of duty." Fulfillment of duty was not, of course, a Jewish monopoly. In fact, it was a value greatly stressed in German life. Perhaps here it is just another concession to the imaginary anti-Semite.

***

MORITZ FRIEDLÄNDER's (1848-1919) *Apion* (1882) relates the evil-doings of the notorious anti-Semite of antiquity, Apion of Alexandria. The style and structure of the novel are awkward and the approach to anti-Semitism is simplistic. Friedländer attributes Apion's fanatical hatred of Jews to his intense rivalry with Philo, the distinguished Jewish philosopher and communal leader in first century Egypt.[5] The plot follows:

Apion returns from Rome to Alexandria where he spreads false stories about his own philosophical triumphs in the world's capital. He is selfish, irrational, and unscrupulous. When he hears of Philo's appointment during his absence as head of the Academy, Apion's jealousy is boundless. Compared to Philo's quiet, humane thoughtfulness, Apion cuts a sorry figure. But, obviously, Friedländer intends him to be pure villain, as he wants his readers to equate anti-Semitism with personal corruption, dishonesty, and evil. As Apion's viciousness now totally directs him, he resorts to bribery and blackmail. The weak Roman governor accedes and the Jewish population is mercilessly assaulted. Finally, Apion's lies are exposed. Rome intervenes and order is restored.

Friedländer's purpose is publicistic more than literary. As a result, the novel suffers from the unrelieved villainy of Apion. All subtlety is discarded as Friedländer teaches his gentile German readers not to listen to Apion-like leaders in their midst. Through Apion's critics, Friedländer rhetorically addresses the Germans of his day. Do Germans want to be guided by the likes of this false philosopher? Is the manner in which Germans meet their religious needs to interfere with their civil and political duties? Can't Germans see how the Jews have always lived by the highest standards of morality, which alone have enabled them to survive continuous neglect and maltreatment by others?

Friedländer makes mention of the Essenes, identifying them as early Christians. He uses them as the link that binds Jews and Christians together in brotherhood. These fraternal religions should never compete with one another, according to Friedländer. They should respect one another and desist from proselytizing. Like the other German-Jewish writers of historical fiction, Friedländer uses his *Apion* as an argument against apostasy, adducing many of the arguments used by Friedländer's young German-Jewish contemporaries in explaining their baptism. Philo's nephew, son of the Alabarch of Alexandria, says he was influenced, on the one hand, by the low self-esteem of Jews as an oppressed group and, on the other, by outside efforts to convert him. Philo's arguments in dissent are those that any modern rabbi could use in a Saturday morning sermon.

***

MARCUS (MEYER) LEHMANN (1831-1890), the author of *Jüdische Erzählungen* (1964) (Selections from his *Aus Vergangenheit und Gegenwart*, 1872-1876), was born in Hannover and studied secular subjects in Berlin and theology in Prague. From 1853 until his death, he occupied a pulpit in Mainz. He was the long-time editor of *Der Israelit*, the organ of Orthodox Jewry and its response to Ludwig Philippson's Reform journal, *Allgemeine Zeitung des Judentums*.

The historical tales in *Jüdische Erzählungen* feature improbable plots, suggesting that the author cared little for the refinements of literature and viewed it solely as a means of teaching and moralizing. In "Der Fürst von Coucy," the famed Tosaphist, Rabbi Samson of Coucy, has been asked by his wealthy brother Chaim to accompany him on a business trip to London. Since Chaim has always supported him and his family, Samson agrees to escort his brother. En route, they are seized by pirates who are willing to release only one of the brothers. Since Chaim can support his family and he cannot, Samson voluntarily goes into slavery. The time is that of the Crusades and Samson is sold to an emir. By chance, he manages to save the life of no less a person than Richard the Lion-Hearted. In deep gratitude, Richard elevates him to princely status.

Rabbi Samson, the unlikely warrior-prince, arrives home just in time to prevent his only daughter's marriage to the Talmudically untutored, but wealthy, Abel, Chaim's choice of a groom. Chaim had broken a promise made before the earlier departure that his daughter would only marry a scholar. As a prince, Samson is now more powerful than Chaim. Samson prevails and his daughter marries Jitzchak, Samson's prize pupil, whom she loves and who loves her. All ends well.

Thus, even fiction by an orthodox rabbi may express a subconscious wish for Jewish physical daring and power. For what other reason would Lehmann have converted his quiet, impractical scholar into a bold fighter and even a prince? Lehmann also cannot resist the temptation of preaching against conversion. While Samson is in slavery, the noble and beautiful daughter of the emir, who is in love with him, promises him high positions if only he will marry her. But Samson will not relinquish the ancestral religion for which the emir threatens to kill this "wretched dog from the despised tribe of the Jews." But Fatima, his daughter, respects Samson all the more. She suggests that perhaps the Jewish popes will grant him a dispensation and allow him to marry a Moslem girl. Samson enlightens her proudly: "We Jews have no priests whom we empower to bind us to – or release us from – our obligations."

Samson's love for the Holy Land is expressed when he visits it in the chains of a slave. "So this is the land of my fathers," he exclaims emotionally, "the blessing of the entire world. For the possession of this tiny land, most powerful peoples are fighting to this very day.... So beautiful and attractive to all since time immemorial, but, alas, Israel's sons eat the bitter bread of exile in alien lands."

Finally, Lehmann asserts the supremacy of the scholar over the businessman, while still giving the latter his due. The rich man chosen by Chaim for his daughter cannot be the equal of the learned man, whom Samson has decreed for her. Again and again, spirit triumphs over the material in this and in other tales in the collection, nearly all of which are equally close to the fairy tale and equally illustrative of rabbinic concerns. Whether the setting is Spain or Poland, the Jewish male or maiden is a credit to parents and God.

However great the peril or the temptation, he or she will remain loyal to Israel. Moreover, the man of spirit will triumph over the man of mere wealth. Even the trappings of royalty – nearly all his Jews confront kings and princes – will not seduce the morally stable and always endangered young Jew.

***

LUDWIG PHILIPPSON (1811-1889) was a distinguished rabbi, editor, and scholar, when he began to write historical fiction. From 1833 to 1863 he officiated from a Reform pulpit in Magdeburg. Within the Reform he had the reputation of a moderate. Between 1839 and 1853, he translated the Bible into German, and until his death, he edited *Die Allgemeine Zeitung des Judentums*. His most impressive scholarly endeavour was *Die Entwicklung der Religion im Judentum, Christentum und Islam* (1847).

As with other rabbi-novelists of historical works, his most cherished ideas permeate the story line. Philippson, more than his colleagues, was genuinely interested in history and respected the accuracy of his facts. Among his prime targets were baptized Jews who appear to him as potential foes. In whatever historical settings he placed these apostates, they emerged as tormentors of their former co-religionists. He depicted their cupidity, vindictiveness, guilt, and criminal intent vis-à-vis Jews. Though a liberal and apologist, Philippson was uninhibited in his denunciation of monks, the Church, and Christianity. He was, however, infinitely more cautious in his attitude towards Germans. To be sure, he admonished them to practice tolerance and eschew fanaticism and persecution of Jews, but he had to prove to them that Jews have always led virtuous lives, and demonstrated good citizenship. He too, was trying to convince an absent or imaginary anti-Semite to change the nature of his ways. Philippson's plots are less contrived than Lehmann's, though he, too, could not seem to tell a continuous tale. Often he paused, inserting an essay, thereby disclosing his real purpose: to use fiction as a popular mode of instruction.

"Die Marannen," the first novella of *Sarom* (1843), is representative of Philippson's fiction. The novella treats the plight of the Jews in Spain, the machinations of Torquemada and other monks, former Jews who now bring misery to their people. It also rivets attention to the efforts of powerful royal advisers such as Don Abravanel to forestall expulsion. Finally, when expulsion occurs, it zeroes in on Abravanel's family and a young Jewess in love with a Judeophile Christian knight.

The portrait of the elder Abravanel is more subtly drawn than is the rule in historical tales of this type. He is an observant Jew, yet can distinguish between man-imposed religious laws and those others which, in their magnitude, derive directly from God. Though he is the royal financial adviser, highly esteemed by the king, Abravanel knows he is resented by noblemen and bishops alike – all of whom feel themselves unjustly taxed by the Jew. Moreover, in their eyes this adviser even had the audacity to keep the noblest of grandees waiting, while he continued reading in his cursed Talmud. Abravanel entertains no illusions about his personal security; on the contrary, he senses danger lurking everywhere. The monk Torquemada keeps pleading in the king's ear that there can be no Catholic Spain while Jews thrive on her soil. Abravanel knows the king is kind, but he is weak, and eventually the order of expulsion is issued. Abravanel submits, but first offers his entire fortune if he may keep inhaling the air of Iberia. His offer is rebuffed. He embarks on his Italian exile with the words of resignation spoken by Jews in comparable situations: "You have given, oh Lord, and now you have taken. Praised be the name of the Lord."

Other stories in the collection are of more than passing interest. "The Refugee from Jerusalem" offers a Jewish variant of the Wandering Jew, a man who had watched the razing of the Temple and lived on to see other telling events of Jewish history. "The Rabbi and the Minister" has an eighteenth-century setting – otherwise it contains the same elements as the Abravanel story. A young rabbinic student, himself the son of a rabbi, returns from his studies in Strassburg to find his father in jail, maligned both by an unscrupulous minister and the disgruntled president of the congregation. (In fiction by rabbis, the rabbi is often a victim of either hostile Christians or hateful members of his flock.) The story shows how the student, with the help of an ambassador, manages to clear his father and the Jewish community from blame, and have an edict of expulsion cancelled. At the end, the ambassador compliments the young Jew; he would make a splendid diplomat. "To survive," the youngster responds, "a Jew must be born a diplomat."

Though Philippson is not a very talented story-teller, his fiction is somewhat more mature than that of his colleagues. Yet, his work is uneven and more didactic than dramatic. Also, he is all too willing to sacrifice fictional needs to the demands of religious argumentation.

***

Like Philippson, D. HONIGMANN (1821-1885) published his works under the auspices of the *Institut zur Förderung der israelitischen Literatur*. His purpose was more narrowly historical, with moral preaching clearly subordinated. A strong romantic current runs through his novels, which are too long for what little they have to say. His best-known effort, though hardly a literary achievement, is *Das Grab in Sabbonieta* (n.d.), situated in the Venice of Leon Modena. Honigmann transformed Modena, a secondary figure in the novel, into a more perfect man than he was historically. In general, his characters are extreme types, bordering either on total perfection or total villainy. The book's view of Jewish destiny is one of moral grandeur in the face of suffering. A faint Reformist note is discernible: the letter of the law must yield to its spirit, as well as to the times. The author also cannot suppress his resentment at Christian proselytising, which is conducted by most of the Venetian clergymen he depicts.

***

Simon Eichelkatz (und anderes) (1903) by ULRICH FRANK (pseudonym for Ulla Wolff [1850-1924]), which is on the borderline between ghetto literature and historical fiction, is a more lively work than most, but the novella is lacking in a clear and sharp focus. The narrative, though interesting, is not powerful enough to obscure the absence of a center.

The tragedy of Simon Eichelkatz is related by a narrator-physician, who describes Eichelkatz as an old man, unschooled in all but religion, rich in common sense and plain human wisdom. Yet, Eichelkatz, with all his moral simplicity, is less unique than the narrator would have us believe. Our hearts reach out to Eichelkatz, when we learn that he is the father of a famous professor who broke away from Judaism and that there is no longer contact between father and son. Eichelkatz's tactical skill and humanity appear more as a result of the narrator's assertion than in fact is the case.

Like other historical novelists, Frank repeated the ideas closest to him. Eichelkatz cannot bear the notion of Jewish collective responsibility for the misdeeds of one of their own. For example, he asks: "Does a Jewish innkeeper blame all Christians when a Christian drunkard has started a brawl? Or does he merely think this man, whatever his name, is a drunkard, and the innkeeper has to watch him the next time he comes in?" On internal Jewish questions, Frank sided with the Reformers. His Eichelkatz applauds rabbis who prefer a broadly human outlook, rejecting congregants who cling to the letter of the law and disregard its humane universalist spirit.

***

To sum up, German-Jewish historical fiction was neither good literature nor good history. But, it is historically significant to those who wish to understand the psyche of nineteenth-century Jewish intellectuals, eager for normalcy, for making themselves as "German-like" as possible, while retaining a modicum of Jewishness. The writers of Jewish historical fiction – in fairness to them – defended that modicum with loyalty and steadfastness.

Notes

1 See Lothar Kahn, "Tradition and Modernity in the German Ghetto Novel," *Judaism*, XXVIII, No. 1 (1979), 31-41.

2 Kings and their fateful attraction to beautiful Jewesses have often been treated in German literature, especially in relation to Rahel, the Jewess of Toledo. See Franz Grillparzer, Lion Feuchtwanger, and several others.

3 An English translation of this novel was published by Bloch in 1923.

4 It is difficult to avoid the impression at times that these apologetic Jewish writers were pleading with an imaginary anti-Semite, whom they wished to convince of the error of his ways. Berthold Auerbach and Gabriel Riesser belong to this type of mentality, whereas Heinrich Heine and Ludwig Börne were defiantly "aggressive," caring little about the reaction of men they thought beyond hope.

5 Men known for their fanatical Jew-hatred-such as Apion, Torquemada, Chmelnicki – tend to recur in Jewish historical fiction well into this century.

Wilhelm Raabe and his Reputation Among Jews and Anti-Semites

Jeffrey L. Sammons

I.

That Wilhelm Raabe was not an anti-Semitic writer and *Der Hungerpastor* is not an anti-Semitic book in its intention has been so well established in literary scholarship for so long that it would seem redundant to argue the point any more. Nevertheless, legends of reception are often tenacious; for example, in Gordon Craig's widely acclaimed book, *The Germans*, it is said that Raabe, Gustav Freytag, and Felix Dahn "resorted in their most popular books to the technique of parallelism, placing in contrast the careers of their Christian protagonist, who was always portrayed as being honorable, idealistic and dedicated to the service of others, and his Jewish counterpart, who was self-centered, cowardly, materialistic, and unscrupulous," as though Raabe, or, for that matter, Freytag, had done nothing but write such novels their whole lives long.[1] Therefore, it is perhaps not superfluous to make the case again; but in reopening it, we will find that the matter is rather more complicated than it is normally made out to be. Neither the anti-Semitic view of Raabe nor its refutation in their conventional presentations have exhausted the subject of Raabe and his reputation in regard to Jews and anti-Semites.

II.

The case that Raabe cannot be regarded as an anti-Semitic writer was made long ago.[2] It can only be sketched in the briefest terms here; in fact, to my knowledge, there has never been a thorough study on modern principles of Jewish characters and their situations and Jewish references in Raabe's works, but the point is that positive as well as neutral Jewish figures appear in numerous places. The first example is in Raabe's second novel, *Ein Frühling* (1857), written well before *Der Hungerpastor*, in which the Jewish old-clothes dealer Rosenstein, though portrayed with some stereotypical features, is nevertheless a positive figure amiably regarded by his fellow gentiles, and his two kindly, well-bred daughters quite clearly belong to that community of the good and gentle that from beginning to end in Raabe's work distinguishes ideal humanity from the common run of mankind. *Holunderblüte* (1863), written during the genesis of *Der Hungerpastor*, is the reminiscence of an elderly doctor who recalls with sorrow how, as a young student, he aroused the feelings of a girl he met in the Jewish Cemetery of Prague, but did not love her, and she dies, like her prefigurative ancestor, the dancer Mahalath, of a symbolically enlarged heart. This does not strike me as one of Raabe's most successful works; it suffers from the sentimentality that plagued his writing in its first phases, and it falls into the pattern commonly met with in nineteenth-century German fiction of regarding the Jew as exotic or "oriental," and thus foreign and inaccessible. All the same, despite the stress on the filth and nastiness of the Jewish community and the stereotyping of the girl's pawnbroker father, the novella expresses sympathy and understanding for the plight of the Jews, as well as respect for Jewish dignity in the image of the grave of the great rabbi Judah Löw.[3] In fact, the symbol of the enlarged heart – which inspired the narrator to become an accomplished heart specialist – refers not only or even primarily to obstructed love, but to grief at the sufferings of the Jewish people, who, it has been argued, are portrayed as the suffering servants of the world.[4] It is here as well as anywhere that one can see the two reasons why Raabe could not have been an anti-Semite even had he wanted to: his strong feelings about the integrity and just rights of a *Volk*, an extension of his own pronounced nationalism,[5] and his profoundly sympathetic nature that vibrates through his entire *oeuvre* with human suffering, despair, and oppression.

Three other works must be mentioned in this connection. One is *Gedelöcke* (1866), a farcical and improbable story, which, like many of the most improbable fictions, is drawn directly from real life, described in a book Raabe found in a flea-market. The Danish freethinker Gedelöcke, owing to his friendship with Jews and his interest in learning from them, has put himself into the reputation of having virtually converted to Judaism; while he has not actually done so, the very idea of it drives the community (and his wife) into hysterics of gossip, zealotry, and superstition. He creates a situation that makes it impossible to bury him either in Christian or in Jewish ground, and so he is buried and dug up and buried again and dug up and finally deposited in the common field. Here we have an expression of Raabe's secular and often aggressively anti-clerical outlook: the religious Jews, who expel their cantor from the community for bringing this trouble by associating with Gedelöcke, are no better than the religious Christians, but, on the other hand, the Christians are no better than the Jews, and Gedelöcke's whipsawing of his fellow men with their own prejudices certainly has the effect of making anti-Semitism one more symptom of a mean and trivial spirit.

Of particular interest is the novella *Frau Salome* (1875), whose title figure is in some ways the most remarkable Jewish character I know of in nineteenth-century German fiction. Not only is she intelligent and energetic; in her capacity for handling herself in a chaotic disaster and as a refuge for the bewildered daughter of the half-mad sculptor Querian, she is quite clearly a member of the Raabean community of the good, the generous, and the sympathetic. But even more remarkably, she is the millionaire widow of a Jewish banker, the kind of person who would almost never appear in a positive light in the fiction of the time. That she can exchange urbane repartee about her Jewishness with her gentile friend, the *Justizrat* Scholten, merely expresses her and her author's sovereignty over common prejudice. Salome, Scholten, and the girl Eilike are bound together by the central, original symbol of the novella: the "ichor," the blood of the gods that flows in their veins and sets them apart from vulgar mankind. The characterization of Salome not only exhibits Raabe's cross-grained opposition to cliché and convention; I rather suspect that she may have been conceived out of a bad conscience about *Der Hungerpastor*. The novella, incidentally, is full of reminiscences from Heine's *Harzreise.*[6]

Finally, there is the splendid historical novella *Höxter und Corvey* (1875), one of Raabe's several evocations of the bloody misery of the historical past. As is frequently the case in his historical fiction, the blood and misery are the consequence of Catholic-Protestant conflict, but here both factions turn on helpless and harmless Jews, and the protagonists risk life and limb in an attempt to shield an elderly woman and her granddaughter from murderous ruffians and howling mobs. To these cases may be added the painter Rudolf Haeseler, the spirit of shrewd wit and realism in *Der Dräumling* (1872), whose mother, the daughter of a converted Jew, was "schwarzlockig, korpulent, und ästhetisch"; (10: 32)[7] his gentile father is the money-changer, i.e., banker.[8] It is important to observe here that Haeseler is one of the alter egos of Raabe's own personality encountered in various disguises in his works.

It is true that there are scattered, occasionally disrespectful passages in Raabe. As an example one may take a quotation from *Die Leute aus dem Walde* (1862), since it has sometimes been cited by anti-Semitic admirers: "Auf das Haus in der Stadt hielt mehr als ein schwarzhaariger, krummnasiger Geschäftsmann die scharfen semitischen Augen gerichtet." (5: 177) Apart from the fact that, in this case, it is actually the gentile servants who are systematically robbing the property, an examination of such passages, which has never been undertaken, would show that in almost every case they reflect the association of Jews with money and commerce, graspingness and greed, and in spirit they differ in no way from often harsher passages in Heine or Marx. This is not meant to be an excuse but simply an observation necessary to place these stereotypes in their historical context. Social, class, ethnic, and national typing is virtually universal in nineteenth-century literature, a central feature of its anthropology and, if one will, "realism"; it appears in Raabe in many forms, among which the Jewish types are neither prominent nor striking. Furthermore, one must bear in mind the sarcastic edge of Raabe's temperament, most acidly articulated in his social satire. That the Jews have it worse than all the other human types falling under his scourge no one could plausibly claim. There are several instances in which anti-Jewish feeling characterizes negative figures.[9]

As far as his personal life is concerned, Raabe's acquaintances and connections included a substantial number of Jews. In his diaries we find several Jewish names among his social relations in Wolfenbüttel and Stuttgart, in which latter place he met the half-Jewish

Marie Jensen, one of the dearest friends of his whole life, and the vastly expanding correspondence during his Braunschweig years contains exchanges with a number of Jewish people, from literary figures such as Gustav Karpeles and Karl Emil Franzos to a rabbi in Galicia.[10] With the most prominent German-Jewish writer of his time, Berthold Auerbach, he stood in the same politely distant relationship that he maintained with almost every contemporary writer; his only book review is a notice of an anthology edited by Auerbach.[11] Raabe has Eyring, the amiable eighteenth-century narrator of *Die Gänse von Bützow* (1866), reading the poems of the Jewish aphorist Ephraim Kuh (9/2: 69); this at least suggests an acquaintance with Auerbach's novel *Dichter und Kaufmann* (1840). There are other scattered references to Auerbach, for example, in *Deutscher Adel* (1878/79; 13: 211). Always grateful for recognition, Raabe wrote Auerbach a most cordial letter of thanks for his review of *Das Horn von Wanza* (1880).[12] The community of admirers that clustered around Raabe in his late years and became the core of the Raabe-Gesellschaft included people of Jewish origin;[13] I will have more to say about the most prominent of them farther along. There is not one shred of evidence that his associations with Jewish people differed in the slightest nuance from his habits of personal relations generally.

III.

In the light of all this, *Der Hungerpastor* (1863/64) comes to look like an anomaly in Raabe's career, an eccentricity that we might justifiably put to one side if it were not for the reception history, which made of this episode in his grueling search for his own voice and posture his most famous work, at home and abroad, one relatively youthful novel out of sixty-eight works of fiction that has shadowed his reputation to the present day. By the 1950s it had appeared in over sixty editions totalling well over a quarter of a million copies.[14] It is a double-plotted *Bildungsroman* paralleling the development of a model German youth, Hans Unwirrsch, to that of an exact Jewish contemporary, Moses Freudenstein. The poor shoemaker's son Hans, in his hunger for light and truth, passes through a series of discouraging and sobering social experiences, until he finds his vocation as a pastor in a bleak community of fishermen on the remote shores of the Baltic; Moses, in his hunger for power, status, and worldly goods, transforms himself into a Frenchified Catholic intellectual named Théophile Stein, ruining various women along the way. He eventually becomes a social success and a political agent of the oppressive German governments, but, in the narrator's judgment, "bürgerlich tot im furchtbarsten Sinne des Wortes." (6: 461)[15]

It would certainly seem that anyone familiar with mid-nineteenth-century German literature must be struck by the similarity in pattern of this novel to the great best-seller of those times, Gustav Freytag's *Soll und Haben* (1855). Strangely, this connection has been treated gingerly,[16] and though it seems to be accepted by now,[17] to my knowledge a thorough comparison has never been undertaken. The reason may be that, although Raabe met Freytag personally on his mini-grand tour in 1859, the two writers did not admire one another very much;[18] furthermore, a comparison may have seemed odious to Raabe admirers, for, whatever the failings of *Der Hungerpastor*, as a work of literature it is undoubtedly superior to *Soll und Haben*. But Freytag's novel, too, pairs the exactly contemporaneous careers of an innately good, if somewhat priggish and occasionally slow-witted bourgeois gentile and a crudely ambitious, unethical, and greedy Jewish boy. In both novels the career of the Jew keeps impinging on that of the gentile, creating nasty complications that require to be repelled and set right. In neither novel is there any pronounced sense of the Jews as a religious community; they are an ethnic foreign body in a German nation struggling for an elusive identity and cohesiveness. Both novels have very much the cast of ideological tracts in the interest of German nationalism and a liberal bourgeois ethos, although the tenets of classical liberalism are much more explicitly articulated by Freytag, whereas Raabe has a scene of a proletarian revolt that the protagonist observes sympathetically. Both novels understand the condition of the Jews to be historically and socially determined but nevertheless pass ethical judgments on them. Freytag was no more of an anti-Semite or racist than Raabe; he was a national and class partisan. But despite nuances in the texts sometimes adduced in defense of both, despite their authors' subsequent embarrassment and implicit disclaimers, the books took on lives of their own and nourished calamitous prejudices.

While this is not the place for a detailed comparison, some differences might be mentioned, apart from the considerable qualitative gap in style and thoughtfulness.[19] In the first place, Freytag was much more extensively concerned than Raabe with the Jews as a social problem. Apart from minor figures, there are six important Jewish characters in *Soll und Haben*, distributed along the ethical spectrum that is a horizontal axis of the novel: three negative ones – the antagonist Veitel Itzig, the oily financier Hirsch Ehrenthal, and the *gonif* tavern-keeper and fence Löbel Pinkus; and three, in a qualified way, positive ones – the ethically assimilated but physically feeble scholar Bernhard Ehrenthal, the comic and sleazy but ultimately Biblically righteous Orthodox peddler Schmeie Tinkeles, and a Jewish innkeeper who represents an outpost of *German* ethics in the even more degenerate environment of the Poles.[20] In *Der Hungerpastor*, Moses Freudenstein is the only important Jewish figure. Otherwise there are Moses's father, who hoped by avarice and labor to win strength and survival for his son, only to earn his son's contempt and to die of horror when he realizes what a monster he has sired, and the Jewish housemaid of the family, who abhors Moses as a renegade (both motifs are prefigured in *Soll und Haben*). In Raabe's overall scheme of things Moses is less a Jewish type than an example of the *canaille* that he found infesting mankind everywhere; there are parallels to his brutal cynicism in other, wholly gentile figures, such as the obnoxious swindler and loan shark Pinnemann in *Drei Federn* (1865), the corrupt Baron von Glimmern in *Abu Telfan* (1867), or the terrifyingly invincible Dietrich Häussler in *Der Schüdderump* (1869/70). It might be added that there is a non-Jewish parallel to the exotic, mistreated, ultimately vengeful racial outcast in the Wendish piper Kiza in *Die Hämelschen Kinder* (1863).[21]

On the other hand, however, Moses is a much more serious and impressive antagonist than Veitel Itzig. Freytag's Jew, though he has a disagreeable capacity for hard work and self-improvement, remains an unappetizing and inferior character throughout; he has no dialectical relationship to the protagonist Anton Wohlfart, who is never attracted to him, and he represents nothing in the realm of ideas. But,

Moses is a forceful and elegant personality, with a strong if egocentric imagination, quick in learning and in the acquisition of Epicurean taste and *savoir faire*, a juggler of Machiavellian and cynical ideas of some penetration. While Itzig's chief intellectual accomplishment is to learn standard German and commercial correspondence, Freudenstein becomes a scholar of Semitic languages and aspires to a professorship. Despite his conversion to Catholicism and change of name, Moses does not hide his Jewishness but employs it, for example, in his seduction of the excessively emancipated Kleophea Götz, when he stresses the heroism and stoicism of the Jewish people (6: 264-5; cf. 271). Hans, who has been his protector against anti-Semitic roughhousing in his boyhood (another motif prefigured in *Soll und Haben*), feels an unrequited friendly attachment to him and has some difficulty arriving at a true assessment of his character – an aspect of the novel rather poorly handled by Raabe. In fact it is Hans's envy of Moses's humanistic education and Latin studies that impels him to rebellion against his destiny as a shoemaker (6: 63). The figure of Moses has absorbed some of the dexterity and mental sharpness of Freytag's other parallel figure, the renegade aristocrat Fink, who despite his need for some instruction in bourgeois ethics, rather overshadows the boring Anton Wohlfart, even in the narrative voice, in attractiveness and ultimate competence. It has even been suggested that Moses's demonically nihilistic nature and his sarcastic vengefulness represent a fraction of Raabe's own spirit.[22] I find this hard to accept, for Raabe really goes to extremes in making him a villain, but his stature and role are certainly more imposing than Itzig's. Finally, Raabe disposes of him differently. Itzig, while being pursued by Anton, drowns, with more melodramatic than poetic justice, in the same place where he had drowned his mentor, the degenerate gentile Hippus. Raabe had originally planned to have Moses shipwrecked and washed up on the hunger pastor's shore, to die in his arms, but wisely thought the better of it and let him live on, "bürgerlich tot," perhaps, but nevertheless surviving as an image of the endurance of human evil in the world, which continues to balk the supersession of bourgeois values.

As in the case of Freytag, critics have from time to time attempted to mitigate the effect of this portrayal, for example, by pointing to the fact that Moses is a renegade Jew, not a representative one (the tack Raabe himself took in self-defense, as we shall see), or by citing the passages about the mistreatment of Jews, now fortunately in the past, and about Moses Mendelssohn's humiliations, passages clearly showing Raabe to have been a supporter of Jewish emancipation (6: 41, 47). But the case is not wholly persuasive. Repeatedly, Moses's characteristics are identified as "Semitic": his intellectual quickness, seen as sophistry and Talmudic quibbling (6: 130); his unchildlike nature, even as a boy; his tendency to materialism; his vengefulness; the cynicism with which he turns Catholic and becomes a government agent, thus in both ways an enemy of the liberal, Protestant, progressive, bourgeois German; his rootless cosmopolitanism. It is a curious fact, however, that all of this diction is on the authorial level of narration; good Hans never employs it, even when he is at last obliged to turn against Moses. In one odd passage, Hans finds himself on a train with some Eastern Jews in caftans, who, we are told, do not smell very agreeably, but Hans converses with them in Hebrew (6: 364).[23] This distinction might give pause to a subtle reader, aware of the complexities of Raabe's narrative technique; nevertheless, the overall effect comports too well with what Mark Gelber has defined as "literary anti-Semitism": "the potential or capacity of a text to encourage or positively evaluate anti-Semitic attitudes or behaviors."[24] Undoubtedly, at the center of the portrayal lies Raabe's nationalism, his deepest ideological commitment. Moses himself has an interesting speech in which he talks of the freedom of Jews, who are Germans only insofar as it pleases them, passengers on the ship of liberalism, cosmopolitan adherents of the idea rather than the nation (6: 130). But, as strong as the nationalistic affect was in Raabe, elsewhere in his works it does not commonly overrun his deep sympathy with the fragility and sorrowfulness of the human condition, which in fact he expresses, perhaps somewhat uneasily, in the motto to *Der Hungerpastor*, from Sophocles's *Antigone*, line 523: "Nicht mitzuhassen, mitzulieben bin ich da." (6: 5) How, then, did the literary anti-Semitism of *Der Hungerpastor* come into being?

The answer, I am certain, lies in Raabe's life-long dilemma of his relationship with the public. On the one hand, he was extremely ambitious for standing as a major writer, with a voice and a message that demanded to be heard in Germany, and, not incidentally, he was determined to make his living exclusively as a writer of fiction. On the other, he was insistent upon his own integrity, his own sense of excellence, his refusal to accommodate to the tastes, the complacencies, the horizons of expectation of the reading public. This dilemma runs through his whole life like a *Leitmotiv*, generating perpetual quarrels with publishers and editors, episodes of despair and sometimes of fury and *Publikumsbeschimpfung.*[25] *Der Hungerpastor* is impaled on one horn of the dilemma. As I imagine it, Raabe read *Soll und Haben* and observed its success, then said to himself quite rightly that if that was the sort of thing the public wanted, he could do it better.[26] As far as I can see, this is the only time in his whole long career that he drew inspiration from the immediate German literary environment, from which he normally kept aloof. The result shows that it was a compromising mistake, for, perhaps subliminally, he drew into the undertaking some of the prejudices of a public with which, in his deepest instincts, he was out of harmony. The dilemma continues in the ambivalence of his subsequent estimation of the novel. At times he appeared to repudiate it as immature along with almost all his earlier writing before he began to find his way to his own voice and form in the later 1860s; at other times, his longing for recognition made him more indulgent of a work that had contributed to his fame and saw thirty-five editions by the end of his life.[27] Walking a tightrope, he fell off into a trap, but that it was a trap was far from evident for a long time.

How enduring the dilemma remained appeared in an episode in 1903, when Raabe received a letter from a Jewish lady, Philippine Ullmann. She must have been quite elderly, for she begins with reminiscences of Raabe's family during his earliest childhood in Stadtoldendorf. Then she goes on to express her concern about the effect of *Der Hungerpastor*, asking whether in his long life he has never met a Jew with character.[28] In connection with this there emerges a set of curious parallels and coincidences. For the same thing had happened to Dickens forty years before: he received a letter from a Jewish lady, Eliza Davis, observing that the portrayal of Fagin in *Oliver Twist* "has encouraged a vile prejudice against the despised Hebrew," and rather pertly suggesting that he atone with a charitable donation.[29] The repetition is not without significance, for it is well known that Raabe owed much to Dickens, and in fact he reread *David Copperfield* while working on *Der Hungerpastor*; furthermore, it has long been established that *Soll und Haben* was structurally modeled on *David Copperfield.*[30] If, as I suppose, *Frau Salome* was meant to be some kind of compensation for *Der Hungerpastor*, this would constitute yet another parallel – to Dickens's creation of the kindly, upright Jew Mr. Riah in *Our Mutual Friend* as an antidote to Fagin in *Oliver Twist*. That the correspondence of Mrs. Davis and Dickens is virtually contemporaneous with the publication of *Der Hungerpastor* may be mentioned as a detail.

Dickens replied to Mrs. Davis that if the Jews feel wronged, "they are far less sensible, a far less just, and a far less good-tempered people than I have always supposed them to be." He defended himself on the grounds of realistic typology.[31] But his sense of justice must have been touched all the same, for he revised *Oliver Twist* to remove some of the direct references to Fagin's Jewishness.[32] Raabe, in his response, went even more on the offensive. He thanks Philippine Ullmann for her reminiscences of his boyhood milieu, but then his reply turns testy. He says it is the Jews' fault if they count the renegade Moses as one of their own, and adds that she seems to have an accidental acquaintance with his writings, calling her attention to *Frau Salome* and *Höxter und Corvey*. He denies that he is to be counted among anti-Semites and says that Jews have always been among his best friends and most appreciative readers.[33] Here Raabe's irritable obsession with his sense of having been neglected rises to the surface again. He quite evaded the question that had been put to him, but one wonders whether it was completely settled in his own mind. When a rabbi raised it with him in 1902, asking whether Moses was meant to be a representative figure and apparently pointing to the rise of political anti-Semitism and the agitation of the Prussian court preacher Adolf Stöcker, Raabe replied with one of the rudest letters of his life.[34] However, it is also true that Raabe made a spirited reply to a man who solicited an anti-Semitic novella from him in 1883. Here he rejects the anti-Semitic writings and illustrations sent to him, observing that he does not think they will do the Jews much harm and adding that Israel does no harm to the real German people.

He is not a partisan writer, and, if he wrote *Der Hungerpastor*, he also wrote *Frau Salome*. He ends by firmly rejecting the request.[35]

As is well known, Raabe's reputation was long in the hands of the *Gesellschaft der Freunde Wilhelm Raabes*, a society of admirers that grew out of the entourage that gathered around him in the latter part of his life. The Raabe-Gesellschaft has many achievements to its credit in preserving his memory, researching his life and works, and making his texts available in good editions. That it developed a narrow, proprietary vision of Raabe as a coterie writer of wisdom literature affirming conservative values and an intact world of the past, and maintained an anti-intellectual hostility to literary criticism and inquiry emanating from outside its ranks might be regarded indulgently by a later generation with more modern interests and values, if it were not for the notorious fact that the Raabe-Gesellschaft became completely Nazified.[36] The successors of the Raabe-Gesellschaft would have us believe that this was unavoidable; like all similar corporate entities in Nazi Germany, it was placed under the cultural institutions of the Third Reich and forced into conformity. But the record in the *Mitteilungen* of the Raabe-Gesellschaft does not bear this out. It reveals instead a spontaneous and servile collaboration. In the third issue of 1933, the most intelligent and deeply learned of the Raabe scholars of the older generation, Wilhelm Fehse, published, of all things, a *sonnet* to Adolf Hitler.[37] In 1939, to support Germany's aggression against Czechoslovakia, he contributed another poem denouncing the Czechs – and Woodrow Wilson.[38] And there was worse.

In 1932, after what seems to have been some sort of internal crisis, a sixty-six-year-old schoolteacher named Franz Hahne became president of the Raabe-Gesellschaft. Hahne was a Nazi and a raging anti-Semite. He could hardly discuss any subject without connecting it to a denunciation of the Jews; he regarded himself as an expert on race theory[39] and prided himself on having been one of those who introduced the ideas of Gobineau into Germany.[40] In his younger days Hahne had met Raabe, who assured him that he was in no way anti-Semitic, but Hahne would not believe him.[41] Instead, he asked himself why Raabe had never "attacked the Jews" after *Der Hungerpastor* and guessed that the reason might have been Raabe's fear of

Jewish power.[42] For Hitler's fiftieth birthday in 1939, Hahne arranged to have a Hitler Youth prepare a calligraphic manuscript of Raabe's novella *Des Reiches Krone* (1870) as a gift,[43] and upon Hitler's escape from the assassination attempt in the Bürgerbräukeller, Hahne sent congratulations on behalf of the Raabe-Gesellschaft.[44] The *Mitteilungen* carried an essay entitled "Raabe und Hitler."[45] One might imagine this ludicrous concept to have been a parody composed by some Tucholskyan saboteur, but no: it is the work of yet another of those egregious schoolteachers, who, we are told, joined the Nazi movement "mit fliegenden Fahnen."[46] Throughout the war Hahne's contributions to the *Mitteilungen* reflected the Nazi government line, become, naturally, more and more estranged from reality. In the last issue in 1944, before the encroaching catastrophe made it impossible to publish anymore and the bombing of Hahne's home obliged him to retire from the presidency, he inserted a bitter denunciation of the United States as a land devoid of culture, tradition, history, liberty, or German lawfulness, ruled by Mammon and misgoverned by a warmongering Roosevelt in thrall to evil Jewish advisers.[47]

Needless to say, the Jewish members of the Raabe community had no role to play in this phase. Most striking is the case of Heinrich Spiero, a modestly talented but productive literary historian who met Raabe during the seventieth-birthday celebration in 1901 and subsequently devoted a quarter-century of service to the cause. He became vice-president of the Raabe-Gesellschaft and was for many years president of the Berlin chapter. Among more than forty publications, he wrote the first general biography of Raabe,[48] composed a lexicon of Raabe's cultural allusions,[49] and edited an elaborate Festschrift for the hundredth anniversary of Raabe's birth in 1931.[50] Spiero was completely assimilated – loyal, patriotic, and conservative. In his memoirs, published in 1929, he does not refer to his Jewish origins with a single word, presenting himself as an active liberal Protestant; after World War I he was a member of a committee that tried without success to devise a progressive constitution for the Protestant Church.[51] No matter; he was unceremoniously forced out when the Raabe-Gesellschaft was "Aryanized."[52] In 1937 Fehse gave him a little kick when he was down by writing dismissively of his pioneering biography.[53] As far as I can see, only one Raabe enthusiast was sufficiently offended to make a gesture: Constantin Bauer, who resigned the editorship of the *Mitteilungen.*[54] His name will crop up again a little farther along.

After World War II, the shattered Raabe-Gesellschaft found its first priority to be the restoration of continuity rather than reflection on its years of treachery to Raabe's spirit. The Braunschweig professor Ernst-August Roloff, who, under the "Führerprinzip," had been appointed, not elected, as president after Hahne's retirement, understandably found himself in the position of picking up the pieces. His achievement of re-organizing the remnants and convincing the occupation authorities to permit the society to be registered deserves acknowledgment. But, in the process, the Raabe-Gesellschaft fell into a state of near amnesia. The impossible Franz Hahne was installed on the shelf as "honorary president."[55] Among the retrospective obituaries in the post-war *Mitteilungen* there is one of Spiero, who died in Berlin in 1947;[56] it remarks that he was working on a new edition of his biography to the end, but wastes no words on an ejection that must have been traumatic for him. Instead of an explicit stock-taking, there was an oblique gesture of *Wiedergutmachung*: one of the stalwarts of the Raabe-Gesellschaft took up a previously tabu subject, the influence of Heine on Raabe.[57] The first, very brief reference to the evils of the Nazi period was contributed by a member in *New York*;[58] then Roloff's son devised a rather euphemistic account of those years, making it appear that the Raabe-Gesellschaft was helplessly under duress, mentioning Spiero's expulsion along with Bauer's departure "ohne äußere Nötigung," praising Hahne for the resourcefulness of his leadership, and even suggesting a resistance legend.[59] Finally, in 1956, the admirable Bauer cited some of the Nazi passages in the *Mitteilungen* and observed that this past history was a burden for Raabe's reputation in foreign countries.[60] The amnesia itself is un-Raabean; to be sure, "die arme gequälte Menschheit vergißt gottlob leicht und schnell," he wrote in *Der Marsch nach Hause* (1869/70; 9/2: 257), but his own writing, especially in his historical fiction, works against the forgetting of human suffering and brutality.

Many people will of course be inclined to say that this failure of responsibility and contrition was characteristic of the whole atmosphere of West Germany after World War II, and indeed that the evolution of the Raabe-Gesellschaft was wholly congruent with the evolution of the German bourgeoisie to fascism. That may be, but it would be unfair and unreasonable to put the burden on Raabe himself. To have associated him, with his tolerant, sympathetic, and pacific nature, his hatred of despotism and brutality, his subtle moral sensitivities, even remotely with the band of gangsters, lunatics, petty tyrants, and homicidal maniacs who made up the bulk of the Nazi leadership was not only reprehensible but bizarre. One would have thought it self-evident that Raabe himself would not have touched the Nazi phenomenon with a ten-meter pole. The members of the Raabe-Gesellschaft, whose only appropriate course under the circumstances would have been to dissolve, therefore forfeited their claim to be so-called *Raabemenschen*, successors to his spirit. And yet the matter is not entirely that simple; for a particular reason that no one in the modern phase of Raabe scholarship has thought worthy of attention, he is linked to the subsequent development.

V.

When Raabe replied to the Jewish lady who raised the questions about *Der Hungerpastor* that, like our Lord God, he let his light shine upon the just and the unjust,[61] he was not turning a phrase. For not only were there numerous Jews in his circle of acquaintance; there were also numerous anti-Semites. It will be remembered that the Raabe-Gesellschaft grew out of that circle of acquaintance, the clubby atmosphere of his entourage in Braunschweig. It therefore had some reasonable claim to succession and its members to special privileges as initiates. Both Fehse and Hahne, along with others who participated in the Nazified phase, had been in his circle. The author of the essay on Raabe and Hitler is found among his correspondents in 1908. One surprising character encountered here is Adolf Bartels, the popular, hysterically anti-Semitic literary historian who devoted some two dozen publications to a campaign to destroy Heine's reputation; this is a bit odd, since Raabe's admiration of Heine is now well-established.[62] Perhaps one might mention here also Raabe's encouragement of Gustav Frenssen and his novel *Jörn Uhl*;[63] while the latter is not an uninteresting work, and especially in its dénouement does not wholly deserve the opprobrium of *Blut-und-Boden-Literatur* into which it seems to have fallen, Frenssen did evolve into a Nazi supporter of a particularly fatuous kind, judging from his memoirs.[64] The circumstance is striking because Raabe was normally very chary of interest in and critical approval of the work of his German literary contemporaries, having, for example, strenuously evaded any critical approbation of the most ancient and enduring of his friends, Wilhelm Jensen.

In the writings of Raabe's closest personal friend of his old age and the real founder of the Raabe-Gesellschaft, the schoolmaster, Latinist, and occasional poet Wilhelm Brandes, I do not find much of an anti-Semitic nature, but there is one passage that shows how the conservative ideological attitude of that class of men in those times became second nature: while attempting to distinguish Raabe's humor from the liberal succession to Jean Paul, Brandes remarks on "dem jüdischen Flügel des jungen Deutschlands."[65] What can this possibly mean? None of the Young Germans was Jewish. Brandes mentions Saphir and Glassbrenner, but Saphir had nothing to do with Young Germany, and Glassbrenner, who in any case was not Jewish, can, in my opinion, at best be seen as located on the periphery of the movement. It is a defamatory transference of the Young Germans' model figures, Heine and Börne, and a continuation of the strategy of Wolfgang Menzel in the 1830s of denouncing Young Germany as "Young Palestine." This, too, strikes me as unfaithful to Raabe's origins and foundations. For, apart from his demonstrably positive relationship to Heine and hints that he was also an admirer of Börne, with the sarcastic and bitter tone of the innumerable political observations in his works he seems to me to preserve more of the Young German spirit than any other post-mid-century writer I know.

If the keepers of Raabe's reputation were guilty of a breach of faith, Raabe was not without complicity in it, insofar as he welcomed such people into his fold. But I do not think this indicates a change in Raabe, an accommodation on his part to the Wilhelminian ideological atmosphere. His ideological commitments and social views were formed early in life and thereafter changed some in form and perspective, but not very much in substance to the end of his days. Furthermore, we do not know what Raabe, in his innermost heart, thought of any of these people. His extraordinary gregariousness and sometimes rather brittle politeness were accompanied by an extraordinary reticence in his personal relations, which were easy-going, passive, and noncommittal to a degree that suggests uncommon introversion amidst an outward appearance of uncommon conviviality. It is important to remember that many of his associates were successful men of affairs, less "provincial" than they are often made out to be, but such people hardly ever appear as characters in his fiction, and when they do, rarely as positive ones.

The answer must lie again in Raabe's need for an audience. He made his light to shine upon the just and the unjust, as long as the just and the unjust were his readers and adherents. I think he knew perfectly well that this is what he was doing, and that it accounts for the combination of tolerant conviviality and mild aloofness in his relations with his friends. This would explain Bartels, for example, who wrote positively of Raabe during the revival of which the high point was the birthday celebration of 1901.[66] Raabe obtained and himself nurtured a reputation as an inner-directed individualist, indifferent to literary and intellectual fashions, sternly insistent on going his own way regardless of public and publishers. This is almost exactly half-true. The other half of the truth is that he was deeply ambitious of audience and influence, and he suffered protracted episodes of angry despair when he found himself isolated and neglected; thus he was profoundly grateful for response and discipleship. This is perfectly understandable; writers who are absolutely indifferent to readers are more common in legend, sometimes of their own making, than in reality. But he not only sought popularity; he also feared it, and in this he was right also. Like many major authors, Raabe was both of his time and out of phase with it, as the critical renaissance of recent years amply proves. His desire for a public created dangers that I believe he sensed but did not fully grasp. As he did not see the extent to which he had trapped himself in his one imitative excursion into the commonplace with *Der Hungerpastor*, so he was in no position to see the risk of imprisoning his reputation by encouraging a band of disciples who were not content to admire and enjoy, but who enhanced their own self-regard as a chosen people, *Raabemenschen*, while grafting their more petty vision and their parochial preoccupations onto his supple, subtle, and, above all, questioning art. The damage has been very great, for Raabe's community of "friends," for all its indubitable achievements, nevertheless, by its own ultimately unatoned ideological, ethical, and human failures, its own perpetually unacknowledged involvement in the sequence of events that made Raabe's beloved Germany the most hated nation on the face of the earth, has obscured from the canon of world literature one of the truly outstanding nineteenth-century novelists. It has been the painful task of modern criticism to rescue Raabe from his reception – a struggle on two fronts, against his "friends," although this confrontation has been easing, decade by decade, into convergence, and against those many serious and estimable minds that have come to be wholly disposed against him. It is only just and realistic to recognize, however, that Raabe cannot be separated or isolated from the first phases of his twentieth-century reception, that his involvement in it was rooted in his own ambivalent but intense manner of coping with the threatening isolation and homelessness of the nineteenth-century bourgeois artist.

Notes

The following abbreviations are used:

BA = Wilhelm Raabe, *Sämtliche Werke*, Ed. Karl Hoppe et al. Göttingen: Vandenhoeck & Ruprecht, 1960 –.

Mitt. = *Mitteilungen für die Gesellschaft der Freunde Wilhelm Raabes*; after World War II, *Mitteilungen der Raabe-Gesellschaft.*

RJ = *Jahrbuch der Raabe-Gesellschaft.*

Diary = Wilhelm Raabe's unpublished diary, 1857-1910; transcript in the Braunschweig Municipal Archive. I should like to take the opportunity to thank the officials of the Archive for permission to use the diary and for all their helpful assistance to me.

[1] Gordon A. Craig, *The Germans* (New York: Putnam, 1982), p. 139. This, to my mind, rather overpraised book is especially disappointing when it turns to literary matters. However, the view of Raabe is of long duration. Ernest K. Bramstedt, in his useful book, *Aristocracy and the Middle-Classes in Germany: Social Types in German Literature 1830-1900*, rev. ed. (Chicago: University of Chicago Press, 1964), p. 148, n. 1, refers to arguments against *Der Hungerpastor* as an anti-Semitic book as "whitewashing." A more balanced view is given by Pierre Angel, *Le Personnage juif dans le roman allemand (1855-1915): La racine littéraire de l'antisémitisme Outre-Rhin* (Montreal, Paris, and Brussels: Didier, 1973), pp. 22-34, 182-87.

[2] The first detailed argument of the case appeared in a Jewish periodical: Josef Bass, "Die Juden bei Wilhelm Raabe," *Monatsschrift für Geschichte und Wissenschaft der Juden*, 54 (1910): 641-88. The most recent contribution of note in this area is: Dieter Arendt, " 'Nun auf die Juden!' Figurationen des Judentums im Werk Wilhelm Raabes," *Tribüne*, 19, No. 74 (1980), 180-40.

[3] Raabe visited the cemetery in 1859 and his diary (May 18, 1859) shows his particular interest in Rabbi Löw's grave.

[4] Josef Kunz, "Wilhelm Raabe, 'Die Holunderblüte.' Versuch einer Interpretation," *RJ (1973)*, pp. 72-86.

[5] Raabe made this connection in his first novel, *Die Chronik der Sperlingsgasse* (*BA* 1: 167), where he quoted Psalms 137: 5: "Vergesse ich dein, Jerusalem, so werde meiner Rechten vergessen," remarking that this sentiment kept the pieces of a people together through the millenia, and adding: "Vergesse ich dein, Deutschland, großes Vaterland: so werde meiner Rechten vergessen."

[6] See Adolf Suchel, "Literarische Einflüsse auf Raabes Novelle 'Frau Salome,' " *Mitt.*, 35 (1948): 7-19, and, more persuasively, Katherine Starr Kaiser, "Structure and Narrative Technique in Wilhelm Raabe's *Krähenfelder Geschichten*" (Diss., Brown University, 1974), p. 60.

[7] All references in parentheses in the text are to volume and page number of *BA*.

[8] A parallel between Haeseler's early life and that of Heine has been suggested by Gerald Opie, "Raabe and the Classical Tradition: Some Reflections on *Der Dräumling*," in *Wilhelm Raabe: Studien zu seinem Leben und Werk* (Eds., Leo A. Lensing and Hans-Werner Peter), (Braunschweig: pp-Verlag, 1981), p. 137.

[9] E.g., *Die Kinder von Finkerode, BA* 2:69; *Der heilige Born*, Chapter 21 and especially *BA* 3:320-23; *Der Schüdderump, BA* 8: 84.

[10] His name was Crohn: Diary, Sept. 7, 1906; April 9, 1908; Sept. 27, 1908.

[11] Review of *Deutscher Volkskalender auf das Jahr 1859*, Ed. Auerbach, Wilhelm Raabe, *Sämtliche Werke* (Berlin-Grunewald: Klemm, 1913-16), Series III, Vol. 6: 519.

[12] Raabe to Auerbach, April 22, 1881, *BA* Supplement 2: 221-2.

[13] Among them seems to have been Bass (see n. 2 above). In a monograph of the Nazi period, Günther Vogelsang, *Das Ich als Schicksal und Aufgabe in den Dichtungen Raabes* (Braunschweig: Appelhans, 1942), pp. 207, 209, Bass is

identified as a Jew. A Viennese, Bass appears to have been totally assimilated, judging from his contributions, e.g., "Welsche und deutsche Liebe bei Raabe," *Mitt.*, 19 (1929): 19-36.

14 *BA* 6: 493.

15 This political turn, as an agent of the repressive governments, is the main reason why Moses is not to be identified with Heine, despite Moses's own attempts to so identify himself. There is some reason to suppose that Raabe was thinking of Joel Jacoby, who, during the *Vormärz*, became a police spy and government agent. Raabe's amalgamation of his reprehensible Jew with repressive authority rather than with rebellious opposition, as was common on the right then and later, is a significant symptom of his political location.

16 Walter Silz, "Freytag's *Soll und Haben* and Raabe's *Der Hungerpastor*," *Modern Language Notes*, 39 (1924): 10-18.

17 Originally, Hermann Pongs in *Wilhelm Raabe: Leben und Werk* (Heidelberg: Quelle & Meyer, 1958), p. 215, tried to weaken the connection, but seems to have come to accept it when editing the critical edition (*BA* 6: 469). The connection is stressed by Friedrich Sengle, "*Der Hungerpastor* (1863/64): Zum Problem der frühen Biedermeiertradition," *Wilhelm Raabe* (Eds., Lensing and Peter), pp. 84-87.

18 As part of his pattern of resentment in these matters, Raabe claimed that Freytag had excluded any mention of him from his influential journal *Die Grenzboten*; see Raabe to Karl Geiger, June 29, 1909, *BA*, Supplement 2: 490. The somewhat fluffy Käthchen Nebelung in *Eulenpfingsten* (1874) reads only contemporary literature, such as Gutzkow's *Ritter vom Geiste*, Auerbach's *Dorfgeschichten*, and *Soll und Haben* (*BA* 11:384). In a notebook entry Raabe remarked that some books one reads with the heart, like Goethe's *Dichtung und Wahrheit*, others lying on the sofa, like *Soll und Haben* (*BA* 11: 517).

19 Sharp contrasts, in connection with the *Bildungsroman* tradition, are drawn by Gerhart Meyer, "Wilhelm Raabe und die Tradition des Bildungsromans," *RJ (1980)*, p. 105

20 See my discussion of these matters in "The Evaluation of Freytag's 'Soll und Haben,' " *German Life & Letters*, N.S. 22 (1968/69), 315-23.

21 This was first suggested by Bass, "Die Juden bei Wilhelm Raabe," pp. 658-59.

22 Marketa Goetz-Stankiewicz, "Die böse Maske Moses Freudensteins. Gedanken zum Hungerpastor," *RJ (1969)*, pp. 7-32. It has also been argued that Moses is a Mephistopheles-figure having nothing to do with anti-Semitism: Rudolf Mohr, " 'Der Hungerpastor' – Ein Pfarrerroman?" *RJ (1977)*, p. 62. Cf. also Sengle, *"Der Hungerpastor,"* p. 87, who follows Goetz-Stankiewicz.

23 This scene is implausible for two reasons. For one thing, it seems unlikely that the modestly enthusiastic theology student Hans (who was tutored in Hebrew by Moses) could have learned enough Hebrew to converse in the language; for another, Orthodox Eastern Jews of the time would have regarded Hebrew as a holy tongue restricted to liturgical purposes and would have con-

versed only in Yiddish. There is a somewhat unpleasant coda to the scene: on Hans's return train journey on Christmas Eve, he encounters no unpleasant Jews, who, the narrator suggests, do not seem to travel in the cold (*BA* 6: 418).

[24] Mark Howard Gelber, "Aspects of Literary Anti-Semitism: Charles Dickens' *Oliver Twist* and Gustav Freytag's *Soll und Haben* (Diss., Yale University, 1980), p. 19. Sengle, "*Der Hungerpastor*," p. 86, also speaks of "literarischer Antisemitismus."

[25] The best account of this subject is in an unpublished dissertation, Karl Heim, "Wilhelm Raabe und das Publikum" (Diss., Tübingen, 1953). Heim summarized his findings in "Wilhelm Raabe und das Publikum," *Mitt.*, 42 (1955); 1-12.

[26] Raabe, to be sure, nowhere admits to a dependence on *Soll und Haben*. But in the text of *Der Hungerpastor* there is an obscure joke: one of the odd fellows in the *Stammtisch* fellowship of the *Neuntöter* distinguishes himself by buttoning his coat on the left one day and on the right the other, a habit he refers to as his "Debet" and "Kredit" (*BA* 6: 208). I strongly suspect a buried verbal allusion here.

[27] *BA* 6: 491-3.

[28] Philippine Ullmann's letter was first published by G. Rülf, "Ein Nachtrag zu 'Wilhelm Raabe und die Juden,' " *Monatsschrift für Geschichte und Wissenschaft der Juden*, 55 (1911), 247-51. This is a supplement to Bass's article (see above, n. 2).

[29] Eliza Davis to Charles Dickens, June 22, 1863, *Anglo-Jewish Letters* (Ed. Cecil Roth), (London: Soncino, 1938), pp. 303-4.

[30] Roland Freymond, *Der Einfluß von Charles Dickens auf Gustav Freytag* (Prague: Bellmann, 1912).

[31] Dickens to Eliza Davis, July 10, 1863, *Anglo-Jewish Letters*, p. 306.

[32] Gelber, "Aspects of Literary Anti-Semitism," pp. 78-79, is not persuaded that the revisions did much to relieve the anti-Semitic potential of *Oliver Twist.*

[33] Raabe to Philippine Ullmann, Feb. 4, 1903, *BA* Supplement 2: 445.

[34] Raabe to S. Bachenheimer, Feb. 24, 1902, *BA* Supplement 2: 437-8. Here Raabe refers to the Jews as "Ihre[] Stammes- und Unsere[] Gast-Genossen," which suggests that even then he was far from accepting "Deutsche Staatsbürger jüdischen Glaubens."

[35] Raabe to M. Schulze, Nov. 21, 1883, *BA* Supplement 2: 242-3.

[36] A strictly non-indulgent analysis of this development is given by Eugen Rüter, *Die Gesellschaft der Freunde Wilhelm Raabes: Rezeptionssteuerung als Programm* (Darmstadt: Thesen Verlag, 1977). See also M. Töteberg and J. Zander, "Die Rezeption Raabes durch die 'Gesellschaft der Freunde Wilhelm Raabes,' " *RJ (1973)*, pp. 178-93, and Leo A. Lensing, "Reading Raabe: The Example of Kurt Tucholsky," *Seminar*, 19 (1983), 122-35. For an example of a defense of the Raabe-Gesellschaft as an innocent victim ot the times, see Fritz Meyen's rejoinder, "Einige Bemerkungen zu Töteberg / Zander...," *RJ (1974)*, pp. 105-10. The editorship of the *RJ* found itself obliged to defend the critical position of Töteberg / Zander (*ibid.*, p. 111).

[37] *Mitt.*, 23 (1933): 66. Fehse, as far back as 1924, had argued that Frau Salome is not a representative Jewish figure but had passed out of the "Schicksalsring ihres Rassentums" (*Mitt.*, 14 [1924]: 55). Fehse is the only one of Raabe's "friends" of that epoch to have suffered for his conduct; he died in a Russian internment camp in 1946 (*Mitt.*, 42 [1955]: 21). I have heard that he starved to death. A eulogy of Fehse by a member of the successor generation, Hans Oppermann, not mentioning such things as the sonnet to Hitler, appeared in *Mitt.*, 44 (1957): 66-72.

[38] *Mitt.*, 29 (1939): 1-3.

[39] See *Mitt.*, 25 (1935): 133.

[40] *Mitt.*, 31 (1941): 31. Ludwig Schemann, the translator, biographer, and explicator of Gobineau, was one of Raabe's correspondents (diary, July 11, July 12, 1902; March 11, 1905; May 7, 1907). When he sent Raabe some of his studies, Raabe replied most cordially, remarking that his attention had first been drawn to Gobineau by Schopenhauer (Raabe to Schemann, July 31, 1902, *BA* Supplement 2: 440). Schemann, in *Gobineau: eine Biographie* (Strassburg: Trübner, 1913-16), I: 495, praises his "friend" Hahne for his translations of Gobineau's travel novellas, and in *Gobineaus Rassenwerk: Aktenstücke und Betrachtungen zur Geschichte und Kritik des Essai sur l'inégalité des races humaines* (Stuttgart: Fromann, 1910), p. 174, Schemann cites Hahne as one of the schoolteachers who found Gobineau's race theories pedagogically valuable.

[41] Franz Hahne, "Raabes Stellung im Dritten Reich," *Mitt.*, 23 (1933): 102-3. The whole situation shows that a man like Hahne firmly believed that an ethically admirable position *must* be anti-Semitic.

[42] *Ibid.* In 1939, Hahne found it necessary to defend Raabe against a Nazi attack on him as pro-Jewish: *Mitt.*, 29 (1939): 68-75.

[43] *Mitt.*, 29 (1939), No. 2. It is my guess that Hitler cared about as much for the devotions of the Raabe-Gesellschaft as he did for the man in the moon. He returned a two-line telegram of thanks that has every appearance of having been composed by a member of his staff. The *Mitteilungen* proudly printed it (*ibid.*).

[44] *Mitt.*, 30 (1940): 1.

[45] By Johannes Iltz, *Mitt.*, 24 (1934): 8-17.

[46] *Mitt.*, 30 (1940): 70-73.

[47] Franz Hahne, "Die andre Welt: Eine raabische Betrachtung," *Mitt.*, 34 (1944): 1-15.

[48] Heinrich Spiero, *Raabe: Leben – Werk – Wirkung* (Darmstadt: Hofmann, 1924).

[49] Heinrich Spiero, *Raabe-Lexikon* (Berlin-Grunewald: Klemm, [1927]).

[50] *Wilhelm Raabe und sein Lebenskreis* (Ed. Heinrich Spiero), (Berlin-Grunewald: Klemm, 1931).

[51] Heinrich Spiero, *Schicksal und Anteil: Ein Lebensweg in deutscher Wendezeit* (Berlin: Volksverband der Bücherfreunde, 1929). The assimilation obviously hid nothing; although this book has practically nothing to do with Jews, the copy in the Yale University Library bears the stamp of the "Bibliothek zur Erforschung der Judenfrage, Frankfurt/M."

52 *Mitt.*, 23 (1933): 120; cf. 24 (1934): 61.

53 Wilhelm Fehse, "Dasein und Leben," *Mitt.*, 27 (1937): 2.

54 *Mitt.*, 23 (1933): 66.

55 *Mitt.*, 35 (1948): 37. Hahne contributed one post-war item, "Zu Raabes 'Prinzessin Fisch,' " *Mitt.*, 36 (1949): 72-77. His previously obtrusive anti-Semitism is now nowhere in sight.

56 *Mitt.*, 35 (1948): 36.

57 Suchel (see n. 6 above). One oddity occurs in the retrospective chapter reports: the one for Dessau relates that the chapter had sponsored a talk in 1943 on American propaganda by Colin Ross, absurd imaginer of a Nazi United States in his notorious book, *Unser Amerika*, and that in December, 1947 the chapter had celebrated Heine's 150th birthday (*Mitt.*, 36 [1949]: 38-40). This impressive change of attitude is very likely owing to the circumstance that Dessau was in the Soviet Zone, but even more impressive is the impassive cold-bloodedness with which it is reported.

58 Walter Buchholz, "Ein Nachwort zu Wilhelm Raabes 'Stopfkuchen,' " *Mitt.*, 38, No. 1 (1951): 6-11.

59 E. A. Roloff d. J., "Aus der Chronik der Raabe-Gesellschaft," *Mitt.*, 38, No. 2 (1951): 8-14.

60 *Mitt.*, 43 (1956): 10.

61 *BA* Supplement 2: 445. The phrase is an abridgment of Matthew 5:45; Raabe employs variants of it in several other places.

62 Dieter Arendt, "Die Heine-Rezeption im Werk Wilhelm Raabes," *Heine-Jahrbuch (1980)*, pp. 188-221.

63 See, apart from Raabe's correspondence with Frenssen, Raabe to Siegmund Schott, July 22, 1902, *BA* Supplement 2: 439.

64 Gustav Frenssen, *Lebensbericht* (Berlin: Grote, 1941).

65 Wilhelm Brandes, *Wilhelm Raabe: Sieben Kapitel zum Verständnis und zur Würdigung des Dichters*, 2nd ed. (Wolfenbüttel and Berlin: Julius Zwissler, Otto Janke, 1906), p. 89. Note that this book, first published in 1901, appeared during Raabe's lifetime and, so to speak, under his eyes.

66 See the praise of Bartels on his eightieth birthday on these grounds, by the subsequent post-war president of the Raabe-Gesellschaft, Ernst-August Roloff, *Mitt.*, 33 (1943): 31-33.

Franz Rosenzweig in Perspective: Reflections on his Last Diaries

Stéphane Moses

In the complete edition of Franz Rosenzweig's writings, which is being published at The Hague, there is in the second volume of the *Letters and Diaries* an unedited text of extreme importance. It is a diary, his last, written between March 23 and September 13, 1922.

Rosenzweig had kept a diary between 1905 and 1918. His decision to resume it in 1922 was possibly prompted by the discovery, six weeks previously, that he was afflicted with an incurable disease.[1] According to the testimony of his physician, Dr. Koch, Rosenzweig expected a "quick and almost solemn" death.[2] The notes jotted down between March and September 1922, a sequence of feverish, breathless reflections, of flashing and paradoxical intuitions, are those of a man who feels that his time is running out, and who is desperately trying, before it is too late, to review his thoughts, to reassess their essential themes, and to pursue to their ultimate conclusions the ideas that had always obsessed him.

These reflections are also connected with a lecture course Rosenzweig had planned to give during the third trimester of that same year at the Freies Jüdisches Lehrhaus, which he had founded in 1920 in Frankfurt.[3] In this course, which was to be entitled "The Science of the World" ("Die Wissenschaft von der Welt"), he wanted to apply the theological categories of *The Star of Redemption* and, in particular, the category of creation, to the analysis of the problems posed by the modern world. Chief among them for Rosenzweig was the question of *power* in the modern world – political power, ideological power, and technological power.

These last reflections gain their particular inflection precisely from his wish to apply the principal categories of *The Star* to the reality of the modern world. In them he expressed something of his need to reinterpret his own thoughts in the light of experience – to confirm them, give them different nuances, or even refute them. In contrast to the systemactic structure of *The Star*, in which the philosophical discourse is carried on by a dialectic of extreme rigor, here his thought bursts forth in discrete, unlinked fragments; it proceeds by way of intuitions, aphorisms, and paradoxes, revealing the tensions at work in it.

A critical review of the system of *The Star*, confronting it with questions posed by the modern world, give these last diary pages both a retrospective and anticipatory cast. To the extent that Rosenzweig submits his thought to the scrutiny of new questions, these reflections can be considered an attempt to place his thought in historical perspective. Though not identical with a contemporary perspective fifty years after the catastrophic collapse of the cultural world to which Rosenzweig wanted to bear witness – that of the "Jewish-German symbiosis" – the viewpoint emerging from these last diary notes, the avenues they open up, and the problems they illuminate are nevertheless so close to us that we can use them as a point of departure for a retrospective glance at Rosenzweig's thought. To assess the possible relevance of these notes and reflections for today's reader, I shall consider three themes of great importance for Rosenzweig: first, the conception of revelation as anti-religion, and, in this context, the reference to Freud's theses on the origin of religion; second, Rosenzweig's temptation by "quietism" and, in the same context, his hesitations about history, messianism, and Zionism; and, finally, the meaning in the modern world of the concept of Creation.

II

The notes on dialectic nature and revelation, which culminate in the definition of revelations as "anti-religion,"[4] were put down in the short period from March 26 to April 4, 1922. They pertain to a long letter to Rudolf Hallo, the last paragraphs of which are devoted to this very topic. It seems that these reflections may have been inspired by a passage in a letter from Rudolf Hallo, received in January, 1922, in which he wrote: "Behind Judaism, for me, a millenium, many millenia of pre-Jewish culture are burning more and more brightly. How the aspect changes!"[5]

The problem Rudolf Hallo raises here is that of the *method* to be used for understanding Judaism. He opposes Rosenzweig's religious approach in *The Star* with the historical method which sees in monotheism a stage in the evolution of the cultures of the Near East. Confronted with this methodological problem with which *The Star*, being a work of purely philosophical and theological inspiration, does not deal at all, Rosenzweig reacts, in his reply to Hallo and in his diary notes not by denying the validity of scientific methods for the study of cultures and religions, but by proclaiming that Judaism is neither a culture nor a religion. He adds: "Revelation has only this function: to make the world unreligious again."[6] Seemingly paradoxical, this statement in fact relates to the classical thesis of Jewish theology, according to which the biblical revelation is distinguished from all pagan religions not by any of its specific features but by its very essence; just as the unique God who created the world and who revealed himself on Mount Sinai is of a radically different nature from the false gods of paganism. According to Rosenzweig, all human experiences are necessarily profane, not divine; what is derived from experience is by definition immanent in the world and cannot pretend to any divine status. The cultures and the religions which are the products of the human mind are radically opposed to the biblical revelation which teaches the absolute transcendence of God the creator. Paradoxically, the world of creation would then have to be understood as a purely profane reality, and creation would be identified with nature. On March 26, Rosenzweig writes: "Revelation renews the creation, that is to say, it reestablishes the norm, the natural."[7] In the dialectic of culture and nature, culture (i.e. religion) denies nature, and revelation denies religion, thus reestablishing the world in its original state: "Everywhere created nature has been turned into culture. Revelation has again made nature manifest (*offenbar*)."[8]

This schema is totally different from that proposed in *The Star*, which was as follows: originally, the pagan world was an enchanted world; then science came and disenchanted the world, and finally, man, by spreading revelation among the world, undertakes to make it sacred again.[9] The three stages of this dialectical schema (which is very near to Schiller, Hölderlin, and the German Romantics) appear now to be moved forward by one notch: the holy pagan is no longer the original stage of human history; the norm, the primal stage, is that of the world created as pure nature prior to any religious culture. Then comes religion, which obscures and overshadows this immediate connection with nature; the role of revelation would thus not be to sacralize the world, but on the contrary to de-sacralize it again.

It is this schema which Rosenzweig develops in a diary entry dated April 4, 1922:

> As long as man does *not* know *anything at all* of God, as long as he simply accepts each of his revelations as they occur to him, he is not a pagan. Only with *theology* does paganism actually start, namely, when man begins to make his experiences. Now he prays *to* the angels which God has sent him. Adventavit religio! Only one thing can help now: that God reveals *himself* (not *something* to man), thereby giving man an aim for all projections and substantiations, thus making all "religion" impossible for him.[10]

The primitive state, that which "religion" overshadowed, was that of an immediately significant world. This immediate significance is indeed of a divine nature precisely to the extent that it precedes every culture, every religion, every human institution.

This is the old mystic idea of a *natural revelation*, of an original stage in which mankind, before it had been corrupted by the fall in reflection and in culture, would have directly perceived nature as a manifestation of God. Then the biblical revelation would have the function of delivering the world of the religions which, like an opaque screen, comes between God and nature, and of restoring nature to its original significance. This schema, which Rosenzweig counterposes to the reductionist approach suggested by Rudolf Hallo, is intended to distinguish the monotheistic revelation from all other religious cultures, while nevertheless placing it into the context of the religious history of mankind. Rosenzweig had used this same method in *The Star* to define the non-historical vocation of the Jewish people in opposition to the essentially political reality of the gentiles. As in *The Star*, where Hegel's political philosophy served him as a frame of reference against which he expounded his theory of the non-temporal destination of the Jewish people, here he sketches his thesis of the irreligious character of the biblical revelation in contrast to the concept developed by Freud in his *Totem and Taboo*. After having noticed that it would be fascinating to try a Freudian interpretation of Isaac's sacrifice, Rosenzweig goes on and writes:

> The experience of fatherhood would be an authentic revelation of God, precisely because God is not "contained" in it. (A father can be the representative of God as long as man does not call him "God"). Only the "father substitute," the totem, is idol worship. Only in retrospect from Revelation does the idol appear as a *God*-substitute. In itself, in its *origin*, it is a *reality*-substitute. It disorders reality to such an extent that God no longer can send his messengers; now, God has to reveal himself; he has to establish his own religion (which is merely *anti-religion*) against the "religionitis" of man. (The second commandment is as unpagan as the first.)[11]

Totem and Taboo was published in 1913. Yet Rosenzweig's first reference to the concept of "Totem" was only in this diary entry of 1922. Before then he had never mentioned Freud's name, neither in *The Star* nor in his correspondence. Moreover, he never reverted to this theme again, except by brief allusions.[12] This note of April 4, 1922 is thus unique testimony to Rosenzweig's attitude to Freud's theses about religion. Let us briefly summarize those theses, as developed by Freud in *Totem and Taboo*. According to Freud, totemism is the primitive stage of religion. In totemist religion the tribe is placed under the protection of a sacred animal, the totem, to whom divine qualities are attributed. Freud's central thesis is that the totem is a father substitute. In a primordial stage in the history of mankind, that of the ancestral horde, in which a tyrannical father appropriated all available females, the sons one day staged a revolt in order to take his wives. The totemic religion preserved the subconscious memory of this original murder; the relation of the tribe to the totem expressed the ambivalence of the son's relation toward the father. The prohibition against killing the totem symbolizes the remorse for having killed the beloved and admired father, while the annual sacrificial rite of eating the totem is the necessary symbolic reenactment of this murder so as to be able to lead an independent existence. For Freud this structure explains the nature of all religions, even the most elaborate ones. God is always the father substitute; rites, precepts, and religious morals are always the symbolic expression of mankind's feeling of guilt for the original murder.

What interests Rosenzweig here is less the psychoanalytical interpretation as such than the fundamental ideal according to which the totem, i.e. in biblical language the idol, is a *substitute*. All he retains of the Freudian view is that in religion symbolism interposes itself like a screen between God and the world. As opposed to this role of religious symbols, Rosenzweig poses a natural relation to the real world, which, in its living immediacy, has the character of an authentic revelation. The aim of biblical monotheism is to eliminate this "projective" symbolism, in order to re-endow natural experiences with their spontaneously divine character.

This definition of revelation as "anti-religion" stands in complete contrast to one of the most fundamental conceptions of *The Star of Redemption*, where Judaism and Christianity are described through their rites and religious symbolism, and where the system of ritual and liturgic signs is presented as the very *organon* of the knowledge of Redemption.[13] Here Rosenzweig's thought seems to have followed the fundamental ambiguity of symbolism itself. The symbol both reveals and screens the reality it reflects; it makes its object manifest by hiding it as well. Religious symbols have the function of representing spiritual realities, but in representing them they obscure them. In *The Star* Rosenzweig considered the religious symbols in their transparency as manifestations of the truth. In his diary of 1922 he places the emphasis on their opacity. For Rosenzweig, what makes Jewish revelation "anti-religion" is precisely the awareness of this ambiguity, the fact that for Jewish monotheism God is always beyond the signs that manifest him.

III

The second theme, Rosenzweig's "quietism," is directly related to the previous one. As early as 1931, in an article that appeared on the occasion of the publication of the second edition of *The Star*, Gershom Scholem emphasized the quietist aspect of Rosenzweig's thought, especially in respect to his conception of Judaism. In one of his diary entries of 1922 Rosenzweig seems to confirm this interpretation:

> Redemption delivers God, man, world from the shapes and morphisms that had been forced upon them by Creation. Before and afterwards is "beyond." But the middle, Revelation, though it is entirely here on our side – for I am I and God is God and world is world – nevertheless is quite beyond, for I am with God. God is with me, and where is the world? It overcomes the creaturely death and establishes the rights of the redeeming death. He who loves *no longer* believes in death and *only* believes in death.[14]

These words give evidence to the ambiguity of the notion of revelation, which lies at the heart of *The Star of Redemption* and is the point of departure for Rosenzweig's entire system. In *The Star* this ambiguity already betrays itself through the semantic ambivalence of the very term "revelation," which sometimes refers to the totality of the world of personal experience as it is described in the second part of the work – and sometimes, to the specific experience of the direct relationship between God and man. In its widest sense, revelation describes reality itself, with its three elements: God, the world, and man, and the relations between them. In its narrowest sense, revelation is the quasi-mystical experience of man's encounter with God. In the first case, the philosophical intention of *The Star* would be essentially *realistic*. It would be a matter of demonstrating in what respect the concrete experience of the religious man most spontaneously unveils the immediate reality of things. In the second case, *The Star* ought to be understood as a *mystical* work, since the whole system would lead back to the original experience of the meeting between man and God.

In *The Star* Rosenzweig seems to waver between these two interpretations. At the end, however, he appears to be carried away by realism, since the mystic experience of revelation, even though it is the central moment of the system, is presented as a dialectic moment that must be passed through, as a point of departure destined to lead to *life*.[15] The problem posed by those last words of *The Star* is the point of departure of Rosenzweig's reflections in his diary note of May 1922.

The term "life" seems to contain an ambiguity even more fundamental than that of the word "revelation." *The Star* presents itself as a dialectic of life and death, as an attempt not to deny death in the manner of the philosophy "from Ionia to Jena," but to assume it and to go beyond it. *The Star* traces a road "from death to life." The central stage along that road is revelation, which, as the manifestation of God's love for man, is the victory over death; for love, as it is written in the Song of Songs, "is strong as death." In that diary entry of May 1922, Rosenzweig realizes that this victory is nothing but a metaphor, that the kind of life to which revelation gives access is spiritual life, and that the road "from death to life" is nothing other than the "mystical road" of religion.

Rosenzweig had conceived *The Star* as a history of the Absolute through the three great phases of its development. The first stage was to correspond to the original unity of all things in the bosom of the Absolute; the second, starting with creation and terminating with redemption, was to cover the entire history of mankind; and the third, was to be that of the final reintegration of all reality into the reconstituted divine unity. Only the intermediate stage is that of life; the first and the last are "beyond" (*jenseits*). Yet, to the extent that life is the result of a separation from the original divine unity, it is of necessity bound to limitation, to finitude, that is to say, to death.

In the second part of *The Star*, creation, which is God's relation to the world, separates God the creator from man, conceived here as part of the world, as a thing among things, and consequently doomed to finitude and to death. Revelation in the narrow sense of the term – which is God's relation to man – would thus have a double function: on the one hand, it distinguishes man from the world. It removes him from his condition of being a thing among other things, and in the middle of life invests him with the fullness of his humanity. But, on the other hand, by taking him out of the world and installing him outside it in a privileged relation with God, it also removes him from life itself. Such is the paradox of revelation: it liberates man from death, but at the same time from life. In other words, through revelation man gains access to a timeless life, preserved from the attrition and degradation that characterize natural life. Death does not disappear in revelation, it changes its significance. It is no longer perceived in opposition to natural life, for man himself has renounced the latter in favor of a spiritual life which already appears as some sort of symbolic death. In revelation, man is beyond life and death: "I am near God, God is near me, and where is the world?" There is nothing more authentically mystical than this formulation by Rosenzweig, where the spiritual life is already perceived as a symbolic anticipation of death: "He who loves *no longer* believes in death, and *only* believes in death." Here Rosenzweig no longer hesitates to interpret his own philosophy as *quietism*, as an aspiration to internal peace, to the timelessness of the spiritual life, at the price of renouncing the reality of the world.

That this quietism was one of the deepest foundations of his world view and that he did not cease to question it are attested to by the notes in his diary devoted to Zionism and messianism. Zionism is not explicitly mentioned in *The Star*. The Jewish aspiration for Redemption is deprived there of all its historical impetus by the concept of a quasi-timeless Jewish people, which realizes its religious vocation far from the hazards of history in the ever-renewed eternity of its liturgical time. The idea that the Jew does not have to pursue redemption and, even less provoke it since he lives it in anticipation through the symbolism of rites, the refusal to let the Jewish people compromise itself in the impurity of history, the severe criticism of politics, the view of Christianity as the agent of the historical advent of redemption – all imply the absolute rejection of any attempt on the part of the Jewish people to hasten the advent of the kingdom of God by historical means. Yet, Rosenzweig emphasizes that the symbolic anticipation of redemption through rites – in particular the Yom Kippur rite – is not the same as the real redemption which would put a stop to history and which consequently cannot be anything but an historical event. At the very center of the Jewish experience of eternity there would thus be an aspiration for the future, an expectation – certainly purely passive and disconnected from historic reality – of a redemption that can occur unexpectedly at any moment. This abstract messianism, conceived as a purely religious category without any relation to profane time, became the germ of an intellectual evolution that led Rosenzweig to an almost complete reversal of his position. The diary notes of 1922 are an important milestone in this development.

In letters he wrote in 1917 and 1918, Rosenzweig accused Zionism of being an exclusively political ideology aimed at reducing Judaism to a simple nationalism that would deprive Judaism of its religious vocation, which is the sole guarantee of its eternity. In a note dated April 12, 1922, he seemed to reaffirm this attitude: "If Zionism brings the Messiah, then *The Star* will become superfluous. But all other books, too."[16] Here the opposition between *The Star* and Zionism appears complete. The former is placed on a level with "all other books," i.e. with the whole of universal culture symbolizing a "spiritual" conception of redemption, while Zionism represents an attempt at bringing the Messiah, forcing his coming by purely historical means. But what is important is that the *possibility* of such an attempt is here alluded to for the first time. Messianism is no longer defined as a purely timeless category; although it does not necessarily imply a relation to history, neither does it exclude it. A political and national movement like Zionism is not necessarily messianic; yet it is not a priori excluded from being such. Further on in the same note, Rosenzweig throws light on the fundamental ambiguity of all messianic movements in the history of Judaism. This ambiguity does not detract from them or put into question their messianic character. Such ambiguity is part of the very essence of the messianic event, which is always susceptible to two ways of interpretation – a natural and supra-natural one – which are not mutually exclusive; neither is one more "true" than the other. In the chiaroscuro of history all the great messianic movements *are and are not* what they pretend to be: "Can I dissociate myself from it, because it is only ***possibly*** messianic? Which movement would *not* be only 'possibly'?"[17]

Another diary entry strongly underlines the presence of this historic dimension at the heart of the Jewish faith. The Jewish prayer, says Rosenzweig, contains in its very essence the hope for a return to the Land of Israel. If western Judaism of the 19th century lost the sense of this national dimension, that is due not so much to the process of social emancipation as to religious alienation: "After 1800 we ceased to pray for the Return, because we ceased to *pray*. If we had continued praying, we would have prayed for the Return."[18] Rosenzweig now recognizes the central importance of the national dimension of Judaism. For him, however, the national dimension is a factor in Israel's religious faith, and not the reverse. He thus contends that for the modern Judaism of the Diaspora, the expression of religious faith could, indeed must, survive the loss of the longing for rational redemption: "It was the error of liberalism that we stopped praying, [simply] because we no longer wanted to pray for the return." But three months later, this diary entry of Rosenzweig refers to one of the central ideas of Judah Halevi and of the historiosophical tradition inspired by him – that of the quasi-organic bond of Jewish prophecy with the Land of Israel – and connects it with a classic thesis of Zionism – that of the historic (but, Rosenzweig says, Jewish and religious) sterility of that part of the Jewish people which has decided to strike roots in the Diaspora:

> The connection of prophetism with the land (instead of, as is the case with the Christians, with time) is something which arouses much thought. It is simply true that the Jew who strikes roots in the Diaspora loses his Jewish-religious strength. Without a bit of alienation from the Germans, Hermann Cohen also would not have been such a Jew.[19]

IV

The last theme in Rosenzweig's diaries I want to comment on is that of the meaning of creation in the modern world. In the third trimester of the academic year 1921-1922, Rosenzweig gave his last course of lectures at the Freies Jüdisches Lehrhaus. In the trimester program of the Lehrhaus, prepared by Rosenzweig himself, this course, entitled "The Science of the World," was outlined as follows:

The question: The world as representation
The world as change: Nature
The world as form: Art
The world as order: Law
The world as conflict: Power
The world as a work: Spirit
The world as home: Technique
The answer: The world as creation

A great many of Rosenzweig's diary entires between mid-April and early June, 1922 are devoted to reflections on this subject. The complex concerns one of Rosenzweig's central problems in *The Star of Redemption*: that of the reality of the outside world. This was the fundamental question he had to confront in his polemic against Idealism. "The phenomenon has always been the crux of Idealism,"[20] writes Rosenzweig in *The Star*. Since we perceive the world only through the representation we make of it, how can we be sure that there exists an objective reality beyond that representation? In Rosenzweig's view, this question by its very nature is unsolvable. All the originality of his "New Thinking" lies in his refusal to pose the question of representation and to base the reality of the world on our own intuitive evidence of it. However, in the second part of *The Star*, when Rosenzweig explicates the manner in which this intuition presents itself to us, he has to admit that our experience of the world is incomplete; we perceive it as an appearance whose essence escapes us: "The world is enigmatic, for it reveals itself before its essence exists."[21]

The world is certainly evident, but its evidence is that of an appearance; it has the ambiguous reality of the phenomenon, of the entirely external apparition. Its being, the substantiality the world lacks, must be given to it by man. In the experience of revelation, which raises him above the world of things, man becomes conscious that as a spiritual being he has within himself a part of indestructible reality. To the extent that he turns toward the world in order to humanize it, he confers upon it this reality and gives it the solid substance, the ontological foundation, which it lacks. This projection of revelation onto the world is what defines redemption. But the concrete modalities of achieving redemption are not clearly defined. From *The Star* we only know that there are two modes of reaching redemption: one consists in transforming the world from inside; the other consists in leaving the world behind in order to take refuge in the eternity of sacred, that is, liturgical, time. There are thus two different modes of man's relation to the world: the first is historical; the second symbolical. In the religious typology of *The Star*, the historical relation to the world defines the collective vocation of Christianity; the symbolic relation defines the collective vocation of Judaism. (Although for the individual this schema is quite the opposite: through his faith the Christian is detached from the world;

though his destiny the Jew is obliged to take part in it.) The third part of *The Star,* comparing the ritual structures of Judaism and Christianity, considers the religious dimension of redemption or the symbolic relation of man to the world. It does not concern itself with deciphering the modalities of man's practical engagement in historic reality. It is precisely this question, left open in *The Star*, which Rosenzweig takes up again in his lecture course in the spring of 1922.

Three years after having completed *The Star*, Rosenzweig realized that in his great systematical work he had unwittingly used an idealistic method. The idea that only by projecting his own experience on the world does man endow it with reality would seem to render the very foundations of Rosenzweig's thought questionable. Is it still possible thus to guarantee the external world's objective reality? What is left of the experience of creation, which according to *The Star* unveils itself precisely in the fact that the world is always there *before us*? Such were the questions Rosenzweig was asking himself at the time he undertook to give his course on "The Science of the World."

In his notes of 1922, Rosenzweig first distinguished three aspects of man's perception of reality: nature, law, and art. These three facets are already present in *The Star* in a diffuse and unsystematic form as the profane version of three fundamental religious categories: creation, Judaism, and Christianity. Nature is the form in which creation appears to us when we abstract its negativity, its finitude, and when we are insensitive to the horizon of the absolute on which it is reflected. Law, that is to say, the political organization of society, represents the attempt at controlling historical time from the inside, in contrast with Judaism, which, according to Rosenzweig, creates a parallel, non-historical time, thus escaping the hazards of history. Art plays the same role toward Christianity as law towards Judaism: it is for the individual a quest for salvation, but a profane salvation, that is, a solitary one that does not care for communion with other humans.

But these three experiences do not give us access to the immediate reality of the world. On the contrary, they themselves are constructions of the human spirit. Nature, law, and art are "representations," productions of an original theoretical activity. In his diary notes, Rosenzweig outlines the epistemology of this theoretical activity in its three forms: the scientific, the juridical, and the aesthetic. Each of these three theoretical attitudes has its own axiomatics, by which it constructs its specific field of activity. Science creates its own object, which is nature, through a process of relativization: it relates the image we have of the world to the point of view of the observer. The view of the world art gives us also has no objective reality. Each artist deciphers the world in his own fashion; every viewer interprets the work of art as he understands it. This is a twofold process of appropriation in which everything ultimately leads to the pleasure of the viewer, listener, or reader. Law constructs a specific type of reality for its own use, which is purely abstract, based on the principle of distinguishing and isolating specific cases. As far as law presents itself as general and pretends to apply mechanically to everybody and always in the same manner, it no longer begets justice but injustice.[22]

Thus science, law, and art are abstract spheres which, to be sure, are necessary insofar as they satisfy our needs to understand. They are unreal insofar as they can in no way guarantee to us that an outside world actually exists beyond them. Opposite these three abstract spheres Rosenzweig places the three most concrete realities of all: those of technology, politics, and ideology. These are translations into *praxis* of the three categories of man's theoretical activities. Technology, politics, and ideology (Rosenzweig uses the term *Weltanschauung*[23]), are the practical applications of science, law, and art – this time not intended to *interpret* the world, but to *dominate* it. Praxis, too, is a projection of human activity onto the world; just like theory, it does not encounter its object but creates it. Yet, in contrast to theory, praxis creates the very matter of the world. In this sense it is even more idealistic than theory, but at the same time infinitely more realistic, since knowledge creates only abstract representations, while man's power over the world shapes reality as such.[24]

Thus, precisely to the extent that they *impose* an external order on the world, technology, politics, and ideology violate its natural structure. While knowledge fails the world through its lack of realism (or through an excess of theory), power fails it through an excess of realism (or through a lack of theory). Here Rosenzweig contrasts the *irreality* of knowledge with the *super-reality* of human praxis.[25] The brutality of man's power creates an oversimplified, schematic, but dangerously *real* world. "The superreality of the spirit," writes Rosenzweig ("spirit," to him, signifies "ideology"), "consists in that the world has day and night. But the spirit is always *awake*."[26] This vigilance of the spirit is not that of reason, which incessantly transforms the world through knowledge, but that pitiless vigilance of the ideology which never rests, which watches over the world and supervises it, effacing the difference between the rational and the imaginary, of the diurnal and the nocturnal, depriving the world of its sleep and the night of its mystery, throwing a crude and uniform light on all reality. The same applies to technology: the surface of the globe, says Rosenzweig, is made of lands and seas, or, as it is told in Genesis, of the dry and the wet; not all of it is habitable; nature's subjection by man has its own natural limits; when man oversteps them, he destroys the world which he pretended to tame. But technology is not concerned with natural equilibria; it wants to conquer nature as a whole. As for political power, it ignores the duality of earth and heaven, of the temporal and the spiritual. Political power is totalitarian by nature. Its ambition knows no limits. Far from submitting itself to transcendental exigencies, it pretends, on the contrary, to determine by itself its own scale of values. "Power," writes Rosenzweig, "is prepared to fight for mastery over heaven itself." Wishing to impose order on the world by force, praxis ends up by turning against itself. Technology, politics, and ideology appear in reality less as products of human activity than as autonomous forces that enclose man and reduce him to the status of an object. Technological power, ideological power, political power – these are in the final analysis the true dangers that threaten modern man. "The scholar, the artist, the jurist are only stammering," writes Rosenzweig, "they do not attain reality. Whereas the man of power, the ideologist, the technician, are really frightening."[27]

The dualities of day and night, of dry and wet, of heaven and earth – these three pairs of opposites define Creation in the Bible. For Rosenzweig, the biblical narrative presents us with the most faithful image of reality: a complex network of contrasts, of tensions, of more or less tenuous balances. This complexity, which technology, politics, and ideology try to deny, is inscribed in the heart of creation. Between the brute *super-reality* of praxis and the *irreality* of theory, creation – as the biblical text describes it, but also as we feel it intuitively by our immediate experience – reveals to us the world in its very reality, as something that is at the same time eminently complex and absolutely concrete. This concrete complexity manifests itself in three aspects, which are the true intuitive sources of the three theoretical activities of man: Creation in itself is *arranged in an order*; each being, each thing occupies its proper place. It is this natural order which makes law possible. From another aspect, the existence of the world is spontaneously perceived as something *good*; "And God saw that it was good," says the biblical text after each day of the Creation. In the simple fact that the world is, lies something fundamentally good. This feeling, says Rosenzweig, is the origin of art. Finally, the Bible does not present the Creation as one single *moment* in which Being bursts forth from nothingness, but as a complicated process spread out over time, in which every day produces its own order of reality. It is this original complexity which accords to science its objectivity.[28] This conception of Creation as an intermediary instance between idealism and realism, between theory and praxis, exemplifies Rosenzweig's philosophical position as it emerges from the study of his last diaries. Beyond the systematic, almost dogmatic construction of *The Star of Redemption*, we have here a living tension between opposite poles: contemplation and experience, eternity and history, mystique and life.

Notes

1 Franz Rosenzweig, *Der Mensch und sein Werk, Gesammelte Schriften*, Vol I: *Briefe und Tagebücher*, 2. Band, 1918-1929 (Den Haag: Martinus Nijhoff, 1979), p. 760. (Hereafter B.T.2).

2 B.T.2, p. 822.

3 B.T.2, p. 771.

4 *Ibid.*

5 B.T.2, p. 747.

6 B.T.2, p. 768.
7 B.T.2, p. 760.
8 B.T.2, p. 767.
9 *Der Stern der Erlösung*, 3. Ed. (Heidelberg: 1954), pp. 171-173.
10 B.T.2, p. 770.
11 B.T.2, pp. 770-771.
12 B.T.2, pp. 1003, 1114.
13 *Stern,* 45-46.
14 B.T.2, p. 778.
15 *Stern,* 210-211.
16 B.T.2, p. 774.
17 *Ibid.*
18 B.T.2, p. 769.
19 B.T.2, p. 801.
20 *Stern*, 62.
21 *Stern,* 170.
22 Cf. B.T.2, p. 783, note 747.
23 Cf. B.T.2, p. 775, note 735.
24 Cf. B.T.2, pp. 776-777, note 738.
25 Cf. B.T.2, p. 783, note 747.
26 Cf. B.T.2, p. 785, note 750.
27 *Ibid.*
28 Cf. B.T.2, pp. 791 and 794, notes 764 and 772.

A Dual Voice: Mary Shelley and Bettina von Arnim

Nancy A. Kaiser

Any attempt to characterize Mary Wollstonecraft Shelley or Bettina Brentano von Arnim leads to contradictory statements. The woman who created the monster, and with *Frankenstein* a bold myth embodying the dilemmas of modern existence, is also the woman who stated: "with regard to 'the good cause' – the cause of the advancement of freedom and knowledge, of the rights of women, &c. – I am not a person of opinions."[1] The woman who called the King of Prussia to account and documented squalid conditions of poverty in Berlin is also the woman who indulged in an exaggerated adoration of Goethe, stylizing herself as Psyche, as muse, and as child to the master. In each case, the mixture of unconventionality and adherence to stereotypical roles for women is striking. It is not possible to compare the two women in any narrow sense, but a contrastive study is nevertheless instructive.[2] Each woman had intellectual and personal connections to the Romantic movement in her homeland, to a Romanticism which accorded women a special position. Each outlived that Romanticism on into an increasingly conservative mid-century. As writers, Mary Shelley and Bettina von Arnim expressed themselves in print, in public. This activity was characterized by ambivalence. It is my intention to explore the contradictions in the lives and writings of the two women, the manner in which each asserted her own individual voice, yet implicitly recognized traditional modes of female self-expression.

In an extended study of nineteenth-century fiction by women, Sandra Gilbert and Susan Gubar have identified a concealed plot in such fiction as "the woman writer's quest for her own story."[3] Mary Shelley and Bettina von Arnim represent two versions of such a quest. In Shelley's works, the narrative strategies and recurrent themes betray the author's ambivalence, a dual voice of self-assertion and self-restriction. Bettina von Arnim's literary manipulations of reality in her works, which cannot be assigned to any specific genre, develop a self-conceived persona which transgresses boundaries while adapting elements of established identities for women.

Certain biographical similarities between the two women helped determine my decision to juxtapose them. A brief consideration of their full names is a significant exercise. Mary Wollstonecraft Godwin Shelley was the daughter of Mary Wollstonecraft, whose treatise *A Vindication of the Rights of Woman* (1792) applied principles of the French Revolution to an indignant protest against the oppression of women. Among her other writings, the unfinished novel *Maria; or the Wrongs of Woman* (1798, posthumously) is the most radical, if problematical, extension of feminist themes. Her unorthodox life ended in 1797, when she died of complications following Mary's birth. William Godwin (1756-1836) was a political philosopher and author. His *Enquiry Concerning Political Justice* (1793) had made him a celebrated author with the critical younger generation, although he turned increasingly conservative with age. His second marriage resulted in a confusing step-family situation. It was hardly an optimal environment, and Mary Shelley cultivated her mother's memory. She often read at her mother's grave, and she and Percy Bysshe Shelley spent time there in 1814, the year of their elopement. Percy Shelley is, of course, an additional, vital factor in the biography of Mary Wollstonecraft Godwin Shelley. Their life until his death in 1822 rivals in unorthodoxy anything German Romantics such as the Schlegels had offered in Jena. In their years together Mary Shelley interacted with the younger generation of English Romanticism: Byron, Shelley, and Keats. She achieved literary success with *Frankenstein* (1818). But, she also led an extremely nomadic, financially insecure existence. She went through five pregnancies, experienced one life-threatening miscarriage and the deaths of three children. After Percy Shelley's death, she published five additional novels, a two-volume account of her travels, and several volumes of biographies for the *Cabinet Cyclopedia.*[4] She also edited Percy Shelley's works and raised their surviving son. Mary Shelley never sought a public voice, and her journal and letters sometimes appear to belie the potential conveyed by her extended name. The contradictions are apparent in her fiction, and some of the issues can be related to those implicit in Bettina von Arnim's works.

For purposes of comparison and emphasis, it would be necessary to regard the German author as Bettina La Roche Brentano von Arnim.[5] In her case, the grandmother was the strong female precursor. Sophie von La Roche is regarded as the author of the first German "women's novel," *Geschichte des Fräuleins von Sternheim* (1771). Although by no means radical like Mary Wollstonecraft, Sophie von La Roche was an interesting and independent woman. Her novel presents an admirable heroine who struggles with the pressures of social convention for young women of her class. Since Bettina Brentano's mother died when she was eight, the grandmother and her house in Offenbach were formative influences until La Roche's death in 1807. Bettina's brother Clemens Brentano and her husband Achim von Arnim were also prominent literary figures. They belonged to the second generation of German Romanticism. Brother and sister were close, although the insistent attempts of the elder brother to shape his sister's intellectual development were repeatedly rejected.[6] The marriage with Achim von Arnim did not possess the passion and turbulence of Mary and Percy Shelley. The English couple had caused a scandal by running away to the continent while Percy Shelley was still married. Achim and Bettina von Arnim staged a secret wedding in 1811, although there was no scandal involved. Their marriage brought seven children and intermittent financial worries. They spent much of their married life with two households, as Bettina lived in Berlin and Achim on the family estate in Wiepersdorf. Their letters attest to sustained marital affection.[7] Bettina von Arnim first began to publish after her husband's death in 1831. She eventually edited his works, but she clearly and persistently claimed a public voice for herself. Her dedicated efforts to political and social causes are radically different from Mary Shelley's "great horror of my name being in public."[8] Despite obvious biographical parallels, therefore, the contrast between the two women seems unmistakeable, and yet elements of Bettina von Arnim's self-presentation reveal the residual contradictions. A section of the published version of her correspondence with Karoline von Günderode illustrates this point and also indicates the complexities of the historical context.

In one of the letters to Günderode, Bettina von Arnim proposes a new religion, "die Schwebereligion." With characteristic enthusiasm, she explores the potential challenge to a reality she otherwise finds confining. She and Günderode are to be both priests and laypersons, and the basic principle of the religion denies categorization at the same time that it demands action: "ein erstes Grundgesetz. Nämlich: Der Mensch soll immer die größte Handlung tun und nie eine andre, und da will ich Dir gleich zuvorkommen und sagen, daß jede Handlung eine größte sein kann und soll."[9] She continues with diatribes against pedantic education and a stolid work ethic, equating God with "Poesie" and deducing that all human beings created in God's image must therefore all be potential poets. She calls for an intellectual bravery which might even engage in somersaults of logic to prove that humankind can indeed live on air alone. Her intent with such a proof is to confound those who maintain the opposite, "um den Menschen die Sklavenkette zu legen des Erwerbs."[10]

"Unsere schwebende Religion" occupies the two women for only a brief segment of the volume. Yet it is, in context, appropriate for the topic I am developing. The letters were originally written between 1802 and 1806, and the rhetoric of German Romanticism is readily apparent. The primacy of "Poesie," the rejection of hierarchical categories, even the indeterminate state of "schweben" are all reminiscent of the early stage of Romanticism centered in Jena. So are the discontent with prosaic social conventions and the critique of a society increasingly based on isolated functional units, capitalist division of labor, and economically determined status. The laws of the religion were to guide the development of a young prince into a supremely beneficent ruler. While recognizing the playfully speculative side of the discussion, the letters rather defensively assert the two women's right to such topics: "es ist ein schöner Scherz, aber nehm's nur nicht für Scherz, es ist mein Ernst, denn warum sollten wir nicht zusammen denken über das Wohl und Bedürfnis der Menschheit?"[11] The interesting question is not so much why they should or should not undertake such a task, but rather why she felt it necessary to ask that very question and why the "Schwebereligion" took the form of educating a male ruler.

The answer is complex, partly because Bettina von Arnim also assumed a more radical role, both publicly and in imaginary scenarios, than such passages indicate. She did not publish the volume of revised correspondence, *Die Günderode*, until 1840. By then the political and intellectual climate was decidedly different. German Romanticism, in all its phases, belonged to the past; Karoline von Günderode had committed suicide in 1806, and prominent figures of the early Jena circle had turned conservative. Friedrich Schlegel had done so long before his death in 1829. Bettina von Arnim retained her Romantic unconventionality. She updated the political and social provocation in 1840 by dedicating *Die Günderode* to students, whom she compares to flowers carrying dreams of the future. Despite the elaborate imagery, the references to the former political role of the student fraternities in the dedication were unmistakeable. 1840 was a propitious year in German history, and many intellectuals shared the sanguine dreams of the future. Friedrich Wilhelm IV had ascended to the throne, and there were fleeting hopes for liberalization. They soon proved to be illusory, and Bettina von Arnim's next volume, *Dies Buch gehört dem König* (1843), was an attempt to call the king to account.

Her self-assigned role as an exhortative voice to the king was in reality more radical than the education of a young prince envisioned in *Die Günderode*. In his enthusiastic review of *Dies Buch gehört dem König*, Karl Gutzkow found it a sad commentary that a woman could get away with a critique which would have sent a man to prison.[12] His criticism is of the system of censorship. The implication is that a woman's critique was not taken as seriously. Bettina von Arnim did have trouble with the authorities in other instances, and it is difficult to assess her effect.[13] Gutzkow's comment and her own hesitancy in *Die Günderode* concerning the two women's right to conjecture on topics of social and political relevance indicate at least an ambiguity inherent in asserting an individual, public voice as a woman in the nineteenth century. They also illuminate the political, intellectual, and social-historical contradictions of German lands in Bettina von Arnim's lifetime (1785-1859).

Such issues of private self, public voice, socially-determined identity, and an eventful, contradictory biographical context are shared by Bettina von Arnim and Mary Shelley. Shelley's lifetime (1797-1851) ranges from Romantic ferment to Victorian propriety, and her attempts to find an appropriate mode for self-expression are equally instructive. I began with *Die Günderode* because it is less well known. I could have begun with the tangled contradictions of self-assertion and gender identity in Mary Shelley's *Frankenstein*. Both works have their roots in Romanticism, and the relative freedom and progressive function accorded women in certain aspects of German and English Romanticism formed an early context for the two writers. There was a pronounced influence of eighteenth-century ideals of equality, coupled with a repudiation of social conventions and mores. In Germany, women took an active part in the intellectual salons and cultural life. Nevertheless, the role of women in Romantic theory entailed an ambivalent message for real women in a nineteenth-century context. Specific writings of Friedrich Schlegel and Percy Shelley illustrate the difficulties and ambiguities.

Schlegel has been designated as a proponent of women's emancipation, as has Percy Shelley.[14] In both cases, the title is apt. The two writers castigated a social order which subordinates women, and both were vehemently negative in the portrayal of conventional marriage.[15] In Percy Shelley's "A Defence of Poetry" (1821), historical progress is noted partly in terms of the "abolition of personal and domestic slavery and the emancipation of women."[16] Such a view is consonant with Schlegel's call for "die Vollendung des Männlichen und Weiblichen zur vollen ganzen Menschheit" in *Lucinde*, the Romantic novel which he published in 1799.[17] *Lucinde* is generally assigned central importance in considering the role of women in Romanticism. The work has a biographical basis and was regarded as shocking in its open eroticism. More significant, however, is its evocative illustration of the statement from the 1795 essay "Über die Diotima": "Nur selbständige Weiblichkeit, nur sanfte Männlichkeit, ist gut und schön."[18] The advocacy of the interchange of supposedly male and female character traits and of traditional roles, the recognition of all the facets of a woman in the title figure, and the presentation of the relationship of Julius and Lucinde as one of equality and mutual enrichment and pleasure are definitely progressive traits. However, the limitations to Schlegel's depiction must also be mentioned, and they modify the independence ("selbständige Weiblichkeit") which he espouses. The connection of women and nature is problematical, as illustrated by the lesson which Julius learns from (through) Lucinde about women and nature in opposition to society: "daß die Frauen allein, die mitten im Schoß der menschlichen Gesellschaft Naturmenschen geblieben sind, den kindlichen Sinn haben, mit dem man die Gunst und Gabe der Götter annehmen muß."[19] The passage, and the adjective "childlike," are meant to be read positively. The concept of nature in early Romanticism includes an implicit critique of the historical development of exploitation and domination of nature. At the same time, the function of woman as the projected ideal external to social reality is a highly ambivalent concept for real women living in society. When one is praised for an identity essentially beyond society, attaining a public, social voice is a contradictory process. It is an issue which is difficult to resolve and one which figures in the designation of Bettina von Arnim as "Kind," as "Kobold," as a voice to be tolerated but perhaps not heeded.

Percy Shelley also idealizes feminine traits in his poetical works, with somewhat different implications. The composition offering the clearest comparison to *Lucinde* is *The Revolt of Islam* (1817/1818). This epic poem is a reluctant revision of the work originally entitled *Laon and Cyntha* and is dedicated to Mary Shelley. It is a vision of revolution and also of passionate love, in the original version between brother and sister. As in Schlegel, the demand for independent womanhood is strong, perhaps even more forceful:

> 'Can man be free if woman be a slave?
> Chain one who lives, and breathes this boundless air,
> To the corruption of a closed grave!
> Can they whose mates are beasts condemned to bear
> Scorn heavier far than toil or anguish, dare
> To trample their oppressors? ...'[20]

The love between Laon and Cyntha is portrayed with erotic clarity parallel to that in *Lucinde*. Cyntha, however, speaks the words just quoted. She assumes a dynamic leadership role, and her voice dominates in several of the cantos. Her figure is consistent with Percy Shelley's approval of outspoken women, his great admiration for Mary Wollstonecraft, and his support for Mary Shelley.

At the same time that Percy Shelley was occupied with *The Revolt of Islam*, Mary Shelley must have been finishing *Frankenstein*. The ambivalence regarding self-assertion and creative production in this most famous work by Shelley would lead one to suspect that women, even as the embodiment of Romantic ideals, still struggled to develop their own mode of self-expression. The novel epitomizes the dilemma of women authors and the dual voice with which they responded. Not that women characters play a determining role in *Frankenstein*. Caroline Beaufort, Elizabeth Lavenza, Justine Moritz, and Safie are all stereotypical characters, notable perhaps for their passivity and for their fate as victims. The unfinished female partner for the monster shares the same characteristics. All three narrators are male: Robert Walton, Victor Frankenstein, and the monster. Their interlocking narratives are about the quest for identity, for "one's" own story, to adapt the phrase from Gilbert and Gubar, and the process reveals Shelley's ambivalence regarding her own audacity of authorship. In her introduction to an 1831 edition of the novel she emphasizes her personal reticence: "It is true that I am very averse to bringing myself forward in print."[21] Her narrators in *Frankenstein* are anything but reticent. Walton, a failed poet, is attempting a passage around the North Pole, seeking "the dominion I should acquire and transmit over the elemental foes of our race." (p. 26) Victor Frankenstein designates himself as "the author of unalterable evils." (p. 87) He states his family name for the first time, thereby bringing himself forward verbally, when he tells Walton of his Promethean vow: "So much has been done, exclaimed the soul of Frankenstein – more, far more, will I achieve: treading in the steps already marked, I will pioneer a new way, explore unknown powers, and unfold to the world the deepest mysteries of creation." (p. 47) His creation, the monster, also refers to himself as an author when he threatens Frankenstein with becoming "the author of your own speedy ruin." (p. 97) He eventually asserts himself solely through destructive behavior.

All three figures are functional story-tellers and also self-designated authors. In each case the self-assertion, the lack of reticence, results in intense isolation. Walton writes to his sister: "I bitterly feel the want of a friend." (p. 18) The monster demands of Frankenstein a companion monster, as he is "alone and miserable." (p. 137) And, Victor Frankenstein loses his brother William, the servant Justine, then his friend Clerval, his bride Elizabeth, and (indirectly) his father to his own creation. The cost of authorship is high. The novel connects the three author-narrators in the icy Arctic seas, and apparently only one of them will survive. Walton, significantly also a failure as a poet, gives in to the pleas of his crew and will return southward to civilization. The other two figures are connected in a more intimate fashion, as Frankenstein is parent to his monstrous creation. The novel has been termed a "birth myth" and a "parable of motherhood"; in her 1831 introduction Mary Shelley refers to the book itself as "my hideous progeny." (p. xii)[22] Barbara Johnson has suggested reading it "as the study of the experience of writing *Frankenstein*," which in turn is a dramatization of the problems of women's autobiography.[23] The novel is then very much a book about female authorship, and the message is mixed.

The monster is the agent of destruction, truly a murderous creation. His existence would seem to negate any legitimacy of his creator's efforts. Because of his extended tale of development and woe, however, our sympathies as readers lie with the ostracized, persecuted monster at the same time that we abhor his deeds. In a way, the "unnatural" deed is the rejection of the well-spoken, cultured being (a reader of Plutarch, Milton, Goethe) simply because his appearance is deviant. He had tried to assimilate himself, except for the evidence of monstrousness which he could not conceal. Only after he is violently ejected from the cottage of his imagined "protectors" does he experience "the feelings of revenge and hatred." (p. 132) The narrative strategy of divided perspective and insight into the monster's story means that we can neither totally reject the monstrous product of Victor Frankenstein's presumptuousness nor accept it. The monster, simultaneously assimilated and unacceptable, and the ambivalence which is inherent in the structure of the book are indicative of Mary Shelley's fears regarding her own literary production and her ambivalence toward her self-assertion as a woman writer.

Mary Shelley never again wrote anything like *Frankenstein*. The five additional novels published during her lifetime lack the combination of such vivid imagery with thematic and structural complexity: *Valperga* (1823), *The Last Man* (1826), *Perkin Warbeck* (1830), *Lodore* (1835), and *Falkner* (1837).[24] In addition, there is *Mathilda*, the story of a father's incestuous love for his daughter. Written in 1819 and not published during Shelley's lifetime, it reflects her complex relationship to William Godwin. All the novels are less well-known than *Frankenstein*, and deservedly so. Rather than consider each work separately, I prefer to discuss common aspects which express what Mary Poovey has analyzed in Shelley's character as "a remarkable combination of stereotypical feminine reticence and unconventional self-assertion."[25] This dual voice is more subdued in the novels after *Frankenstein*, but the issues remain.

One strategy shared by several novels is an equivocation on the question of responsibility for a story. Victor Frankenstein abdicates responsibility for the product of his labors. He flees the laboratory after animating his creation and is later curiously unable to acknowledge his deed. A related evasion of responsibility is evident in Mary Shelley's explanation of the origin of *Frankenstein*. In the 1831 introduction she ascribes the conception of her story to a "waking dream," (p. xi) in which "my imagination, unbidden, possessed and guided me." (p. x) The denial of conscious responsibility allows her simultaneously to restrict and to assert her authorship. The equally equivocal acknowledgment of Percy Shelley's role both credits and belittles his aid: "I certainly did not owe the suggestion of one incident, nor scarcely of one train of feeling, to my husband, and yet but for his incitement it would never have taken the form in which it was presented to the world." (p. xi) She does credit him with writing the Preface under her name, but a curious dialectic works here to transform the denial of responsibility for the Preface into a virtual reaffirmation of her participation in the novel's message. The Preface included a disclaimer: "The opinions which naturally spring from the character and situation of the hero are by no means to be conceived as existing always in my own conviction;...." (p. xi) By disowning the disclaimer, she in effect can reassert an affinity with the hero's character and situation.

Similar strategies for limiting responsibility for a story while ultimately claiming it are evident in *Valperga, The Last Man*, and *Perkin Warbeck* as well. *Valperga: or, the Life and Adventures of Castruccio, Prince of Lucca* is an historical novel of the struggles of the Guelphs and Ghibellines in fourteenth-century Italy. The Preface documents Shelley's sources for her material and quotes in full a brief biography of the Ghibelline captain Castruccio. She thereby claims an outside source for her story and outlines its inevitable course. The final sentence of the Preface, however, directly follows the biography and abruptly reasserts her authorial liberty: "The dates here given are somewhat different from those adopted in the following narrative."[26] The three-volume novel turns out to be equally, perhaps more essentially, about the fictional character of Euthanasia, Countess of Valperga. The "or" of the title juxtaposes the authority of historical fact with the product of the author's own creation. Similarly, the original impulse behind *The Fortunes of Perkin Warbeck* had been an historical study of the supposed pretender to the throne of Henry VII. She deviated because she felt restricted by the traditional genre, by "any narration, that should be confined to the incorporation of facts related by our old Chroniclers."[27] Her author's conclusion indicates an additional, even more personal reason of masked self-justification for her conventional life after Percy Shelley's death. In a direct appeal to the reader, she attempts to exculpate Lady Katherine for remaining at the court of Henry VII after he beheaded her husband. The fictional episode in the final chapter, the request of Elizabeth, wife of Henry VII, to Richard (Perkin Warbeck) that he command Katherine to remain with her, could not have taken place in a narration of facts. The (self-)defense of Lady Katherine is conventional: "a woman's tutelage in my early years, a woman's education in the world, which is that of the heart – alas! for us – not of the head."[28] With *Perkin Warbeck*, Shelley deviates in order more fully to defend conforming.

The issue of authorial responsibility in *The Last Man* is complex. In the Introduction she claims to have discovered a fragmentary manuscript in the Sibyl's cave in Naples in 1818. She can again disclaim responsibility for conceiving of her story. The vacillation is between the restrictive statement that "I have faithfully transcribed from my materials" and the assertion "that, obscure and chaotic as they are, they owe their present form to me, their decipherer."[29] The novel itself contradicts the legitimacy of the introductory disclaimer with its "sacred remains" because *The Last Man* is the first-person narration of events in the future, leading up to the extinction of the entire human race except the narrator in the year 2100. Its existence as a document in 1818 is patently false, and creative responsibility must reside with the author, or with the narrator Lionel Verney, who is *à clef* for Mary Shelley herself.

Claiming responsibility for a story involves acknowledging one's own individual voice. It is a matter of self-assertion, and Mary Shelley equivocates. Within the narratives themselves, the analogous issues include the responsibility of characters for their own lives and questions of legitimacy, of acquaintance with one's heritage. In *Mathilda*, the narrator begins her tale with a disavowal: "My fate has been governed by necessity, a hideous necessity."[30] The motif of unalterable destiny runs through all of the novels, effectively excusing the characters from liability for their own actions. In *The Last Man*, Lionel Verney can still assert the possibility of "an active principle in man which is capable of ruling fortune," but he is countered by the course of the novel itself.[31] A world-wide plague inexorably annuls the efficacy of individual assertive action. In the following novels, the role of fate and circumstances beyond the individual's control is increasingly prevalent. In *Perkin Warbeck*, the omniscient narrator repeatedly reinforces the theme with imagery of entanglement and mechanistic determination. In Shelley's final novel, *Falkner*, the entire elaborate plot mechanism manipulates the characters who believe that they are acting independently. Elizabeth Raby's desire to support Gerard Neville in his search to acquit his mother of charges of adultery leads directly to the inadvertent exposure of her foster-father Falkner as the woman's abductor and unintentional destroyer. The betrayal was not her conscious intention. Mary Poovey's skillful analysis of the novel as a surreptitious punishment of the father figure and assertion of the "indirect but undeniable power of women" demonstrates that the question of determinism versus self-assertive action is as ambivalent and complex as the issues in *Frankenstein.*[32] In *Falkner*, unconscious desires are asserted and accomplished without direct responsibility.

Gerard Neville is obsessed in the novel with clearing his mother's name, and Mary Shelley has a decided predilection for misrepresented or uncertain parentage and for orphans. Certainly the themes have a biographical connection to her own life. They are also related to the elusive "woman writer's quest for her own story," especially since "orphan" is often defined as having a father but no mother. Orphans include Caroline Beaufort, Elizabeth Lavenza, Justine Moritz, Safie (*Frankenstein*), Mathilda (*Mathilda*), Castruccio, Euthanasia, Beatrice, Arrigo Guinigi (*Valperga*), Lionel and Perdita Verney (*The Last Man*), John (Rupert) Falkner, Elizabeth Raby, Gerard Neville (*Falkner*). Ethel Fitzhenry (*Lodore*) is virtually motherless for most of the novel. *Perkin Warbeck* centers on the related question of legitimacy, and *Falkner* and *Lodore* are partly narratives of finding and restoring to honor a "lost" mother.

The theme of re-legitimating the maternal heritage is an ambivalent issue in Mary Shelley's works. It is connected to the lack of a female tradition for women writers, but it is also allied with conventional values of motherhood and domesticity. *Lodore* reunites mother and daughter, providing a spouse and fortune for each. The novel, however, leaves a loose end. It concludes with the uncertain future of Fanny Derham, the scholarly, more independent woman figure. She had been described as a woman more appreciated by other women than by men due to her "superiority of intellect."[33] In *Lodore*, the superiority of intellect is joined with an exemplary docility of character, and Fanny Derham reinforces the feminine ideal of propriety in the novel, even if she does not share in all the rewards. In other novels, Mary Shelley portrays independent women who transgress the boundaries of domesticated femininity. Her attempts to justify their transgressions characterize her ambivalence, the dual voice of self-assertion and self-restriction.

The protagonist in *Perkin Warbeck* has a system of female supporters in his attempt to gain the throne. Two women play prominent roles, Lady Katherine Gordon and Monina de Faro. Richard (Perkin Warbeck) marries Lady Katherine, but the commoner Monina continues to fight actively for his cause. Her efforts are characterized by bold behavior, courage, and an ability to incite others with her words. She has a "public career," even if often underground or in disguise. Lady Katherine comes to advocate abandoning the cause, and her purpose as stated to Richard is "to draw you from the uneasy throne to the downy paradise of love."[34] Richard is eventually executed by Henry VII, at whose court Lady Katherine remains.

Monina, as she had vowed, does not outlive him. The political cause of Richard is, however, hardly justifiable. It is an ambition which costs many more lives than Victor Frankenstein's presumptuousness.[35] Monina's fervor is therefore misplaced, and her assertiveness is justified only because it originated, not in ambition but in love for Richard. It is sublimated love and therefore still within the realm of feminine propriety. Shelley creates the assertive female character and simultaneously restricts her motives and the legitimacy of the cause for which she fights.

The earlier historical novel contains an even stronger castigation of ambition but also a stronger role for women. Euthanasia, Countess of Valperga, is the Guelph Republican pendant to the Ghibelline Castruccio. She had loved him and attempts to restrain and counsel him as he becomes a tyrant. When her efforts fail, she resolutely puts duty and principle in primary position, even joining a conspiracy against the man she loved. Beatrice of Ferrara, the other principal female in the novel, is tied to Castruccio by passion and devotion and ends tragically. Both women are exceptional, as Beatrice is a self-proclaimed prophetess, daughter of Wilhelmina of Bohemia, who believed herself "the Holy Ghost incarnate upon earth for the salvation of the female sex."[36] In all of her works after *Valperga* (1823), Shelley never again allows such unorthodox beliefs and strong behavior for her female characters.

To a certain extent, Bettina von Arnim could be a figure in one of Mary Shelley's novels. Euthanasia and Monina share some of her traits of character: the energetic activity for a political cause, the persistent effort to counsel historical figures, the reluctance to compromise. The similarities are, however, limited. Mary Shelley curtailed her characters' realm of action. Bettina von Arnim would have rebelled, just as she chafed under the admonishments of her brother, Clemens Brentano. When he chided her for associating with an impoverished Jewish girl, she responded as none of Shelley's characters would: "Aber Sittlichkeit und Anstand, das sind zwei dumme Wächter, die dem menschlichen Sein und Willen den Weg verwehren."[37]

Her anxieties were less about the propriety of self-assertion and more about the effect: "Und dies ist, was mich oft vor mir erschreckt, daß ich im Lande der Phantasie mir eine große Rolle auserwählt habe, die ich zwar ohne Gefahr spiele, die aber nicht die Wirklichkeit berührt."[38]

Bettina von Arnim was anything but reticent. Both in her fantasies and in reality she sought an active, public role. Specific features of the role she created remain contradictory. Paradoxically, such features may have insured her the liberty to speak while undermining her influence. In her commentary to a collection of Bettina von Arnim's writings, Gisela Dischner notes that she apparently never felt herself disadvantaged or repressed as a woman, in contrast to other prominent women in German Romanticism.[39] She never engaged in the ambivalent tactics of Mary Shelley to mask her self-assertiveness. Yet, the persona she presented also elicited assessments of conventional female behavior, as in Heinrich von Treitschke's evaluation: "Bettina's Stärke lag wo das Genie der Weiber immer liegt, in der Kraft des Verstehens und Empfangens; sie wußte das und blieb immer der Epheu, der sich am festen Stamme emporrankt. Männerarbeit zu thun hat sie sich nie erdreistet;...."[40] Such assessments are often based on her first book, *Goethes Briefwechsel mit einem Kinde* (1835). In all four of her published volumes of re-edited correspondence, Bettina von Arnim took great liberties with chronology and with the original texts of the letters. In so doing she emphasized the persona she wished to present as "Bettine." Such a fictionalization of self underscored traditionally accepted roles for women and it embodies the contradictions in Bettina von Arnim's position.

The personal attachment to Goethe was a life-long fixation, although a dispute with Goethe's wife effectively ended their reciprocal correspondence in 1811. Bettina continued to write and to cultivate the connection, eventually designing a Goethe-monument in which she figured as Psyche. Her self-designation as "child" in the title of the published volume indicates the role she assumed, although she was twenty-two years old when the correspondence began in 1807. She refers to her letters as "das unmündige Stammeln eines unbedeutenden Kindes," as a melody to accompany his songs.[41] Such phrases reflect a stereotypical female role, as do the constant assurances of her devotion. Unorthodox in her insistent imposition upon Goethe, she equivocates in the conventional tone of the role she assumes.

It is, however, insufficient to dismiss the puerile posturing as gender-determined behavior in contrast to her assertiveness. The ambivalence is more complex. In the correspondence with Günderode, Bettina von Arnim explains how her behavior could sometimes be advantageous, because "sie halten mich doch für ein Kind, weil ich keine Gesellschaftsmanieren habe."[42] A tacit critique of the superficiality of prescribed social conduct also functions in the persona of "Bettine." Nor is her role in the Goethe book solely that of the clinging ivy of Treitschke's description. She also reasons and disagrees with Goethe, albeit effusively, on subjects such as music, the Tyrolean struggles for independence, or education and civil rights for Jews. Certainly she stylizes herself as Mignon, but she also rewrites the part. The enigmatic figure from Goethe's *Wilhelm Meister* turns militant, and Bettina also addresses the title character, exhorting him to participate actively in the world: "Die Melancholie erfaßt Dich, weil keine Welt da ist, in der Du handeln kannst."[43] She complains to Goethe that she herself is denied an active role: "Staatsangelegenheiten vertraut man mir nicht, aber Herzensangelegenheiten."[44] The immature role is both assumed and imposed. The author's ambivalence and the contradictions of her times find expression in the dual voice of "Bettine," assertive and yet "Dein Kind, dein Herz, dein gut Mädchen, das den Goethe über alles lieb hat und sich mit seinem Andenken über alles trösten kann."[45]

A more muted ambivalence characterizes the other volumes of rewritten correspondence: *Die Günderode* (1840), *Clemens Brentanos Frühlingskranz* (1844), and *Ilius Pamphilius und die Ambrosia* (1848). They present a curious genre. Epistolary novel is an appropriate designation only if novel is understood in the Romantic sense as defined by Schlegel: "einen sentimentalen Stoff in einer fantastischen Form."[46] The author reworks her relationship to Goethe, to Karoline von Günderode, and to her brother by re-ordering, sometimes rewriting their correspondence years later. Her partner in the final volume is Philipp Nathusius, a man thirty years younger than she. Here her role is that of female mentor. All of the volumes affect a latent eroticism and a distinct self-stylization. Ingeborg Drewitz emphasizes Bettina's instinct for reflecting her own image in the correspondence with others, and another biographer terms it "der Kult des Ichs."[47] In a positive sense, her epistolary novels illustrate Schlegel's statement: "daß das Beste in den besten Romanen nichts anderes ist als ein mehr oder minder verhülltes Selbstbekenntnis des Verfassers, der Ertrag seiner Erfahrung, die Quintessenz seiner Eigentümlichkeit."[48]

Repeatedly in the volumes she engages in a verbal tug-of-war with her partners, testing her own strength against their ideas. With her brother Clemens she resists the attempts to channel her energies, whether in her style of life, her writing, or her music lessons. With Günderode she confronts pressures to occupy herself with history and philosophy. The confrontation is productive. She rebels against a hierarchical system of thought, insisting that philosophy nauseates her and rejecting history as the study of names and epochs. Günderode quotes Bettina von Arnim's own words in order to convince her of the necessity of studying history: "Da führt der Wind der Vergangenheit Samen in die Zukunft."[49] In Günderode's formulation, the urgent task is the incorporation of the unfulfilled promise of the past into present impetus toward building the future. It is this sense of history to which she wishes to arouse her friend.

Bettina von Arnim never developed a traditional intellectual sense of history. Yet, she shared Günderode's vision, and Hölderlin's friend Sinclair once defended her against the reproach of an insufficient sense of history with a fitting characterization: "Gebt ihr eine Fahne in die Hand und laßt sie uns voranschreiten, so führt sie uns sicher, trotz ihrem Mangel an historischem Sinn, zu einem gesunden Wendepunkt der Geschichte."[50] Both in fantasy and in reality, Bettina von Arnim sought such a bold role, and the uncertain efficacy of her efforts is indicative of the contradictions, both of her epoch and of the self which she presented.

One role which she consistently claimed was that of advisor to Friedrich Wilhelm IV, whom she had known as crown prince before his ascension to the throne in 1840. She dedicated two books to her advisory endeavors: *Dies Buch gehört dem König* (1843) and *Gespräche mit Dämonen* (1852). The figure and ingenious wisdom of Goethe's mother ("Frau Rat") provide the continuity to the loosely structured volume of 1843. Much of the book is in dialogue form, and the central theme is the role of the king. The monarch is seen as a positive figure, unfortunately alienated from his people by his ministers and the state bureaucracy. The 1852 volume is even more unstructured, definitely to its disadvantage. The dialogue form is again prevalent, and the "Dämon" having the major role is Bettina's persona. In the latter section she is joined by numerous other voices. The villians are again the ministers, and the sense of crisis between monarch and populace is stronger. By 1852, the reactionary character and policies of Friedrich Wilhelm IV were hopelessly evident, and Bettina von Arnim's attempted exhortations seem accordingly strained.[51]

The initial volume had been received with great interest; the second volume was decidedly unsuccessful. In the elaborate discussions with Frau Rat in the first book, Bettina's social and political concerns become evident. She argues against religious dogmatism, against the death penalty, and in favor of judiciary reforms and freedom of thought and expression. The supplement to the book is a documentary section entitled "Erfahrungen eines jungen Schweizers im Vogtlande." Written by a Swiss acquaintance of Bettina, it depicts the conditions in the poorest sections of Berlin. Both the topic and the documentary genre were to occupy her further in 1844. She intended to compile a public report on poverty and advertised in regional German newspapers to solicit data. Contributions came from Silesia concerning the misery of the weavers, and when the Weavers' Revolt broke out, Bettina von Arnim was suspected of inciting the disturbances. She was forced to abandon her project, and "Das Armenbuch" was never completed.[52]

Her activities in 1844 were indicative of her assumption of an active, public role. In contrast to Mary Shelley's characters, her initiatives were neither camouflaged nor ambiguously motivated. She attempted to wield what influence she had in the cause of issues which concerned her. During the cholera outbreak of 1831, she actively assisted in nursing the poor. The victims of industrialization and capitalist expansion occupied her in both volumes to the king and in "Das Armenbuch." Before Friedrich Wilhelm IV's ascension to the throne, she had already interceded for the "Göttingen Seven," professors who had been dismissed in 1837 for protesting the abrogation of the constitution in Hanover. Her efforts contributed to having two of them, the Grimm brothers, later called to the university in Berlin. In the revolutionary fervor of the 1840's her salon was a center of progressive intellectuals. In 1848 she wrote the anonymous brochure "An die aufgelöste preußische Nationalversammlung: Stimmen aus Paris," which defended the Polish striving for independence. She had actively defended one of the Polish leaders, Ludwig von Mieroslawski, and clearly took the progressive side in this controversial issue which characterized the failure of the 1848 revolution in Germany.[53] Not only did she claim for herself in all such activities the right to conjecture "über das Wohl und Bedürfnis der Menschheit," as she had written to Karoline von Günderode, but she vigorously assisted in advancing the cause.

Yet the ambivalence in her writings remains. "Bettine" as "Kind," as "Kobold," as "Dämon," as companion to the whimsical figure of Frau Rat Goethe all attest to contradictory elements in Bettina von Arnim's public voice. Christa Wolf has emphasized the freedom which such identities afforded her, and her thesis is convincing.[54] Yet, reading Bettina's works is at times an unsettling experience. The Minister of the Interior remarked concerning *Dies Buch gehört dem König* that it would be a dangerously radical work except for its being written "in dem für nur einen kleinen Leserkreis geeigneten Tone prophetischer Exstase" and for "der abentheuerliche Charakter" of the author.[55] Bettina von Arnim's life-long romanticized persona, the "Naturkind," resulted in a conflicting message. Her outspoken assertiveness was upon occasion dismissed too easily. The contradictions are different from those in Mary Shelley's fiction, but the issues are related. For Shelley, an assertive woman was unnatural, and her attempts to restrict her characters and herself result in the contradictions in her life and work. For Bettina von Arnim, self-assertion came naturally, but the assessments accorded her character and writings and the stylized self she presented indicate similar tensions. The editor of Bettina von Arnim's works characterizes her as living in the world which she would like to create.[56] Mary Shelley inhabited all too consciously the society which she perceived and acknowledged. The dual voice perceptible in the lives and writings of both women demonstrates their personal contradictions and those of the worlds they inhabited.

Notes

[1] *Mary Shelley's Journal* (Ed., Frederick L. Jones), (Norman: University of Oklahoma Press, 1947), p. 204.

[2] The topic is perhaps also appropriate for a volume of essays in honor of Professor Liptzin. His book, *Shelley in Germany*, traces the influence of Mary Shelley's husband in Germany. See Solomon Liptzin, *Shelley in Germany* (New York: Columbia University Press, 1924). Chapter six contains interesting descriptions of versions of Mary Shelley in works by German authors.

[3] Sandra M. Gilbert and Susan Gubar, *The Madwoman in the Attic: The Woman Writer and the Nineteenth-Century Literary Imagination* (New Haven: Yale University Press, 1979), p. 76.

[4] According to one biographer, she was the only woman asked to contribute to *The Cabinet of Biography* edited by Rev. Dionysius Lardner and published during the 1830's. Jane Dunn, *Moon in Eclipse* (London: Weidenfeld and Nicholson, 1978), pp. 282-283. Shelley's additional works include short stories, some poems, and two blank-verse dramas.

[5] Her full name was Elisabeth Catharina Ludovica Magdalena Brentano. She signed her name in correspondence as Bettine, and both Bettina and Bettine are used in references to her.

[6] Bettina von Arnim reworked their correspondence from 1800 to 1804 and published it in 1844 as *Clemens Brentanos Frühlingskranz*. Clemens had died in 1842, but brother and sister had been estranged for many years, Bettina being unable to accept her brother's Catholic mysticism.

[7] *Achim und Bettina in ihren Briefen* (Ed., Werner Vordtriede), 2. vols. (Frankfurt: Suhrkamp, 1961). There is also a selection of her letters to him in volume five of: Bettina von Arnim, *Werke und Briefe* (Ed., Joachim Müller), (Frechen/Cologne: Bartmann Verlag, 1961). This is the final volume of the Konrad edition.

[8] Letter of January 7, 1830 to John Bowring, quoted here from the newest edition of the letters: *The Letters of Mary Wollstonecraft Shelley* (Ed., Betty Bennett), (Baltimore & London: Johns Hopkins University Press, 1983), II, p. 99.

[9] Bettina von Arnim, *Werke und Briefe* (Ed., Gustav Konrad), (Frechen/Cologne: Bartmann Verlag, 1959), I, p. 327.

[10] Arnim, I, p. 331.

[11] Arnim, I, p. 326.

[12] Karl Gutzkow reviewed the book for the *Telegraph für Deutschland*, Nr. 165 (October 1843). The review is quoted at length in Konrad's notes: Arnim, III, pp. 468-470.

[13] Her quarrels with the censors are documented in: H. H. Houben, *Verbotene Literatur von der klassischen Zeit bis zur Gegenwart* (Berlin: Rowohlt, 1924), I, pp. 29-41. Her dispute with the Berlin magistrature is analyzed in: Gertrud Meyer-Hepner, *Der Magistratsprozeß der Bettina von Arnim* (Weimar: Arion Verlag, 1960).

[14] For Schlegel: the commentary by Ernst Behler in volume V of the *Kritische Friedrich-Schlegel-Ausgabe* (Ed., Ernst Behler), (Munich: Schöningh, 1962), pp. xxvi-xxxv; the collection of writings and commentary *Friedrich Schlegel Theorie der Weiblichkeit* (Ed., Winfried Menninghaus), (Frankfurt: Insel, 1983). Also relevant is Hannelore Schlaffer, "Frauen als Einlösung der frühromantischen Kunsttheorie," *Jahrbuch der deutschen Schillergesellschaft*, 21 (1977), pp. 274-296. A critical view is offered by: Bärbel Becker-Cantarino, "Schlegels *Lucinde* Zum Frauenbild der Romantik," *Colloquia Germanica*, 10 (1976-77), pp. 128-139. For Percy Shelley: Nathaniel Brown, *Sexuality and Feminism in Shelley* (Cambridge, Mass.: Harvard University Press, 1979).

[15] Their views on marriage are found, for example, in Schlegel's Athenäumsfragment 34 and in Percy Shelley's essay "On Marriage." They also both addressed the question of women in antiquity; Schlegel in the two essays "Über die weiblichen Charaktere in den griechischen Dichtern" (1794) and "Über die Diotima" (1795), and Percy Shelley in "A Discourse of the Manners of the Antient Greeks Relative to the Subject of Love" (first published in unexpurgated form in 1931).

[16] *The Complete Works of Percy Bysshe Shelley* (Eds., Roger Ingpen & Walter E. Peck), (London: Ernest Benn Ltd., 1930), VII, p. 127.

[17] *Kritische Friedrich-Schlegel-Ausgabe*, V, p. 13.

[18] *Kritische Friedrich-Schlegel-Ausgabe*, I, p. 93.

[19] *Kritische Friedrich-Schlegel-Ausgabe*, V, p. 55.

[20] Canto II: XLVIII *The Complete Poetical Works of Percy Bysshe Shelley* (Ed., Neville Rogers), (Oxford: Clarendon, 1975), II, pp. 141-142.

[21] Mary Shelley, *Frankenstein* (New York: Signet, 1965), p. vii. All further references to this work appear in the text.

[22] The "parable of motherhood" is in: Marc A. Rubenstein, " 'My Accursed Origin': The Search for the Mother in *Frankenstein," Studies in Romanticism*, 15 (spring 1976), 187. The "birth myth" is in: Ellen Moers, "Female Gothic," in *The Endurance of Frankenstein* (Ed., George Levine & U.C. Knoepflmacher), (Berkeley: University of California Press, 1979), p. 79. Of the other essays in this volume, the following is most relevant to my analysis: U.C. Knoepflmacher, "Thoughts on the Aggression of Daughters," pp. 88-119. Mary Poovey has an excellent analysis of the original and the 1831 versions: Mary Poovey, *The Proper Lady and the Woman Writer* (Chicago: University of Chicago Press, 1984), pp. 114-142. Related articles include the chapter by Gilbert and Gubar,

pp. 213-247 and Devon Hodges, "*Frankenstein* and the Feminine Subversion of the Novel," ***Tulsa Studies in Women's Literature*, 2 (Fall, 1983), pp. 155-164.**

[23] Barbara Johnson, "My Monster/My Self," *Diacritics* (1982), p. 7.

[24] Biographical turbulence was most certainly a factor in the production of the novel, begun as part of a ghost-story competition with Byron, Percy Shelley, and Byron's physician Polidori. During the writing of *Frankenstein*, Shelley's half-sister Fanny Imlay learned of her illegitimacy and committed suicide, as did Percy Shelley's wife Harriet, supposedly pregnant. Mary and Percy Shelley finally married and tried in vain to adopt his two children by Harriet. Mary Shelley's other half-sister by marriage gave birth to Byron's daughter. Shelley herself, having already given birth to two illegitimate children and watched one die, was pregnant again. The questions of parenting and legitimacy are related to the doubts concerning a woman's self-expression in writing and to the contradictions of *Frankenstein*.

[25] Poovey, 115. Her study is extremely perceptive, with clear analyses of *Frankenstein, The Last Man*, and *Falkner*.

[26] Mary Shelley, *Valperga: or, The Life and Adventures of Castruccio, Prince of Lucca* (London: Whittaker, 1823), I, p. iv.

[27] Mary Shelley, *The Fortunes of Perkin Warbeck: A Romance* (Philadelphia: Carey, Lea & Blanchard, 1834), I, p. 3.

[28] *Perkin Warbeck*, II, pp. 236-237.

[29] Mary Shelley, *The Last Man* (London: Henry Colburn, 1826), I, pp. x-xi. See also: Gilbert and Gubar, pp. 96-104 and Poovey, 157-158.

[30] **Mary Shelley, *Mathilda* (Ed., Elizabeth Nitchie), *Studies in Philology*,** Extra Series 3 (Chapel Hill: University of North Carolina Press, 1959), p. 2.

[31] *The Last Man*, I, p. 131. The assertion is made in a discussion with Lord Raymond, the Lord-Byron figure who argues for the determination of human character and actions.

[32] Poovey, 163.

[33] Mary Shelley, *Lodore* (New York: Wallis & Newell, 1835), p. 153. As in all of Shelley's novels, the characters have corresponding figures in her life. It has been suggested that Fanny Derham is *à clef* for Fanny Imlay. At times biographical identification obscures other issues, and I have not engaged in it extensively.

[34] *Perkin Warbeck*, II, p. 112.

[35] Regarding the political message of *Perkin Warbeck* see: William A. Walling, *Mary Shelley* (New York: Twayne Publishers, 1972), pp. 101-104, and Betty Bennett, "The Political Philosophy of Mary Shelley's Historical Novels: *Valperga* and *Perkin Warbeck*," in *The Evidence of the Imagination: Studies of* ***Interactions between Life and Art in English Romantic Literature*** **(Ed., Donald H. Reiman, Michael C. Jaye, and Betty Bennett), (New York: New York Univer**sity Press, 1978), pp. 354-371.

[36] *Valperga*, II, p. 26.

[37] Arnim, I, p. 156.

[38] Arnim, I, p. 92.

[39] Gisela Dischner, *Bettina von Arnim: Eine weibliche Sozialbiographie aus dem neunzehnten Jahrhundert* (Berlin: Wagenbach, 1984), pp. 11-15.

[40] Heinrich von Treitschke, *Deutsche Geschichte im neunzehnten Jahrhundert*, 4th ed. (Leipzig: Verlag v. Hirzel, 1897), IV, p. 418.

[41] Arnim, II, p. 68, 69.

[42] Arnim, I, p. 250.

[43] Arnim, II, p. 181: letter dated 20. März.

[44] Arnim, II, p. 181: letter dated 15. März.

[45] Arnim, II, p. 73.

[46] *Kritische Friedrich-Schlegel-Ausgabe*, II, p. 333.

[47] Ingeborg Drewitz, *Bettine von Arnim. Romantik, Revolution, Utopie* (Düsseldorf: Eugen Diederichs Verlag, 1969), pp. 13, 30, 34. Gertrud Mander, *Bettina von Arnim* (Berlin: Stapp Verlag, 1982), p. 115.

[48] *Kritische Friedrich-Schlegel-Ausgabe*, II, p. 337.

[49] Arnim, I, p. 295.

[50] Arnim I, 307. She refers to the incident in a letter to her brother as well: Arnim, I, p. 160.

[51] For a detailed study of Bettina von Arnim and the King of Prussia see: Ludwig Geiger, *Bettine von Arnim und Friedrich Wilhelm IV* (Frankfurt: Rütten & Loening, 1902).

[52] The materials are collected in: *Bettina von Arnims Armenbuch* (Ed., Werner Vordtriede), 2nd. ed. (Frankfurt: Insel, 1981). Professor Liptzin refers to Bettina von Arnim's efforts in: Solomon Liptzin, *The Weavers in German Literature* (Göttingen: Vandenhoeck & Ruprecht and Baltimore: Johns Hopkins Press, 1926), pp. 16, 25, 42.

[53] See Ursula Püschel, *Bettina von Arnims Polenbroschüre* (Berlin: Henschelverlag, 1954).

[54] Christa Wolf, "Nun ja! Das nächste Leben geht aber heute an. Ein Brief über die Bettine," in her *Lesen und Schreiben: Neue Sammlung* (Darmstadt: Luchterhand, 1980), pp. 284-318. It was originally the afterword to her edition of Bettina von Arnim's *Die Günderode* (Leipzig: Insel, 1980).

[55] Houben, p. 35.

[56] Arnim, III, p. 446.

The Changing Image of the Jew: Nathan the Wise and Shylock

Ludwig W. Kahn

1.

I would like to start with an observation neither very new nor very surprising – namely that the fortunes and reputations of literary figures tend to change as we, the readers, change or, more precisely, as our consciousness and our outlook change. As an illustration let me offer my own changing perception of a well-known poem by Theodor Fontane. The great German novelist had written mostly about the Prussian nobility and, on the occasion of his 75th birthday, he had every right to expect the Prussian squires and Junkers to acknowledge and repay the literary homage he had paid to them and their circle for so long a time. Instead, he says in his poem, his real literary constituents turned out to be members of a much older aristocracy, namely the descendents of Abraham and Isaac, with names ending in "berg" and "heim," people called Meyer and Pollack, Fontane's Jewish publishers, critics, and readers. To the Jewish readers his books had meant something; *they* had read him:

> Jedem bin ich was gewesen,
> Alle haben sie mich gelesen,
> Alle kannten mich lange schon,
> Und das ist die Hauptsache... Kommen Sie, Cohn.

Fontane withheld his poem from publication, allegedly because he did not want to publicize his final break with the Prussian aristocracy.[1] But is the poem really a turning away from the aristocracy and a welcoming of the Jews? I must confess that, when I first read the poem many years ago, I had an uneasy sense that it came close to some form of benevolent anti-Semitism. First, there is an implication that Fontane would, after all, have preferred Prussian Junkers as readers and that the Jews were only accepted by default, as a second choice, so to speak. But what bothered me even more was that Fontane was so aware of the Jewishness of his readers, that the Jews were singled out as a group distinct, different, and alien, set apart from other Germans. In my circle, it was polite to be blind to color, creed, and national origin of the other person – after all, we were all equal human beings. But, since then we have learned that it will not do to pretend that differences do not exist; our religious, racial, and ethnic consciousness has been raised and, with it, our literary perception. Today, I think, if we tend to feel more positively about Jewish identity, Fontane's poem now reads quite differently; it is with pride that we read his testimony to Jewish literary sensitivity and taste. The image of the Jew has changed – for social, historical, and political reasons that regretfully cannot be discussed here – and with it our response to a work of literature.

2.

Before turning to Lessing's Nathan, let us take a quick look at the one-act comedy that Lessing had written thirty years earlier, *Die Juden* (1749). As the play begins, we hear that a baron had been murderously assaulted the night before and had been rescued by a traveler who happened to pass by. Since the robbers had worn beards, they are believed to be Jews; as a servant remarks, all Jews without exception are cheats, thieves, highwaymen (scene 2). The traveler soliloquizes that, if a Jew commits a crime, he has probably been compelled to do so seven out of nine times by some action of a Christian (scene 3). Not only the uneducated and unenlightened servant spouts bigotry; the baron himself is convinced that all Jews seek profit by any means, legal or illegal, and that their very facial features betray their malice, perjury, selfishness, and moral turpitude. In vain the traveler interjects that there are good people and bad people among all nations and religions.... (scene 6) As it happens, the traveler saves the baron a second time by discovering that the robbers of the night before were not Jews, but members of the baron's household – one of the criminals is, ironically, the very servant who made the anti-Semitic remarks. In gratitude the baron proffers the hand of his daughter, but this offer the traveler cannot accept because – he is a Jew. Since marriage is thus out of the question (after all, Lessing pleads for tolerance, not for miscegenation), the baron offers all his worldly possessions; these the Jew also politely declines:

> Auch dieses Anerbieten ist bei mir umsonst, da mir der Gott meiner Väter mehr gegeben hat, als ich brauche. Zu aller Vergeltung bitte ich nichts, als daß Sie künftig von meinem Volke etwas gelinder und weniger allgemein urteilen. (scene 22)

With greatest fairness and noble-mindedness Lessing shows the absurdity of religious prejudice. Yet, the very plot of the play rests on the assumption that the Jew is not recognizable as a Jew: – he looks, dresses, speaks, behaves in such a way that no one suspects him of being a Jew. The only dietary law he observes is the avoidance of pork; otherwise he apparently joins his gentile host for all meals. The Jew's servant complains that on all their travels he has to carry a heavy baggage of books – and they certainly are not Judaica. Lessing himself, in a later defense, points to these books as evidence that his Jew is educated and cultured in addition to being wealthy.[2] In brief, the plea for tolerance is not for all Jews, not for Jews as such, but for the one Jew who is affluent, educated, and assimilated to the rising German bourgeoisie. Today, such tolerance at the price of the suppression of all distinctive Jewish traits, tolerance that does not allow for heterogeneity, has become somewhat questionable.

In his early play, *Die Juden*, Lessing dealt with the social and legal emancipation of the Jews. Thirty years later, in *Nathan der Weise*, he is ostensibly concerned with a theological question –: which religion is the true and genuine one? It seems obvious, however, that considerable political, economic, social, and legal advantages would accrue to those of the true faith. The scene is set in Jerusalem during the Crusades which makes it easy to bring together representatives of the three great monotheistic religions: Saladin, the Mohammedan sultan; Nathan, the rich and wise and good Jewish merchant; and a Christian Knight-Templar. In the end, of course, it turns out that the putative daughter of the Jew, the Christian knight, and the Mohammedan ruler are all members of one and the same family –

the family of the universal brotherhood of all men that undoubtedly embraces Nathan both literally and figuratively (the final stage direction reads "allseitige Umarmungen"). Early on we learn something about Nathan's religion: his daughter, Recha, has been saved from a fire by the Christian Templar, but in a state of exaltation she believes that it was an angel who came to her rescue. Nathan tries to dissuade her because, as he puts it, we can dream and emote about an angel but we cannot *do* anything for him as we can for a mortal man. Ecstatic feelings are cheaper than good deeds (v. 360-61), and Nathan's religion demands good and humane actions rather than pious visions. Again and again the concept of humanity, of being a "Mensch," is emphasized throughout the play. To give just one example: when the dervish, Nathan's Mohammedan friend, professes that he feels bound to do, not what the Koran, but what his conscience demands ("was er für gut erkennt," v. 387), Nathan exclaims: "Lass dich umarmen, Mensch," and the emphasis is clearly on "Mensch": Jew and Mohammedan meet on the common ground of humanity. As a magnanimous humanist Nathan always tries to put the best possible face on other men's actions. Thus, at one point he imputes very noble motives to the Templar's not so noble disdain of, and discourtesy towards, Jews. Surprised, the Templar acknowledges: "Ich muss gestehn,/Ihr wisst, wie Tempelherren denken sollten." To which Nathan replies:

> Nur Tempelherren? *sollten* bloss? und bloss
> Weil es die Ordensregeln so gebieten?
> Ich weiss, wie gute Menschen denken; weiss,
> Dass alle Länder gute Menschen tragen.

The repeated emphasis on humaneness and humanity may seem almost over-deictic. When the Templar reacts with some jibes at the sectarian exclusiveness of Jews, Nathan answers with what some readers have considered an expression of loftiest sentiment:

> Wir müssen, müssen Freunde sein! – Verachtet
> Mein Volk so sehr Ihr wollt... Was heisst denn Volk?
> Sind Christ und Jude eher Christ und Jude
> Als Mensch? Ah! wenn ich einen mehr in Euch
> Gefunden hätte, dem es g'nügt, ein Mensch
> Zu heissen! (V. 1306-13)

Let us remember this strange concession of Nathan's: "Disdain my folk as much as you will" – to modern ears it does not sound like a very persuasive argument for tolerance. The rest of the speech, of course, states unequivocally that Jew and Christian and Mohammedan should rise to some transcendent and undistinguishable, and ultimately reductive, form of universal humanity. How man can aspire to such humaneness and rise above the claims of his religion is exemplified in Nathan's own story. Eighteen years ago, during a pogrom, Christians had burned to death Nathan's wife and their seven sons; Nathan had cursed the world and himself and had sworn irreconcilable hatred towards all Christians. Just then a groom brought him a Christian baby girl, a few months old. What would a Jew have done, acting merely as a Jew, as nothing but a Jew, as a "Stockjude" (v. 1885)? Would he not have taken bloody revenge? But Nathan thanked God for having returned to him one girl for his seven murdered sons and brought her up as his own daughter. This, then, is how all men should act everywhere and at all times, not because their religion commands it so, but because the human voice within them tells them to.

In the middle of the play, at its very center, Nathan tells Saladin the famous parable of the three rings. Its source is, of course, to be found in the third story of the first day of Boccaccio's *Decameron*: Saladin, in need of money, tries to trap a rich Jew; he asks him, since the Jew is considered wise and well-versed in religious questions, which of the three religions he believes to be the true one. The Jew escapes the dilemma by telling a story: a rich man of olden times possessed a precious ring which he desired to remain forever in his family. Therefore, he stipulated in his will that to whichever of the sons he should leave the ring, that son should be his heir and the head of the family, and he asked that the same provision should be made by all his descendents. So it went, until the ring came to a father who had three good and obedient sons, all of whom he loved equally well. Each of the sons begged that he should be left the ring, and the father promised it to each in turn. Secretly he had two counterfeit rings made, so like the original that he who made them could hardly tell them apart. After the father's death each son produced his ring and claimed to be the rightful heir. To this day it is impossible to decide which is the genuine ring, just as – the Jew concludes – it is impossible to decide which of the three religions is genuine; just as the three brothers with their rings, Jews and Christians and Mohammedans each believe to have received their religion directly from God. Nathan retells Boccaccio's story rather faithfully, but makes two significant additions. First, in Nathan's version the original ring has the magical power to make its wearer beloved by God and men. Secondly, Nathan's story has a continuation: the three sons go to court; the judge, remembering the magical power of the original ring, asks which brother is beloved by the other two – for such love would prove the power of the original ring. Since each seems to love only himself, the judge concludes that all three rings must be false. The judge, however, has some advice:

> 'Es eifre jeder seiner unbestochnen
> Von Vorurteilen freien Liebe nach!
> Es strebe von euch jeder um die Wette,
> Die Kraft des Steins in seinem Ring an Tag
> Zu legen! Komme dieser Kraft mit Sanftmut,
> Mit herzlicher Verträglichkeit, mit Wohltun,
> Mit innigster Ergebenheit in Gott,
> Zu Hilf'! (v. 2041-48)

He who wins the love of God and his fellow-man will thereby demonstrate the genuineness of his religion. Superficially this sounds like the saying that the tree shall be known by its fruit (Matth. xii, 33), i.e. *that* religion is best which produces the best and wisest human beings. But the meaning of Nathan's parable is precisely the reverse –: neither Torah, nor Gospels, nor Koran lead us to righteousness. It is the other way round: a man's righteousness ultimately reflects credit and honor on his religion. Explicitly, Lessing rejects the notion that any religion can serve as guide to the erring and perplexed. Saladin castigates the Christians because they wish to be nothing but Christians and take pride in obeying Christ's teachings, not because these teachings are good and humane, but merely because Christ taught them. (v. 871-2) This Christian attitude is carried to the absurd when the Patriarch maintains that, in matters of morality and conscience, a Christian ought to obey blindly when God deigns to speak through one of his messengers, i.e. through a servant of the Church. (v. 2480 ff.) It is to this tradition, which accepts religion as a spiritual vademecum, that Nathan opposes his conclusion: a man's righteousness does not depend on his religion, – the worth and value of his religion depend on his righteousness. To be sure, Lessing is tolerant in granting all religions equality, but they are equal because they are neutral and basically irrelevant. If every Jew, like Nathan, would shed his Jewish idiosyncrasies, surrender his Jewishness, and strive by pure humaneness to win the love and goodwill of God and men, he would prove his ring to be genuine. What, in the last analysis, it really amounts to is that noble-mindedness, humaneness, moral excellence, humility, charity, and brotherly love can turn even the counterfeit ring into a genuine one.[3]

For a hundred years after Lessing and down to our own day *Nathan* was the canonical text of tolerance, and a great source of self-respect and pride for many Jews who accorded *Nathan* a place of honor on their bookshelves and in their hearts. Assimilation was the watchword of 19th century Jewry, and Nathan, anxious to tone down Jewish distinctions and differences, could serve as the prototype of assimilation. Hettner states: "Nathan der Weise war das Evangelium der Liebe und Duldung, das der innerste Kern des gesamten Zeitalters war."[4] Korff calls *Nathan* "das hohe Lied der Menschenverbrüderung."[5] In his *History of the Jews*, Abram Leon Sachar characterizes *Nathan* as the "song of songs of tolerance" (although Sachar puts it into quotation marks).[6] Such, then, was the commonly held opinion – a few anti-Semitic cranks notwithstanding.[7] But today we must take a second look at Lessing's advocacy of tolerance. For one thing, Lessing neither is, nor should be, tolerant of anti-humanism, superstition, or intolerance. Furthermore, does not tolerance imply the accepting of the otherness, the separateness, and uniqueness of the Jew? And, in this respect Nathan is less than a perfect exemplar; remember his concession to the Templar: "Disdain my folk as much as you will!"

Modern critics have indeed begun to chip away at the monumental figure of Nathan – for various, and sometimes questionable, reasons. Within a year of Hitler's seizure of power, Gerhard Fricke, an excellent literary historian and politically a most dubious character, explored in a number of articles the significance of classical German humanism for his day.[8] Since Fricke begins by praising the National-Socialist regime for rejuvenating Germany and leading it towards its own destiny and its own future, towards its "eigene Bestimmung," (p. 252) he must reject Lessing's ideal of universal humanity – "eigene Bestimmung" does not go with equality and the brotherhood of all men: "Aber wir empfinden ..., dass wir von der Idee und Verwirklichung der Humanität, wie sie im *Nathan* ... Gestaltung gefunden hat, unwiderruflich entfernt sind." (p. 253) The substance of our thoughts and actions, Fricke maintains, is determined not by abstract reason, but by the transcending, fateful, superindividual realities of folk, race, and religion. By contrast, Fricke argues, Nathan is detached from the human condition and from the forces of nation, tradition, and religion:

> Er besteht im Grunde, gelockert und grundsätzlich losgelöst von allen konkreten Bindungen seines menschlichen Schicksals, von Nation, Rasse, Überlieferung, Religion usw. aus der schlechthin überindividuellen "Reinheit" des sittlichen Handelns ... Das Ich, das in Nathan beispielhaft dargestellt ist ... hat damit eigentlich alle menschliche Bestimmbarkeit, Wirklichkeit und Existenz verloren. (p. 274-76)

In addition to the nationalistic jargon, there are obvious overtones of the existentialist outlook so popular in the thirties and forties.

Fricke's strictures were taken up a few years later in America by Meno Spann, albeit without invoking nation or race.[9] For Spann it was not the German mystique, not "deutsche Wesensart," but the need of preserving the true and distinctive essence of a person that militated against Lessing's humanism. "Lessings Toleranz," Spann insists, " ist eine Toleranz durch Aufhebung der Gegensätze im reinen Vernunftreich. Von Toleranz im eigentlichen Sinne des Wortes, d.h. dem Erleiden dieser Gegensätze kann im 'Nathan' wohl kaum die Rede sein. ..." (p. 155) Lessing, the son of the Enlightenment, had considered differences, such as those between Nathan and the Templar, or between Nathan and the Patriarch, merely the result of faulty thinking or feeling – as mistakes that can and should be corrected, as "korrigierbare Denkfehler," (p. 157) not as what they really are, namely, irreconcilable opposites, i.e. "Wesensgegensätze." By contrast, Spann, also under the influence of existentialism, defines tolerance as a suffering of the otherness of the other: "ein Leiden am andern." (p. 158)

More recently, Hans Mayer based his objections to Lessing on the same existential, as well as on sociological, grounds.[10] Nathan himself regards his religion as accidental and exchangeable: "Sind Christ und Jude eher Christ und Jude als Mensch?" Hans Mayer controverts: "Das Aussenseitertum der Juden ist nicht ein *mentaler Spleen*, weniger noch eine *emotionale Idiosynkrasie*, wie etwa beim *Misogyn* des jungen Lessing: sie ist in der damaligen Gesellschaft existentiell, folglich unlösbar." (S. 334) Lessing is faulted for premising his plea for tolerance on an intolerant postulate, namely, that the Jew must pay for his civil rights by surrendering his existential otherness: "[Lessing] gründete andrerseits aber *Toleranz* auf ein *Postulat der Intoleranz*, indem für Shylock und seine Geschwister die Gleichstellung nur denkbar sein sollte um den Preis der Aufgabe der Nationalität, im Grunde der existentiellen Besonderheit in der europäischen Gesellschaft. ..." (p. 343) Lessing's expectation that individual Jews, if they are educated and wealthy, could become naturalized members of the German bourgeoisie disregards, according to Mayer, the social and historical realities, disregards the outsider status of the Jew.

On existential grounds, Fricke and Spann come to the conclusion that the ideas of the Enlightenment are no longer applicable to our times. Mayer seems to argue that they *are* applicable, but that they have not been realized and that, therefore, the enlightenment has failed: "Wenn Aufklärung mit dem Grundsatz einer Gleichheit alles dessen, 'was Menschenantlitz trägt,' wahrhaft Ernst machen will, muss sie die Juden als Anderssein, als Volk, in ihren gesellschaftlichen Gewordensein akzeptieren." (p. 329) In fairness to Lessing, however, it must be remembered that he does not discriminate against the Jews or single them out – he asks of the Jews, and expects from them, no more and no less than he does of the Christians or Mohammedans. In simple terms, Lessing did not wish to assimilate the Jews or to integrate them into a German and Christian bourgeoisie; rather he envisioned their meeting on some common higher ground.

Reviewing a performance of *Nathan*, Friedrich Torberg wrote probably the most eloquent, the most passionate, and the most consciously "Jewish" denunciation of Lessing's philosemtism:[11]

> Wir stehen hier einer höchst seltsamen Form von Toleranz gegenüber, die demjenigen, dem sie gilt, erst dann zugute kommt, wenn er darauf verzichtet, das zu sein, was er eigentlich ist. Also eine Toleranz um den Preis der Selbstaufgabe. Also eine Toleranz, die nicht bereit ist, Andersartigkeit zu akzeptieren. Also keine Toleranz.

And Torberg submits the rather startling thesis:

> ...dass nämlich dieser Philosemitismus im Grunde nichts anderes ist als ein Antisemitismus mit verkehrtem Vorzeichen. Er glaubt den Juden einen Gefallen zu erweisen, wenn er ihr Jude-Sein nicht zur Kenntnis nimmt – und da er immer wieder auf Juden stösst, denen er damit tatsächlich einen Gefallen erweist, glaubt er es sogar mit Recht. Er akzeptiert den Juden als Deutschen, als Menschen, sogar als Christen – als alles, nur nicht als Jude.

And to Lessing's undoubtedly noble humanism he replies:

> Kann man denn nicht Mensch *und* Christ, Mensch *und* Jude sein. Muss man das eine um des andern willen hintansetzen oder gar aufgeben? Und ist es die wahre Toleranz, die eine Antithese herstellt, wo es auf Synthese ankäme?

Torberg's question may betray a certain lack of 18th-century thought, but it does show how much of its lustre the great image of Nathan has lost over the years.[12]

If the literary fortunes of Nathan have declined, the reputation of Shylock has correspondingly improved.[13] Of course, the interpretations of *The Merchant of Venice* and of Shylock diverge considerably – all the way from chafing at the play's blatant anti-Semitism to finding in it a deep sympathy for the Jew. Still, as Shakespeare wrote the play (not necessarily as we read it today), we very definitely find a Christian society permeated by love, friendship, light, music, grace, beauty, harmony, and liberality. This aristocratic society is threatened by something plebeian, alien, and dark – by the Jew Shylock who has neither love nor mercy, and least of all generosity. Not just two religions, but two life-styles oppose each other. As Gustav Landauer has pointed out, the very names show Shylock's outcast state: where all the male names end in "o" – Antonio, Bassanio, Lorenzo, etc. – the Jew's cacophonous name is Shylock.[14] Surely, Shylock's obsession with profit and money is meant to betray a base trait of his character:

> I hate him for he is a Christian:
> But more, for that in low simplicity
> He lends out money gratis, and brings down
> The rate of usance here with us in Venice. (I,iii)

It has been argued that Shakespeare is prejudiced against Shylock, not because he is a Jew (how could a man like Shakespeare be bigoted?!), but because he is a usurer.[15] But it does not matter, since Jew and usurer are obviously synonymous. Antonio, the grand seigneur, is forced to deal with Shylock and to sign the infamous bond, just as poor and desperate people in folk tales are occasionally driven to pacts with the devil. Just as we are supposed to applaud when in such a tale the devil is finally outmanoeuvred, there can be little doubt that we are supposed to feel deep satisfaction when Shylock in the end is cheated and outwitted. When Shylock is frustrated in his evil designs, the world of Antonio is rid of the alien threat and is once more whole: harmony is reestablished. Can there really be any doubt that the Jew was conceived as a sinister and monstrous figure of malice, as the very incarnation of avarice and cruelty?[16] Even his famous and over-quoted remonstration that Jews are, after all, human beings is not as redeeming as it sounds:

> He hath disgrac'd me, and hind'red me half a million, laugh'd at my losses, mock'd at my gains, scorned my nation, thwarted my bargains, cooled my friends, heated my enemies, – and what is his reason? I am a Jew. Hath not a Jew eyes? hath not a Jew hands, organs, dimensions, senses, affections, passions? fed with the same food, hurt with the same weapons, subject to the same diseases, healed by the same means, warmed and cooled by the same winter and summer as a Christian is? – if you prick us do we not bleed? if you tickle us do we not laugh? if you poison us do we not die? and if you wrong us shall we not revenge? – if we are like you in the rest, we will resemble you in that. If a Jew wrong a Christian, what is his humility? revenge! If a Christian wrong a Jew, what should his sufferance be by Christian example? – why revenge! The villainy you teach me I will execute, and it shall go hard but I will better the instruction. (III,i)

Jews usually applaud the speech. Yet, the wrongs that Shylock enumerates consist for the most part of interference with his business. The whole speech, moreover, is made by Shylock to justify his cruelty and hatred. Finally, with Lessing's *Nathan* in mind, we cannot fail to see that the claim of a common human bond between Jew and

Christian is here based not on some lofty form of humaneness, but on the lowest common denominator of physiology: on the vulnerability of the body, on hunger and thirst and the need for warmth. The true bond between Christian and Jew is their non-denominational vindictiveness.

In fine, Shylock is an abject figure. Yet, he shows traits that demand our attention. First, his hatred, his desire for revenge are always in the open; he does not dissemble as does Jago, or Edmund Gloucester, or Marlowe's Jew of Malta; his enemies ought to know what to expect.[17] Secondly, inspite of what we have just said, he does after all point out that Jews are human beings. Thirdly, and perhaps most importantly, in some rather famous lines he eloquently and passionately states the case for the despised and abused Jewish pariah:

Signior Antonio, many a time and oft
In the Rialto you have rated me
About my moneys and my usances:
Still have I born it with a patient shrug,
(For suff'rance is the badge of all our tribe)
You call me misbeliever, cut-throat dog,
And spet upon my Jewish gaberdine ...
Well then, it now appears you need my help:
Go to then, you come to me, and you say,
"Shylock, we would have moneys," you say so:
You that did void your rheum upon my beard,
And foot me as you spurn a stranger cur
Over your threshold, moneys is your suit.
What should I say to you? Should I not say
"Hath a dog money? is it possible
A cur can lend three thousand ducats?" or
Shall I bend low, and in a bondman's key
With bated breath, and whisp'ring humbleness
Say this:
"Fair sir, you spet on me on Wednesday last,
You spurn'd me such a day, another time
You call'd me dog: and for these courtesies
I'll lend you thus much moneys"? (I, iii)

Shylock is neither a servile coward nor a hypocrite; he does not fawn upon his enemies; mistreated and execrated, he stands up to his persecutor and fights back. Most unlike Nathan, he would never say: "Disdain my folk as much as you will." He snarls at his enemy:

> Thou call'dst me dog before thou hadst a cause,
> But since I am a dog, beware my fangs – (III, iii)

This, then, is the rehabilitated image of Shylock as it emerges – the man who refuses to be treated like a dog, who takes up the fight for the whole injured and down-trodden Jewish race.

Admittedly, we would admire Shylock even more if, in the trial scene, he were to fight to the bitter end and buy his pound of flesh even at the price of his life. – But let us look at this much-discussed trial scene. Does not Portia, as the judge, goad Shylock on by repeatedly declaring his bond legal, valid, and enforceable? Does she not reenforce his trust in the law – only to trick him in the end by the cheapest and flimsiest sophistry? In all likelihood this trial scene filled the Elizabethen spectator with glee, but it has jarred the sensibilities of more modern audiences, most notably those of Heinrich Heine:

> Als ich dieses Stück in Drury Lane aufführen sah, stand hinter mit in der Loge eine schöne blasse Britin, welche am Ende des vierten Aktes heftig weinte und mehrmals ausrief: "The poor man is wronged!" Es war ein Gesicht vom edelsten griechischen Schnitt, und die Augen waren gross und schwarz. Ich habe sie nicht vergessen können, diese grossen und schwarzen Augen, welche um Shylock geweint haben... Shakespeare hegte vielleicht die Absicht, zur Ergötzung des grossen Haufens einen gedrillten Werwolf darzustellen, ein verhasstes Fabelgeschöpf, das nach Blut lechzt und dabei seine Tochter und seine Dukaten einbüsst und obendrein verspottet wird. Aber der Genius des Dichters, der Weltgeist, der in ihm waltet, steht immer höher als sein Privatwille ... und sein Drama zeigt uns eigentlich weder Juden noch Christen, sondern Unterdrücker und Unterdrückte und das wahnsinnige schmerzliche Aufjauchzen dieser letztern, wenn sie ihren übermütigen Quälern die zugefügten Kränkungen mit Zinsen zurückzahlen können.... Wahrlich, mit Ausnahme Portias ist Shylock die respektabelste Person im ganzen Stück. Er liebt das Geld, er verschweigt nicht diese Liebe.... Aber es gibt etwas, was er dennoch höher schätzte als Geld, nämlich Genugtuung für sein beleidigtes Herz, die gerechte Wiedervergeltung unsäglicher Schmähungen....[18]

And, Heine points out that Shylock's Venetian antagonists are playboys, fortune hunters, and common thieves. In short, Heine raises Shylock from a comic figure to a tragic hero.

The most weighty vindication of Shylock, however, came in 1872 in a book by the German jurist, Rudolf von Ihering, entitled *Der Kampf ums Recht* – a much translated, often re-edited, and most influential bestseller.[19] In simplest terms, Ihering (who was writing, after all, in the heyday of rugged individualism) argues that when a person is denied his right, and when such denial implies a denial of personhood and human dignity, he is not only entitled to fight for his right, but is actually under a moral obligation to do so – not to fight under such circumstances is a dereliction of duty towards oneself. In support, Ihering cites Kant: "Wer sich zum Wurm macht, kann nachher nicht klagen, wenn er mit Füssen getreten wird." (p. 6) Ihering illustrates with two figures from literature: Shakespeare's Shylock and Heinrich von Kleist's Michael Kohlhaas. Indeed, Michael Kohlhaas gives the classical definition of man's utter existential loneliness when he is deprived of his rights. When asked why he risks reputation, property, family, and life in the fight for his rights, he replies: "Weil ich in einem Lande, in welchem man mich, in meinem Rechte, nicht schützen will, nicht bleiben mag. Lieber ein Hund sein, wenn ich von Füssen getreten werden soll, als ein Mensch."[20] (p. 162) And to Luther he explains:

> Verstossen nenne ich den, dem der Schutz des Gesetzes versagt ist. Denn dieses Schutzes, zum Gedeihen meines friedlichen Gewerbes, bedarf ich; ja, er ist es, dessenthalben ich mich, mit dem Kreis dessen, was ich erworben, in diese Gemeinschaft flüchte; und wer mir ihn versagt, der stösst mich zu den Wilden der Einöde hinaus. (p. 183)

Like Kohlhaas, Shylock refuses to be treated like a dog or a worm. He fights for his integrity, his dignity, his Jewish identity. To paraphrase Ihering: Shylock speaks the language which an injured sense of right always speaks; and when Shylock is defrauded of his right by a miserable quibble and staggers off-stage, his tragedy (according to Ihering) is not that he has lost his money, his daughter, his religion – his tragedy lies in the fact that he believed in the law, that he was sustained in this belief by Portia herself, only to be taught in the end that he is nothing but the despised Jew whose rights are in the same breath acknowledged and denied (p. 54). The tragedy is that he who fought for his manhood finds himself an outlaw beyond the pale of mankind, that he is banished from the community of men and (in the words of Kohlhaas) cast to the wild beasts of the wilderness. By birth Shylock is an outcast and fights for rights he never really had; and the modern reader's sympathy for, and acceptance of, Shylock has come about because we are prepared to accept the outsider and no longer require that he be assimilated.

After Ihering it was almost commonplace to side with Shylock and to denigrate, as Heine had done, his antagonists. So Alfred Kerr, Berlin's most influential theatre critic: he sees Antonio's and Portia's circle consisting of idlers, pimps, fortune hunters who borrow, steal, and waste money, while only the Jew is willing to forego a fortune in order to obtain his right: "Der Wucherer dünkt mich in diesem Werk der einzige Edelmann."[21] Finally, to Alfred Polgar Shylock is the one man who defends his own, individual, and unique existence:

> Aber der Schwarzalbe ist der einzige Mensch in dieser Komödie, der einzige Mann, der einzige Charakter. Er is böse, finster, hässlich, aber treu sich selbst ... die einzige Figur, die ein Schicksal durchleidet und in Verstrickung gerät, deren Fäden aus ihrem eigensten besondern Sein gesponnen sind. ... Die Andern? Dutzendmenschen, Lebemänner, Beaux, Spieler und Springer, übermütige, reiche Mädchen, Karnevalsfiguren, umkreist von einem Schwarm von Narren, Tänzern, Musikanten, Köchen und Liebedienern.[22]

Polgar fails to see that *The Merchant of Venice* is a comedy and that Bassanio and Portia and the rest of them are figures in a comedy; but, his Shylock is what Nathan no longer can be: a militant Jew aware of his existential Jewishness.[23]

Shylock and Nathan have not changed, but our perception of them has – the self-image of the Jew has changed. We may look back nostalgically to a time when we could identify with Nathan rather than with Shylock, with noble humaneness rather than with Jewish militancy. Perhaps it is one of our tragedies that the realities of the world have limited our options. Such, at least, is the conclusion arrived at by Ernst Simon in 1929:[24]

> Viel eher ist Shylock ein Jude als Nathan. ... Wir sollten uns heute zu diesem tragischen Bruder Shylock bekennen, statt ihn apologetisch abzuschütteln. ... Wir sollten verzichten auf Nathans blasse Judenschemen. ... Wir aber, die wir Lessings tapfere Humanität nur allzusehr, gerade in unserer jungen Nationalbewegung, brauchen könnten, wenden uns dennoch von seinem blas-

sen und blutlosen Judenbild ab und hören lieber mit Heinrich Heine in der Nacht des Jom Kippur Shylock's Stöhnen und Rufen: "Jessica, mein Kind!" (pp. 218-219)

In these dark times Nathan is rejected by Gerhard Fricke, the National-Socialist, as well as by Ernst Simon, the Zionist: and the human race is once again divided into a multiplicity of nations, races, and religions.[25]

Notes

[1] *Erinnerungen an Theodor Fontane, 1819-1898. Aus dem Nachlass seines Freundes und Testamentsvollstreckers Justizrat Paul Meyer* (Berlin: 1936). In the chapter "Fontane – der Antisemit," (pp. 13-15) Meyer reports that he warned Fontane that the poem was derogatory to Jews; Fontane agreed and did not print the poem.

[2] An account in English of *Die Juden* and Lessing's defense of his protagonist can be found in George Alexander Kohut's introduction to Gotthold Ephraim Lessing, *Nathan the Wise*, Tr. Patrick Maxwell (New York: Bloch Publishing Co., 1917), pp. 37-40.

[3] For a further discussion of humanism and *Nathan* in particular, see Ludwig W. Kahn, *Literatur und Glaubenskrise* (Stuttgart: Kohlhammer, 1964), pp. 17-45.

[4] Hermann Hettner, *Geschichte der deutschen Literatur im achtzehnten Jahrhundert. Zweites Buch; Das Zeitalter Friedrich des Grossen*, Zweite Auflage. (Braunschweig: Vieweg, 1872), p. 551.

[5] H.A. Korff, *Geist der Goethezeit,* II. Teil. (Leipzig: J.J. Weber, 1930) p. 156.

[6] A.L. Sachar, *A History of the Jews* (New York: Knopf 1948), p. 273.

[7] Documents concerning the "Wirkungsgeschichte" of *Nathan* are reprinted in Peter von Düffel (Ed.), *G.E. Lessing: Nathan der Weise. Erläuterungen und Dokumente* (Stuttgart: Reclam, 1972), pp. 138-139: see the anti-Semitic diatribe of Eugen Dühring.

[8] Gerhard Fricke, "Das klassische Humanitätsideal und die deutsche Gegenwart," in *Vollendung und Aufbruch* (Berlin: Junker und Dünnhaupt, 1943), pp. 251-327. (The article first appeared in 1934-5 in *Zeitschrift für Deutschkunde.*) Around the middle of the nineteenth century, Heinrich Heine, in his poem, "Lied der Marketenderin" had poked fun at the Enlightenment's ideal of tolerance and humanity. The promiscuous female camp-follower proves her tolerance by sleeping with any and every man, without respect to military rank, nationality, or religion; she loves and values man as such, as "Mensch":

Der Mensch, er ist mir lieb und wert ...
Das Vaterland und die Religion,
Das sind nur Kleidungsstücke –
Fort mit der Hülle! dass ich ans Herz
Den nackten Menschen drücke.
Ich bin ein Mensch, und der Menschlichkeit
Geb' ich mich mit Freude.

9 Meno Spann, "Der Nathan im heutigen Literaturunterricht," *The German Quarterly*, XII (1939), 153-59. The article provoked an exchange with Harold Lenz, *GQ*, XIV (1941), 121-7, 170-75; Spann, *GQ*, XIV (1941), 211-16; Lenz, *GQ*, XIV (1941), 216-18.

10 Hans Mayer, *Aussenseiter* (Frankfurt: Suhrkamp, 1975).

11 I quote from Torberg's article in the weekly *Christ und Welt* of April 16, 1969.

12 In the past few years a number of studies have appeared that try to show the world of Lessing and Nathan not as an utopia where humaneness and reason reign supreme but as a world where emotions, traditions, blood bonds, loyalty to one's heritage and religion demand an equal hearing. Most persuasively, Ruth Angress, " 'Dreams that were more than dreams' in Lessing's *Nathan*," *Lessing Yearbook*, III (1971), 108-27; also Benjamin Bennet, "Reason, Error and the Shape of History: Lessing's Nathan and Lessing's God," *Lessing Yearbook*, IX (1977), 60-80; and others. In the parable of the rings, Heinz Politzer, "Lessing's Parabel von den drei Ringen," *German Quarterly*, XXXI (1958), 161-77, discovers a sense of the numinous and the ineffable, a sense of eternity. These are attempts to rescue Nathan for the modern reader by emphasizing the background of existential realities, of prejudice and warfare and unreasonableness.

13 The juxtaposition of Shylock and Nathan has become somewhat of a commonplace. To mention only two critics: Kuno Fischer, *G.E. Lessing als Reformator der deutschen Literatur, Zweiter Teil: Nathan der Weise* (Stuttgart und Berlin: Cotta, 1905). According to Fischer, if a Jew, whose religion makes him the elect of God, is vilified, despised, and rejected, he can react either with hatred and revenge (Shylock) or with patience, suffering, and tolerance (Nathan); David Friedrich Strauss, "Lessings Nathan der Weise: ein Vortrag," in *Kleine Schriften* (Bonn: Emil Strauss, 1898). Strauss flatly states that Shylock's Jewishness has almost completely superseded his humaneness, whereas Nathan's humaneness has almost completely superseded his Jewishness.

14 Gustav Landauer, *Shakespeare*, Erster Band (Frankfurt: Rütten und Loening, 1920), pp. 50-51.

15 Bernard Grebanier, *The Truth about Shylock* (New York: Random House, 1962). – The New Variorum Edition of *The Merchant of Venice* cites in the appendix selected commentaries and documents for the history of Shylock's literary reception – among them Heine and Ihering, to be discussed later, are excerpted here in English translation.

16 The title-page of the earliest edition (1660) confirms this view of Shylock. It reads: "The most excellent history of the *Merchant of Venice*, with the extreme cruelty of Shylock...."

17 Shylock possibly hides his true intentions when he tells Antonio: "I would be friends with you" (I, iii) and calls the bond a "merry sport." But what *were* his intentions? Could he really have foreseen that wealthy Antonio would default, that none of his friends would come to his aid, that, miraculously, all of Antonio's ships would be shipwrecked – to be equally miraculously restored later on?

18 The chapter "Jessica" of Heinrich Heine, *Shakespeares Mädchen und Frauen*, first published in 1839.

19 I am quoting from Rudolf von Ihering, *Der Kampf um's Recht*, mit einem Vorwort von Dr. Rudolf Wassermann (Berlin: Philo-Verlag, 1925).

20 H.v. Kleist, *Werke* (Ed., Erich Schmidt), (Leipzig und Wien: Bibliographisches Institut, n.d. [1904].) Page references are to volume three of this edition.

21 Alfred Kerr, *Die Welt im Drama, III: Das Neue Drama* (Berlin: Fischer, 1917), p. 301.

22 Alfred Polgar: *Ja und Nein, I: Kritisches Lesebuch* (Berlin: Rowohlt, 1926), p. 31.

23 To a literary historian, Heine and Ihering and their followers miss the point if, for example, they question the legality or morality of Portia's judgment as if it were a real trial in the real world, say in the law courts of Venice, London, or Berlin. It is a trial in the theatre, on the stage, in a comedy.

24 Ernst Simon, "Lessing und die jüdische Geschichte," in *Brücken. Gesammelte Aufsätze* (Heidelberg: Lambert Schneider, 1965), pp. 213-219. The essay was first published in 1929.

25 An earlier version of this text was presented in October, 1982, as a lecture at the Leo Baeck Institute in New York. I would like to refer the reader to two important contributions which have appeared since I prepared my lecture: Mark H. Gelber, "Wandlungen im Bild des gebildeten Juden in der deutschen Literatur," *Jahrbuch des Instituts für deutsche Geschichte*, XIII (1984), 165-78; and Wilfried Barner, "Vorurteil, Empirie, Rettung. Der junge Lessing und die Juden," *Bulletin des Leo Baeck Instituts*, 69 (1984), S. 29-51.

The Austro-American Jewish Poet Ernst Waldinger

Harry Zohn

In a lecture delivered in 1960 at Skidmore College in Saratoga Springs, New York, the Viennese-born poet and American college professor Ernst Waldinger described himself as "a confirmed maverick, a hybrid poet with scholarly inclinations, an inveterate and ardent teacher (who knows how little can be taught), a conservative liberal ... a cosmopolitan, and, at the same time, an Austro-American."[1] Waldinger was also aware that he was "a double-faced creature, a highly suspect animal, a person called a hyphenated American."[2] While he was engaged as a cultural mediator and literary and psychological bridge-builder between his old and new homelands, Ernst Waldinger, the poet and the man, remained very conscious of his Jewishness, which to him meant the urge and the obligation to preserve a great heritage and to lead a life of high moral standards, as well as chosenness for suffering and bearing witness. In his poem "Aus Davids Geschlecht," he refers to Jesus as a suffering Jew: "... bin ich nicht wirklich auserwählt? Als Jude leiderprobt, das Kreuz zu tragen, gleich jenem Jesus, der von David stammt?"[3] ("Am I not truly chosen, as a Jew tried by sorrow, to bear the cross, like that Jesus who was descended from David?") He expressed the same insight more powerfully in another poem:

Quam Olim Abrahae Promisisti

Als ich zum ersten Mal als Bub dies lernte
Hebräisch und mit Gleichmut, wußt ich erst
Nur halb, was dies bedeutet: auserwählt!
Es wog noch leicht auf meinen Knabenschultern.
Als mir's im ersten Jahr des ersten Weltkriegs
In Mozarts Requiem im strahlen-hellen
Konzerthaus nun lateinisch und fugiert
Entgegendröhnte, dies, was meinem Stamme
Seit Abraham versprochen ward, erahnt
Ich's besser schon, obwohl der Neue Bund
Gemeint war, nicht der meine, und obwohl

Dann Christi Leidenslast vier Schreckensjahre
Wir teilten. Doch als ich das Requiem
Heut hörte nach dem unvergeßnen Grauen,
Nach jener Schmach der Nazisintflutzeit,
Da wußt ich, daß zum Leiden auserkoren
Nur wir, das wirklich auserwählte Volk, sind,
Obschon das Leid der Dinge Wesen ist –

Nur wir verkörpern seit der Kreuzigung
Die Imitatio Christi, wir allein![4]

(When as a boy I learned it, hardly yet
With interest, in Hebrew at that time,
I only grasped half of the words' importance.
This "chosen" was no load yet on my shoulders.
When it reverberated in my ears
At the beginning of the First World War,
In Mozart's Requiem once in Vienna,
In Latin and as a fugue in the bright light
Of our concert hall, what has been promised
To our tribe since Abraham already
Was better rooted in my mind, although
It was not our covenant, although
We shared Christ's burden many bitter war years.
But when I heard that Requiem today,
The unforgotten horror in my heart,
The shameful age of brown barbarity,
I knew: to suffer *we* are chosen only,
Though suffering be the essence of all things.
And since the crucifixion we alone
Have represented the "Imitatio Christi."

Translated by the poet)

No limitation of Waldinger's stature in modern literature in the German language is intended if one calls him the most distinguished Austrian poet who found a new home in the United States after 1938. The list of such lyric poets, after all, includes such notable figures as Guido Zernatto, Heinz Politzer, Franz Golffing, Berthold Viertel, Friedrich Bergammer, Max Roden, Margarete Kollisch, Alfred Farau, and Mimi and Norbert Grossberg. (Richard Beer-Hofmann, the patriarchal figure among the Austrian writers exiled in the United States, was not primarily a writer of verse.)

Waldinger was one of the great "adepts at self-portraiture," "Dichter ihres Lebens," to use Stefan Zweig's phrase. About his romantic name with its sylvan connotations ("forest-dweller") he wrote two poems – one in which he muses on the way in which one of his ancestors might have been given that name ("Der Name Waldinger"[5]) and another ("Mein Name"[6]) in which he credits his name with implanting the spirit of poetry in him. Even though Waldinger's only published autobiographical work is an essay entitled "Darstellung einer jüdischen Jugend in der Wiener Vorstadt," which he contributed to Josef Fraenkel's compendium *The Jews of Austria* (London: Vallentine, Mitchell, 1967), and which is a warmly evocative description of a Jewish boyhood in Neulerchenfeld, part of one of the outlying districts of Vienna, his life was "no more and no less than the history of our time," and many aspects of it are preserved, interpreted, illuminated, and transmuted in his poetry.

Ernst Waldinger was born in Vienna on October 10, 1896, as the oldest of four children. Both his parents were natives of Galicia. His father's Orthodox background became somewhat attenuated over the years, but Ernst did receive a good Jewish education and later remembered, in addition to joyous Seder evenings, his studies at a Beth Hamidrash in the Leopoldstadt, Vienna's largely Jewish second district, giving warm though far from uncritical pen portraits of various religious leaders and teachers. Waldinger's mother, who had recognized the dreamy nature and rather impractical bent of her oldest son at an early age, hoped that he would become a rabbi. Waldinger's childhood was not exactly idyllic, but it was full of relationships, ideas and images, sights and sounds that he later used in his poetry. After graduating from the Gymnasium, Waldinger volunteered for military duty in 1915. While serving as an officer in Rumania, Waldinger received a head wound in August, 1917 which paralyzed his right hand and the right side of his face and temporarily deprived him of the faculty of speech; this injury constituted a lifelong, albeit comparatively minor, physical impediment. Waldinger was hospitalized until 1919 and then studied German literature at the University of Vienna, where he was awarded a doctorate in 1921. Two years later he married Rose Beatrice Winternitz, an American-born niece of Sigmund Freud.

Even though Ernst Waldinger had written verse since the age of seventeen, he was "An Unknown Poet" when he was visited in 1926 by the noted Berlin-born American-Jewish critic Ludwig Lewisohn. The American wrote about the Austrian in the influential weekly *The Nation*; the essay was subsequently included in Lewisohn's collection *Cities and Men* (New York: Harper, 1927). Lewisohn found Waldinger "sweet and indomitable and incorruptible," (p. 214) and was delighted to discover in his work "a union of precise fidelity to fact with plasticity of contour and musical resonance of texture." (p. 219) He described one of Waldinger's poems, which he saw in manuscript form, as being "as severe as a canto of Dante and as rich in vowel-music as a sonnet of Rossetti, and yet there blows through it a bleak wind of modern life." (p. 220).

Waldinger's first collection of poetry did not appear until 1934 and bore the title *Die Kuppel* (The Cupola); it secured for the poet the Julius Reich Prize of the University of Vienna. A second collection, *Der Gemmenschneider* (The Gem-Cutter), was published three years later.[7] Waldinger's early publications already stamp the poet as a consummate craftsman, a cosmopolite of experience, whose work is imagistic, rhythmic, and infused with a profound sense of ethics and an abiding humanitarianism. In making "music for our time" (*Musik für diese Zeit* is the title of a collection issued in 1946), Waldinger is aware that, in the final analysis, it is the inner music that will prove to be the most enduring. Because of his inherent realism, Waldinger never was a mere aesthete, not even where he cast his poetry in strict and artful forms, trying his hand at a ghazal or a *Siziliane*, or writing cycles of sonnets about colors, flowers, and months. The majority of his poems are rhymed, and again and again he used the sonnet form which gave him "the intellectual bliss of a strict, clear order" and which, to him, "can encompass everything, even simple things." In a letter to Ludwig Lewisohn dated May 19, 1946, Waldinger described as his aim "the subtle simplicity of the [Matthias] Claudius type to which German poetry is so perfectly suited." One of his poems is entitled "Die Heilkraft der Sonette"[8] ("The Curative Power of Sonnets"). On numerous occasions the poet availed himself of what he characterized as the "kelch-kristallene Kraft" of this form, and in "Warum ich Sonette schreibe" ("Why I Write Sonnets"), a poem included in the collection *Gesang vor dem Abgrund* (1961), he wrote: "Ich kehre zum Sonette stets zurück/ In unsrer Zeit, die aller Helle bar,/ Zur Form, die meine erste Liebe war,/ Zur scharfen Schau und zum Gedankenglück."[9]

If some of Waldinger's earlier poems, bearing such titles as "Ode to International Traffic," "The City Dwellers," and "Song of the Mythical Threshers," are expressionistic in outlook and style, many of his most characteristic lyrics are eminently musical, expressing the spirit of music, reflecting on the special quality of an instrument or on the meaning of a musical form, communing with the great masters of music, or interpreting specific compositions by Schubert, Mozart, Tartini, Vivaldi, or Chopin. Beginning in 1929, Waldinger gave himself a foretaste of his future homeland by translating, over a period of two decades and under the title *Prairie and Skyscrapers*, about one hundred poems by such eminent American poets as Edwin Arlington Robinson, Robert Frost, E.E. Cummings, Edna St. Vincent Millay, Emily Dickinson, Marianne Moore, and Archibald MacLeish.[10]

Having earned a living in a commercial establishment in Vienna for many years, Waldinger emigrated to the United States with his wife and two children in September, 1938. While living in New York City, he had a variety of occupations, working as a librarian, in a department store, and as a government clerk before being appointed, in 1947, to a full professorship at Skidmore College in Saratoga Springs, New York. During his tenure there, Waldinger published four collections of his poetry (*Glück und Geduld,* 1952; *Zwischen Hudson und Donau*, 1958; *Gesang vor dem Abgrund*, 1961; *Ich kann mit meinem Menschenbruder sprechen*, 1965). He gave numerous public lectures and readings at home and abroad, and was awarded several prizes and decorations by the Austrian government, including the Goldenes Ehrenzeichen für Kunst und Wissenschaft in 1962. Following his retirement from his academic position in 1965, Waldinger and his wife lived in New York City again. The last year or two of the poet's life brought him untold sorrow: the untimely death of his daughter Ruth, a talented artist, and the illness of his wife and her death during an Austrian vacation a few days after Waldinger himself had suffered a stroke. The poet's death came in a New York hospital on February 1, 1970.

If the First World War had been the decisive experience that gave Waldinger his poetic voice after a period of speechlessness, his expulsion from his homeland and the necessity to fashion a second homeland for himself was an equally decisive experience, one that was as difficult as it was fructifying. Waldinger became a cultural mediator "between the Hudson and the Danube," and surely there were few in his generation who had such a positive attitude toward America, while preserving vivid memories of a nostalgically cherished native land, in particular the mellow, idyllic beauty and comforting solitude of the Danubian and Alpine regions. At first Waldinger was somewhat repelled by the boundlessness of the American landscape and the seeming formlessness of American life, but later he wrote perceptively and even lovingly about his new homeland – even though an occasional elegiac tone indicates that he regarded America as the land of his old age in contrast to Austria, the nostalgically evoked land of his youth. In the "insular heat of Manhattan" he longed for "the cool rooms in the farmhouses" of Austria (*Die kühlen Bauernstuben* is the title of a collection issued by the Aurora-Verlag, New York, in 1946); a room in his Saratoga Springs home was a replica of such a *Bauernstube*. In the Berkshires or the Canadian Rockies, he dreamt of the Semmering. With equal empathy and zest he wrote about a cemetery in the mountains of the Eastern Tyrol and a village in New England, the Golden Gate Bridge and a summer afternoon in Lower Austria, a choral society in Neulerchenfeld and a Quaker Meeting in Haverford, the Wolfgangsee and Saratoga Lake, a horse on 47th Street in New York and a blackbird in Salzburg, a beach in Santa Barbara and a swimming pool in Sauerbrunn, the Musikvereinssaal in Vienna and Lewisohn Stadium in Manhattan. Even as he was alive to the sights, the sounds, and the spirit of his new homeland, he kept recalling a Vienna that really no longer existed, a city which, as he put it, he had saved and preserved by taking it to another country and enshrining it in truth itself, in his heart. He revisited his native city for the first time in 1958, and, predictably, with mixed emotions; his attitude may be summed up by the title of one of his poems: "Verzeihen, aber nicht vergessen."[11] As late as 1967, Waldinger described himself as "noch so stark in Wien verwurzelt, daß diese schicksalshafte Anhänglichkeit alle verständlichen Ressentiments überwunden hat und daß mir allgemein versichert wird, daß in meinen Versen Wiener Wesen und Landschaft in Wort, Bild und Melodie stets mitschwingt." As he intoned poetic paeans of praise to his mother tongue, Viennese German, an idiom that shaped and colored even his utterances in English, he was careful to point out that he was "a son of the German language only" ("Ich bin ein Sohn der deutschen Sprache nur...").[12] Elsewhere he apostrophized the German language as "O great, good spiritual motherland."

Many of his bittersweet poems reflect poignant memories of his childhood, but Waldinger had the rare faculty of endowing a personal, local experience with universal, timeless significance. Moreover, throughout his work, it is evident that Ernst Waldinger was not only a *homo austriacus* and a *homo americanus*, but a *homo judaicus* as well – a constellation rare enough among German-Jewish writers. Waldinger never forgot that he was a member of the People of the Book, that his background and his gifts inextricably bound him to the word. In his poem "Kol Nidre," he writes about "diese menschlichste der Bitten," ("this most human of all supplications") and says about the haunting melody: "Selbst in der banalsten Tätigkeit wie die alltägliche Rasur ermahnt sie mich an unsrer Sendung Judenschicksal."[13] Waldinger's poem "Der Handlee" memorializes what was once a familiar figure in the streets of Vienna, the Jewish peddler, who was referred to by his cry, which means "I trade (in old clothes)."[14]

Der Handlee

Der Mann mit dem alten Schlapphut,
Ausgefranstem Kragen,
Fettigem Rock und verbeulten Hosen,
Vertretenen Schuhen,
Der Handeljud, der durch die Höfe zog
Und durch die engen Wienergassen:
Sein Kaufruf durchgellte die Luft
Wie ein Peitschenschlag,
Daß das Echo fast die Fenster erklirren ließ:
Handleeee!

Als Junge schämte ich mich seiner sehr –
Aber dann wußt ich,
Daß er zu meinem Stamme gehörte,
Unwiderruflich, der bescheidensten einer.

Vielleicht saß er allein am Abend
Über Thora und Talmud

Und holte sich Trost in den guten Legenden,
Und an der Sabbattafel
Fühlte er sich wie ein König.

Mit Tausenden seinesgleichen
Erlitt er das Martyrium in Auschwitz und Mauthausen,
Auf daß der Name des Herrn geheiligt werde.
Aber wollte der Herr wirklich dieses Opfer?

Wenn ich seiner gedenke,
Schäme ich mich, der ich entkam,
Und neige mich in Ehrfurcht
Vor seinem Schatten
Und verfluche seine Mörder,
Denen ich vergeben muß,
Weil das Unheil und ihre Schuld
Zu gewaltig sind, daß sie gesühnt werden könnten.

(The man with the old broad-brimmed hat,
With the frayed dirty collar.
Greasy jacket and rumpled pants
And the worn, shapeless shoes,
The peddler who moved through the courtyards
And the narrow lanes of Vienna,
His trade call whizzed through the air
Like the stroke of a whip
That its echo almost rattled the windows:
"Handleee ....!"

As a boy I was ashamed of him,
But then I knew
That he belonged to my people,
Irrevocably, as one of the humblest of my people.

Perhaps he sat alone in the evening,
Bent over the Torah and the Talmud,
And was consoled by the good legends.
And at the Sabbath table
He felt like a king.

Together with hundreds and thousands of his faith
He suffered the martyrdom of Auschwitz and Mauthausen
That the name of the Lord be sanctified.
But did the Lord really demand this sacrifice?

When I recall him
I am ashamed for having escaped
And bow in awe and reverence

Before his shade
And curse his murderers
Whom I have to forgive
Because the evil they committed and their guilt
Are too tremendous ever to be expiated.

Translated by the poet)

"Wenn ich auch nicht die alten Psalmen summ'/ Ich wandle auf der Ahnen Tränenspur" ("Even though I do not hum the old psalms, I walk along my ancestors' trail of tears"), Waldinger wrote.[15] A poem of consolation and encouragement in dark times is entitled "The People of Millenial Hope":

Das Volk der tausendjährigen Zuversicht[16]

Wenn soviel Jammer auf der Erde ist,
Wie soll ich da mein eignes Los beklagen!
Laß mich gefaßt die Bürde weiter tragen,
Soweit das Schicksal meinen Pfad bemißt.

Als kleines Kind schon – was man nicht vergißt –
Hört ich des Todesengels Schwingen schlagen;
Mich traf das Schwert in meinen Kriegertagen;
Ich stöhn, weil Schwermut mir am Herzen frißt.

Und Lahmheit schlug mich, Armut und Exil,
Und wie im Mächtespiel der Würfel fiel,
Fast immer stand ich, wo ich mitverlor –

Doch flüstert eine Stimme mir ins Ohr:
"Kannst du denn nicht die Zuversicht bewahren?
Dein Volk hat sie seit dreimal tausend Jahren."

(Seeing all earth so overwhelmed with woe,
I cannot stoop my own lot to bewail
Nor let the strength to bear my burden fail
As long as destiny will have it so.

My unforgotten childhood felt the low
Pinions of death's dark angel near me sail;
The sword of war struck me and left me pale.
Shall my sad heart not fill to overflow?

Shattered, exiled, in need – I paid the price.
Whenever the insensate powers played at dice
I was where losers were, where losers lie –

Yet in my soul a whisper will not die:
"Cannot *that* faith master thine own poor fears
Which kept thy people firm through thrice a thousand years?"

Translated by Ludwig Lewisohn)

Waldinger's last and most comprehensive collection of poetry, truly his poetic testament, characteristically entitled *Ich kann mit meinem Menschenbruder sprechen*, and published in Vienna in 1965, contains a section entitled "Aus Davids Geschlecht," ("From the Line of David") including such poems on Jewish themes as "Hebräisch" ("Nicht meine Muttersprache, dennoch heut gesprochen vom Volk, dem ich entstamme heilig-herbe Sprache...Erzväterzunge"[17] /"...not my mother tongue, yet spoken today by a people I spring from, holy and acerbic tongue...patriarchal tongue of my forefathers"), "Siebenarmiger Leuchter" ("So versöhnend wie der Regenbogen... widerlegst du des Verneiners Wut"[18] /"as conciliatory as a rainbow... you refute the negator's rage"), "Sabbatausgang," Die Leopoldstadt" ("fand... das Judenviertel gänzlich judenrein...und dünkte sich so grenzenlos allein"[19] /"...found the Jewish district completelz *judenrein*...and felt so boundlessly lonely"), and "Anlässlich des Auschwitz Prozesses" (concerning T.W. Adorno's dictum that after Auschwitz it is no longer possible to write poetry: "So mein ich, daß es gerade deshalb notwendig ist, Gedichte zu machen, damit dem Unmenschlichsten in jedem von uns das Menschlichste, die Sehnsucht nach dem, was der Mensch sein sollte, entgegengehalten wird."[20] ("I think it is necessary to write poems to confront what is most inhuman in all of us with our most human quality, the yearning for what a human being ought to be.") Other poems memorialize Maidanek, Lidice, Theresienstadt, and the Warsaw Ghetto fighter, Simon Feigenblatt.

Waldinger's lighter side and his vibrant sense of humor are illustrated by his charming versification of a little conversation reported by Marion Mill Preminger in her autobiography *All I Want is Everything:*

Albert Schweitzers Kravatten

Als sie ihm lächelnd einen Vorwurf machte,
Daß zwei Kravatten doch zu wenig seien,
Altväterische schwarze Schlipse, die er
So lange trug, bis sie ins Grüne spielten,

Erstaunte er: "Wieviele sollt' ich haben?"
Drauf sie naiv und leicht kokett versetzte:
(Der weise Mann, geduldig, wie sichs ziemt,
Gab er ihr Recht der Dummheit) "Manche Herren
Vermögen zwischen hunderten zu wählen,
Wenn sie am Morgen vor dem Spiegel stehen,
Um ihre Toilette zu vollenden.
Sie tragen freilich nicht die Dreieckschlipse
Wie die Gelehrten von vor anno Schnee."
Doch kurz und kehlig sagte Albert Schweitzer:
"Was, hundert Schlipse? Und für *einen* Hals?"

(When, smiling and reproachful, she told him
That two neckties were not nearly enough,
Old-fashioned black cravats which he
Kept wearing till they were faded and threadbare,
He was astonished: "How many am I supposed to have?"
Whereupon she naively and a bit coquettishly replied,
[While the wise man, in seemly patience, conceded
Her the right to be stupid]
"Some gentlemen I know have hundreds to choose from
When in the morning they stand before the mirror,
Completing their toilette.
Of course, they don't wear the stocks
That scholars used to wear way back when."
But pithily and throatily said Albert Schweitzer:
"What, a hundred ties?! And all for one neck?!"

Translated by Harry Zohn)

A revealing statement about Waldinger's conception of himself is contained in a letter to the author of this article dated June 26, 1964, and referring to a reading by a celebrated contemporary novelist sponsored in Cambridge by the Goethe Society of New England: "Ich bin zwar keine Kanone wie Günter Grass... aber in meiner altmodischen Art glaube ich mehr dem, was mit dem Namen Goethe symbolisiert ist, zu entsprechen." Waldinger was a poet's poet and strove to remain in the literary mainstream, though he was aware that he was fighting a rearguard action, as it were. In many of his poems he communes with or apostrophizes an array of intellectual-spiritual *compagnons de route*, such great figures of the past and present as Franz Kafka, R.M. Rilke, Freud, Thoreau, Bertrand Russell, O.M. Graf, Ernst Schönwiese, Hermann Broch, Mark van Doren,

Theodor Kramer, Joseph Weinheber, and Max Mell (the last two, to his consternation and poetic disapproval, sometime adherents of Nazism).

The eight volumes published during Waldinger's lifetime were joined in 1982 by *Arabesques*, a selection in German and English edited and translated by the poet's cousin, Rudolph Lindenfeld.[21] Both before and after his death, Ernst Waldinger has increasingly attracted critical attention, although he has yet to be recognized on both sides of the Atlantic in his full stature. In an article written on the occasion of the poet's sixtieth birthday and published in *Books Abroad* (Winter, 1957, p. 28), Jacob Picard hailed him as "one of the foremost representatives of all the pure poets writing in the German language in exile and, in fact, in some respects the voice of his former compatriots who found refuge in America." The Viennese critic Otto Breicha wrote that, along with Theodor Kramer, Waldinger exerted the greatest influence on the post-World War II generation of Austrian poets. Writing in *The German Quarterly*, in January, 1972, Alexander Kallos discussed the poetry of this "defender of literary tradition" under these rubrics: Permanency and Healing Power of Nature; Preservation of Tradition in Art; Purity of Language; Musicality; Metaphysics; Religion; and Death. Kallos descerned in Waldinger's work "a Horatian buoyancy, evenness, and clarity, the beauty, serenity, and perseverance of Hölderlin and Weinheber; a healthy and down-to-earth simplicity, hiding some deep thought, reminiscent of Robert Frost." (p. 102) Frederick Ungar, who published collections of Waldinger's poetry both in Vienna and in New York, wrote in 1984: "Waldinger's clear and pure voice was the noblest of the Austrian and German emigration. It is our own fate, poetically heightened, that we confront in his work."[22] Waldinger's literary remains repose in the Dokumentationsstelle für neuere österreichische Literatur in Vienna and include much unpublished material: three to five thousand poems, fourteen autobiographical essays and an equal number of other articles, a memoir of Sigmund Freud, a great deal of material on the situation of exile writers, and over a thousand letters from such correspondents as Albert Einstein, Thornton Wilder, Hermann Broch, Kurt Pinthus, Franz Theodor Csokor, and Ernst Krenek. It is to be hoped that scholars will not neglect this valuable material and that some of it will appear in print.

Ernst Waldinger will be remembered as a man of letters who sought to stem the tide of rampant materialism and combat the dehumanizing tendencies of modern life by reasserting, in the face of "modernity" and untrammeled subjectivity, the great traditions of Western civilization, a man who defined his ideal of *Gestalt* as "the humane synthesis of emotion and reason." In a poem entitled "Programmatisch" he said: "Auch ich könnte von den Waben der Verwirrung schwarzen Honig saugen."[23] ("I, too, could suck black honey from the honeycombs of confusion.") Instead, however, he chose to place himself in ideological and formal opposition to the mainstream of contemporary poetry, which is informed by cynicism, despair, and nihilism and often makes a cult of egotism, hedonism, formlessness, alienation, dissolution, absurdity, and atavistic brutishness. A foe of obscurity, esotericism, and opaque symbolism, Waldinger stove to achieve his poetic effects through lucidity and communicativeness. "In this age of withdrawal, anarchy, and extreme conformity," he said in *Tradition and Poetry*, "tradition may be a strong counterbalance to the overpowering forces of levelling – *if* we can revive it. Our period, the most revolutionary since man learned to tame the flame and to make tools, is also one of rapid disintegration of all values which we were accustomed to deeming essential for civilization."[24] Beyond this conservatism, which stamps this child of the Austro-Hungarian empire as one of the great classicists in modern Austrian letters, Waldinger deserves recognition and wider dissemination as a poet who poignantly chronicled Jewish fate in our time and touchingly articulated the feelings of many of those whose taste of the bitter bread of expulsion and exile led them to a reaffirmation of their Jewish heritage.

Notes

1 "Tradition and Poetry," *Bulletin of Skidmore College*, Vol. 46, No. 1, September, 1960), p. 13.

2 *Ibid.*, p. 2.

3 *Ich kann mit meinem Menschenbruder sprechen* (henceforth referred to as *Menschenbruder*), (Wien: Bergland Verlag, 1965), p. 136.

[4] *Ibid.*, p. 152.

[5] *Glück und Geduld* (New York: Frederick Ungar, 1952), p. 117.

[6] *Zwischen Hudson und Donau* (Wien: Bergland, 1958), p. 31.

[7] Both books were issued by F. Ungar's Saturn Verlag in Vienna.

[8] *Menschenbruder*, p. 14.

[9] *Gesang vor dem Abgrund* (Ed., Ernst Schönwiese), (Graz: Stiasny, 1961), p. 63.

[10] Some of these are included in *Gesang vor dem Abgrund*.

[11] *Menschenbruder*, p. 150.

[12] *Glück und Geduld*, p. 8.

[13] *Menschenbruder*, p. 44.

[14] *Ibid.*, p. 146

[15] *Glück und Geduld*, p. 8.

[16] *Die kühlen Bauernstuben* (New York: Aurora Verlag, 1946), p. 90.

[17] *Menschenbruder*, p. 135.

[18] *Ibid.*, p. 139.

[19] *Ibid.*, p. 145.

[20] *Ibid.*, p. 147.

[21] Santa Cruz: Bayshore Press.

[22] *Encyclopedia of World Literature in the 20th Century* (New York: Frederick Ungar, 1984), Vol. 4, p. 581.

[23] *Menschenbruder*, p. 22.

[24] *Tradition and Poetry*, p. 6.

Bialik on America: The Transformation of an Inner Experience

Efraim Shmueli

I.

A short visit to the United States changed the attitude of Chaim Nachman Bialik, the father of modern Hebrew poetry, towards America and its technological achievements. He had been a vehement critic of the American way of life until his visit in the first half of 1926. The result was his transformation into a most enthusiastic admirer of American life. Yet, his poem, "The Sound of the Multitude" (see Appendix), in which he expressed his feelings about his experience in America, sharply contradicts opinions uttered by him both at the time and on his subsequent return to Palestine. The poem is an apocalyptic vision of doom: the mechanized metropolitan city characteristic of America will perish like Nineveh and Sodom leaving only its God-made counterpart, the tender elm, to survive the destruction. This article is an attempt to clarify the inner experience of the poet's dual and contradictory expression. How can we reconcile his praise of America in talks and public addresses with the dark tone of the poem? I wish to suggest that by city and city life, Bialik meant "Galut," the age-old Jewish experience of life in an urban gentile environment. The elm, as an image of growth and creativeness, symbolizes both America and the rebuilding of the Jewish home in Palestine. His perception of the ultimate doom of "Galut" was given form in an image of apocalypse which contrasted the pastoral pattern of a God-given world with the excessive industrial rationalization of a man-made metropolitan way of life. Bialik's initial "fear of America" was born of inner doubt and intensified by outer constraints, which hindered his using the clear-cut Zionist ideology of his time.

II.

The attitude of Bialik to the world of modern technology, of industry and of the big city, all of which, in his eyes, symbolized America, sheds light on his character and his poetic genius. Familiar with the countryside in his boyhood, in adulthood he was inclined to be a homebird – in Odessa where he lived from 1900-21, he changed house only once in twenty years. He envisaged life in a big city as uncongenial to his poetic muse. Bialik did spend some time in Warsaw, Moscow, Berlin, The Hague, London, and New York. In Moscow he did not compose poetry. He lived in Warsaw for less than two years, at the peak of his poetic creativity. However, the name of the city occurs only at the end of "And Should the Angel Ask." The main part of "The Brook" was inspired and written in a country place in the woods, and only the opening lines were written in Warsaw in the autumn of 1904.

The big city did not have a depressing effect upon him. Bialik is quoted as saying: "It is possible that the environment of Warsaw is more satisfying than that of Odessa, but this is not my place." (Fichman, "Bialik's Poetry" (Hebrew), p. 342). Yet, in the poem "As the Days Lengthen," from *Visions of the Latter Prophets*, in which he pictures the desolation which seizes "man and beast together, one finds the sea-shore, the threshold of a tent, and the other side of the small patch which is behind its enclosure," but no city streets such as we find, for example, in the poems of Shneour. In The Hague he wrote the poem "You go from me," in London "My Mother of Blessed Memory" and "When he Bares Himself Before Your Eyes." On the basis of these poems, one may say that the city awakened within him a need to turn inward and back to memories of the countryside of his youth. Life in the modern big city was the subject of the one and only poem he wrote in New York in Sivan, 1926: "Let it Erupt as it Will." This was his first poetic encounter with the modern metropolis.

N.H. Rosenblom ("America in the Eyes of Bialik" in "Sura," Vol. 3) has attempted to evaluate this poem and to clarify its background and the feelings and ideas which preceded its composition. He describes the prejudice regarding America which was prevalent in the Jewish community in Russia, prejudice which Bialik had absorbed unthinkingly:

> They were not able to grasp [the idea of] a responsible, stable government which did not interfere with the personal lives of its citizens or regulate their conduct from waking until sleep through a detailed body of laws. American freedom was therefore understood by them as a throwing off of the yoke, libertarianism, and the rule of the servant in place of the master.

Whether a prejudice as described in these terms existed in reality is doubtful. But there is no doubt that there were indeed prejudices to which Bialik gave expression in his letters: "The big fair," "vulgarity and commotion," (the phrase he used to describe the daily press) "lack of taste," and "noise, noise, noise," are typical epithets. Elsewhere in one of his letters, he wrote:

> American ways and habits are an abomination to me. I hate their crowds, their tumult, and the noise of their wheels mordantly. And I am about to fall into their hands and mouths and to become prey to their golden teeth and the pens of their journalists. God help me, for I am very sore afraid.

This fear was reiterated time and time again before his journey and even after his return. Rosenblom felt that "besides the concrete factors there existed a deeply hidden psychological cause rooted in his inner consciousness and afflicting him with an irrational terror of America." The poem, "Let it erupt as it will," is, in his eyes, an expression of a "fear, psychological and primitive, lacking form or content." This fear burst forth and was articulated, expressing in rhyme a generalized hate of the city. The entire poem thus constitutes a catharsis from some nameless fear.

In contrast to the city, "nest of Satan," source of all the pain of man and the very bosom of all its outcries, the poet juxtaposed "a young elm, a plant in the street, planted between walls, not begrimed by the city's billowing smoke," which renews itself every spring. It is a symbol of eternal youth, donning white blossoms "from the very hands of God for His glory." Here we have depicted the work of man, as against Bialik's vision of the work of God. Rosenblom moreover considers the elm to symbolize for the poet the American Jewish community, and, especially, the group of faithful Hebraists in its midst.

III.

Different is the picture of the American Jewish community to be found in his letters:

> The notion of America immediately brings to mind noise, bustle, and confusion, which holds sway in America in many areas of life; these are the very things to which we assign terms of reproach such as "bluff," devious business practice, and the like. Everything there is inflated, exaggerated, and essentially hollow. American Jewry is a Jewry of tailors and shoemakers, who have achieved status through the mighty dollar and have no other values but those expressed by the dollar.

This picture of American Jewry haunted him. The obvious association is the Biblical depiction of the sinfulness of Sodom and Gemorrah and of the Talmudic description of city-dwellers who are "robbers, men given to immorality, who will readily take an oath in vain and swear to falsehood." (Eruben 21;6) New York conceivably called up for him the image of "a city with a tower with its top in heaven," and of Nineveh, Tyre, and the accompanying prophecies of anger and retribution. Time and again Bialik mentioned to his friends his fear of America. Thus he told Jacob Fichman:

> I am afraid of America – God knows, that everything in me objects to this trip. But they have set Achad Ha'am on me, and the old man says: Go. And since he enjoins me to go, I cannot refuse. I have never turned him down. (Rosenblom, p. 369)

When, on his return, he spoke in the Beth Am in Tel Aviv he confessed:

> I went to America in fear and dread, I would almost say a bestial fear. I cannot explain to myself the reason for this fear.

Personal psychological causes were added to the notions he derived from ancient Hebrew literature. He had been living in Israel but a short time and it was hard for him to leave it. When he first came to Israel, he had secretly hoped for a renewal of his literary talents, but this failed to come: "I hope for the day on which I may be able to dedicate myself completely to my literary work in Eretz Israel." Actually, he hoped for more than this: for new revelations of his own genius. In 1923 he had written "The Soul is Bowed Down in the

Dust," a break in the years of silence dating from 1915. He saw himself bereft of significant achievement.

> Why have you set upon my abode? What my sin – what my strength?
> Neither poet nor prophet – a hewer of wood am I.

In answer to an anniversary greeting he wrote to Ben Ami sadly and despondently:

> Your letter and your written greeting are very precious to me. For I know they come from a loving and loyal heart. But I won't hide from you that I would much more that the cymbals did not beat around me. In my present condition I need complete rest, and what I said in my short poem, believe me, came from the heart.

Here we see the apprehensive perplexity caused by his failure to accept the loss of his creativity, together with his adulation by others as national poet. The praise of the public was for him a mockery. His fear of being swallowed by the big city and his fear of being expressively conspicuous in public may be similar in origin:

> America always casts some fear upon me. I, being slow to move, fear that I will be lost in the speedy tempo of America, lost like a drop in a big sea.

This was his fear of an anonymity, in which both body and soul would be lost in the big city with whose language, customs, and manners he was unfamiliar.

IV.

The poet stayed in the U.S. for almost six months and was received by the Jewish public with great enthusiasm. To be sure, his first appearance in New York, before an audience of four thousand which awaited his words in eager anticipation apparently turned out to be disappointing. He was introduced by the leaders of the community in terms such as "prophet," "the leader of the nation," "the poet laureate," but his speech did not get "a good press." It was not to be expected that the communist *Freiheit* or the Bundist *Forverts* would in those days receive enthusiastically a Zionist poet, who had come to conquer souls for the upbuilding of Eretz Israel. Bialik himself confessed that his first speech was not very successful. He had hardly rested from the wearying journey. He had been in New York only one day. His speech, as printed in "Devarim She' Beal Peh," (Pt. I, p. 19) was undoubtedly a good one and full of content. An examination of this speech will readily show that the poet did not saccharify his remarks to suit his audience. It may have been hard for many to hear doubts voiced about the continued existence of the great Diaspora.

The unenthusiastic reception of his words aroused in him a better understanding of his audience, a greater identification with them, and "opened him up" to America and its Jewish community. He seemed to become firmer and surer, and he discarded his already prepared speeches:

> They were gracious to me and encouraged me with their looks and with their gestures. The American public was kinder to me than were the journalists and writers, and they forgave me my initial "flop."

But, in fact, his personality had greater influence than his words, which, to them, lacked understanding. Bialik glimpsed and was influenced by this reaction:

> This thing, namely this favorable attitude, perhaps immediately changed my mind for the good towards the Jews of America. I too saw them in a more favorable light, and many of the phenomena of Jewish life there now appeared to me in a completely different aspect than in the recent past.

V.

However, he had not really changed his opinion that centers of Jewry in the Diaspora would not endure endlessly. After having visited many Jewish communities, his feeling intensified that

> even in America itself the future of the Jews is not fully secure. Its present greatness, no matter how much we rejoice over it and wish it length of days, is really no more than a soap bubble – which disappears with one breath; and, despite all its contrived serenity, one feels even there a lack of strength and no inner assurance.

He felt that American Jewry was obliged to watch over the welfare of the Jewish nation not merely out of concern for the fate of others nor for considerations of pity:

> They themselves needed to be aroused to the cause of their own survival, to a revival of the Jewish spirit, the Hebrew language, and Jewish national identity. Children cannot be educated through vicarious identification with others' troubles: they must be charged with the joy of a positive creative identity and national pride. And this cannot be done without Eretz Israel. Moreover, only in Eretz Israel it is possible to build from the foundation, to create *ex nihilo*, and only there is blessing to be found.

By contrast, gentile America was a revelation, broad and big, a land of unlimited possibilities, which gained his lavish praise in speeches and letters: "A community with an enormous potential, it is still in its early youth." That vulgarity which he had noticed at first seemed to him now the natural phenomenon of youth: "If this is natural, then there is nothing more appropriate and beautiful than this naturalness." The bustle is no longer artificial or mechanical. It flows from the essence of American life, from its inherent standards. He wrote:

> You walk through the streets of New York and, in the midst of this wild hubbub, a boy of nine or ten walks among the many automobiles, his bag on his shoulder without any fear and readily makes his way ... and I say that here we have a great stride forward....

Americans seemed to him to feel at home in the hurly-burly "with a genius-like simplicity and great serenity." Bialik saw:

> a new civilization developing, whose great potential can hardly be conjectured. For the time being, the American people is blossoming in terms of bigness and height, without a wrinkled brow, as if entirely involved with material things, in a fever of building and materialistic acquisitions alone.

He thought it had within itself adequate power to reach a second stage, in which things of the spirit begin to grow and flourish. He found similarity in what he perceived to be the American attitude towards material needs to those of the Jew's forebears who

> took a serious attitude to two matters: livelihood and the future world ... they understood that the relationship of man to his natural needs is both natural and necessary and would that he were so faithful to higher needs as he

is to his bodily needs. In this respect, we might say that our forebears were unhypocritical. They knew that there is a constant tie which binds the material and the spiritual. And this is also the American attitude.

VI.

Bearing in mind the view of the modern metropolis expressed by Bialik shortly before leaving the United States, the contrary tone of the poem, "The Sound of the Multitude," is, at the very least, surprising. It was written in the last month of his stay in New York and the poet's main ideas about the big city and America had already crystallized in large measure. In the poem, in contrast to the primordial works of creation which are considered to be eternal, the works of man, as exemplified in the cities which he has built, are doomed to perish. The same attitude is inscribed large in the words of the prophets, repeated by the rabbinic sages, and reiterated in the religious and ethical literature. Spengler's "Decline of the West," popular in the twenties, which pictured the big cities as symbolic of the beginning of the decline of the great powers and of their civilization, may also have influenced Bialik. The green, young elm, symbolic of eternal youth, is rejuvenated each spring, and draws its nourishment from the depths of God's earth. The metropolis is destined to destruction and its latter end is like that of Sodom, Pithom and Raamses, Carthage and Palmyra. At the final judgment it will fall apart from the weight of its burden like a mere lodge of thatch. Yet, this is delayed:

> ...but there are still days stored by God,
> and His quiver yet holds arrows, He has lightning and thunder.

And the elm, which is attached to its mound of earth, is afraid and "stands as a frightened child." There are thus two visions in this poem: a vision of retribution for the city and a vision of hope and comfort for that which the tender plant symbolizes. Judging by the language and imagery of the poem, the poet may be regarded as having captured the spirit of the prophet of doom, on one hand, and the prophet of solace, on the other. The predominant tone of the poem is strident and taut, while the idyllic-pastoral aspect is sparse.

The anti-urban stand, even if we take it literally, is not alien to the Hebrew ear. A careful reading will confirm this, e.g. in the first line we find the expression "the sound of the multitude of the city." In the Talmud (Yona 20b), this phrase refers to the din of the city of Rome, which is said to be louder than the sound made by the rotating orb of the sun. (The sun's rotation is described as producing a buzzing like that of a saw felling a cedar, as it creates rays of light.) Again the poet adopts the stance of the prophet in his simile, "like an idol formed by the craftsman." (cf. Isaiah 10:15)

In its simplest sense, the poem is an apocalyptic vision of the future, side by side with a vision of development and growth. Hidden in this vision of the future surely lies the poet's fear for the Jewish community in America. Though his fear of the new world of technology and its example in America had evaporated, there remained the fear for the future of the Jews while they remained on alien soil. In his last words to the Jews of America, at his farewell appearance, he expressed his ultimate public stand on the problem of Galut as follows:

> Do not build Eretz Israel out of fear for the fate of the various segments of the nation, nor even out of concern for your own fate, lest you delay too long. Nay, it is in revival itself – a revival of the spirit, the language, and the honor which you have lost; only from such positive motives can you approach the upbuilding of the land.

Appendix

The Sound of the Multitude

By Chaim Nachman Bialik Translated by Jenny Macklowitz Klein

Let the sound of the multitude of the city erupt as it will,
Let the oppressed and the wicked rot together in the stench of its desire for gain
And the vomit of its furnaces make filthy the purity of the seven heavens.
The spring in its eternal way, sweet, pure, tender
Peeps from all the cracks and from the myriad of crevices.

And a plant in the street, planted between walls, a young elm,
Not begrimed by the city's billowing smoke,
On a mossy carpet, yesterday's blossom, pure green,
Spread yard on yard at its feet –
It, too, like its forebears before it
Myriads of years before in the eternal woods,
Arrayed itself in festive garb in honor of the festival,
And bound to its mound of dust as a babe at the breast,
Stirring on its many roots, blossoming and shining,
And in all its branches and boughs lights up
And each vein and each member quivers with joy.

And opposite this tree with its carpet of grass,
Which stream in their wonted innocence
To the light of God and the grace of its redeeming ray
From the narrow streets – paved with flint and iron, like armor,
From the roar of the market, from the filth and impurity of the city and its people,
A full moment it appears to me, but one small moment,
Suddenly cut off, no one knows wherefore,
Even while yet in the fullness of its strength, the noise of the city,
And the world around lies dead, like an idol formed by the craftsman,
And there is silence!

And there, deep from within the silence – deep, deep within
There came to me for a fleeting moment, as through a crack in the curtain
Piercing me like an arrow – a bit of the vision of the future.
And I called from my heart: Nest of Satan!
Source of all the pain of man and the very heart of all its outcries,
The city, wherein the Grace of God refused to swell,

Nor would His eye everlastingly lodge in it, or rest therein –
Your end is the latter end of Sodom and of Nineveh!

Even now, amidst all your change, fleeting moments,
In all your thundering noise and in all the confused murmur
Of your days, miracle upon miracle,
Smitten by a strong hand and skilled palms,
Swift currents and mighty waves –
Behold how faded and weak you are
Against the merest of God's creations!
Your wheel yet turns, but there are still days stored up by God,
And His quiver yet holds arrows, He has lightning and thunder.
And when that day comes, the day of judgment and testing,
Though you wax great, and the burden is too much to bear,
And the yoke very heavy, you shall be suddenly shattered
As a hut of straw.

And like all your brothers, fastnesses of iron and stone,
Carthage, Tadmor, Palmyra, Raamses, and Pithom,
You, too, in the depths of Sheol will find surcease from your wrath.
But even at that time and after
When your last remnant perishes and you are destroyed –
Inasmuch as it is folded in God's bosom and under His heaven
Yet one more tree on one more mound,
Like its forebears in the eternal forests of yore,
On the hill of its roots, green and moist, will flourish.
And as a symbol of eternal youth, neither fading nor rotting,
With great might, will be drawn from the darkest depths,
With an ever renewing spring – even be made visible,
Will wake and stir to new life.
It will cleave to its mound; its clods will be sweet,
And will drain to satiety the marrow of its innards,
And the hidden treasures of the deep will enter into its flesh
And it will swallow them and take suck of their plenty;
And when it dons its festive garments, white blossoms,
A garb of purity, embroidery from the very hands of God, for His glory,
It will tremble and shine and stand as a frightened child,
And every bird and leaf will swallow His glory with a full mouth,
And all the nectar of its innards will stir as a vine
And it will be as one who is lost because of his wealth and glory
And every vein and every bough will quiver for joy.

The Beginnings of Hebrew Literature in America

Gershon Shaked
(Translated and Edited by
Evelyn Ben-Shim'on and Ruth Toker)

Hebrew Literature and the American Environment

In 1927, L.A. Arieli-Orlov, who had emigrated to the United States in 1923, wrote to Menachem Ribalow, editor of the journal *HaBrit HaIvrit*:

> You ask me whether I have smashed my pen to pieces. Not quite, not for the time being, but rather I'm on the verge of smashing my pen to pieces. There are a number of stories in my travel bag, but I don't have the courage to finish them. I lack faith in the urgent need to finish, and more than that, I lack the environment. Here in busy America, I don't have an environment. I have not found my bearings yet. I live a lonely life such as you cannot imagine. Don't confuse this with being a "greenhorn," as if I were an emigrant recently arrived. I already speak proper English, and I have learned the manners of the place. But – how should I put it to you – all groups are alien to me, including the average Jew for whom the pursuit of the dollar has removed all former grace and benevolence; the rabbi who constantly preaches insipid stuff, rubbish, to his flock, and the callow youth, and even our common acquaintances, the teacher and the principal. It is true that loneliness encourages a more powerful imagination, but it depresses the spirit too much, and every work of art demands an exaltation of the spirit.[1]

Most writers of modern Hebrew literature in the United States underwent this experience of loneliness. They felt more and more and from year to year like writers who had lost their addressees, like voices crying out in a cultural wilderness, whose true spiritual arena was Eastern Europe or the Near East. This experience was expressed not only privately, in the writers' letters to correspondents in the United States and in Israel, but also publicly, in articles printed in Israel and the Diaspora.[2] In 1957, thirty years after Arieli-Orlov's letter to Ribalow, Hillel Bavli wrote an article entitled "B'Shlichut

HaLev" ("On an Errand of the Heart"), which included remarks that Bavli had made at a reception on behalf on the Bialik Institute in Jerusalem. He wrote: "If the price of creation is loneliness, then the lot of the Hebrew writer in America is a loneliness of loneliness, since no Hebrew atmosphere surrounds him, and no instruments for absorbing it are at hand."[3] The experience of loneliness of the Hebrew author in the United States did not diminish over the years; it actually grew and increased. At the beginning of the century, Hebrew literature was marginal to a flourishing Yiddish culture and literature[4] and to a Jewish-American literature (in English),[5] which had just begun to sprout up; by the time Israel was established in 1948, Hebrew literature in the United States, like Yiddish literature, had disappeared from the stage, and Jewish-American literature took the place of its two sisters.[6]

The decline of Hebrew literature and original Jewish culture in America stands almost in opposition to the demographic and social development of American Jewry, though, as Halkin claimed, it concurs with its spiritual development.[7] The number of American Jews between 1880 and 1955 had increased from 275,000 to 5,200,000. In 1880, American Jewry was 0.55% of the population; in 1955, 3.15%. In 1880, 3.44% of the Jewish people in the world lived in America; in 1955, 43.2%.[8] East European emigrants to the United States went through processes of acclimatization, usually with the aid of *landsmanshaftn*. They struggled for economic and social gain, and many succeeded.[9] That was precisely the trouble. Economic and social security signified the end of a particular cultural identity. As early as 1919, a Hebrew teacher and publicist, S. B. Maximon, wrote on this subject in an article, "Al HaChinuch HaIvri B'Amerika" ("On Hebrew Education in America"), first printed in the journal *HaToren*.[10]

For Maximon and many others, the decline of Hebrew education aptly depicted the cultural setting in which Hebrew literature in the United States found itself. Moreover, if in Eastern Europe the Hebrew language was the crowning achievement of the enlightened Hebrew intellectual, in the United States it was pushed into an unobtrusive corner, an object to be whittled away in the hands of tutors in Sunday and Hebrew schools or by teachers in Rabbinical colleges. The organization which bore Hebrew on its shoulders, *HaBrit HaIvrit*, supported and maintained the major Hebrew newspaper *HaDoar*, in which a large portion of modern Hebrew literature in the United States was published.[11] It tried to establish ties between local writers or writers in the land of Israel and the members of the organization, who tried to express their identity by cultivating the Hebrew language. Most of the active writers were Hebrew teachers in different levels of Jewish education. Some, like E. E. Lisitzky, regarded the task of Hebrew teaching as a holy mission and not a temporary business: "Pioneering spirit – that is the essence of teaching Hebrew in America – a pioneering spirit such as in Israel, except that it is remote."[12] The existential situation of the teacher-storyteller became a principal topic in many stories.

Despite repeated attempts, these writers did not manage to establish a literary center in the United States.[13] After the first generation of emigrants or their children either died or immigrated to Israel, these attempts provided no continuity. Today, Gabriel Preil (Estonia, 1911 – U.S.A., 1922 –) is certainly the last Hebrew poet in the United States.[14] The life of the Hebrew newspapers *HaDoar* and *Bitzaron* was tenuous, and they were supported more by the "leftover" writers of Israel (writers who wrote in Israel or emigrated from Israel to seek their way in the U.S.A.), rather than by the late flourishing of "Hebrew" America.

"A Procrustean Bed and the Space of God"

In 1927 Menachem Ribalow published "Mitat S'dom U'Merchav Yah" ("A Procrustean Bed and the Space of God"), in which he presented the literary expectations of local criticism that tried to express the needs of the intended audience. Ribalow's premise was that literature had moved Eastern Europe to America and to Israel, and that it had to adjust to the new circumstances in America:

> Is there any hope here for any undertaking, economic or cultural, if it will not be done in accordance with the requirements of the era? ... At a time when we are surrounded with a space of God, we cannot not lie in a procrustean bed.[15]

The problem of the Hebrew writer in America was that the model of the shtetl and its anti-model were no longer meaningful to the generation of addressee-immigrants. Some of the culture and language they had brought along survived in their world; but the writers knew that unless they changed their materials, they would lose the second-generation immigrants, who were drifting away from their roots and who did not have a real affinity for the cultural and linguistic tradition and its social contexts. The older reader, steeped in Hebrew literature and his home *shtetl*, needed the original forms and content of the *shtetl* literature. When he changed his manners and morals, he asked for new answers to the new issues of emigration and acclimatization.

Ribalow raised questions, therefore, that dealt with the very cultural existence of the diaspora. He was aware that in the United States, Hebrew literature did not have the breathing space between the beginning of the Enlightenment and the period of assimilation that it had had in Eastern Europe, and that the demand for close cultural contact with the environment was liable to do away with the need for Hebrew literature and culture: "And if we are so 'expansive' in literature, why do we need this 'reduction' of the [Hebrew] language which is foreign here?" Ribalow's answer to the difficult problems he raised was unambiguous: "We shall never return to Israel." The Jewish people, he claimed, have existed in the diaspora because of Messianic prophecy and are likely to continue their existence in this way:

> A flourishing, inhabited Israel is likely to be a source of inspiration for the West. At the same time, the connection to the source of Russian influence must be cut off. An English-American orientation must be adopted in order to effect redemption from the enslavement of a tradition now antiquated and to adjust Hebrew lives to the ordinary human life.[16]

In Ribalow's words, the spiritual secularism of Ahad Ha'am and the ideas of the Hebrew Enlightenment come together in a strange mixture, and they are a profound expression of the distress of a cultural group in the face of the freedom and abundance that America bestowed on its Jews. In 1944 Ribalow tried to sum up the features of "Hebrew literature in America." He compiled a long list of different types of writers, novelists, Zionist-publicists, essayists, and critics.[17] In the course of his discussion, he presented a few major writers of fiction: B. Isaacs, Y. Twersky, R. Wallenrod, S. Halkin, and E.E. Lisitzky. To these, one must add writers such as H. Sackler, L.A. Arieli-Orlov, H.A. Friedland, S. Damesek, and others. There was quite a large group that contributed to journals, newspapers, and literature in the United States and in Israel.

Dramaturgy, Poetry, Fiction

Most of these writers contributed in different literary genres, and many of their stories have some link with American-Jewish fiction in other languages. One of the most colorful figures in this group of writers is H. Sackler, who wrote in Hebrew, Yiddish, and English and realized in his work what Dov Sadan has regarded as the unity of Jewish literature – above and beyond its languages.[18] Although Sackler wrote novels, stories, and an essay-diary,[19] he was mainly a dramatist of some stature, one of the leading figures in the history of Hebrew dramaturgy between the two World Wars.[20] Lisitzky, Efrat, and Halkin were primarily poets; Wallenrod was a storyteller, an essayist, and a scholar.

The writer's creative power is revealed not only in fiction, but also in the narrative poem.[21] The paramodern narrative poem typical of the Enlightenment (Jehuda Leib Gordon's "In Deep Waters," "Between the Teeth of Lions," "Zidekiah in Prison") found its way to the generation after Bialik, mainly in some of Tchernichowsky's works, such as *Baruch MiMagenza* and *The Idylls*, and in young Shneour's poems, such as *Matana* (Gift), and Shimoni's *Idylls (BaYa'ar B'Hadera* [In the Forest in Hadera], *Matzeva* [Monument], etc.). A discussion of the changes occuring in the structure and forms of the poem in transition from Eastern Europe and the United States is beyond the scope of this paper. What is important is that in most of these poems, the heroes and heroic acts are dominant. They have epic amplifications or deviations, large or small, according to the poetic type and structure. Moreover, in many poems, there is an attempt to realize Ribalow's plea to bring together Old-World (East European Jewish) and New-World culture. An attempt was made here to relate the two cultures in such a way that any connection between them – for example, between the Hebrew language and Indian society, had to be absolutely accidental. The Jewish Hebrew poets wrote many long poetic romances about the persecuted Indian minority. It is not certain whether they were attracted to this theme because they identified with the persecuted minority or because they wished to continue an American tradition of the Indian epic, founded by H.W. Longfellow in "The Song of Hiawatha" (1855). (This was translated into Hebrew by Saul Tchernichovsky in 1913.[21]) Long narrative poems were written by the fathers of Hebrew poetry in the United States – B.N. Silkiner ("Mul Ohelei Timmora" [Opposite the Tents of Timmorah] or *Shirim* [Poems]) and E.E. Lisitzky, who wrote many long narrative poems and gave this self-testimony:

> Round and round blows the wind, from a native town in Russia to cities and towns in America; from the Jews in them to the Indians; from the Indians to the blacks; around and back blows the wind, to the same native town in Russia which was wiped out, and to its Jewry who were annihilated.[22]

Lisitzky, in fact, published two volumes of long narrative poems. Of interest in the first volume is the Indian world (*Medurot Doachot* [Dying Campfires]) and in the second, the Black world (*B'Ohalei Kush* [In the Tents of Cush]).

Another writer who treated this theme extensively is I. Efros. In his work, there are certainly parallels between the Indian "human condition" and the Jewish "human condition," for example, in *Silent Wigwams* (first printed in Tel Aviv in 1933). Here, the relationship between the Indian girl Lelarry and her Indian lover, Tiger Killer, resembles the relationship between a Jewish girl and a gentile boy, depicted quite often in the poetry and fiction of Eastern European Jewish literature and in the American-Jewish novel (for instance, *Father and Daughter* by R. Grossman [1934]).

The combination of the Hebrew language and Indian material fulfills several functions: it brings this language closer to the indigenous local culture; it creates a common identity between two wretched and depressed minorities; and it paints an exotic background for an heroic and romantic plot. The author requires a technique and a plot-device which is typical also of Tchernichovsky (his idylls) and his generation. The narrative factor materialized, of course, not only in Hebrew-Indian poems, but also in long narrative poems about other topics, from Silkiner's Biblical narrative poems and Halkin's Biblical and biographical poems (*Baruch ben Neriah, Ya'akov Rabinowitz B'Yarmuth*) to Efros's historical poems (*Zahav* [Gold] and to nostalgic poems, such as Lisitzky's *People of Morals*, which is about the world of the poet's home-town.

The elevated language and exotic material or material from remote sources – history, the model of the *shtetl* – suited, perhaps, the different narrative possibilities of this literature better than realistic and unmediated material, since Yiddish and English features were familiar to the audience of addressees. While Hebrew fiction and, alongside it, narrative poetry developed independently, it seems that narrative poetry in Hebrew-American literature absorbed, for some of the above reasons, part of the story-telling effort of the writers.

The American Genre and its Attributes

In a certain way, Hebrew fiction in the United States is close to realistic Hebrew fiction in the land of Israel. The latter does not advance new literary forms or create literary "models"; rather it draws extensively on the generation preceeding the modernistic *min haMartef* ("cellar authors") generation. Brenner's fragmentation, Genessin's "stream-of-consciousness," Steinberg's and Shofman's complex impressionist stories, and Agnon's stylish irony did not influence most Hebrew writers in the United States, with the exception of Shimon Halkin. It is possible to say that most of the writers returned to the repertory of pseudo-realism founded by Ben Avigdor, Goida, and Y. Steinberg. Yiddish poetry of the period had reached its climax of modernity; the Yiddish play (Gordin, Cobrin), in fact, continued the tradition of Goldfaden's melodrama, and realism dominated the Hebrew and Yiddish story and novel.

The repertory of the semi-realistic tradition is limited, nevertheless, it is precisely here that Hebrew fiction in the United States comes close to Hebrew fiction in Israel. In order to understand thoroughly the thematic and formal limitations of this fiction, which lagged years behind its time, one must remember that from the beginning of the century until the 1940s – the years it came into existence – a realistic trend in American literature also developed. In the early twentieth century, American realists included William Dean Howells (1837-1920), Hamlin Garlan (1860-1940), Stephen Crane (1871-1900), Frank Norris (1870-1902), Jack London (1876-1916), and Theodore Dreiser (1871-1945). But between the two World Wars, the writers of more complex works dominated, from the naturalist-realists like Sherwood Anderson (1876-1941), Sinclair Lewis (1885-1951), John Dos Passos (1896-1970), James T. Farrell (1904-), and John Steinbeck (1902-1968) to the three important representatives of what Americans called "the lost generation" – Ernest Hemingway (1899-1961), William Faulkner (1894-1962), and F. Scott Fitzgerald (1896-1940). To this list, one should, perhaps, add Thomas Wolfe (1900-1938).

The "naturalist" option, concurrently open to the Hebrew writers as a continuation of a certain tradition in Hebrew fiction, paralleled generic narrative in Israel and bore an affinity to various American writers such as Dreiser, Dos Passos, Lewis, Sinclair, Farrell, and Steinbeck. The writers were attracted to this form but used it superficially, with the exceptions of Anderson/Wallenrod, Wolfe/Halkin, and others.

The language of the Hebrew writers limited their themes. Jewish-American and even Yiddish writers could write works praising absolute "enlightenment." They could relate to young Jews breaking out of ghetto walls.[23] But, the Hebrew language seemed to limit the degree of thematic daring. Anyone writing in this language would not have been satisfied with a successful "breakthrough" and could describe it only as an irreparably negative or a distorted process. The thematic limits of the narrative work of art in Hebrew were evident in immigrant novels, such as Henry Roth's *Call it Sleep* (1934), or in acclimitization and progress novels, such as A. Cahan's *The Rise of David Levinsky* (1917). This book, and those like it, had a decisive influence on Hebrew and Yiddish fiction in the United States. Written in the first person, it opens in a *shtetl* in Eastern Europe, continues in the sweatshops of New York, and ends in the capitalistic elitism of Jewish New York. The narrator prevails over the obstacles he faces and reaches the summit of American capitalism. He is "making it," since he succeeds in achieving substantial economic gains. This is a sign of social and personal achievement, which in the novel's world view yields spiritual emptiness. The suffering and success of the American Jew in the new land is undoubtedly the main theme of most Hebrew, Yiddish, and American-Jewish fiction, from the beginning of the century until the twenties. This theme shapes a large portion of the narrative structure in the various genres. Most of the works are like the stories of character formation in the sense of the *Bildungsroman*, which is also a story of immigration and wandering.

Some of the stories are comic or pathetic anecdotes which try to describe conventional, familiar models from the American-Jewish way of life. The structure of these short stories is based on the "Pointe." The "Pointe" gives these semi-documentary stories their literary pattern. It is difficult to determine whether authors such as Friedland and Isaacs were following the tradition of the "Pointe" used frequently by Shofman, whose influence on Hebrew fiction between the two World Wars was greater than his stature in the history of fiction, or whether the "Pointe" device derives from the common reservoir of all fiction everywhere and at all times.[24]

Still, the "Pointe" is only a minor device. Most stories are semi-documentaries and their major goal is to bear witness to the miracle of Jewish emigration and to the establishment of a vital Jewish community in America. H. A. Friedland wrote stories according to this formula. In *Miktavim* (Letters), a Reform rabbi sends love letters to a non-Jewish girl and finds, to his great satisfaction, that she has instructed that they be buried with her. The "Pointe" is that the rabbi is requested to execute her will. In "Miss Rose," the best friend of three sisters who all find husbands is left alone. The story "Pine Town" from Shlomo Damesek's book *Here and Now* is also a major example of this trend. Set in the Catskill Mountains in upstate New York, "Pine Town" is also the name of one of those resorts which were virtually out of bounds for Jews. The ironic "Pointe" is that in time, following the Second World War, Pine Town and places like it were gradually taken over by Jews.

This story is a sociological paradigm (Blank's novel *Al Admat Amerika* [On American Soil] was written according to it) that is based on personal testimony, uses almost exclusively social-documentative material, and reduces other narrative factors. The social-documentative material does not allow for a narrative plot. The story becomes social reportage and exposes what other stories of this kind concealed. In most works, the fiction – a man's fate in a social situation – somewhat balances the social-paradigmatic aspect; in Damesek's works, the documentary dominates and changes the delicate balance. The use of documentary material serves a social function for the readers: it becomes a symbolic synecdoche of the sufferings which every immigrant has to go through in order to "make it."

Most of these fictional and semi-documentary works are written in a realistic style, and the choice of documentative materials is based on a genuine affinity for extra-literary materials. The addressees are requested, as it were, to "re-organize" a familiar reality, to "reconstruct" the experience which they and their ancestors had gone through (if they still remembered the language in which their ancestors used to pray). In these stories there is a tendency to present to a Hebrew-reading, "foreign" addressee (the reader in the land of Israel and in Eastern Europe) the American immigration model as it was perceived by Hebrew writers. The local reader in America probably recognized this model much better through Yiddish and American-Jewish English fiction, rather than through the local Hebrew literature.

The *Shtetl* in Contrast to the Land of Opportunity

In most Hebrew literature in America, the new model was presented in contrast to the model of the *shtetl:* "the American genre and its attributes" turned out to be the reverse of the *shtetl* model. This contrast is a leitmotif, a theme, and frame of reference in most of these works. Thus, these works may also be described as works which aspire to give form to the process of severance from the *shtetl.* The affinity to the old model exists, therefore, as a theme which helps shape the work, leaving its mark on the different views in the text. Thus, for example, an affinity to the old model appears as the theme in the following passage from R. Wallenrod's novel, *B'Ayn Dor* (In the Absence of a Generation):

> Woe to you, *shtetl* near the Visnika river, running on the Prifet that was so engraved in your son's consciousness, who left you without returning. Woe to you, *shtetl* of the native land and to what has become of you. There was in you an abundance of afternoon sunlight. In you were the shining greenery of forests dripping resin, of meadows and valleys, redolent of the fragrance of hay. In you there were both weekday dances and sacred dances on Sabbath and on Simchat Torah. Woe to you, quaint and simple *shtetl* of Polesia, whose sons would dance....[25]

In the old model, the nostalgic element is secondary. The main factor is what may be called "the comparative factor." Thus, for example, in H.A. Friedland's stories, *Sofer Stam B'Nechar* (A Scribe in a Foreign Country) and *Machol HaPrayda* (The Dance of Parting), there is a constant comparison between the old model, a model of the sacred, and the new model, a model of the secular. This contrast is well presented in the comparison between the different occupations of Rabbi Mordechai. Once he was a scribe, but when he found himself in America, he was condemned to other work:

> And thus, these hands which served all their days in sanctity have begun to serve profanity. These fingers which tied phylacteries have begun to pull ropes and cables and hold a broom. And as he used to rise early, in the distant past, to the entrances of synagogues and to the houses of study, he now rises early to the factory, because he took it upon himself to wash the floor in the morning before the workers arrived.[26]

This type of contrast is also seen in the occupations of Rabbi Baruch Shlomo. In his home town, he had been a cantor; thirty years later, having abandoned the work cycle, he returns to his prayers and intonations in the United States: "And he is now once again in his small town."[27] One can see other Friedland stories from this point of view – *Medoro Shel Rabbi Meleck* (Rabbi Meleck's Compartment), *Mumcheh Min HaChutz* (An Expert from the Outside), and others – all of which describe life in the sweatshops or in the Hebrew schools in America. The values of the new reality stand in contrast, or in a paradoxical relation, to the traditions of the old model.

These contrasts appear in two of B. Isaac's stories – *BaGolah* (In Exile) and *HaYenuka* (The Child-*Rabbi* [of *Hassidim*]). These stories, written with linear continuity, present characters through external characterization and create seemingly authentic situations. *BaGolah* is a story of immigration that focuses on the contrast between Vilna and New York. Rabbi Yankele arrives at his relatives' house in order to serve as a Rabbi in New York. He seeks out and finds Rabbi Wolf, the great cantor of Vilna, who "sold out" greedily to a rich community which lacked all Jewish content. Rabbi Yankele's discovery of the wretched cantor and the dismal Jewish content lead to thoughts of retracing his steps, but he comes to the conclusion that remaining in America is a Jewish "mission":

> Judaism is in peril, her sons are coming closer to conversion, the Sabbath is nullified, the earth is shaking under their feet, and I, I am seeking a way to escape, to hide, to grasp the horns of the altar and to be saved! Why have I come and why am I running away? To abandon my brothers under these circumstances and flee for my life![28]

Further on, he thinks, "I need Vilna, but America needs me." (p. 96) This is the polarization between the *shtetl* model in the hero's conscience and the Jewish-American anti-model. He sees himself as a messenger of one reality to a counter-reality, and he takes upon himself an impossible mission. The story of the hero striving to continue the traditions of the old country in the new is the story both of the Rabbi and of the author himself. The polarization is an expression of the author's and his hero's social situation – the author, like his hero, is serving as a messenger of one culture in a different cultural context but is not prepared to accept it as it is.

The polarized contrast between the old model and the new also appears in Isaac's interesting story *HaYenuka*, which is a mixture of the usual Hassidic story and an immigrant one. What at first seems to be a story of apostasy, together with a story of immigration, turns out to be only a Hassidic story. It begins in the Hassidic mode, in the Peretz and Yehuda Steinberg tradition: "The dance had ended. The Hassidim wiped the sweat off their faces, crowded around the Rebbi, lending an ear to his words."[29] The child, the Rebbi's son, does wonders in the Hassidic dance; but the devil prevails over him, and he joins a dance troupe and dances in theaters. He arrives in "New

York in America," performs alone in the theater, and attracts an audience. When he stops attracting the crowds, he is advised to add girls to his show; but, he refuses. He decides to establish his own art center. His son Marvin inclines to modern dancing, and the pupils turn to the son and abandon the father. The son defies the father, saying he is out of date: "He found that his father had never danced but one long dance, a dance he feared to name – a Hassidic dance." (p. 72) In the end, the [former] "child" is left isolated. He feels that he has extinguished the godly spark he had received from his father.

It would seem that this is a story in the pattern of stories by Frishman and his literary group. Those stories, printed in the "Agora Books," deal with Hassidism and the Enlightenment.[30] In actuality, *HaYenuka* is also an immigration story that describes the secularization processes of religious immigrant–Jews in the course of their acclimatization. Integration in the United States means estrangement from the *shtetl* model. The Rebbi's son is still guilty of heresy, according to the tradition, but all the same, he carries the tradition along. The Rebbi's grandson, however, is no longer faithful to this tradition. He has detached himself from the tradition but feels sorry for those who have totally cut themselves off from it. The "child" saw in his art a transformation of his faith, while his own son has severed his ties with the heritage of his forefathers.

In the selection of narrative material, in the anecdotes, and in the way he ended the story, Isaacs exposed one of the fundamental problems that he and his social group represented: American "enlightenment" was the exit from which there was no return. This group began to realize that immigrants who sought to transform the old model ended up breaking away from it altogether. Without the spark of tradition, the Hebrew author and his friends in America were drowning men grasping at a straw. They did not have a future, for their heritage had no hope. The story is an expression of deep despair at the dim chances for the survival of a heritage. Isaacs complied, as it were, with Ribalow's critical demand that one write about the confrontation between the *shtetl* tradition and the new American context. Herein lies the trouble. One learns from Isaacs's works that the *shtetl* tradition had no future in the American configuration. The father's generation indeed tried to carry on the tradition in a secular way, but the third generation broke away from it completely.

In many stories from the collection, *Amos Mocher HaTapuzim* (Amos the Orange Merchant), Isaacs depicts the situation of the second generation after it has broken off from the *shtetl* model and from tradition.[31] The Jewish spark which remained in Amos's heart after he escaped from the Jewish seminary is all but extinguished. He goes from New York to Florida to deal with matters of real life on earth, not Jewish matters, which, in his opinion, have become out-dated and obsolete: "That's how I referred to your Jerusalem. Do you know that you can stick the whole of Jerusalem with its crumbling Wall into one apartment building in New York?"[32] Amos becomes an orange merchant. The Jewish part of his character expresses itself in the fact that his non-Jewish friends and neighbors see him as a kind of peace-maker. The priest announces that he is none other than a reincarnation of Amos the Prophet. Isaacs uses the theme of transformation, but this transformation is far from complete. All that remains of Amos is a minor "Jewish quality," the signs of which are recognized more by his non-Jewish friends than by the hero himself.

The story *HaRomsim V'Ha Nirmasim* (The Tramplers and the Trampled) in this collection of stories by Isaacs also moves between proximity to and distance from Judaism. The contrast is expressed in an affinity to Jewish cooking. Whereas Yehuda Quint, who has recently immigrated, enjoys his aunt's Jewish dishes, her son Robert detests them and prefers American food instead. The impoverishment of the "Jewish quality," expressed in the heroes' attitudes to food and in the Jewish "quality of kindness," is saliently expressed in *Pega Rah* (Evil Spirit). Bill's Americanism is expressed in the "Americanization" of different phenomena:

> Bill is a typical American Jew. There are characteristics that mark him as an American, which are apparent, as well as those which are concealed. The apparent characteristics are, for example: great love for hot dogs, passion for the national desert, pie. On this list of American "commandments" concerning the stomach, and by which his Americanism becomes apparent, belong the Thanksgiving Day meal and Christmas Dinner.[33]

The hero's Judaism is thus expressed in his eating behavior. He likes gefilte fish with horseradish and challah, and he loves lox and bagels: "But it's just ritual, the worship of God, and it's taught in

Sunday School that our fathers and forefathers suffered for their Judaism, so why should good fortune befall them?" (p. 31) In addition, his relationship to religious observance is not very strict. The ritual still exists, but it has been emptied of content: "...Equipped with tickets [for synagogue seats], prayer books, and prayer-shawls, Bill and his friends stand on Yom Kippur in the synagogue's corridor, surrounded by others in conversation, discussing current events, from basketball, whose season ended then, to television, etc. ..." (p. 32)

The contrast between hot dogs and pie, and gefilte fish and lox and bagels, is a contrast between the customs of the American group and those of the Jewish sub-group within it. This is the "tension" that remained, according to this literary model, in American-Jewish society. The contrast between the *shtetl* model and its anti-models, expressed in the Hebrew literature of the Eastern European diaspora in the confrontation between Jewish values of spirit, religion, and family, and their counter-values in the United States, has been reduced to a limited pattern of behavior (the "eating" paradigm). Isaacs has tried to save something of the Jewish "spark," while emphasizing that Bill (the same "Evil Spirit") gives anonymous donations to two lonely women, who regard him as an "Evil Spirit." This story is not entirely satirical (the portrayal of patterns of behavior lacking in content) and not entirely apologetical (an anonymous donation as the transformation of a Jewish epoch). The author needed this anecdote and the others in order to cope with and justify his way of life, which he felt was an endless polarization. Still, he tried to find a justification for life, the crux of which is the series of attempts to mitigate that polarization.

It seems that the nostalgic longings for the *shtetl,* the contrast of its American anti-model, and the justification of the American-Jewish "achievement" are the main themes that concern writers such as Isaacs, Friedland, Sackler, Blank, Wallenrod, Grossman, and others. Of these, Friedland is a sophisticated story-teller, and Isaacs, a profound designer of the "naturalistic" anecdote.

The most important theme (it also determines novelistic form) in Hebrew-American fiction is the saga of the integration of the Jewish immigrant in the new country. This theme, as stated earlier, is dictated largely by A. Cahan's book, *The Rise of David Levinsky*. Three other related samples will be discussed, although they differ from Cahan's book in their literary levels, characterization, and scope of documentative and thematic material.

Grossman's *Av Uvito* (A Father and his Daughter), which appeared in 1934, contains a trivial story without any counterbalancing narrative features. (It is difficult to determine the intended audience.) The father, Rabbi Mordechai, a widower, and his daughter, Leah-Lucy, immigrate to New York. They come up against all the difficulties new immigrants are likely to face – death (of Rabbi Mordechai's friend); illness (of the daughter); work in a sweatshop. These melodramatic features appear one by one in the first part; in the second, which takes place in a small town, a love plot ensues between James, an eccentric gentile, and the daughter. The daughter goes off with the gentile, becomes pregnant and gives birth to a child, who dies. The two wander west, but James deserts Leah-Lucy after revealing (suddenly and without any warning) his latent anti-Semitism. The Ku Klux Klan appear in the father's town. The anti-Semitism of the lover and the anti-Semitic actions of the Klan lead the father and daughter, who, meanwhile, has returned home, to consider immigration to Israel.

Almost everything imaginable has been incorporated in this story: an immigration melodrama, a love plot (also melodramatic, between a Jew and a non-Jew), anti-Semitism, Zionism, a complicated intrigue (all its components are artificial and unconvincing), and an ideology forced onto the plot. This trivial novel par excellence exposes the major features of the "sociological melodrama": the orphan and her father; the Jewish orphan caught between the father and a non-Jewish lover; the dead child or a deserted woman; the return of the lost daughter. These features are found in many Hebrew, Yiddish, and non-Hebrew immigration stories, and many of the authors depend on those components and try to deal with them in different ways.

This formula worked well in S.L. Blank's *Al Admat Amerika* (On American Soil), published in 1958. Blank was a Bessarabian writer, who immigrated to the United States. In his best works, he wrote about Bessarabia, in the style of Hamsun's *Blessing of the Earth,*[34] although he wrote about the United States in works such as *Mister Kunis* (1934), *Ee HaDemaoth* (Island of Tears, 1941), and especially, *Al Admat Amerika*. The picaresque novel of crime, *Mister Kunis*, has quite an original message. It utilizes the trivial conventions of the crime story in order to describe the rise, fall, and repentance of the Jewish immigrant as a young criminal. The main theme of *Al Admat Amerika* is the consolidation and establishment of American Jewry, moving from an immigrant neighborhood on the Lower East Side to a new suburb, which they gradually infiltrate family by family and finally take over. While depicting "the transition," the author reconstructs in a long series of flashbacks how each family congealed, established itself, and got a foothold on a flourishing business. These are no longer immigrants struggling for a piece of bread, but satisfied middle-class Americans growing more and more self-assured in a middle-class neighborhood. Blank likes to describe the process of the consolidation of families and their integration in the land. The Bessarabian novels are settlement stories. One can say they depict how a barren land becomes inhabited. These novels describe how Jews struck roots, established themselves, and prepared to pass on their property to their sons' sons. Socially, *Al Admat Amerika* is a middle-class novel with a structural narrative pattern formed by many strands of plot. These strands are connected to the new, open space where everybody meets:

> Our brothers, children of Israel, may they live long, since fortune smiled upon them on American Land – they left their meager residence and the noise of the market, a place where they toiled and labored for many days, and sought their profits. One who had the money would get an apartment immediately, and the other was a temporary tenant until the blessing of the place would fall on whatever he did.[35]

In the new, open space, marriage plots develop among members of the second-generation families, who have already entered the liberal professions or are continuing their fathers' businesses. (Thus, Sammy, son of Mike and Sadie, marries Perle, daughter of Hank and

Mary Friedmann; and Martin Friedmann marries Bertha, daughter of Itchie and Minnie Mayer; and Sidney, son of Uncle Menashe, marries recently orphaned Hannah, etc....) This is also a humorous novel of becoming rich, established, and successful. The aim of the novel is to celebrate the spiritual and economic establishment of the immigrants and to depict the heritage they hand over to their sons. It is a positive, humorous perception of reality. The author does not spare his criticism, but the satiric element disappears because of the humorous enjoyment of success and abundance. Personal, social, and economic productivity fascinate Blank, and he likes to describe the "productivity rites" everywhere. The structure of this novel is more fragmented than that of his Bessarabian works. The fates of the families portrayed are similar – the families move from failure to success, from desolation to productivity; however, there is no central family around whom all strands of the plot are woven. The sociological process itself, the transition from Second Street to the "neighborhood," is the theme and "hero" of the novel.

The style of Blank's novel differs from that of the short stories of Friedland, Isaacs, and Damesek, or the novels of Grossman or Sackler. In all these works, style is only functional: it does not draw attention to its expressiveness, and its uniqueness lies in the attempt to express the fact that it is "translated." With the aid of "Americanisms," the authors indicate that, like Yiddishisms, Russianisms, and Arabicisms in other literary contexts, the speakers do not speak in the language that is written. The written language is "translated" from a different, colloquial speech. Blank's style is close to the stylized language, but he needs different styles to create a humorous atmosphere. Two examples follow:

> It has been said of their women, yesterday their dwelling was in the pigsty, somewhere in paupers' neighborhoods; today – Woe, their dishes, furniture, clothes are bought at a very high price – Please ask the baker, the butcher, the grocer, and they will tell you their nature and essence. They'll change their character in front of your face, if you don't pay them the degree of respect they believe they deserve. If they expressed their disgust, it would be better for a man to fall into the gutter than be offended by their speech. With their trimmings, powder, and adornments, they prance in precious jewels – not like us! To what has his Uncle Menashe compared them? To those primping swans, covering their ugly legs with their wings. (pp. 86-87).

> ... and among the worthy people of the city is the editor of "Dos Folk," in person. And how will he present himself to them? He is altogether lovely, from head to toe – sparkling, including his moustache, as if he has just come out of the bath. And the way this guy articulates and has a pair of black smiling eyes. If he were a woman, Uncle Menashe would have fallen in love with him immediately. Willy sings his greatest praises. He once was a "socialist" who sought to turn this world into complete chaos. The folk-pleasers [figuratively "bullies" – Trans.] stand on a crate on Second Street and bark loudly, pour tubs of sewage water of "bassiem" on the authorities, and everybody is boils-stricken. Well, how then will he put it to them? One who wants to make of all gentiles one nation! "A Tale of *Yachlach*" he writes in his manner of speaking, and the "cooking spoon" in our city; instead of two, there he is shoving his nose into every cooking-pot and expressing his opinion. (p. 106)

These two humorous passages relate to two stereotypes in the social inventory of American Jewry – women who belong to the nouveau riche and the professional "socialist." They are written in Hebrew in a stylized language, for the author needed a formula in order to create humorous effects. Original phrases like "change their character" (lit. invert their placenta), "be convenient for a man," "trimmings," "to what he has compared it to" – are restrained, conventional Hebrew idioms that have roots in the cultural tradition. Add to these the rhetorical questions ("please ask" and "they will tell you"), the rhetorical-catalogical exaggerations ("powder...," "precious jewels"), the comic metaphor ("primping swans"), and the humorous style of the first passage is nicely elicited. In both passages the author needs the special relationship with an inner addressee-reader to construct his humorous attitude ("has been said of," "please ask," "if they expressed their disgust," "to what has he compared them"). The second passage is also based on the rhetoric of the transferred dialogue, which needs a certain comic, rhetorical relation to an inner addressee ("how will he be laid," "Willy sings his praises," "how will he put it to them" "in our city," etc.). Here, too, the author needs the idiomatic style of language ("worthy of the city," "in person," "will be laid before them," "altogether lovely," "come out of his bath," "sings his greatest praises," "folkpleasers" [instead of bullies], "tubs of sewage water"), which functions within a mixture and play of Yiddishisms (*kaliker, kachlefl*, meaning both "cooking spoon" and "shoving his nose into every pot"). This is a style which calls attention to itself. More than Isaacs, Friedland, Grossman, or Sackler, Blank is attached to the literary-stylistic tradition of Hebrew literature. In this group of writers, he is the exception. The style of these writers is similar to that of some of the "Agorah" writers who lacked style. What the writers wished to provide were pictures from life, just as American writers did.

The greatest writer in the context of the Jew as an immigrant is Harry Sackler. He wrote mostly plays, but he also wrote a collection of stories, *HaKeshet B'Anan* (The Rainbow in a Cloud, 1948), an historical novel about the forefather Abraham, *U'Sfor HaKochavim* (And Count the Stars, 1961), and *Hilula B'Meron* (A Celebration at Meron, first printed in English in 1963). It is his novel of American Jewry, *Beyn Erets V'Shamayim* (Between Earth and Heaven, 1964) that is of specific importance. Kabakoff comments:

> For many years [Sackler] kept in the drawer of his desk the manuscript of this comprehensive novel of the life of the Jews in America, which he first wrote in English. For some reason or other, he was not able to find a publisher for this novel, despite the success of his first historical novel *Hilula B'Meron* in its English version. The new novel was emended in its Hebrew translation when it appeared in 1964 under the name of *Beyn Erets V'Shamayim.*[36]

What is of interest here is the fate of the text and the novelistic material. The novel is written in the tradition of *The Rise of David Levinsky* and is perhaps closer to that novel than to any other piece of Hebrew fiction. Like the fiction of the "Agorah writers" of the late nineteenth century, Sackler's novel is also based on documentation, ideology, and intrigue. The extra-literary allusions are numerous, and the author tries to encompass most types of occupations and the existence of Jewish immigrants in the United States. The main character is the young immigrant, Avner Stern. The author depicts him as a picaro in all levels of the new society. The hero starts out in a clothes factory as a cutter and presser and becomes involved in the struggle of the new trade unions. He fights against the Mafia, which was hired to break up the strikes. He becomes an English teacher of young immigrants and studies law. Along the way, he arrives at a typical, small American town and tries his luck there. He falls in love with a non-Jewish married woman and is smuggled out of town (after being injured by the woman's husband). He stays for a while with a Jewish farmer and then returns to New York, where he finds his way to the Jewish press and becomes a journalist of status. He fights different Jewish public figures and finally joins the American army in the First World War.

The layers of society in this documentary novel are quite rich and variegated: a Jewish bourgeoisie in opposition to a Jewish trade union; Jewish *landsmanshaftn* (reminders from Stern's small town, Dubrovin); a closed gentile society banishing a Jewish sinner; a Jewish bohemian; and intellectual journalist circles. The documentary material in this novel is dominant. Sackler wished to create models from "the world of yesterday." He did not seek a special vantage point, but one which would recall that world to his readers, who were aware of its existence and shared that experience.

The novel's intrigue revolves around four women. The first is Avner's girlfriend, Malkah Zilberhacken, who becomes Molly Zilber and, in the end, Madeline Stahl. Malka was the girlfriend of the town hero, and now she exploits her looks to survive and progress in America. She begins as a worker, and with the help of a married man who is very attached to her, she becomes a model. In the end, she opens a boutique, which all the society women want to patronize. Her relationship with the married man, at different stages of their lives, is an expression of the struggle of small town people to survive. To such people, the goal of American success ("making it") justifies all means.

The second woman in Avner's life is a small Italian girl named Celia. Their relationship raises a problem the young immigrant faces – Jewish identity and loyalty to the ethnic group. Love and loyalty to the other group (religion) are woven into the plot, and the intrigue tries to emphasize that ethnic identity comes before any love.

The third woman in the hero's life is Corry Wharton, a married woman. All the hero's relationships with the local non-Jewish world, with WASP society, are revealed in seductions and consenting affairs. Avner's stay in Eureka on Long Island with his schoolmate Bruce Caldwell is connected with this woman and her husband. Avner's attitude toward Corry is an expression of his strong attraction to that enchanting world. When he is rejected by it, he arrives at a Jewish farm and finds himself a Jewish wife, Elka Alpert, his partner in life.

The intrigue is clearly an expression of the novel's ideology, which is the ideology of the American Jew who seeks to preserve his Jewish identity. The picaresque journey is paved with social and sexual temptations (capitalism, socialism, complete assimilation, etc.). In the end, after military service, Sackler's hero finds the path to his sought-after identity. In contrast to other novels of "success," like *The Rise of David Levinsky*, Sackler's novel, in spite of its socialist chapter, does not condemn the frivolity of achieving or present a counter-moral to "Social Darwinism." What is important in Sackler's view is how a man in the land of opportunity will be a Jew and survive. The object is not survival without moral corruption, but survival without the necessity of complete assimilation. In short, the novel *Beyn Erets V'Shamayim* is a story of personal enlightenment (in the nature of "Haskalah" literature). It is the story of a hero trying to preserve his Jewish identity.

One of Isaac's longest immigration novels, *Yada'im* (Hands), is close in spirit and form to Sackler's great novel. Bianca, son of Shmerl the shoemaker, is a shoemaker-apprentice accused in his home town of participating in revolutionary circles. He arrives in the United States, becomes a peddler and a dish-washer, and manages to find a job in a shoe shop. As happens in every melodrama, the landlord's daughter, against her father's wishes, falls in love with Bianca. He studies and becomes an expert in orthopedic shoes. Together with his wife, he takes over the shop and a chain of shops, until he becomes a wealthy man, donating a large sum of money for building a synagogue for the *landsmanshaft*. The motif of "hands" is the leitmotif of the story; the hero longs for gentle hands, in contrast to the rough ones of the nearby environment. The Rabbi and the Rabbi's son are the ones with gentle hands, and to them, Bianca is willing to donate his money, once he has settled down to a peaceful, prosperous life. The main theme of the short novel is, again, the relation between economic survival and cultural survival. "The common people" express their cultural survival in economic identification with a "religious enterprise."

The aesthetic model here expresses American modes of living and is close to the given social model. The author aims at the addressee, who identifies himself as a Jew mainly in two ways: affiliation with the *landsmanshaftn*, which connect him to the country of origin, and affiliation with the "religion of origin." The connection between the two is almost an ideal act of identification under American circumstances. The author took this identification ritual from the available models in the social inventory and utilized it as a "happy end" in his work, in order to create an identification between the assumed addressee and the work. His aim was to convert the act of reading into a pseudo-ritual of identification with the "cult" of dual survival. This is the only innovation in the story.

Conclusion

Hebrew literature in America reflects a "generic" model – the American-Jewish way of life. It tries to create an identification between the audience of readers and the model which this literature has tried to convey and glorify, by the fact that it is in Hebrew and by the identification with the community's culture more than with the next generation. Admittedly, the authors discussed here are second-rate writers. But, from them one learns more about fiction in the United States than from the major authors who, to a certain degree, succeeded in breaking through the limitations of Hebrew-American literary provincialism. Three who did break through the limitations of place and generation were Reuben Wallenrod, E. E. Lisitzky, and Shimon Halkin. A discussion of these three is a chapter in itself, and each one deserves separate consideration. The general fictional norm from which these three have distinguished themselves has been presented here. Authors such as Isaacs, Friedland, and Sackler represent and typify in different ways the average level of this fiction, which lacked a cultural background, a natural audience, and a real chance for any literary life. What began in Hebrew fiction at a very early stage passed on to Yiddish fiction later. American-Jewish fiction gradually discarded its original native languages and dedicated itself to the alien English language.

Notes

[1] L.A. Arieli-Orlov to M. Ribalow from Syracuse, Fast of Gedaliah, 1927, "Genazim" archives, No. 2635. There are many similar and parallel letters of Arieli-Orlov. See Gershon Shaked, *HaSiporet HaIvrit* (Hebrew Narrative Fiction), 1880-1980, Vol. 2, pp. 118-119, 369-370.

[2] Cf. *ibid.*, pp. 247-248. In 1946, Eliezer Z. Friedland tried to revive a journal in the United States (following upon *Niv*) named *Alil*, and his loneliness is reflected in Friedland's letter to A. Aharoni. Friedland to A. Aharoni, "Genazim" archives, 29 Shvat, 1946.

[3] Hillel Bavli, "*B'Shlichut HaLev*," *HaDoar*, Vol. 34, No. 39, 28 Tishrei, 1956, p. 783.

[4] See Abraham Epstein, *Sofrim Ivrim B'Amerika* (Tel Aviv: 1952), p. 9.

[5] On the penetration of Jews into the American culture and its sociological consequences, see James Yaffe, *The American Jews* ("Portrait of a Split Personality"), (New York: 1968), esp. pp. 221-229.

[6] Many books have been written in English about the development of a Jewish-American literature. See Max F. Schulz, *Radical Sophistication, Studies in Contemporary Jewish-American Novelists* (Ohio: 1969).

[7] Halkin explains very well the decline of Hebrew literature in America. Read B. Shahevitch, *Ya'arot Metohamim* (Abbyssed Forests), Simon Halkin, Jubilee Volume (Jerusalem: 1957), pp. 151-153

[8] Ya'akov Leschinsky, *HaT'futsa HaYehudit* (The Jewish Diaspora), (Jerusalem: 1960), p. 111.

[9] Leschinsky, *ibid.*, pp. 202, 227.

[10] *HaToren*, 6 yr., Vol. 25, 10 Elul, 1909. Maximon wrote: "In the state of Ohio, for example, Jewish people from three countries have gathered in the capital city. There are about two hundred thousand Jews, ninety percent of whom are concentrated in seven communities: Cleveland, Cincinnati, Columbus, Toledo, Youngstown, Akron, and Dayton. Nearly forty thousand of them are school children attending the public school. How many of them are sent to a Hebrew school or afternoon school? In Cleveland, a thousand; in Toledo, two hundred; in Akron, two hundred; in Dayton, a hundred and fifty; in Youngstown, about a hundred; and in Cincinnati and in Columbus, there is not a trace of Hebrew education." And furthermore, "the tutors ... are wretched peddlers who, by chance, sell "Hebrew" and a Bar Mitzva. ... The Reform rabbis, the majority of whom shout "Judaism, Judaism," have neither the taste nor the smell of Judaism." S.B. Maximon, *Gvilim* (Parchments), (New York: 1925), pp. 111-113.

[11] The *"Brit Ivrit Olamit"* (World Hebrew Covenant) was a central cultural organization in the Jewish world and especially in the U.S.A. It is now a small, minor group.

[12] E.E. Lisitzky, *Eleh Toldot Adam* (Jerusalem: 1953), p. 287. All of the

following either taught school children or were Hebrew tutors in other frameworks: L.A. Arieli-Orlov (1886-1943), B. Isaacs (1884-1975), S. Damesek (1896-1963), H.A. Friedland (1891-1939), R. Wallenrod (1899-1966), S. Halkin (1898 -), E.E. Lisitzky (1885-1962), H. Bavli (1893-1961), I. Efros (1891-1981), Y. Zilberschlag (1903-), and many others.

[13] See. J. Kabakoff, *Shocharim V'Ne'emanim* (Jerusalem: 1978), pp. 333-339.

[14] Many American Hebrew writers immigrated to Israel or wished to immigrate at some time in their lives. Y. Twersky, S. Halkin, and I. Efros finally arrived in Israel. R. Wallenrod tried several times to immigrate to Israel. For most of them, writing in the American vacuum was difficult, and most of them tried to have their work printed in Israel.

[15] M. Ribalow, "Mitat Sdom U'Merhav Yah" ("A Procrustean Bed and the Space of God"), *HaDoar's Jubilee Book* (New York: 1927), pp. 11-12.

[16] *Ibid.*, p. 15.

[17] M. Ribalow, *Hebrew Literature in America*, "Ahisefer," (New York: 1944), pp. 99-101.

[18] *HaSiporet HaIvrit, 1880-1980*, Vol. 1 (1977), pp. 22-23.

[19] *Sof Passuk* (Full Stop), (Tel Aviv: 1960).

[20] G. Shaked, *HaMakazeh HaIvri HaHistori B'Tkufat HaTchiya* (The Hebrew Historical Play in the Renaissance Period), (Jerusalem: 1970), pp. 145-150, 179-184, 218-226, and *passim.*

[21] On the development of Hebrew poetry in the United States, see some of Abraham Epstein's important comments, *Sofrim Ivrim B'America* (Hebrew Authors in America), (Tel Aviv: 1952), p. 10

[22] E.E. Lisitzky, in the Introduction to the collection of poems, *Anshei Midot* (Men of Stature), (Tel Aviv: 1958).

[23] For example: S. Ornitz, *Haunch, Paunch and Jowl* (An Unsentimental Classic about the Ghetto that was the Lower East Side), (New York: 1963), First Ed. 1923).

[24] G. Shaked, *HaSiporet HaIvrit, 1880-1980*, Vol. 2, p. 270.

[25] R. Wallenrod, *B'Ayn Dor* (Tel Aviv: 1968), p. 79.

[26] H.A. Friedland, "Sofer Stam B'Nechar," in *Sipurim* (Stories), (Tel Aviv: 1939), p. 49.

[27] H.A. Friedland, "Micol HaPreydah", in *ibid.*, p. 171.

[28] B. Isaacs, *Bagola*, in *Bein Shtey Olamot* (1969), p. 95.

[29] B. Isaacs, *HaYenuka*, in *ibid.*, p. 60.

[30] *HaSiporet HaIvrit 1880-1980*, Vol. 1, pp. 122-124; 232-237.

[31] B. Isaacs, *Amos Mocher HaTapuzim* (Tel Aviv: Newmann, 1953).

[32] *Ibid*, p. 9.

[33] B. Isaacs, *Pega Rah* in *ibid.*, p. 30.

[34] *HaSiporet HaIvrit 1880-1980*, Vol. 2, p. 298.

[35] S.L. Blank, *Al Admat Amerika* (Tel Aviv: 1958), p. 78.

[36] J. Kabakoff, *ibid.*, p. 187.

Of History, Literature, and Charles Reznikoff (1894-1976)

Milton Hindus

"To elaborate is (of) no avail," wrote Walt Whitman, and he promptly proceeded to elaborate his greatest poem. Without fear of contradiction, then, I wish to elaborate a thought I expressed at Charles Reznikoff's funeral. It was a thought about the tricks that history plays, and appropriate perhaps because Reznikoff's first ambition was to become a professional historian. In his early years, he had planned to take a doctorate in history and in the course of his life he translated some histories and wrote some himself. Poetry was apparently a second thought, a happy second thought. At the funeral, I spoke of well-known contemporaries who "will have plenty of time in which to be forgotten" and contrasted them with the glorious "unknowns" among us (some unrecognized, some little recognized, some unpublished as yet) who will have "an eternity in which to be remembered."

A hundred years ago, at the time of the first American centennial in 1876, who were the poets whose names were "household words" in America? They were, of course, the so-called "Fireside Poets" whose names are not easy to recall today. They were *not* the names of the period that we think of first today. Emily Dickinson was then forty-six years old and still had ten years in which to live. She was "nobody" outside the limited circle of her family and friends, and would remain that for years after her death, since she steadfastly refused to publish in her lifetime and regarded publication as an intolerable indignity: "Publication is the auction of the mind of man," she wrote, and refused to put herself on the auction-block where the only fate worse than being bought is not being bought. In 1876, Whitman was 57 years old and unfortunately only too well known. Outside a small circle of family, friends, and "disciples," he was widely regarded as an eccentric and indecent pretender to the title of poet, with an insatiable appetite for publicity, self-promotion, and advertising. "Poverty be justifying for so vile a thing" (as the quest for publicity), Emily Dickinson hat written, but she could afford to be disdainful, while Whitman, of course, was poor. Even so loyal an admirer of Whitman as John Addington Symonds complained that "the ways he chose for pushing his gospel and advertising his philosophy put a severe strain on patience...." In 1876, Melville was working (had been working for ten years) in the New York Custom House and had virtually been forgotten as a writer, since he had had the temerity to publish *Moby Dick* a quarter of a century before. He was destined to sink still more deeply into obscurity until his death in 1892, after which he remained virtually unnoticed for another thirty years, before being rediscovered by a new generation in the 1920's.

But while the new "Jazz Age" was congratulating itself complacently on doing belated justice to Melville, Whitman, and Dickinson, at the same time as it was downgrading spitefully the Fireside Poets whom the 19th century had worshipped, it was busily losing track of some authentic literary phenomena in its own midst, just as its forefathers had once done. In 1926, one finds Scott Fitzgerald writing plaintively: "Of all the work by the young men who have sprung up since 1920, one book survives – *The Enormous Room* by E.E. Cummings. It was swamped in the mediocre downpour, isolated – forgotten. But it lives on, because those few who cause books to live have not been able to endure the thought of its mortality." Perhaps Fitzgerald even then (only a year after the appearance of *The Great Gatsby*) could foresee that his work, too, was fated before his death to be "swamped in the mediocre downpour" and would survive eventually only because of the efforts of "those few who cause books to live and who could not endure the thought" of their mortality. Of those blessed with such vision and enthusiasm, Gertrude Stein was surely one, and she tells us in her *Autobiography of Alice B. Toklas* of an argument with Hemingway as to the merits of E.E. Cummings, whom he had at first undervalued and then, in reaction, overpraised. On the same page on which Gertrude Stein records this incident, she also states her own prophetic conviction that "Fitzgerald will be read when many of his well-known contemporaries are forgotten."

So the tragicomedy continues – an endless succession of false recognitions and belated recognitions and attempted reparations, always coming too late or almost too late for the most important person involved. Whitman, for one, knew all about it, by experience as well as in theory, as we can see in his saying to Traubel: "There are always the unknown men ... often essentially greater than those with boisterous reputations... (men) without a name, unknown, eclipsed by the formidable reputations of mostly lesser people.... It can't be helped, but we should contribute nothing ourselves to such a falsifying human habit."

Of all the "vanities" of Ecclesiastes, surely the most vain is the desire for fame, immediately or posthumously. Milton in *Lycidas* calls it "the last infirmity of a noble mind." And then there are those whose minds can hardly be described as noble but who nevertheless cherish the pitiful ambition to "go down in history" and sometimes succeed, alas, like the Titanic! History is a tangled tissue of crimes, follies, and catastrophes, interspersed now and again with intelligent inventions and memorable virtues. There is a difference after all between being remembered and being remembered *for good*. What should Hitler not have given, had he had any semblance of sanity or sense, to be simply forgotten instead of leaving a name that has become a synonym for infamy. On the other hand, one remembers the story by Anatole France of the Procurator of Judea, Pontius Pilate, who, years after the event, could not "recall the name" of a little-known "prophet" who had died on a cross during his term of office.

Real fame, worthy fame, for which the "noble mind" need not be ashamed of striving, sometimes strikes like lightning (as it did Byron) and at other times grows so slowly that it is impossible to be aware of its progress. It is that which is capable of proving itself to the candid mind over and over again, generation after generation. Its grounds and reasons should be self-evident to anyone who cares to look into them deeply enough. It belongs, for example, to him of whom Phaedo spoke with Echecrates 2,500 years ago and said with the careful phrasing he had learned from his master: "Of all the men of his time whom I have known, he was the wisest and the justest and the best." It is something rare and deserved and infinitely precious bestowed on the choicest, the most sensitive, and intelligent spirits, and it is not to be confused (except by an obtuse, undiscriminating, vulgar world) with the little, temporary, ephemeral triumphs or notoriety that are so mercilessly clawed for by the crude and the loud. Real fame, as distinguished from the simulacrum often mistaken for it, is what Emily Dickinson must have had in mind when she wrote to a concerned and admiring well-wisher and friend: "If fame belonged to me, I could not escape her."

Charles Reznikoff was one of those who knew the gulf that separates well-merited renown from well-merited oblivion. This may be inferred from one of his wry, pointed, charming epigrams (the 23rd of the "inscriptions" which are gathered into the little volume of his selected poems, which he called *By the Waters of Manhattan*):

> Scrap of paper
> blown about the street,
> you would like to be cherished, I suppose,
> like a banknote.

Surely he must have taken pleasure, as we continue to do, in the possession of an "eye for resemblances," which could take the most commonplace scene and transform it with an unforgettable metaphor, as he does in an untitled poem:

> Feast, you who cross the bridge
> this cold twilight
> on these honeycombs of light, the buildings of Manhattan.

Reznikoff's "letters to the world" (in prose as well as in poetry) are now committed, as we all must be eventually, to hands he cannot see and that even the living may not see for some time, may never see. These hands belong to all of us who treasure the English language and the memory of those who have also treasured it and have left lovely written records of precisely how they felt. According to Louis Zukofsky, Ezra Pound, who did not choose his words casually, has described the writing of Reznikoff that he had seen as "good." Reserved but high praise indeed from a critic and connoisseur who had once hailed Robert Frost's first book as the work of a man who was not a fool. More important, perhaps, Pound also discerned in Reznikoff a portent and a harbinger of a development that has since become literary history. In 1931, after reading Reznikoff, Pound was quoted in the Objectivist issue of *Poetry Magazine* (Chicago) as voicing a "suspicion" that "the next wave of literature will be Jewish." In retrospect, it is indeed possible to see in Reznikoff the first native American writer of East European derivation capable of writing the English language with enough felicity and distinction to impress the most demanding judge of style (that is to say, as Pope did, one and only one who has himself "written well"). After a couple of generations, he still remains to my mind among the very best. For about twenty-five years (between 1936 and 1961), this fact was almost totally obscured in a world with many other things on its mind and other writers now themselves forgotten or close to being forgotten. But I venture to predict that the same fate is not likely to be visited on him again. Though relatively few are aware of him or of his work even now, these few are keenly enough aware to make it entirely possible, even likely, that they will beget literary progeny who will carry on and continue to remember. It may be a valid generalization, incidentally, that writers, artists, and composers who have been "rediscovered" are less likely to be neglected a second time. The classic examples that may be adduced to prove this are some of those cited earlier (Melville, Dickinson, Whitman) and others whose names now come to mind: Vermeer, Bach, even Rembrandt, who, despite the luster of their names at present, have all had to undergo their intermittent "crooked eclipses."

Everything I knew of Charles Reznikoff in the many years I knew him and everything I have learned of him since his death lead me to believe that he was something even more rare than a good writer (which, as the world goes, is rare enough). He was a good man. In the language of his ancestors, which he worked diligently to comprehend though he never mastered it to his own satisfaction, he was a man exceptionally endowed with joy in his *nishmas chaim*, a Biblical expression which my dictionary translates as the "breath of life," the word *nishmas* in other contexts also signifying spirit or soul. *Zaicher l'vracha*. May his memory be blest....

It is fitting perhaps to conclude with the beautiful conclusion of his own poem, "Rashi," written in the speech of the strangers he had married," as he calls the English language in one of his other poems:

Jacob is like the stars
Which rise to their station,
Which the winds cannot blow away
Nor clouds extinguish.
But we become names upon gravestones and upon books,
Our desire for the law an inheritance
Among our grandsons.
It was good to labor, and after labor
It is good to rest.

Cynthia Ozick and the Jewish Fantastic

Joseph Lowin

Cynthia Ozick has recently been accorded wide recognition as a major writer of American fiction. William Abrahams, the editor of the *O. Henry Prize Stories* of 1984, commenting on the selection of a story by Ozick as the best short story of the year, went so far as to call her "one of the three greatest living American writers of short fiction."[1]

Likewise, she has been acclaimed as a Jewish writer. If there is indeed – as Ruth R. Wisse has asserted – a movement of Jewish writers who identify themselves self-consciously as Jews and whose fiction draws extensively from the Jewish tradition, then Ozick is their acclaimed leader. According to Wisse, Ozick's "most effective stories and novellas are not only steeped in internal Jewish life and lore to a degree that sets them apart from the work of her contemporaries and predecessors; they are actually Jewish assaults on fields of Gentile influence."[2] It is not clear that such aggressive language is appropriate to describe Ozick's contribution to western, or American, literature. What is apparent is that Ozick has chosen to treat what are accepted as western literary genres from a Jewish perspective. An attempt has recently been made to demonstrate that in her novel, *The Cannibal Galaxy* (1983), Ozick has created a Jewish mimesis by elaborating a Jewish model for the representation of reality.[3]

In addition to her realistic fiction, there are many stories in the Ozick canon that have supernatural elements; indeed, several of these may be counted among the most masterful representations of the fantastic short story. As Ozick's fiction reminds us, traditionally Jewish subject matter also contains golems, dybbuks, and other gradations of the supernatural. This essay is an attempt to analyze and assess Ozick's contributions to the fantastic short story by examining two of her most powerful and representative efforts, "The Pagan Rabbi" and "Levitation."[4]

For many years, Cynthia Ozick has been posing the question: how is it possible to be both Jewish and a writer? For her, the very term "Jewish writer" is an oxymoron – like "pagan rabbi." If writing is anti-Jewish, how is a Jew to handle the overwhelming need to write? One answer is to stifle one's impulses, and many of Ozick's stories are, paradoxically, polemics against story-writing. Another response is to compose tales that fall within the Jewish textual tradition. In either case the Jewish writer writes.

"The Pagan Rabbi" and "Levitation" are both difficult and compelling: difficult because they contain polemics against writing; compelling because they have a problematical, mystical element that lies within the Jewish textual tradition. Cynthia Ozick's comments on the mystical tendency to be found in many of her stories are crucial to an understanding of the role of the supernatural in her writing:

> I myself am hostile to the mystical enterprise. I'm a rationalist and I'm a skeptic. But there's something in me that is fascinated by the surrender to the mystical blur between the creator and the created. It's really a fictional theme for me. I reject it intellectually and emotionally. But it's where the stories come from.[5]

Is this statement a confession? Or is it a literary *profession de foi*? The narrator of "Puttermesser and Xanthippe," another of Ozick's fantastic stories, commenting on the pervasiveness of golem-making in Jewish history, makes an observation similar to the one offered by Ozick concerning her own writing:

> Puttermesser was no mystic. ... Her mind was clean; she was a rationalist. ... What interested Puttermesser was something else: it was the plain fact that golem-makers were neither visionaries nor magicians nor sorcerers. They were neither fantasists nor fabulists nor poets. They were, by and large, scientific realists. ... Even Rabbi Elijah, ... the Vilna *Gaon*, once attempted ... to make a golem! And the Vilna *Gaon* ... was ... the scourge of mystics. ... If the Vilna *Gaon* would contemplate the making of a golem, ... there was nothing irrational in it.[6]

Obviously, there is "something" in the Vilna *Gaon*, in the most Jewish of "Jewish Writers" (here the term is *not* an oxymoron), that is also "fascinated by the surrender to the mystical blur between the creator and the created."

The fantastic is an elusive genre. It is elusive, as Tzvetan Todorov has explained, because by its very nature, it is fluid, dynamic, evanescent – characterized by change.[7] The fantastic, Todorov writes, does nothing more than occupy a duration. It is characterized by a blur, by the hesitation of the reader implicit in the text as to whether the incident he is reading about will resolve itself into one of two neighboring genres, what Todorov calls the uncanny (*l'étrange*) or the marvelous (*le merveilleux*). The uncanny (a term taken from Freud's essay [1919][8]) describes a situation in which a supernatural event is explained rationally. The marvelous describes a situation in which the supernatural is simply accepted as such. In his analysis of the *problems* posed by the fantastic, Todorov emphasizes that it is a literature "which postulates the existence of the real, the natural, the normal, in order to attack it subsequently." (Todorov, p. 173)

For Ozick, there is a nuance of "the real" that may be of consequence. She answers the question "What is Art?" with a liturgical, almost homiletical, declaration: "It is first noticing, and then sanctifying, the Ordinary. It is making the Ordinary into the Extraordinary. It is the impairment of the distinction between the Ordinary and the Extraordinary." She goes on to say that the Jew has a very important trait in common with the artist: "Nothing that passes before him is taken for granted, everything is exalted."[9]

The plot of "The Pagan Rabbi" offers a case in point. Two young men, sons of prominent rabbis, had been classmates together at a rabbinical seminary. One – the narrator – drops out of school and marries a gentile girl – an incident which causes his father to sit *shiva* (mourn) on his account. He subsequently goes into his uncle's fur business in upstate New York, is miserable in his marriage because his wife is frigid (he calls her a puritan), gets divorced, moves back to New York City, and, deciding to deal in writers and writing, opens a bookstore. The other classmate – Isaac Kornfeld – continues his rabbinical studies, becomes a professor of "Mishnaic history," publishes brilliant monographs on Jewish subjects, and causes his father to beam broadly with pride. He subsequently marries Sheindel, a *sheitel*-wearing Jewish woman, and together they have seven daughters. Kornfeld winds up committing suicide by hanging himself from a tree with his *tallit* (prayer shawl).

Almost everything about these two parallel lives is plausible, recognizable, sociologically accurate, and, until the strange, brutal fact and manner of the suicide, utterly realistic. The element which moves the tale from the realistic to the fantastic is the tree from which Isaac Kornfeld hangs himself. He may have been a rabbi, but, as the narrator learns when he goes to pay a condolence call on the widow, he had become a "Pagan Rabbi" – a teller of seemingly supernatural stories and a person who had himself lived inside these stories. Sheindel describes a series of her husband's literary inventions:

> These were the bedtime stories Isaac told Naomi and Esther: about mice that danced and children who laughed. When Miriam came he invented a speaking cloud. With Ophra it was a turtle that married a blade of withered grass. By Leah's time the stones had tears for their leglessness. Rebecca cried because of a tree that turned into a girl and could never grow colors again in autumn. Shiphra, the littlest, believes that a pig has a soul. (*The Pagan Rabbi*, p. 13)

The difference between Ozick's fiction and classical 19th century fantastic literature is apparent. Reality is not merely social order. It is also natural, cosmic order. The fantastic in Ozick's tale resolves itself into something more than the marvelous, and, despite appearances, into something more than mere fairy tale. What Ozick is describing in her story about Isaac's own stories is the development of the narrative of the family life of Rabbi Isaac and Sheindel Kornfeld into a story belonging to the Jewish fantastic, with its judgment of the world.

The seemingly insignificant fact that Isaac Kornfeld would frequently go out into the field to daydream truly bursts with significance and places the tale firmly within a certain Jewish textual tradition. The epigraph to Ozick's story, taken from *Mishna Avot*, performs the first step of this function: "He who is walking along and studying but then breaks off to remark, 'How lovely is that tree!' or 'How beautiful is that fallow field!' – Scripture regards such a one as having hurt his own being." (p. 3) The connection is clear: there is a danger to one's very Jewishness inherent in an esthetic appreciation of nature.[10]

Cynthia Ozick has made much of the fundamental opposition between paganism and the Jewish idea. In this story, the very choice of the name "Isaac Kornfeld" places Ozick in the Jewish textual tradition, in the company of no less a Jewish writer than Rashi. "Isaac Kornfeld" clearly alludes to the Scriptural tale of another Isaac, young *Yitzhak*, son of Abraham, who, awaiting the arrival of his bride, goes out into the field to meditate. There is, first, the linguistic connection between "Isaac Kornfeld" and *vayetzeh Yitzhak lasu'ah basadeh.*" (Gen. 24: 63) And, there is a connection between Rashi and Ozick. Rashi recalls a midrash on what Isaac was "doing" in the field. Rather than have him daydream on the erotic consequences of a marriage, Rashi reins in the dreamer and has him praying instead of dreaming ("*lasuah: leshon tefila*"). Ozick's tale, a kind of midrash, tells what happens when one goes out into nature for "non-liturgical purposes."

Isaac Kornfeld, it must be emphasized, was also a writer – and not only of scholarly monographs. The story contains, *mise en abyme,*[11] Isaac's text. This text may be interpreted, variously, as the suicide note of a madman (and thus the fantastic story resolves itself into the uncanny), as the description of a supernatural occurrence (in which the story would resolve itself into the marvelous), or as an allegory or parable. Isaac's text is reproduced verbatim in Ozick's text, and has three "readers." Sheindel, who knows the text by heart, reads the first half to the narrator; the narrator reads the other half out loud. The reader implicit in the text, the reader who knows that he is in the genre of the fantastic, wavers between Sheindel's marvelous reading and the narrator's uncanny one. The "letter" is addressed to someone called "creature" and "loveliness." It is nevertheless a Jewish text and like many Jewish texts it begins inside the story of the Exodus. It contains a brilliant midrash against diaspora living (based on a highly intuitive, almost pantheistic mysticism). The two philosophical points of Isaac's midrash are that idolatry does not exist – because death does not exist – and that, in the plant world, in the world of trees, in the world of nature, the soul is able to be free.

The next stage in Isaac's *itinerarium mentis* (and in the reader's road to the fantastic) is his "discovery" (on the outside as it were, in the field) of wood nymphs. He has seen a nymph save the life of one of his daughters drowning in a stream. He comes to the conclusion that there are only two ways to communicate and commune with these free-floating souls. To experience ecstasy (to stand outside of himself), he must either die or copulate with nature.

He tries the latter first. In what Ozick could only have meant to be the description of an abomination, Isaac Kornfeld fornicates with an oak tree and succeeds in achieving some sort of ecstasy this way. He even conjures up the presence of a pagan girl, Iripomoňoéià (the "apple of his eye"), who informs him that his soul has stepped out of his body and is now visible. Isaac looks at his soul and is mortified by what he sees. Isaac Kornfeld's soul, walking in the field, studying Talmud, is Jewish! The soul does not even notice Iripomoňoéià, denies her, "passes indifferent through the beauty of the field," (*The Pagan Rabbi*, pp. 34-5), is faithful to the rabbinic dictum that Ozick had quoted for us in the epigraph of her story. When Isaac Kornfeld confronts his Jewish soul, he learns that to have a Jewish soul is not to be free in nature but to be bound to law. According to Kornfeld's soul, the page of Talmud is a garden, the letters on the page are birds, and the columns of commentary on the page are trees. When Isaac Kornfeld learns that he cannot be a Jew and a writer (a teller of stories) at the same time – when, moreover, he learns that he cannot live inside his stories – he decides to die.

If the story ended here, the fantastic would have dissolved into nothing more than allegory, with a clear message: If you want to be a Jew, give up writing and all that this enterprise entails. Todorov, for whom the end of a work of art is art itself, and for whom the subject of writing is writing itself, warns against the use of the fantastic genre for allegorical purposes. Todorov does recognize that the fantastic lends itself to an allegorical resolution. Cynthia Ozick, who has called for a liturgical component in Jewish literature, balks, however, at the use of the term allegory for her own works:

> Two stories – "The Pagan Rabbi" and "Usurpation" – intend to be representative of certain ideas; but I think of them rather as parables than allegories. In an allegory, the story stands for an idea, and the idea can be stated entirely apart from the story; in a parable, story and idea are so inextricably fused that they cannot be torn free of each other. In this sense I hope I've

written an occasional parable. But I would never seek out allegory, which strikes me as a low form.[12]

Whether we use the term allegory or parable, or indeed neither of these, we can agree with the comment of Ruth Wisse about the ending of an Ozick story: "Her reader is expected at the conclusion of her stories to have an insight, to understand the point of events."[13]

Ozick's warning against allegorical readings is well-taken. The story does not end with the suicide of Isaac Kornfeld. It ends with the reactions of both the narrator and Sheindel to Isaac's tale of the supernatural. Sheindel, it is clear, is on the side of Rashi. There is only one thing a Jew ought to do in a field, and that is to pray. It would be even better to make a fence about the law and not go into the field at all. The fantastic, she seems to be saying, is not a place for Jewish rabbis. For the narrator, and even more for the reader implicit in the text, the ending is more problematical. The narrator is a product of the Enlightenment and has even failed as a product of the Enlightenment. Like the reader, he is involved with writing and books. And yet, when he goes home, the narrator flushes all his houseplants down the toilet. He apparently agrees with Sheindel's judgment of the world, although he does not accept entirely Sheindel's reading of the story. When he first met Sheindel, in the grief of her recent widowhood, he was attracted to her. He fell in love with her and even contemplated marrying her and normalizing his life in Judaism. In the end, however, the narrator rejects Sheindel because he cannot accept her severity. He is aware of the dangers of the Enlightenment, but he would prefer to be ordinary. The act of consigning the houseplants to New York's sewers is a mere gesture, however significant. The narrator will, we are certain, continue to live in the world.

II

The title, "Levitation," places this tale in the "key"[14] of the supernatural, and creates at the very threshold of the story the atmosphere of the uncanny in which the reader expects to find himself immersed. Once inside, however, the reader finds depictions of human beings so ordinary and descriptions of events and surroundings so everyday in nature that the expectations created by the title are contradicted. The reader's hesitation at this point creates the "moment" – amounting to the duration of the reading of the literary text – which Todorov says is a characteristic of the fantastic.

Joseph Epstein has asked whether "The Pagan Rabbi" and especially "Levitation" are examples of a new "liturgical" fiction, a new "literature attentive to the implications of Covenant and Commandment" that Cynthia Ozick has set herself out to write. Epstein finds these stories "willed and schematic ... even where [he] cannot precisely figure out the scheme." Epstein had thought at first that the difficulty lay in what he perceived as Ozick's inability to end a story successfully. (The ending of "Levitation" is given by Epstein as the most blatant example of the defect, but the same charge has been made against many of Ozick's short stories, including "The Pagan Rabbi.") He later came to the conclusion that what he found objectionable in Ozick's writings had to do precisely with the subject that interests us here: Ozick's "fantastical" fiction. "I like Miss Ozick's work least," he writes, "when she is readiest to let her imagination rip; I like it best when she brings her Jews down to earth."[15]

"Levitation" is even more evidently about writers and their writing than "The Pagan Rabbi." It is "about" two writers, second-rate novelists, whose subjects are Jewishness and ordinariness. It is also about contradictions, including the contradiction between Jewishness and ordinariness. The one taboo of Lucy and Jimmy Feingold is that they may not write about writers. To write about writers who do not write about writers – as Ozick does here – is to create an uncanny effect of mirroring, where the mirrors do not so much reflect reality but refract it, causing a feeling of reverberation, of shimmering. In addition, Ozick does not hesitate to include other texts within her text, such as the verbatim quotation of several lines from the writings of her characters and an almost verbatim regurgitation of Jimmy's readings in Jewish history.

The setting for the "levitation" of the title, its shell, is made up of concrete details from the "real" life of two writers living in New York City. Feingold makes his living as a powerless editor at a publishing house. Nervous about his editorial decisions, he rejects manuscripts for ignominious reasons. As a writer, he is ordinary. He has a "nice plain pale face; likeable." (*Levitation*, p. 3) He is recognizable. Ozick's portrayal of the vicissitudes of New York existence is also true to life.

> New York: They risked their necks if they ventured out to Broadway for a loaf of bread after dark; muggers behind the seesaws in the playgrounds, junkies with knives hung upside down in the jungle gym. Every apartment a lit fortress; you admired the lamps and the locks and the police rods on the doors, the lamps with timers set to make burglars think you were always home. Footsteps in the corridor, the elevator's midnight grind; caution's muffled gasps. (*Levitation*, p. 8)

In the intensity of this realism there is a hint of the transformation – if not yet the sanctification – of the ordinary into the extraordinary. As she had done with Isaac Kornfeld, Ozick incorporates the writing of her characters into her own. Lucy, in her novel, turns Ozick's realistic description of New York into a hauntingly Kafkaesque one. Upper West Side apartments, Lucy writes, "have mysterious layouts. Rooms with doors that go nowhere – turn the knob, open: a wall." (*Levitation*, p. 6)

Novelists, it appears, have a power they do not demonstrate in their daily lives. (The word "power" appears in Hebrew, *oz*, in the epigraph of *Levitation*.) Feingold and Lucy do not know how to harness that power; they decide to give a party and invite influential people in the world of literature, from Irving Howe to Philip Roth, from Norman Podhoretz to William Styron. That none of them come is an indication that we are to look for meaning not in the plotting of the protagonists but rather in the plotting of the author. But, what happens is that a story of the ordinary – a party of mediocre people – almost imperceptibly turns into a story of the extraordinary – the levitation of a roomful of Jews.

Ozick delights in portraying the realization of this *tour d'adresse*. The party itself is like a work of fiction in which the characters are seen to come to life. Ozick indicates the point at which this transformation begins to take place by noticing "something in formation." This is precisely like the fantastic moment of a story: "It seemed about to become a regular visit, with points of view, opinions, a discussion. The voices began to stumble; Feingold liked that, it was almost human." (*Levitation*, p. 10) Then Lucy notices distinctions between the three rooms of the party. The central panel of the triptych – the center hall – is empty, waiting to be filled. In the dining room are the non-Jews (and a sprinkling of Jews), talking about theater and film, "junk," according to Feingold. That frame of the triptych contains a portrait of sterile realistic art.

Lucy, the daughter of a minister who read Psalms from the pulpit and unwittingly caused his daughter to convert to the Judaism of the ancient Hebrews and to marry "out of her tradition," observes the scene of the third wing of the triptych from its threshold in the frame. It is through her eyes, the eyes of a novelist (but not of the author of the story), that the reader sees the levitation of the title. It is through her eyes that we see what is going on.

Feingold himself is holding forth in the living room (peopled exclusively with Jews) about "God," which in his case means Jewish suffering at the hands of the Christians. He quotes chapter and verse about the blood libels of the Middle Ages. Among the guests at the party there is a "pagan rabbi," the one who had administered Lucy's conversion. He eats kosher cake brought from home in a plastic bag and at the same time entertains some very serious doubts about the existence of God. This friend from the seminary has brought along another friend, a refugee, a survivor of the Holocaust and witness to it. It is he who urges Feingold in his narration to "come to modern times." For Lucy, this witness is exactly the ingredient needed to give a voice to Feingold's text. It is this refugee's Jesus-like face of suffering and his haunting voice that cause the first stage of Lucy's hallucination and bring the story to its initial fantastic moment. The refugee's voice has the power the Feingolds were looking for in giving the party in the first place. His very whisper can carve statues in which every Jew is for Lucy a Jew on the cross. Thus, after the crucifixion in this triptych comes the ascension. And so, Lucy sees all the Jews levitating on the voice of the refugee.

Lucy fills the central panel by entering with her mind's eye into the shadow of another tale. Turning her back on the first conclusion, Lucy sees herself in a little city park on a Sunday afternoon in early May with her two little boys, to whom she had furtively been telling stories of little Jesus. They are there for an anthropological demonstration of musicians and dancers from Sicily, not "artists" but real peasants who will sing, and dance to, a song that celebrates the Madonna of Love. The primitive folk music of this ancient people is intensely erotic, sending the dancers into a trance, causing in them an ecstasy similar to the one experienced by Kornfeld. Lucy has an illumination:

> Lucy is glorified. She is exalted. She comprehends, ... before the Madonna there was Venus. ... The gods are God. ... Everything is miracle: Lucy sees how she has abandoned nature, how she has lost true religion on account of the God of the Jews. (*Levitation*, p. 18)

Ozick is not merely indicating the essential contradiction between Judaism and Christianity. Nor is she indicting Christianity for its pagan roots. She is positing a fundamental difference between Western and Jewish storytelling. Lucy comes back from her illumination to the reality of a departing female guest who is afraid of being ambushed in the laundry room of her New York apartment house. In the living room, however, all the Jews are still in the air. And that is the way the story ends. We are no longer sure through whose eyes we see these continually levitating Jews. Thus, the story ends without ending, leaving the Jews in a fantastic tale that refuses to resolve itself into either the uncanny or the marvelous.

This is the conclusion that vexes Joseph Epstein. But, he is looking merely for its allegorical meaning: "I recognize that Miss Ozick is reaching for something deep and special here. Can she be referring, metaphorically, to the inherent *luft*iness of the Jews, to the spirituality that can set them apart, especially when they speak of themselves among themselves? No doubt she is, and she is no doubt referring to more as well." (Epstein, p. 67) In his commentary on the tale, Epstein also writes one of the story's possible conclusions. He usurps Ozick's story to compose a midrash on it that urges the Jews to come back down to earth: "I may sound more like a landlord than a critic here, but I react to the story by asking, 'Madam, what is that living room doing on the ceiling? Madam, I implore you, get those Jews down, please!' " (Epstein, p. 67) Epstein's landlord enters into the logic of the text and takes the fantastic seriously, like Sheindel. But he misses the point.

The "point" that Ruth Wisse enjoins us to look for at the end of an Ozick story is not in its possible endings. The point of "Levitation" – and of "The Pagan Rabbi," "Usurpation," and "Puttermesser and Xanthippe," all tales embedded in the genre of the fantastic – is that there is a Jewish way of using the fantastic. As Ozick told Eve Ottenberg in the interview quoted near the beginning of this essay, she "rejects intellectually and emotionally the surrender to the mystical blur between the creator and the created," but "there's something in [her] that is at the same time fascinated" by it. The "something" in Ozick is not necessarily a pagan streak common to all writers of the Western tradition. It may be a hesitation between the rationalistic and the mystical – two contradictory solutions to a literary dilemma. She is like the Vilna *Gaon*, at the same time a rationalist and a mystic, hesitating to choose between rationalism and mysticism. As we have seen, the fantastic short story is characterized by a similar hesitation. One might venture to conclude that in Ozick's esthetic the term "Jewish fantastic" is not an oxymoron.

Notes

[1] William Abrahams (Ed.,) *Prize Stories 1984. The O. Henry Awards* (Garden City, N.Y.: Doubleday, 1984), p. xi.

[2] Ruth R. Wisse, "American Jewish Writing, Act. II," *Commentary*, 61 June, 1976), 41.

[3] Joseph Lowin, "Cynthia Ozick's Mimesis," *Jewish Book Annual*, 42 (1984-1985), 79-90.

[4] "The Pagan Rabbi," *Hudson Review*, 19 (Autumn, 1966), 425-56. Page references in the body of the text are to the Obelisk paperback edition, *The Pagan Rabbi and Other Stories* (New York: E.P. Dutton, 1983). "Levitation," *Partisan Review*, 46 (1979), 391-405. Page references are to the Obelisk paperback, *Levitation: Five Fictions* (New York: E.P. Dutton, 1983).

[5] Quoted by Eve Ottenberg, "The Rich Visions of Cynthia Ozick," *New York Times Magazine*, April 10, 1983.

[6] "Puttermesser and Xanthippe," *Salmagundi*, 55 (Winter, 1983), 163-255. Quoted from the Obelisk paperback *Levitation*, pp. 99-104.

[7] Tzvetan Todorov, *The Fantastic: A Structural Approach to a Literary Genre*, translated from the French by Richard Howard (Ithaca, New York: Cornell University Press, 1975). Page references in the body of the text are to this edition.

[8] See Sigmund Freud, "The Uncanny" (1919), in his *Collected Papers*, authorized translation under the supervision of Joan Riviere (New York: Basic Books, 1959), Vol. 4, pp. 368-407. A psychoanalytic reading of Ozick's use of the fantastic – beyond the scope of this essay – would be fascinating. It is nevertheless instructive to point out that Freud himself, who "collected" uncanny episodes from real life, including his own, recognized the extraordinary power of literature in this domain: "[T]here are many more means of creating uncanny effects in fiction than there are in real life." (p. 404)

[9] "The Riddle of the Ordinary," *Moment*, 1 (1975), 57-58.

[10] One thinks readily in this context of the Talmudic *aggadah* concerning the "Four who entered the Pleasure Garden" (B. Talmud, *Haggigah*, 14b). Without going into the details of the story, we may state fairly confidently that the Rabbis themselves were concerned about the dangers of the mystical enterprise, which they related metaphorically to the esthetic appreciation of nature, to the world of the imagination, and, by extension, to storytelling.

[11] *Mise en abyme*, as the term is used here, is the technique of reproducing within one work of art, another work of art. It has a mirroring function, causes an effect of reverberation, and serves to enlarge the scope of the artistic text beyond its ostensible borders. The technique can be found in a variety of artistic texts, for example, the description of Hephaistos' shield in the *Iliad*, the players' scene in *Hamlet*, and the artist's canvas in Velasquez' *Las Meninas*. The technique is used extensively and masterfully by Cynthia Ozick.

[12] Catherine Rainwater and William J. Scheick, "An Interview with Cynthia Ozick" (Summer, 1982) *Texas Studies in Literature and Language*, 25 (Summer, 1983), 262-263.

[13] Wisse, p. 43.

[14] The term "key" is taken from Erving Goffman, *Frame Analysis* (New York: Harper & Row, 1974), pp. 40-82. He writes: "In brief, a play keys life, a ceremony keys an event." (p. 58) In a similar way, a title keys a story.

[15] Joseph Epstein, "Cynthia Ozick, Jewish Writer," *Commentary*, 77, 3 (March, 1984). 68. In response to a question about her attitude to the beginnings and endings of her stories, Ozick has declared: "I am never attentive to the end, at least not until I get there, because I trust the end to be implicit in the beginning." (Rainwater and Sheick, p. 256) As we have seen in both Todorov's theory and Ozick's practice, the fantastic short story begins in reality, derives from reality, is anchored in reality. As it distances itself from reality, the fantastic transforms the literary text – and all art – into an experience of limits. It is the place where the distinction between the creator and the created is most blurred, and where the ordinary and the extraordinary meet.

Ranter Sexual Politics: Canticles in the England of 1650

Noam Flinker

The political, religious, and social crises of mid-seventeenth-century England are reflected in the use of language from the Bible by writers whose millenarian and antinomian beliefs were at the fringes of the Puritan movement. The large issues that Englishmen were fervently debating concerned the nature of political reality and constitutional rights, the extent and scope of the Protestant reformation, as well as social and economic tensions that included in some cases an assault on public sexual mores not unlike the so-called sexual revolution of the mid-twentieth century. The Ranters expressed views about each of these areas, but by their dramatic use of language they in effect used the hermeneutic tools of more conservative Puritans to call for a revolution that was almost universally condemned by their contemporaries. Their allusive references to Biblical language in general and to the Song of Songs in particular epitomize attitudes to politics, religion, and social mores, and provide striking illustrations of ways in which a crisis in language reflects other aspects of culture. Despite the emphasis on material things in these works, one paradoxical effect of the discourse is to deny the significance of the world outside the consciousness of the imagining "creature." References to women ("fellow creatures") and Jews turn out to be part of a mindset that views events and people as signs that must be understood to signify something beyond themselves.

The Ranters first surfaced on the English scene in the late 1640s. In *The World of the Ranters*, A. L. Morton discusses their political radicalism, but finds "in them all the signs of a revolution in retreat, an abandonment of the rational hope that had inspired men like Overton and Walwyn, a realisation that they were calling upon their last resources when everything else had failed."[1] Such a position neglects the intense mood of millenarian anticipation that the Ranters shared with other more orthodox Puritans.[2] Earlier in the century, Thomas Brightman's commentary on Canticles had predicted: "If you desire the time of this conversion [of the Jews]: God hath very much concealed the moments of time from us. ... But as neer as we can attain to it by conjectures, (and those not light, as they seem to me) it is to be expected about the yeer 1650."[3] Brightman's student, Nathanael Homes (or Holmes) also wrote a commentary on Canticles which he published in 1652 with the rest of his works. Homes was a millenarian and involved in the movement to readmit the Jews to England.[4] The connection between millenial expectation and an interest in Canticles helps to explain the spiritual excitement of a whole range of seventeenth-century English Protestants that includes the Ranters at one extreme. Although the theology of Ranter leaders, such as Joseph Salmon, went considerably beyond the naive anticipation of an immediate end to time and the world, most of their contemporaries were unwilling to relinquish a belief in imminent apocalypse. As mid-century approached, English millenarians were girding themselves for the last days, and their language reflects this tendency. Ranter discourse is thus very far from conveying a mood of defeat. The social and political significance of the doctrines is in some sense secondary to the intense involvement in denying the significance of the entire material universe that ultimately informs these tracts.

The extant texts about the Ranters introduce a series of methodological problems that must be confronted before going on to illustrate the significance of particular doctrines. There are, in fact, at least three different categories of primary sources about the Ranters. Some provide open attacks on the sect and, in so doing, summarize the views they wish to criticize. Less straightforward are the pamphleteers who write to outline what they once believed but have since rejected. This kind of writing is the most complicated for us to evaluate because it presents material from the perspective of a writer's personal experience, and is thus a first-hand account of events. It is nevertheless of questionable accuracy because of the writer's stated desire to illustrate the errors of his previous ways.[5] The third category consists of works written by Ranters convinced of the truth of their arguments at the moment they were writing. This includes books by Laurence Clarkson, Abiezer Coppe, and Joseph Salmon. Only this third category can be taken as direct evidence for Ranter positions and ideas, even though the other kinds of materials can provide significant testimony.

This distinction between different categories of written evidence implies an additional factor that introduces further complication. Although we must depend almost exclusively upon written documents for evidence about ideas in earlier civilizations, it is hardly feasible to search for an exact literary pedigree for any given idea. Such an admission, however, should not be regarded as a temporary excuse to be used only when written evidence is lacking. The survival of published documents about particular religious and theological ideas is largely the result of chance. If we assume that a particular text depicts an idea or movement definitively, we disregard the primarily oral provenance of most such imaginative forces in the Middle Ages and Renaissance. It is therefore important to consider the theoretical implications of the non-written or oral aspect of a movement such as the Ranters. Since there is, however, no available evidence that is not written, it will be necessary to arrive at an estimate of the orality of Ranter discourse on the basis of those written texts that have survived.

An important ploy used by various Ranter leaders involved subversion of traditional approaches to Biblical texts so as to make the radically different new readings appear to be valid understandings of the original. Although this strategem served to justify their ideological positions, it also legitimized a Biblical hermeneutic that was tied to the original Hebrew and Greek texts in only an associative or impressionistic fashion. It also led the way to the Quaker view of the "inner light," which was reputed to be no less reliable than the Bible. One instance of such subversion appears in Joseph Salmon's treatment of the nuptial metaphor in the Bible. Moses and the prophets present relations between God and Israel in terms of a marriage, in which Israel is expected to be a faithful wife to God, and any worship of other gods is described as whoredom and fornication.[6] In *Antichrist in Man: or A Discovery of the Great Whore that sits upon many waters*, Salmon referred to "fornication with the *great whore*, the wisdom of the flesh; attributing all *power, glory, salvation* and *happiness* to selfish wisdome."[7] The "carnall wisdom" that he rejected as fornication is traditional religion. He explained that "it is a property of a *Strumpet* to pretend what she doth not intend to her *Lovers*: behold a Character of the *Mother of Harlots*, thy fleshly wisdom ... she alwaies pretends, what she never intends: So that here, all is well in the history, but meer deceit and delusion in the *mystery*; this *whore*, she will present a glorious shew, but there is nothing but wickedness and harlotry intended. ... Now therefore know, O Christian! that this whore appears to thee in all thy spiritual *performances,* and *sacrifices* to the *Lord*." (*Antichrist in Man*, 13-14) In some sense then, the traditional Puritan, certain of his religious way, was condemned by Salmon as a fornicator, while, according to Clarkson's *A Single Eye*, a Ranter who engaged in extra-marital sex "in light and love, is light, and lovely ... for love in light is so pure, that a whore it cannot indure, but estranges it selfe from darknesse from whence whoredom has its first original."[8]

The most explicit theoretical statement about the relationship between language and the spiritual mindset of the Ranters comes in tracts by Abiezer Coppe. Whereas Clarkson tried to protect himself from persecution for his views by keeping *A Single Eye* somewhat anonymous, Coppe openly acknowledged the tracts he wrote as a Ranter. Nevertheless, he was much more secretive about his views and ideas. He vacillated between a strong drive to tell all and an equally powerful sense of the secrecy of his message.

In his pamphlets *Some Sweet Sips of Some Spirituall Wine* and *A Fiery Flying Roll*, Coppe encouraged his readers to go beyond the conventions of language and religion in anticipating the new order. Established words and symbols take on new meanings and subvert the old forms with hints at something new. The actual words, however, are always ambiguous and incomplete, and thus suggest that the printed text contains only a small part of the message of the prophet. The written word serves to undermine its own conventional world and prepares the reader for an experience that the writer cannot (or will not) articulate in full.

Coppe's "Epistle I" in *Some Sweet Sips* begins with a series of paradoxes that underscore the difficulty of understanding the message. It contains "some things hard to be understood, which they that are *Unlearned*, and unstable, wrest: as they doe also the other Scriptures, unto their own destruction."[9] The language is to be

Biblical, but without citation of "Book, Chapter, and Verse" because "the father would have it so; And I partly know his designe in it; And heare him secretly whispering in me the reason thereof: Which I must (yet) burie in silence, till –...." (*Some Sweet Sips*, 2 [Smith, 47]) This motif of secrecy suggests that God will soon allow his prophet to reveal the truth, but at no point does Coppe dispel the clouds. In fact, his very words imply that language itself is part of the old way which is to be abandoned: "Here is the voyce of one crying; Arise out of *Flesh*, into *Spirit*; out of *Form*, into *Power*; out of *Typs*, into *Truth*; out of the *Shadow*, into the *Substance*; out of the *Signe*, into the thing *Signified*." (*Some Sweet Sips*, 2-3 [Smith, 47-48]). The new order that is intimated here is one that cannot be captured in "forms" or "typs" or "signes." Coppe wanted to go beyond the limitations of conventional religion and language in order to apprehend spiritual reality with no intermediary. On the other hand, he cautioned: "Arise, but rise not till the Lord awaken thee. I could wish he would doe it by himselfe, immediately: But if by these, mediately: His will be done." (*Some Sweet Sips*, 3 [Smith, 48]) That is, it would be better for the reader to perceive these truths without the intervention of the written text, which is also a collection of signs. If this perception is not possible, however, the speaker is resigned to God's will. This, of course, returns us to the secrecy motif, since one can hardly understand what is signified by means of signs that ultimately refuse to reveal their significance.

On one level it is clear that this motif of secrecy is a reflection of Coppe's implicit objections to a reasoned discourse fully revealed to the public. It is one consequence of translating oral sermons into written prose that was, by definition, potentially available to anyone able to read. The form of the discourse thus reflects its political and ideological perspectives. Views expressed about sexuality and the Jews turn out to be part of an antinomian system of Biblical references that reduces all human experience to the inner world of the Ranter's imagination. As the actions that accompany the ideology become manipulative, they also become increasingly dehumanized.[10]

Much of the sexuality that is reflected in the Ranter texts is manipulative in some sense. This aspect finds expression in each of the three kinds of sources mentioned above. Since references to extra-marital sexual relations appear in each type of source, it is reasonable to conclude that this tendency was typical Ranter practice. Some of their more thoughtful critics pointed in different ways to the manipulative aspect of such sexual politics.

Their emphasis on sexual freedom evidently made the Ranters simultaneously attractive and repellent to most Englishmen. Morton reports that "Parliament set up a Committee to enquire into the Ranters and other heretical groups," (*World of the Ranters*, 102) but also quotes George Fox who claimed in his *Journal* that Justice Hotham had "said, if God had not raised up this principle of light and life, [i.e. Fox's Quakerism] the nation had been overspread with Ranterism and all the Justices in the nation could not stop it with all their laws, because they would have done and said as they commanded them and yet kept their principle still." (*World of the Ranters*, 110) Of course, Fox's testimony must be taken in its context and understood to reflect a sustained effort on his part to distinguish between early Quakers and Ranters. Many contemporaries grouped them together because, aside from sexuality, their ideologies were often strikingly similar.

The testimony of the many anti-Ranter tracts is quite explicit about the sexual practices of the group, but as Morton suggests, there is something very unreliable about these documents: "Much of the evidence is, of course, hearsay and grossly prejudiced. We may well doubt the report that at a meeting in Shoemakers Alley their time was spent 'in drunkenness, uncleanness, blasphemous words, filthy songs, and mixt dances of men and women stark naked.' " (*World of the Ranters*, 81) The radical Digger, Gerrard Winstanley, was perhaps less prejudiced a source; yet, he too was bitter about Ranter sexuality. In his *Vindication of Those ... called Diggers*, Winstanley complained about "the immoderate use of creatures, or of the excessive community of women called Ranting."[11] This pamphlet was evidently written after permissive sexual practices had caused the Digger leader to force the uninhibited Ranters out of his radical commune. Other less sophisticated attacks are filled with accusations about sexual orgies and the like, much of which may have been highly exaggerated.

The works of former Ranters likewise abound with references to sexual license. Morton refers to a work of Laurence Clarkson to show "that at times a ritual nudism may have been practised as a symbol of their liberation from the bondage of the moral law." (*World of the Ranters*, 81). A typical example of an attack on the Ranters by "a late fellow-Ranter" appears in *The Ranters Declaration*:

> On the 9 of this instant *Decemb*, a great Company of the new Generation of *Ranters*, assembled together near the *White Lyon* in *Pelicoat-Lane* [sic], where they entred into a large dispute concerning the exaltation of their jolities, affirming that that man who tipples deepest, swears the frequentest, commits adultery, incest, or buggers the oftenest, blasphemes the impudentest, and perpetrates the most notorious crimes, with the highest hand, and rigedest resolution, is the dearest darling to be gloriously placed in the tribunal Throne of Heaven, holding this detestable Opinion, (equalizing themselves with out blessed Redeemer) that it is lawful for them to drink healths to their Brother *Christ*, and that in the bonsing off of their liquor, each Brother ought to take his Fellow-Female upon his knee, saying *Let us lie down and multiply*, holding this lascivious action to be the chief motive of their salvation, &c.[12]

When the complaints of both the anti-Ranters and the "late-fellow Ranters" are compared with statements of practicing members of the sect, it becomes clear that while many of the details referred to by detractors may have been exaggerated, there was probably more involved here than what Morton calls "ritual nudism." Thus, Laurence Clarkson's *A Single Eye* is explicit about the spiritual importance of extra-marital sex: "So that I say, till flesh be made Spirit, and Spirit flesh, so not two, but one, thou art in perfect bondage: for without vail, I declare that whosoever doth attempt to act from flesh, in flesh, to flesh, hath, is, and will commit Adultry: But to bring this to a period, for my part, till I acted that, so called sin, I could not predominate over sin; so that now whatsoever I act, is not in relation to the Title, to the Flesh, but that Eternity in me...." (14 [Smith, 173]) Clarkson was insisting on the spiritual significance of sexuality, but used Biblical language to make his antinomian point. Words such as "spirit," "flesh," and "sin" thus take on meanings that are not in any sense related to their conventional significance. In order to communicate his idea of monistic wholeness, he subverted the words of Biblical texts. This tactic is similar to the practice of other Ranters, such as Joseph Salmon and Abiezer Coppe.

The women with whom Clarkson had sexual relations were theoretically taking part in an act that was significant, not in itself, but rather in terms of its spiritual meaning for the male speaker. Clarkson revealed the manipulative aspect of his actions in *The Lost Sheep Found*, a pamphlet that must be read with greater critical scrutiny than his actual Ranter works. Nevertheless his retrospective view of acts committed years before remains quite striking:

> So coming to *Canterbury* there was some six of this way, amongst whom was a maid of pretty knowledge, who with my Doctrine was affected, and I affected to lye with her, so that night prevailed, and satisfied my lust, afterwards the mayd was highly in love with me, and as gladly would I have been shut of her, lest some danger had ensued, so not knowing I had a wife she was in hopes to marry me, and so would have me lodge with her again, which fain I would, but durst not, then she was afraid I would deceive her, and would travel with me, but by subtilty of reason I perswaded her to have patience, while I went into *Suffolk*, and setled my occasions, then I would come and marry her, so for the present we parted, and full glad was I that I was from her delivered ... and then I heard the maid had been in those parts to seek me, but not hearing of me, returned home again, and not long after was married to one of that sect, and so there was an end of any further progress into *Kent.*[13]

The personal revelations discovered here must, of course, be taken as part of Clarkson's general purpose in this tract. He wished to discredit his earlier experiences in the eyes of his readers; thus, he avoided the excited tones of *A Single Eye*. Nevertheless, it is not likely that the manipulative psychology portrayed here is totally untrue to what Clarkson felt in 1650. It would seem to corroborate what Winstanley claimed in 1649 as he warned women: "Therefore you women beware, for this ranting practice is not the restoring, but the destroying power of the creation. ... This Ranting power, or god, is full of sutletie to deceive others of what they can, and is a nurse of hardnesse of heart against others, when he hath deceived them, for this is his nature, to gets what he can from others, labours to eat up others and make them poore, and then to laugh and rejoyce in others poverty."[14]

Clarkson's comments in 1660 about the manipulative nature of his earlier sexual exploits are part of the satirical, perhaps even ironical, tone of *The Lost Sheep Found. A Single Eye* is highly mystical and concerned with the spiritual intensity of Ranterism, while the later pamphlet deliberately vilifies that which seemed glorious in 1650. He implicitly condemned that which he had written earlier:

> And indeed *Solomons* Writings was the original of my filthy lust, supposing I might take the same liberty as he did, not then understanding his Writings was no Scripture, that I was moved to write to the world what my Principle was, so brought to publick view a Book called *The Single Eye*, so that men and women came from many parts to see my face, and hear my knowledge in these things, being restless till they were made free, as then we called it. Now I being as they said, *Captain of the Rant*, I had most of the principle women came to my lodging for knowledge, which then was called *The Head-quarters*. (*Lost Sheep Found*, 26 [Smith, 181])

Although the texts of believing Ranters are much more insistent upon the spirituality of their sexuality, this very claim carried within it the basis for the manipulative character of Clarkson in *The Lost Sheep Found*. Clarkson and Coppe both referred to the Song of Songs as a Biblical intertext for blending the spiritual and the sexual. By making text and world into signs of something within, they may have become blind to the dynamics of human interaction that they were developing. In any case, their texts are filled with allusions to Canticles that intimate spirituality and thus direct the reader away from a concern for the mutuality of sexual relations.

In Clarkson's *A Single Eye*, Canticles is invoked as part of the argument about the holiness of adultery. Solomon's Song provides a means of establishing Clarkson's central thesis about darkness and light, an ongoing commentary on Isaiah: "I will make darkness light before them."[15] The following passage juxtaposes Isaiah and Canticles to show that the imaginative intentions of a man's sexual acts determine their spiritual signification:

> Observe not the act nakedly, as the act, for we find the Prayer and Prayses of some to be pure, though to others impure: impure to those acting, in relation to the title his apprehension, his Conscience in the improvement of them is defiled and condemned for a Swearer, a Drunkard, an Adulterer, and a theef.
>
> When as a man in purity in light, acts the same acts, in relation to the act, and not the title: this man [no this man] doth not swear, whore, nor steal: so that for want of this light, of this single pure eye, there appeareth Devil and God, Hell and Heaven, Sin and holynesse, Damnation and Salvation; only, yea only from the esteemation and dark apprehension of the Creature.

> *I will make darknesse light, rough ways smooth*; not half light and half darknesse, not part rough and part smooth; but as it is said, *Thou art all fair my Love, there is no spot in thee.* Observe, all fair my Love, in thee only is beauty and purity, without defilement: my love my dove is but one, thou one, not two, but only one, my love: Love is God and God is Love; so all pure, all, light, no spot in thee. (*A Single Eye*, 10 [Smith, 170])

The implicit message here is that the love described in Canticles ("Thou art all fair, my love: there is no spot in thee." [4:7]) is a justification for all acts, as long as they are done "in light and love." Clarkson did not treat the nature of the inner imagination which must provide spiritual meaning to action. If "Love is God and God is Love," then the sexual acts of the Ranters turn out to be "Prayer and Prayses," with the text from the Song of Songs as a crucial nexus between holy and sexual.

For Coppe, too, the Song of Songs was important in establishing his implicit argument for libertinism. Alluding to the Song in *Some Sweet Sips*, he described his work as "a great pounding at the doors, – But it is not I but the voice of my *Beloved*, that knocketh, saying, Open to me, and let me come *In*." (2 [Smith, 47]) Similar allusions appear in the context of a call to the reader to awaken: "Are you asleepe? for shame rise, it's break aday, the *day* breaks, the *Shaddows* flie away, the *dawning* of the day woes you to arise, and let him *into* your *hearts*. It is the voyce of my beloved that knocketh, saying, Open to me my *Sister*, my *love*, my *dove*, for my head is filled with dew, and my locks with the drops of night." (10 [Smith, 51]) This is followed almost immediately with a passage that at first glance seems to be based on an allegorical reading of Canticles: "The day *star* is up, rise up my *love*, my *dove*, my faire one, and *come away*, The day *star* woeth you, it is the voice of my beloved that saith open to me – I am *risen indeed*, rise up my love, open to me my faire one." (11 [Smith, 52]) There are two passages from Canticles that are most obviously relevant here. In one the speaker urges his beloved to awaken and enjoy the spring: "My beloved spake and said unto me. Rise up, my love, my fair one, and come away. ... Until the day break, and the shadows flee away, turn my beloved." (2:10, 17). In the other the beloved recounts an incident in which her lover knocks on her door at night and then disappears before she can unlock it: "Open to me, my sister, my love, my dove, my undefiled: for my head is filled with dew, and my locks with the drops of the night." (5:2)

The contemporary reader's initial response to these references is probably to regard Coppe as a self-proclaimed prophet who claimed to speak in the name of Christ, the bridegroom of Canticles in standard Christian commentaries. The spiritual awakening intimated by allusion to the language of the lover in the Song of Songs ("Rise up, my love...") appears almost too obvious until one asks about the precise nature of the newly evoked state of consciousness. It turns out that the Biblical texts are to be understood in a sexual sense, since the terms used here ultimately lead back to libertinism. The argument of the prophet moves from one set of Christ-like activities to another. In his *Fiery Flying Roll*, Coppe explained that God is "UNIVERSALL love ... whose service is perfect freedome, and pure Libertinisme."[16] This tortuous and circuitous reading of Coppe recalls the secrecy motif that made it possible for him to publish his views at all. He depended upon the reader's difficulties to shield him from the attacks of the uninitiated. The combination of an explicitly sexual understanding of Canticles and an immediate anticipation of apocalypse provided Coppe with a striking means to articulate his own sense of God in himself.

There is tension between the spirituality which is praised and the carnality which is deprecated, especially in Coppe's discussion of the necessity to confound a sense of righteousness with what he called "base things." In his *Second Fiery Flying Roule*, he insisted upon a relationship between his "wanton kisses" and those of Canticles: "And then again, by wanton kisses, kissing hath been confounded; and externall kisses, have been made the fiery chariots, to mount me swiftly into the bosom of him whom my soul loves, [his excellent Majesty, the King of glory.] Where I have been, where I have been, where I have been, hug'd, imbrac't, and kist with the kisses of his mouth, whose loves are better then wine, and have been utterly overcome therewith, beyond expression, beyond admiration."[17] The kisses here allude, of course, to those of Solomon's Song: "Let him kiss me with the kisses of his mouth: for thy love is better than wine." (1:2) In a sense then, Coppe is suggesting that sexual experience is a way to holiness. The kisses of Canticles lead toward heaven, but they are rooted in a natural reading of the sexual imagery that abounds in the Song. Coppe rejected the allegorical conventions that firmly discouraged sexual readings of Canticles and intimated that sexual experience could be a source for spiritual arousal and development. As with Clarkson, the emphasis on sexuality with no concern for the individual Ranter's relationship with his or her "fellow creature," and the breakdown of language into signs whose meaning can only be found within the imagination, combine to undermine the spirituality described.

Another indication of the dangers of Ranter dehumanization can be found in Abiezer Coppe's claim to have been converted from Judaism. On the title page of *Some Sweet Sips* he referred to himself as "אביעזר כף [avi'ezer caf] A Late converted JEW." By having his name printed in Hebrew letters, Coppe upset the normal conventions of reading. The author claimed that he had recently converted from Judaism to Christianity and apparently expected that the visually shocking use of Hebrew letters might lend greater credence to his message.

There is, however, no evidence at all that Coppe had ever been a Jew. Alexander Gordon asserts that "he was first a presbyterian,"[18] but makes no reference to Jewishness. In fact, the title page of *Some Sweet Sips* seems to imply that the same relationship that traditionally obtained between Judaism and Christianity now holds between Christianity and the new religion of Coppe and his followers. The conventions of traditional Christianity are drained of their ordinary signification and simultaneously charged with a new level of meaning. The reader soon discovers that unlike his original assumption about the Jewishness of Coppe, the text implies that he, the reader, is one of "the bewildered Israelites" mentioned in the full title of the tract.[19] Coppe's use of Hebrew letters and Roman capitals for "Jew" operates within a double convention. On one hand, the Jews had been officially banned from England for centuries, and thus served Englishmen as dehumanized symbols for the unregenerate. On the other, the conversion of the Jews was a crucial part of the millenarian myth shared by most Englishmen. Coppe combined these conventions in his own version of the myth that guardedly articulated his own messianic pretensions.

In *A Fiery Flying Roll*, evidently published a few months later, Coppe went one step further in referring to himself as part of his discourse. He translated his Hebrew first name (literally father of help) into its literal Latin equivalent, *auxilium patris*, and instead of referring to himself as a converted Jew, he described a vision that begins with his personal destruction: "First, all my strength, my forces were utterly routed, my house I dwelt in fired, my father and mother forsook me, the wife of my bosome loathed me, mine old name was rotted, perished."[20] This experience is parallel to the conversion in *Some Sweet Sips*, because it fills in the gaps about the speaker's identity in the earlier pamphlet. There the conversion is extra-textual and as such leaves unanswered questions that are to some extent externalized in *A Fiery Flying Roll*, where the rotting of Coppe's "Old name" is part of the conversion pattern.

Coppe's surname, however, appears in Hebrew characters in both pamphlets. Although there is no textual explanation of the significance of the name, the millenarian expectation of the conversion of the Jews is clearly relevant. In their commentaries on Canticles, Brightman and Homes both looked forward to such a conversion, while Homes went so far as to work actively for the readmission of the Jews to England.[21] Coppe was less interested in real Jews, since for him they too were signs or types whose inner meaning signified the imminence of the millenium. Perhaps he elaborated upon this when he spoke to the initiated, but in print Coppe cloaked everything in secrecy. Near the end of the first epistle in *Some Sweet Sips*, Coppe made explicit reference to the closed nature of his discourse: "If I here speake in an unknown tongue, I pray that I may interpret when I may. Only take one Clavall hint. That which is here (mostly) spoken, is inside, and mysterie. And so farre as any one hath the mysterie of God opened to him, *In Him*, can plainly reade every word of the same here. The rest is sealed up from the rest, and it may be the most, – from some." (5 [Smith, 49]) Further on he elaborated: "Thus you have one Claval hint; if the Lord come *in*, it may be an instrumentall key to open the rest. But the Spirit alone is the incorruptible Key." (7 [Smith, 49]) The epistle closes: "And yours, all of ye that are the Lords, by what names or titles soever distinguished, Yours – אביעזר כף *The Key* *Christ* was Re-baptized –

The Lord is my *King*, and my Shepheard, or *Pastor*, &c. – The Eternall God, whose I *Am*, is *Independent*, – &c." (8 [Smith, 50])

Coppe's utilization of Hebrew characters for his name suggests that it may have some special Biblical significance. In the Song of Songs, the word כף [kaf] can mean 'key' in a phrase that literally denotes "handles of the lock." (5:4) In a representative seventeenth-century explanation of these words, Theodore Haak translated a Dutch commentary that saw the handles as a means of facilitating the implicitly sexual union of bride and bridegroom: "understand here the bolts, wherewith the door was bolted within, keeping Christ without doors, and hindering him from coming in, which now being oiled with the oil of myrrhe; that is, her heart being anointed with the oil of grace, and so all locks and bolts, that is all impediments and hinderances being removed, the Bridegroom might come in unto her without molestation, to enjoy the fruits of his grace, which she had received of him."[22] In these terms, Coppe was himself the key or handle that would introduce Christ into the world. Since much of the language of both pamphlets refers directly or indirectly to this Biblical poem, Coppe's name can be read as a key to the significance of these allusions, just as it seems to be a key to the hidden or mystical meaning of the text.

It is fitting that the Hebrew name can thus function as a sign for the interrelation of Canticles, sexuality, and the Jews. All of these functioned for Coppe as indications of an imminent apocalypse, in which he fully expected to play a crucial role. His methodology served to break down all apparent meanings and to establish his own sense of the universe in their place. The way in which his discourse dinstinguished between the sign and the signified, however, led him in the direction of dehumanization. His women and his Jews became objects to be manipulated by and through his imagination.

These texts thus point to an implicit dualistic conflict at the heart of the impassioned Ranter cries for spiritual oneness. While their doctrines suggest that all experience is godly when imagined so, the interpretation of language, acts, and people as signs of greater ends reduces human experience to a series of empty forms which are drained of inherent significance. In some sense, the act of reading Canticles provides a paradigm for the radical millenarian politics and theology which disappeared from the mainstream of English culture after the 1650s. The linking of public sexuality and imagery from Canticles, on one hand, and a view of people as apocalyptic signs, on the other, led the Ranters to embrace the world, while denying the significance of its flesh. The "inner light" of these radicals thus undermined the relations between people and helped to make possible the reduction of human dignity in the name of ideology.

Notes

[1] A. L. Morton, *The World of the Ranters: Religious Radicalism in the English Revolution* (London: Lawrence & Wishart, 1970), p. 18.

[2] Cf. Nigel Smith's introduction to his very important edition of *A Collection of Ranter Writings from the 17th Century* (London: Junction Books, 1983), pp. 9-10, which I didn't see until after the completion of this essay. Since Smith has reprinted most of the Ranter texts cited below, I shall cite page references to his edition in brackets following citations to the original seventeenth-century versions.

[3] Thomas Brightman, *The Workes of that Famous, Reverend, and Learned Divine, Mr. Tho: Brightman...* (London: 1644), 1051. The original Latin reads: "Si quaeris ad quod tempus erit haec prima conversio, Momenta temporum celavit nos Deus ut plurimum. Hujus tamen certam in scripturis designationem arbitror, cui dies appropinquans clariorem lucem afferet, Dan. 12,4. &c. Sed quantum conjecturis assequi possimus, iisque non levibus, ut mihi videntur, expectanda est ad annum MDCL." (Thomae Brightmanni, *Commentarius in Cantica Canticorum Salomonis, Analysi & Scholiis illustratus ...* [Basileae: 1614], 119a [wrongly paginated 120 in Huntington Library copy]).

[4] Cf. Michael Fixler, *Milton and the Kingdoms of God* ([Evanston, III.]: Northwestern U.P., 1964), p. 238. For correspondence between Homes and Manasseh ben Israel, cf. Lucien Wolf, "Introduction," *Manasseh Ben Israel's Mission to Oliver Cromwell ...* (London: Macmillan, 1901), xxv-xxvi, lxxx-lxxxii.

[5] E.g. Gilbert Roulston, who referred to himself as "a late fellow RANTER" on the title page of *The Ranter's Bible, Or, Seven several Religions by them held and maintain'd ...* (London: 1650). Another pamphleteer, one J.M., identified himself as "(a deluded Brother) lately escaped out of their snare" on the title page of *The Ranters Last Sermon ...* (London: 1654).

[6] E.g. Exodus 34:11-17, Deuteronomy 31:16-22, Hosea 1-4, and Ezekiel 16:23-29. All Biblical citations in my text are to the King James translation. I have not, however, changed any of the Ranter Biblical citations which occasionally differ slightly from the Authorized Version.

[7] Joseph Salmon, *Antichrist in Man: Or A Discovery of the Great Whore that sits upon many waters* (London: 1647), p. 12. This pamphlet is not included in Smith's anthology.

[8] L[aurence] C[larkson], *A Single Eye: All Light, no Darkness: or Light and Darkness One* ... (London: 1650), p. 10 [Smith, 170-71]. Clarkson acknowledged writing this pamphlet published under the initials L. C. in *The Lost Sheep Found* (London: 1660), p. 26 [Smith, 181]. There he described his previous life and many beliefs, along with a great many details about his Ranter experience, including his refusal to admit to having written *A Single Eye* when confronted by a committee of Parliament (30 [Smith, 184]). Testimony from *The Lost Sheep Found* must, of course, be regarded as similar to works of other "late fellow Ranters" and does not have the same testimonial validity as *A Single Eye*, which was written when Clarkson was still a believing Ranter.

[9] Abiezer Coppe, *SOME Sweet Sips of some Spirituall "Wine," sweetly and freely dropping from one cluster of "Grapes," brought between two upon a Staffe from "Spirituall Canaan" (the "Land" of the "Living": the "Living Lord.") TO Late "Egyptian," and now "bewildered Israelites"* (London: 1649), 1 [Smith, 47].

[10] Cf. Norman Cohn, *The Pursuit of the Millennium: Revolutionary Millenarians and Mystical Anarchists of the Middle Ages*, revised and expanded edition (New York: Oxford U.P., 1970). Cohn suggests a connection between revolutionary millenarianism and twentieth-century phenomena such as Nazism and Communism (esp. 281-86).

[11] Gerrard Winstanley, *A Vindication of those, Whose endeavors is only to make the Earth a common treasury, called Diggers: Or Some Reasons given by them against the immoderate use of creatures, or the excessive community of women called Ranting; or rather Renting*, (London: 1649), title page.

[12] *The Ranters Declaration, with Their new Oath and Protestation* ...Licensed according to order, and published by M. Stubs, a late fellow-Ranter (London: 1650), p. 2.

[13] Laurence Clarkson (Claxton), *The Lost Sheep Found: Or, the Prodigal returned to his Fathers house, after many a sad and weary Journey through many Religious Countreys* ... (London: 1660), pp. 22-23 [Smith, 178-79].

[14] Winstanley, *A Vindication* ..., G2^{v}-G3^{r}.

[15] Isaiah 42.16. The later reference to "rough ways smooth" is from Luke 3:5, which is a quotation from Isaiah 40:4, where the King James Version renders "plain" instead of "smooth."

[16] Abiezer Coppe, *A Fiery Flying Roll: A Word from the Lord to all the Great Ones of the Earth, whom this may concerne: Being the last WARNING PIECE at the dreadfull day of JUDGEMENT* ... (London: 1649), p. 1 [Smith, 86].

[17] *A Second Fiery Flying Roule: To All the Inhabitants of the earth: specially to the rich ones* ... (London: 1649), p. 13 [Smith, 108]. Although this pamphlet has its own title page, it is bound together with *A Fiery Flying Roll* in the British Museum copy (Thomason Tracts).

[18] *Dictionary of National Biography*, s.v. "Coppe, Abiezer."

[19] Cf. Note 9 above.

[20] "The Preface," *A Fiery Flying Roll*, A2^v [Smith, 82].

[21] Cf. Note 4 above.

[22] Theodore Haak, *The Dutch Annotations Upon the Whole Bible* ... (London: 1657), Nnnnn 1^r.

Biblical Realism in *Silas Marner*

Harold Fisch

I

If the hero of *Silas Marner*, like the author of the book, has broken with evangelical Christianity, he has not rejected the Bible along with it.[1] For him, as for George Eliot, it remains to be re-interpreted and re-understood. When Dolly Winthrop hears of some of the strange practices of the Lantern Yard conventicle, she wonders whether theirs was the same Bible as the one to be found in the parish church of Raveloe. Silas assures her that it was:

> "And yourn's the same Bible, you're sure o' that Master Marner – the Bible as you brought wi' you from that country – it's the same as what they've got at church, and what Eppie's a-learning to read in?" "Yes," said Silas, "every bit the same." (chapter xvi)

The Bible then connects Silas's earlier faith with his life in the present and future. If Eppie signifies, as the epigraph from Wordsworth indicates, the promise of "forward-looking thoughts," then we are here reminded that she has been "a-learning to read" in the same Bible that Silas had known in his dark Puritan past. But, the Bible is more than a key to the characters and their thoughts; it is a key to the conception of the novel itself as a moral history exhibiting the specific kind of realism and economy which mark the Old Testament narratives.

Like the Genesis-stories or those relating to Samuel, Saul, and David, *Silas Marner* is a story of trial, retribution, and redemption.[2] The characters are morally tested, forced to acknowledge their trespasses. "There's dealings" says Silas, or, as Dolly Winthrop puts it in her more stumbling fashion, there's "Them above." Faults hidden in the past come to light. Silas, who has suffered from malice and injustice, lives to gain a blessing. The characters come to us weighted with their previous history; as Auerbach says of the heroes of the Genesis-narratives, they are "fraught with background."[3]

Silas's personality is conditioned by what has happened to him in Lantern Yard and earlier. Similarly, Godfrey Cass's past, which he conceals from his wife, will eventually constrain him and there will be a reckoning. Providence works wonderfully and mysteriously, calling the past to remembrance, turning sin and suffering into a path of salvation.

There is throughout a sense of the momentousness of our moral choices, a momentousness too in the doings of simple people – seemingly trivial doings very often, but loaded with "the intensity of their personal history."[4] This is something that Eliot had learned not only from the Bible but, collaterally, from Wordsworth, whose "Michael" (from which she had drawn her motto) provides examples of the same phenomenon. In that poem, too, a simple act by an unlettered shepherd can take the moral weight of the universe. After Michael's only son Luke leaves him, we are told that the old shepherd returns to the sheepfold they had together begun to build:

> many and many a day he thither went,
> And never lifted up a single stone.

The detail becomes momentous, its power a function of its utter simplicity. But this is not strictly a separate influence: for it is clear that "Michael" too in its "high seriousness" recalls at every turn the Genesis narratives. Michael and his wife, with their only child born in their old age, with their simple loyalties and hopes, recall such patriarchal households as that of Abraham and Sarah. The sheepfold of which father and son lay the cornerstone is to be a covenant – "a covenant/'Twill be between us ..." When they are far from one another, the heap of stones, like that begun by Jacob at Bethel (Genesis, 28:18) in sign of God's promises and his own, or like that raised by Laban and Jacob at Gilead (*ibid.*, 31:51-2), will be a witness to their mutual exchange of vows. When Luke betrays his trust, it becomes the betrayal of a covenant with all the weight of tragic meaning which such a dereliction implies. George Eliot evidently sensed the Biblical element in Wordsworth's poem, and she fortified and enriched it with her own first-hand understanding of the imaginative possibilities of the Biblical mode of narration.

II

It may be worth pointing out some of the specific Biblical echo-structures in Eliot's novel. They are more numerous than critics have hitherto recognized; indeed, in their accumulated force they would seem to have had a shaping effect on the novel as a whole. The coming of the infant Eppie to Silas on New Year's eve bringing to him her gift of love has been termed a "Christ-event,"[5] and perhaps there is some such Christian typology at work here, but the Biblical episode, which is actually evoked in the text, is the rescue of Lot from the cities of the plain in Genesis 19:

> In old days there were angels who came and took men by the hand and led them away from the city of destruction. We see no white-winged angels now. But yet men are led away from threatening destruction: a hand is put into theirs, which leads them forth gently towards a calm and bright land, so that they look no more backward; and the hand may be a little child's. (chapter xiv)

Like the story of the rescue of Lot, Eliot's tale is one of retribution, redemption, and rescue. The angel has been domesticated into a child, but the sense of the wonder and the miracle remains. There is an echo here too of the beginning of Bunyan's *The Pilgrim's Progress*, where we are told that Christian fled from the City of Destruction and "looked not behind him." Critics have been right in emphasizing the importance of Bunyan's presence in the novel.[6] But here too, as in the example of Wordsworth's poem, we are not speaking strictly of a separate influence, because the same Biblical source stands behind Bunyan's text at this point. In the marginal gloss, Bunyan directs us to the story of Lot's escape in Genesis 19:17 as the Biblical analogy for Christian's flight from the City of Destruction.[7]

The Biblical underpinning can be even more unambiguous than this. In speaking to Dolly Winthrop in chapter xvi, Silas recalls the evil done to him by his friend William Dean in his Lantern Yard days, an iniquity which left him friendless and bitter for fifteen years. There was no longer a God of righteousness in whom he could believe. "That," he said, "was what fell on me like as if it had been red-hot iron." And he continues:

"...because, you see, there was nobody as cared for me or clave to me above nor below. And him as I'd gone out and in wi' for ten year and more, since when we was lads and went halves – mine own familiar friend in whom I trusted, had lifted up his heel again' me, and worked to ruin me."

The Biblical language and parallelism ("nobody as cared for me or clave to me") give the passage its particular solemnity, but this is not just a matter of general colouring: there is also the literal echoing of Psalm 41 where the relevant verses read:

All that hate me whisper together against me: against me do they devise my hurt. An evil disease, say they, cleaveth fast unto him: and now that he lieth he shall rise up no more. Yea, mine own familiar friend, in whom I trusted, which did eat of my bread, hath lifted up his heel again against me. (Psalm 41:7-9)

Silas here formulates his trouble in terms of a Biblical verse. But, there is a paradox here: if his bitterness at the outcome of the casting of lots and the evil which he had met with from the members of the Lantern Yard community had led to the loss of his faith ("there is no just God that governs the earth righteously"), it had manifestly not led him to abandon the Biblical sources of that faith. Indeed, we may see Psalm 41 as a key to the understanding of Silas's crisis and its outcome. The crisis is defined by the three verses quoted above, and the outcome of the drama seems to be structured by the continuation of that same psalm. For after the victim's complaint at the evil done to him by those who had devised his hurt, God mercifully raises him up:

And as for me, thou upholdest me in mine integrity, and settest me before thy face for ever. (*ibid.*, verse 12)

The force of these words had evidently not been lost on the author. She conceives Silas's existence as a moral pilgrimage in which there is both judgement and reward. Whatever her theoretical position on such questions, when Eliot came to construct her fictional plot, here and elsewhere, these categories remained meaningful. We are thus not speaking of some secularized "Religion of Humanity,"[8] but of a re-constituted Biblical faith, rather like that which Matthew Arnold was teaching in this same period. In keeping with that inspiration, she speaks in her novels not of blind fate, like Hardy, but of redemption and reward and of moral decisions taken with a kind of Biblical solemnity.

Critical from this point of view is the choice of Hephzibah as the name for the foundling who has come to Marner's door. Dolly doubts whether it is really "a christened name," but Silas retorts by saying that "it's a Bible name." Silas thus establishes the character of his new-found source of comfort by reviving the Puritan fashion of naming. The name, as David Carroll has pointed out, takes on special significance when the Biblical source in Isaiah 62 is considered:

> Thou shalt no more be termed Forsaken; neither shall thy land be any more termed Desolate: but thou shalt be called Hephzibah, and thy land Beulah: for the Lord delighteth in thee, and thy land shall be married. (Isaiah 62:4)

Carroll sees in the name Hephzibah and the verse that it recalls "a reassurance to Silas that his instinctive affection for Eppie will not be betrayed."[9] It is perhaps more to the point that she comes to bring to an end the years in which he has been *Desolate* and *Forsaken*. She represents the promise of joy and delight ("My Delight is in Her"). The giving of a new name – always a covenantal act in the Bible (see Genesis 17:5,16;43:10-11, etc.) – confirms and establishes this promise. When Silas goes to church in the village for the very first time, it is for the christening of Eppie. We are told that he finds the Anglican forms entirely alien – "He was quite unable, by means of anything he heard or saw, to identify the Raveloe religion with his old faith." (chapter xiv) But, the Biblical name he has given the child, we may say, provides the link. Unwittingly, Silas has found a text which will bind his past and future symbolically together. Not only Eppie but the Biblical word, by which she is henceforward denominated, has the saving function of binding his days each to each by natural piety. Eppie will compensate him for past sorrows at the same time as she will afford him the joy of "forward-looking thoughts."

Eppie is indeed the focus of the covenantal pattern of the book; she visibly signifies the redemptive process. The high-point in this respect is chapter xix; there Eppie makes her momentous choice between Silas and Godfrey Cass, giving her loyalty firmly to the adoptive father who has cherished and reared her rather than to her natural father. It has not, to my knowledge, been noted by critics that the high drama of this chapter recalls, and is designed to recall, the story of Ruth and Naomi. In the book of Ruth also, the daughter-in-law chooses her adoptive mother, "cleaving" to her in preference to her natural kin – "Orpah kissed her mother-in-law; but Ruth clave unto her." (Ruth 1:14) Eppie's declaration of attachment to Silas and rejection of Godfrey echo that chapter of Ruth:

> Thank you, ma'am – thank you, sir, for your offers – they're very great, and far above my wish. For I should have no delight i'life any more if I was forced to go away from my father, and knew he was sitting at home, a'thinking of me and feeling lone. We've been used to be happy together every day, and I can't think o' no happiness without him. And he says he'd nobody i'the world till I was sent to him, and he'd have nothing when I was gone. And he's took care of me and loved me from the first, and I'll cleave to him as long as he lives, and nobody shall ever come between him and me.

The last clause recalls the closing verse of Ruth's declaration to Naomi: "The Lord do so to me, and more also, of ought but death part thee and me." (Ruth 1:17) The effect of this echo is to bring into the novel the memory not merely of the two verses (14, 17) which are literally recalled but the entire context of the story of Ruth and Naomi. Naomi who went out full and has come home empty is the prototype of Silas, robbed of his wealth and bereft of happiness. If Ruth brings a blessing and forward-looking thought to the widowed and childless Naomi (see Ruth 4:15), so Eppie proves to be a blessing for barren Silas, holding to him more firmly than a natural child might have done, being better to him indeed than seven sons.

There are also wider reverberations. Eliot seems to wish to endow Eppie's decision in chapter xix with far-reaching historical significance. In her love and loyalty she represents the antitype to the evangelical pieties and superstitions of Lantern Yard, on the one hand, and to the purely "organic" or earth-bound religion of Raveloe, on the other.[10] No less than Hester Prynne and Pearl in Hawthorne's novel of the same period, her heroine is seen as "the angel and apostle of the coming revelation." Eppie's saving message is addressed to natural man, but it signifies the transcendence of the natural in the interests of a higher bond of loyalty. She also challenges a social structure based on class and inherited privilege in this hinting at a new conception of the relations between men. This, too, would seem to owe something to the story of Ruth who is the ancestress of David and whose story marks the beginning of a salvation history which will transform a nation.

If Eppie reminds us of Ruth, her father Godfrey Cass reminds us of another Biblical character, viz. Judah, the ancestor of Boaz. He, too, had secretly "come in unto" a strange woman by the wayside; she had then born him a child whom he had ultimately acknowledged as his own, but only after he had been brought to admit his fault. The Judah-Tamar story (Genesis 38) and the related narrative of Joseph and his brothers seem to lurk behind the whole history of Godfrey and his brother Dunstan. When Dunstan's body is found together with Silas's lost gold, the skeleton is identified by three items of accoutrement, as Godfrey tells Nancy:

> There's his watch and seals, and there's my gold-handled hunting-whip, with my name on. (chapter xviii)

It is the discovery of Dunstan's guilt, confirmed by these three identifying pieces of personal property, which prompts Godfrey to confess his own hidden guilt. The Bible-conscious reader is surely reminded here of Tamar's producing the three identifying personal effects, which confirm Judah's paternity in Genesis 38:

> By the man, whose these are, am I with child: and she said, Discern I pray thee, whose are these, the signet, and bracelets and staff. (38:25)

The acknowledgment of guilt (and in this case the acknowledgment of fatherhood) is, of course, the theme of the whole cluster of narratives relating to Joseph and his brothers. Immediately following the Judah and Tamar episode, we are told how the brothers of Joseph are tested by a series of strange and bewildering mishaps, among them the seizing of Simeon by the Egyptian ruler. This triggers a process of repentance, causing them to remember their crime of many years previously:

> And they said one to another, We are verily guilty concerning our brother, in that we saw the anguish of his soul, when he besought us, and we would not hear; therefore is this distress come upon us. (Gen. 42:21)

There is no logical link between the two episodes that the brothers know of, but chords of memory are struck by the sight of another brother bound and helpless. Similarly there is no logical reason why the discovery of Dunstan's body should have led Godfrey to reveal the matter of his fatherhood of Eppie, but the laying bare of Dunstan's crime triggers off a moral process in Godfrey and causes him to reveal his own guilty secret stemming from the same period. His mood is like that of Joseph's brothers in the above-quoted passage when he says to Nancy:

> Everything comes to light, Nancy, sooner or later. When God Almighty wills it, our secrets are found out. I've lived with a secret on my mind, but I'll keep it from you no longer.

Lot led by an angel out of the city of destruction; Judah made to confess his paternity; Ruth declaring herself for her adoptive mother against the claims of mere nature – all have something in common. All are stories of redemption.[11] Lot and his daughters are saved for the future; Judah redeems Tamar from her widowed and childless state and a future is assured; finally, in the story of Ruth, redemption becomes the central theme. At the simplest level, a parcel of land belonging to Elimelech, the dead husband of Naomi, has to be redeemed. To Boaz (though not the first in line by kinship) belongs the "right of redemption." In performing his duty he also gains a wife and establishes a line which will culminate in the birth of David, the Messianic king. Naomi too, will be redeemed; her *go'el* is the newborn Obed (4:14), who will compensate her for her long years of exile and loss.

Eliot had, it seems, lost her faith in a personal God whom one could address in the forms established by the Church, but, paradoxically, she had not lost her sense of wonder at the mysterious workings of a providence that brings good out of misery in the long passage of years. It would seem that some such movement was for her both a religious and aesthetic necessity. And, the great moments are when the wonder enters into the consciousness of the characters themselves. In chapter xix Silas achieves his awareness of the wonderful as the stolen money is restored to him in time for it to serve as a dowry for Eppie – "It's wonderful – our life is wonderful." And Godfrey, for whom the past has come back with a sterner admonition, has a sense of the awfulness and mystery of those same "dealings":

> The eyes of the husband and wife met with awe in them, as at a crisis which suspended affection. (chapter xviii)

III

It should be emphasized, however, that the wonder and the awe that the characters feel do not transport them – or us – beyond the visible and material world. Coleridge, speaking of Wordsworth's achievement in the *Lyrical Ballads* remarks that the realism of every-day is enhanced and deepened by "a feeling analogous to the super-natural."[12] This feeling is just as powerful in George Eliot's story, but the realism is even greater, for she has chosen the medium of the novel to give expression to the "unassuming commonplaces" of village life. In the nature of things, the world of the novel is a prose world, one of material things, of small, contingent particulars rather than symbols. The leech-gatherer whose appearance and speech Wordsworth describes in "Resolution and Independence" was, we know, drawn from life,[13] but in the emphatic imagery of the poem he achieves a larger-than-life quality – he becomes a prodigy, a portent, his coming and going equally mysterious:

> As a huge stone is sometimes seen to lie
> Couched on the bald top of an eminence;
> Wonder to all who do the same espy,
> By what means it could thither come, or whence.

Characters in a novel necessarily have a more quotidian character than this; their sublimity, if they have it, is pitched nearer to that of our own lines. Eliot seems to have had a problem here, a problem of finding the exact mode of realism for her tale. She tells her publisher in a letter dated February 24, 1861 of the way the idea of *Silas Marner* came to her:

> It came to me first of all, quite suddenly, as a sort of legendary tale, suggested by my recollection of having once, in early childhood, seen a linen-weaver with a bag on his back; but as my mind dwelt on the subject, I became inclined to a more realistic treatment.[14]

A "legendary tale" of Silas would have made him more like the leech-gatherer; indeed, Silas's catalepsy may have been suggested by another passage in that some poem of Wordsworth:

> Motionless as a cloud the old Man stood,
> That heareth not the loud winds when they call;
> And moveth all together, if it move at all –

But, she was anxious to bring Silas out of the legendary Wordsworthian state into the orbit of ordinary everyday concerns – those of the villagers who sit and converse in the Rainbow where we are not likely to find Wordsworth's huntsmen and shepherds and certainly not his leech-gatherer.

The felt need to overcome the propensity to the fabulous in the tale as it had originally "come to her" thus becomes a central problem in the strategy of composition; more than that, it becomes in a sense the theme of the novel! We are told in the first chapter how the Raveloe folk had at first found Silas strange and portentous. The word "mysterious" occurs four times in the account of their first impressions of him:

> for the villagers near whom he had come to settle [his appearance] had mysterious peculiarities which corresponded with the exceptional nature of his occupation. (chapter i)

They see him as in league with the Devil, an impression strengthened by Jem Rodney's account of having met him in one of his cataleptic fits. But the effect of the narrative as it proceeds is to demystify Silas as he comes nearer to the people of the village and as they draw closer to him after the robbery. By chapter x, the village-folk, following the lead of Mr. Macey the parish-clerk, have decided that there is nothing portentous about him and that he is nothing more than a "poor mushed creatur." The transition from the legendary to the realistic is here a matter of the attitude of the villagers to Silas; they now begin to see him as one of them.[15] But, in the metapoetics of the narration this process of demystification signifies the determination to adapt and recast the high invention of the ballad of mystery or the "greater romantic lyric" so as to bring it within the confines of everyday reality. This was the task the author set herself and it was a remarkably difficult one.

I would wish to argue that the Biblical narratives – the parables of the New Testament but, more particularly, Ruth and the Genesis narratives – provided her with the key to that balance of the wonderful and the everyday, the fabulous and the realistic, that she was seeking. The story of Ruth has epic overtones; it situates itself at the crossroads of history "in the days when the judges ruled" and in the days before a king reigned in Israel. Mysteriously, the story of the choices made by Ruth and Boaz will mingle with this larger theme. Not merely will a broken line be restored, but a world will be made new. And yet attention focuses itself on the matters of everyday, on the gleaners in the field, on legal forms and modes of greeting in a rural society, on the passage of the seasons from the barley harvest to the wheat harvest. We seem to be in a real world of struggling men and women.

Bible stories also exhibit human weaknesses and confusions. Judah's embarrassment at the loss of his seal, his bracelets, and staff has the force of the actual; his history, like that of a character in a novel by Iris Murdoch, is not smoothed over or harmonized in the manner of a legend. So much, says Auerbach of the Genesis stories, is contradictory, so much is left in darkness.[16] This is precisely the comment of Dolly at the end of George Eliot's novel: "It's the will o' them above as many things should be dark to us." There are many loose ends, as in real life; many things are left unexplained. What became of the people Silas knew in Lantern Yard? Was the secret villainy of William Dean ever discovered? Silas will never know, nor shall we. Only those matters which need to be illuminated are illuminated. And, what is illuminated in the tangle of circumstances which makes up the lives of men and women is the strange twisting path of salvation itself, a path marked out by a very small number of obstinately significant details, such as Silas's catalepsy, or Eppie's golden hair, or Godfrey's hunting-whip. These details are illuminated because on them, strangely, the whole history of trial and suffering and redemption seems to hinge. Here the fabulous and the realistic combine. They are like the ram caught in the thicket in the story of the Binding of Isaac, or the coat which Joseph leaves in the hands of Potiphar's wife, strangely recalling the coat of many colours, which his brothers stripped off him earlier in the story, or like Absalom's long hair. With such few details, trivial and yet portentous, the Old Testament narratives concern themselves. They give these stories their special kind of realism. Eliot has struggled to capture the same kind of realism in the rigorous selection of details which make up her spare narrative and she has succeeded to a marvellous degree. It is what makes this novel not only unique in her writings, but practically unique in English literature. Joan Bennett asserted that it is "the most flawless of George Eliot's works,"[17] and Walter Allen went even further and claimed that "*Silas Marner* is as perfect a work of prose fiction as any in the language, a small miracle."[18]

IV

In the same letter to John Blackwood cited earlier, Eliot speaks not only of the need to arbitrate between a legendary and a realistic treatment, but of the opposing attractions of verse and prose as the medium for her tale:

> I have felt all through as if the story would have lent itself best to metrical rather than prose fiction, especially in all that relates to the psychology of Silas; except that under that treatment, there could not be an equal play of humour.[19]

The reason she gives here for her choice of prose is a bit lame, for the fact is that there is little humour in the treatment of her main characters. Humour is mainly confined to the villagers in the Rainbow tavern. In this, *Silas Marner* is strikingly different from *Brother Jacob*, another moral tale of trial, sin, and retribution from the same period,[20] where the jocular tone is very marked throughout. It would thus seem that her choice of prose in preference to metre in *Silas Marner* was determined by other considerations. What one would want to say is that the attempt to capture the "still small voice" of the narrative portions of the Hebrew Bible dictated an utter simplicity and directness of style and the avoidance of anything suggestive of artificiality. The archness, for instance, of Fielding's "comic epic poem in prose" would have been incompatible with George Eliot's purpose here. At the same time, she needed height, sublimity. She found the answer in the utterly simple prose of the Bible, the *sermo humilis*, which some of the Church Fathers upheld in opposition to the high rhetoric of the Ciceronian tradition. The lowliness of the *sermo humilis* enabled one to invest the trivial things of everyday with a certain sublimity.[21] It was prose reduced to its simplest elements, and yet it could be pregnant and lyrical in the manner of poetry.

While the *sermo humilis* of the Bible had been part of the tradition of the English novel from the time of Bunyan and Defoe, the fact is that it had never been totally assimilated. At some point the literary tradition of the West resists such a radical canon of simplicity. Even Eliot, who uses it as her standard in this novel, does not apply it consistently. Her narrative voice, for instance, is not that of the Biblical narrator. Moreover, if we analyse the different stylistic strands in the prose of the novel, we find that the Biblical combination of loftiness and simplicity is really specific to Eppie and Silas and the scenes in which they appear. It becomes, we may say, not so much a way of telling the story, as a "criticism of life." The style itself is foregrounded and is beheld in contrast to other styles. In the confrontation between Eppie and Silas, on the one hand, and Godfrey and Nancy, on the other, in chapter xix, we become aware that the feelings and expressions of the "upper class" pair are cruder and more vulgar than those of Eppie and Silas. Nancy and Godfrey belong to the class of what Matthew Arnold called the Barbarians – they were, he says, much given to field sports – and their language is to that extent differentiated from that of Eppie and Silas.

Let us see how the stylistic aspect of the confrontation is exhibited in chapter xix. Godfrey is voluble at first on the subject of the robbery and discusses the hardships of the weaver's life which he would like to do something to ease. The something, of course, is his plan to take Eppie from him, though he says nothing of this at first. Marner's responses are brief and awkward:

> Silas, always ill at ease when he was being spoken to by "betters" such as Mr. Cass – tall, powerful, florid men, seen chiefly on horseback – answered with some constraint – "Sir, I've a deal to thank you for a'ready. As for the robbery, I count it no loss to me. And if I did, you couldn't help it: you aren't answerable for it."

Godfrey then reveals the main object of his visit. Saying nothing at this stage about his fatherhood, he proposes simply that, being themselves childless, they take Eppie away to live with them and make a lady of her. Marner would be rewarded for the trouble of bringing her up. He concludes:

> she'd come and see you very often, and we should all be on the look-out to do everything we could towards making you comfortable.

The moral insentivity here is compounded by the easy clichés which Godfrey uses ("be on the look-out," "making you comfortable"). The narrator's comment draws attention to the clichés:

> A plain man like Godfrey Cass, speaking under some embarrassment, necessary blunders on words that are coarser than his intentions, and that are likely to fall gratingly on susceptible feelings.

In a reversal of the traditional division of styles as taught in the ancient schools of rhetoric and as practised in the theatre or in the literature of romance,[22] here the upper-class character is the "plain man" whose expressions are "coarser than his intentions," while Silas, the handweaver, has the "susceptible feelings" and the language that goes with them. The reader is now being prompted at every stage to observe the manner of speaking of the different characters. Eppie's first real speech in this meeting is marked by a Wordsworthian simplicity and a Biblical cadence; above all, it is free of cliché:

> "Thank you, ma'am – thank you, sir. But I can't leave my father, nor own anybody nearer than him. And I don't want to be a lady – thank you all the same... I couldn't give up the folks I've been used to."

Godfrey, angered by their refusal to accept what he has persuaded himself is a generous offer, now declares the truth about his "natural claim" to Eppie. He is, he says, her real father. The simplicity and truth of Silas and Eppie have now forced Godfrey to reveal his truth, his manifest claim as well as his sin. But, Silas's is still the higher truth, as he angrily opposes to the claims of "nature" – claims long concealed – the power of those august signifiers by which human relations are fundamentally ordered and which are in a sense independent of the natural relations which they signify. In this case, the word "father" has its own peremptory rights of love and authority, drawn as much and perhaps more from the sphere of the sacred as from biology:

> "Your coming now and saying 'I'm her father' doesn't alter the feelings inside us. It's me she's been calling her father ever since she could say the word."

Nature must bow to the language of the heart – is what Silas seems to be saying. And again, the narrator's comment serves to foreground the stylistic aspect of this extraordinary confrontation:

> "But I think you might look at the thing more reasonably, Marner," said Godfrey, unexpectedly awed by the weaver's direct truth-speaking.

He ends by denying that Eppie will really be separated from Marner, even though Godfrey will have taken over the word "father" as his natural right.

> "She'll be very near you, and come to see you very often. She'll feel just the same towards you."

In the great speech which he now utters, Marner exposes the shallowness of Godfrey's sentiments – his upper-class complacency, as well as the idleness of his rhetoric:

> "Just the same? " said Marner, more bitterly than ever. "How'll she feel just the same for me as she does now, when we eat o' the same bit, and drink o' the same cup, and think o' the same things from one day's end to another? Just the same? that's idle talk. You'd cut us i' two."

Again, it is to Silas's simple language with its Biblical cadences that our attention is drawn, a language to which Godfrey is unattuned:

> Godfrey, unqualified by experience to discern the *pregnancy* of Marner's *simple* words, felt rather angry again. (emphasis added)

The express link with the Bible and its style is made clearer when we find the author commenting in precisely the same terms on the language of the Bible and the Collects, as she had heard them read one Sunday in the Little Portland Street Chapel. The letter – to Sarah Hennell – was written in July, 1861, just a few weeks after the publication of *Silas Marner*:

> What an age of earnest faith, grasping a noble conception of life and determined to bring all things into harmony with it, has recorded itself in the *simple pregnant, rhythmical* English of these Collects and the Bible.[23] (emphasis added).

Eliot's moral and linguistic criticism in this chapter is very much bound up with the sociological aspect of the confrontation. The ultimate point of insensitivity in Godfrey's discourse is reached when he remarks that if Eppie fails to accept his offer, "she may marry some low working-man." It is this fate that the "high society" of Godfrey and Nancy's home, with its balls, its horse-riding, and its drinking, will preserve her from! In short Godfrey and Nancy stand not only for natural bonds, but for natural bonds linked to a system of class gradations which are likewise held to be natural. Opposed to this in the dramatic evolution of the dialogue, is the Biblical, covenantal system of relations which cuts across the rights of class and property. The kind of love and loyalty to which this system has reference is that implied in Ezekiel's parable of the foundling girl whom the passerby finds and adopts and finally takes for his wife (Ezekiel 16:5f) – it is his way of talking about the covenant between God and Israel. And this same higher loyalty finds expression in the story of Ruth and Naomi. It is, of course, the latter text which Eppie's reply immediately calls to mind in the passage already quoted. It merits citation once again:

> "And he says he'd nobody i' the world till I was sent him, and he'd have nothing when I was gone. And he's took care of me and loved me from the first, and I'll cleave to him as long as he lives, and nobody shall ever come between him and me."

While Nancy still attempts to counter this by an appeal to such terms as "nature," "duty," and law," Godfrey has nothing more to say. He is silent. It is the victory of language and, specifically, the language of those lively oracles, which Silas had salvaged from the ruins of Lantern Yard and brought with him to furnish his onward pilgrimage.

Notes

[1] Cf. Q.D. Leavis, Introduction to George Eliot, *Silas Marner, the Weaver of Raveloe* (Harmondsworth: Penguin Books, 1967), p. 14.

[2] Cf. Walter Allen, *The English Novel* (Harmondsworth: Penguin Books, 1958), p. 227.

[3] Erich Auerbach, *Mimesis* (Trans., W. Trask), (New York: Doubleday, 1957), p. 10.

[4] *Ibid.*, p. 15.

[5] J. Wiesenfarth, "Demythologizing *Silas Marner*," ELH, XXXVII (1970), 242. The fact is, however, that the arrival of Eppie occurs not at Christmas, but, somewhat pointedly, a week later, on New Year's Eve (see chapter xii).

[6] Cf. Q.D. Leavis, pp. 7,13.

[7] See John Bunyan, *The Pilgrim's Progress* (Ed., E. Venables), (Oxford: The Clarendon Press, 1900), p. 13.

[8] Bernard J. Paris in "George Eliot's Religion of Humanity," ELH, XXIX (1962), 418-443, argues for a practical identity between Eliot's views on religion and those of the materialist philosopher Ludwig Feuerbach. There is textual evidence for this in her letters. See letter to Mrs. H.F. Ponsonby, dated December 10, 1874 in *The George Eliot Letters* (Ed., Gordon S. Haight), (New Haven: Yale University Press, 1955), Vol. VI, 98f. It does not seem to me, however, that the matter is nearly as simple as this and in any case, where poets and novelists are concerned, it is unwise to draw conclusions from their theoretical positions and apply them directly to their literary productions. In the case of Eliot, Paris himself recognizes that her being a theoretical determinist does not prevent her, as a novelist, from emphasizing the importance of virtue and free choice (440). He might have extended this insight to include her recognition of the action to divine providence in the lives of her characters.

[9] David Carroll, "Reversing the Oracles of Religion," 1967, reprinted in *George Eliot: The Mill on the Floss and Silas Marner: A Casebook* (Ed. R.P. Draper), (London: Macmillan, 1977), p. 212.

[10] John Holloway, *The Victorian Sage* (London: Anchor Books, 1962), p. 114: "The little village [of Raveloe], off the beaten track in its wooded hollow, is half submerged in the world of nature. ... The passage of time and the rotation of the seasons affect humans and animals and plants all alike."

[11] As a matter of fact all three stories, those of Judah and Tamar, Lot and his daughters, and Ruth and Naomi are part of a single family history, for Lot is the primitive ancestor of Ruth the Moabitess, while Judah is the direct ancestor of Boaz, the husband of Ruth. There are important structural parallels between the three stories. (See Harold Fisch, "Ruth and the Structure of Covenant History," *Vetus Testamentum*, 32 [1982], 425-437.) But, it would be fanciful to suggest that these links were present to George Eliot or that they communicate themselves to the reader of the novel. What the various echoes from different parts of Scripture have in common is the general theme of redemption.

[12] S.T. Coleridge, *Biographia Literaria* (1817), chapter xiv.

[13] See *Journals of Dorothy Wordsworth* (Ed., Mary Moorman), (London: Oxford University Press, 1971), p. 42 (for Friday, 3rd October, 1800).

[14] *Letters*, III, 382 (to John Blackwood). For useful discussion, see Lilian Haddakin, "Silas Marner' in *Critical Essays on George Eliot* (Ed., Barbara Hardy), (London: Routledge and Kegan Paul, 1970), pp. 61-62.

[15] Cf. Wiesenfarth, pp. 237-240.

[16] *Mimesis*, pp. 7-9.

[17] Joan Bennett, *George Eliot: Her Mind and Art* (Cambridge: Cambridge University Press, 1962), p. 138.

[18] Walter Allen, *George Eliot* (New York: Collier Books, 1967), p. 118.

[19] *Letters*, III, 382.

[20] Written in 1860, published in the *Cornhill*, July 1864.

[21] Cf. Erich Auerbach, *Literary Language and Its Public in Late Antiquity and in the Middle Ages* (Trans., R. Manheim), (New York: Pantheon Books, Bollingen Series, 1965), chapter I, *passim*.

[22] *Ibid.*, p. 38.

[23] *Letters*, III, 442.

The Representation of Biblical Women in Israeli Narrative Fiction: Some Transformations and Continuities[1]

by
Esther Fuchs

Biblical themes, episodes and characters have inspired modern Hebrew literature since its inception at the end of the eighteenth century. Not unlike their rabbinic predecessors, however, modern Hebrew writers use Biblical materials in order to express and legitimize their own ideologies. The difference between traditional midrashic stories on the Bible and the treatment of Biblical materials by *Maskilim*, like Yehoshua H. Schor or Avraham Mapu, consists in the fact that the latter often used Biblical materials in order to criticize the theocentric and sacral belief-system of traditional Judaism in the name of humanistic secularism. The literary treatment of Biblical women by writers like Y.L. Gordon, David Frishman, Yehudah Steinberg, Saul Tchernichovsky, and Jacob Fichman is an attempt to fill in the gaps left open by the Biblical text.[2] Also, they reflect a concern with and a protest against the status of women in traditional Judaism.

While it can be argued that the tendency of the *Haskalah* and *Tehiya* authors to romanticize Biblical women rests in essence on an androcentric perspective which perceives women as helpmates, mothers, or lovers (namely as auxiliary agents in the drama of man's life), it is illuminating to compare that perspective with the tendency in Israeli male-authored narrative fiction to depict Biblical women negatively.

This essay is concerned with the way in which major contemporary Israeli writers represent Biblical women and with the implicit androcentric and, at times, quasi-misogynous assumptions this representation reveals. The question I would like to raise here concerns the extent to which Israeli narrative fiction perpetuates Biblical patriarchalism and the extent to which it criticizes or opposes it. My purpose here is not to argue that Israeli authors are willfully or consciously distorting Biblical female characters. Neither am I arguing that Israeli authors have invented the tendency to demean Biblical women. This tendency is well entrenched in the Judeo-Christian tradition, as is the opposite proclivity to idealize them. The point is not to examine the literary tradition extending from the Biblical to the contemporary Hebrew text, but rather to investigate the ancient and the contemporary texts synchronically. The synchronic juxtaposition of the Biblical and the contemporary representation of the "same" female characters will permit us to explore some ideological continuities and some differences between both ends of the Hebrew literary continuum in regard to the nature and status of women.

A comparative study of Biblical characters in Israeli fiction reveals a discrepancy in the treatment of male and female characters. Whereas male secondary (or peripheral) characters from the *Tanach* often become central characters in the modern text, secondary female characters, even when wrested from their Biblical anonymity, remain essentially secondary, serving as foils to their male counterparts. When the biblical judgment of a female character is ambiguous, the modern Israeli narrative tends to condemn rather than condone her, and whereas negative male characters (e.g. Abimelech, Saul) are often absolved, if not elevated to heroic status, female villains (e.g. Jezebel, Delilah) rarely receive literary rehabilitation in contemporary Israeli literature. Female characters continue to be evaluated in relation to their male counterparts: as wives, mothers, daughters, or lovers. The modern Israeli story is often less tolerant and more dogmatic in its presentation and evaluation of Biblical women than the original narrative. To exemplify this point, I will focus on three major female role-models – the wife, mother, and daughter – as they appear in the Hebrew Bible and in related works of contemporary, mainstream Israeli writers.[3] The first role-model will be exemplified by Bathsheba, Uriah's wife, in Moshe Shamir's *The Poor Man's Lamb* (1956); the second by Abimelech's mother in Pinhas Sadeh's *The Death of Abimelech and his Ascent to Heaven in his Mother's Arms* (1969); and the third by Jephtah's daughter in Amos Oz's "Upon this Evil Earth." (1976)

The book of Samuel presents David as a sinner and Uriah as his victim, while Bathsheba appears mainly as a sexual object; at most, she functions as the catalyst of the conflict between the two males. While the story condemns David's treacherous victimization of his loyal subject, Uriah, it is highly ambiguous in its treatment of Bathsheba's victimization: "It happened, late one afternoon, when David arose from his couch and was walking upon the roof of the king's house, that he saw from the roof a woman bathing and the woman was very beautiful. And David sent and inquired about the woman. And one said, "Is not that Bathsheba, the daughter of Eliam, the wife of Uriah the Hittite?' So David sent messengers, and took her; and she came to him and he lay with her." (II Samuel 11:2-4)[4] It is not known what Bathsheba feels or thinks about the event. The only thing Bathsheba does in this chapter is send a message to King David concerning her pregnancy: "And the woman conceived: and she sent and told David 'I am with child.' " (II Samuel 11:5) In this story, adultery is presented as a sin committed by one man against another; the woman is merely an object through which the offender perpetrates his sin.[5] Nathan's allegorization of Bathsheba as the poor man's lamb (II Samuel 12) underscores the Biblical conception of the wife as her husband's property. (II Samuel 12) Nathan excoriates David not for abusing Bathsheba, but for stealing another man's wife, while possessing several wives of his own. (The rich man in the parable has "very many sheep and oxen.") Bathsheba appears chiefly as a peripheral character whose motives and moral liability are immaterial to the plot.

In Moshe Shamir's version of the Biblical tale, Bathsheba plays a much more central role. *The Poor Man's Lamb*, presented from the point of view of Uriah the Hittite, the protagonist-narrator, describes at length Uriah's love for Bathsheba and her great impact on his life. For the Hittite, Bathsheba represents a hope for the future: "I cannot stop thinking about her. For me she is more than a desirable woman, more than a beloved wife. She is my soil in the people of Judah. If she does not accept me, if she does not absorb my sperm, I will be [like] a dry tree."[6] But Bathsheba disappoints Uriah; she fails him both as wife and mother. She does not return his love and gives him no offspring. The story implies that Bathsheba marries Uriah only after he becomes one of David's major officers. Bathsheba's ruthless pragmatism seems to have been molded by her insidious grandfather, Ahitophel the Gillonite, but the novel fails to explain why Bathsheba is predisposed to Ahitophel, rather than to the benevolent Eliam, her father, and Uriah's best friend.

The combination of Bathsheba's irresistible beauty and ruthlessness presents the Biblical character as a *belle dame sans merci*. It becomes clear that her interest in Uriah stems from his association with the king, whom she idolizes as a power symbol. The expositional material that elaborates on Bathsheba's interest in David leaves no room for ambiguity concerning the motives for her adultery. Whereas the Biblical text refrains from dealing with the woman's motives (in all probability, because these are irrelevant to the story), the modern version makes it clear that Bathsheba purposely bathes in the open, so as to be noticed by the king. This is conveyed in Absalom's report to the shocked Uriah (p. 175), and later again in Uriah's reconstruction of the temptation scene (p. 246).

Shattered by his wife's disloyalty, the crestfallen Uriah refuses to follow Joab's advice and escape from the battlefield, because life without Bathsheba's love appears to him worse than death. What dooms Uriah in the long run, the novel implies, is his love for a fickle, ambitious, and disobedient woman: "Who is to blame? Not David. He loved me with his heart's blood, and sealed my death sentence with his tears. Bathsheba is to blame. This bloodthirsty woman who coveted royalty from the day her body matured for a man. [The blame is] in Bathsheba who accepted me only in order to get closer to the throne...She told the king: 'Kill him.' " (p. 246)

At one point, Uriah blames himself for his wife's faithlessness. Adapting the Nietzschean motto concerning recalcitrant women, Shamir ascribes the following thoughts to his protagonist: "I am to blame...I did not do the one thing that a man who wants to survive must do; I did not subjugate her with force...I did not act like a man. I was gentle...I wanted her love, instead of instilling in her the fear of my whip." (pp. 248-249)

The narrative evidence substantiates Uriah's suspicions and validates his view that a better use of his whip could have saved his life. This suggests that Uriah is giving expression not merely to his own figural point of view, but to that of the implied author as well. The latter, it would seem, argues the case of modern male chauvinism, while appearing to dramatize an ancient patriarchal consciousness.

The expanded literary treatment that Bathsheba receives in the modern story does not enhance her moral stature, but rather the opposite – it presents her as a scheming temptress.[7] By highlighting Bathsheba's interest in David, the novel suggests that David is merely a victim of her "feminine" wiles. Whereas the novel's focus on Uriah turns him into a hero, its treatment of Bathsheba transforms her into a villain. In the modern version, the woman evolves into an active and independent agent; she is made to bear the greater share of responsibility for the disastrous events that follow. The modern Bathsheba presents a portrait of the new woman as a willful shrew, whose independence undermines her husband's interests and even threatens his life. As such, she reflects, among other things, contemporary male anxiety over woman's liberation from patriarchal authority. Bathsheba's independence is portrayed as the source of her lasciviousness, treachery, and ruthless ambition. The implied author censures Bathsheba according to patriarchal standards; he criticizes her, because she dares to love someone other than her husband, and because she fails to fulfill woman's traditional domestic and maternal roles. The fundamental definition of woman as wife and mother remains the same in the modern version of the Biblical tale, but here the valuative implications of this definition are by far graver than those suggested by the original story.

Amos Oz's "Upon this Evil Earth" is a modern version of the Biblical story of Jephtah. In Judges 11, Jephtah's nameless daughter appears as a courageous and noble character.[8] In fact, her calm response to her father's outburst of anguish presents her as one of the most outstanding daughter-figures in the Bible: "My father, if you have opened your mouth to the Lord, do to me according to what has gone forth from your mouth, now that the Lord has avenged you on your enemies, on the Ammonites." (Judges 11:36) Yet in Amos Oz's story, Jephtah's daughter's valiant self-abnegation emerges in a considerably different light.

Pitdah (topaz), the name that Oz confers on Jephtah's daughter, is evocative of the luxury in which she was born and of the materialism characteristic of the life-style of her hedonistic mother, one of Jephtah's numerous Ammonite concubines. Pitdah is also the name of Jephtah's mother, Gilead's concubine, who is portrayed as a witch and a devotee of Milcom, the god of sensual pleasure. The association of Pitdah, the daughter, with Ammonite hedonism and witchcraft persists throughout the story. For example, the young girl often plays on a pipe songs that the Ammonite "harlots and concubines sang in the city square at night."[9]

Pitdah's fragility and sensuousness are incongruous with the arid, stark desert conditions, in which she is living with her father. While the nomads fight off their enemies and lead a tough battle for survival, the spoiled girl is busy "playing, dreaming, and laughing irrationally." (pp. 202-203) Although the narrative describes Pitdah's development into maidenhood, it seems rather that the older she becomes, the more she regresses into childhood. Her playfulness, silly giggles, and egocentricity are only a few of her childish features. The response of Jephtah's daughter as recorded in the Biblical narrative reflects extreme self-control and selflessness. Oz's Pitdah is childish and narcissistic: "...I love you, Father. And I love myself, too. And the places where you never take me, where the sun sets in the evening. Now, put this cloak over your head and moo, and I'll watch you and laugh." (p. 205)

Like Pitdah, Jephtah appears to be an outsider in his society, but whereas her exceptionalism stems from her meaningless behavior, his is of a different nature. Jephtah is the epitome of the existential outsider who finds society conventional and hypocritical, and he refuses to conform to it. He is a tragic hero, caught between his love for his pagan mother and the monotheistic heritage of his father. The story makes it clear that he becomes a leader not because of opportunism or through political maneuvering, but due to innate qualities and talents that inspire awe and respect in those around him. In contrast to the sensuous female characters – Nehushtah, Pitdah, his mother, his daughter, and his concubines – Jephtah is a spiritual man, a true servant of God.

The tragedy in the modern story is wholly Jephtah's. The climatic scene showing Pitdah in a bridal gown, coming out to greet her victorious father upon his return from the battle with the Ammonites, focuses on him. Jephtah "collapses to the ground" and "howls like [a] wolf pierced by an arrow," (p. 215) whereas his daughter continues to demonstrate thoughtless glee. In response to her father's anguished exclamations, "the girl laughed and answered: 'Put this cloak over your head and eyes and moo, and we'll watch you and laugh.' " (p. 216)

A considerable distance separates Oz's irrational Pitdah from the daughter of the Biblical narrative. Oz reduces the unforgettable response of a remarkable Biblical woman to the frivolous prattle of a silly girl. The Bible notes that Jephtah's daughter asks her father for two months in which to mourn for her youth and her virginity. (Judges 11:37) The modern version omits the daughter's request, probably because it would seem to contradict her depiction as a thoughtless character, incapable of appreciating life over death. Instead, it describes her mourning period on the mountains as filled with cheerful and aimless excursions. Like the mad and lovely Ophelia, Pitdah was "beautiful as she walked and laughed in her bridal wreath." (p. 216) While her madness and frivolity reduce the stature of Pitdah to that of a flat and rather predictable character, her depiction as a bride, and the emphasis on her sensuous attractiveness bring her within the stereotypical confines of woman as sex object.[10] From this viewpoint, the terse biblical description is more suggestive and less male-centered in its treatment of the female character than the modern version.

Biblical mothers are not exempt from the androcentric bias which seems to inspire the contemporary Israeli treatment of Biblical wives and daughters. A case in point is Pinhas Sadeh's characterization of Abimelech's mother in his novella, *The Death of Abimelech and his Ascent to Heaven in his Mother's Arms*. The Biblical story about Abimelech, who seizes control of the city of Shechem and ruthlessly kills seventy of his brothers, does not pay much attention to Abimelech's mother. (Judges 8:31) The modern writer, however, in his attempt to explain Abimelech's deeds, not only endows Gideon's concubine with a name; he also presents her as a savage girl, who rejects the luxury and comfort of her home and the eager courtiers who pursue her. At the early age of fourteen, according to Sadeh's narrative, Estehar sets fire to her father's barn and takes up a nomadic life-style, roaming the fields, and occasionally indulging in witchcraft. It is Estehar's emotional instability, her scorn for civilized conventionality, and her ardent belief in magic and witchcraft, which foreshadow the fundamental psychological make-up of her son, Abimelech. Apologizing for the somewhat lengthy description of Estehar, Sadeh's narrator admits that it is meant as an introduction for the real hero of the novella: "Perhaps it would be worthwhile to conclude with the comment that we expatiate on the history of Estehar, an embittered concubine who got lost in the intricate ways of this painful world, only because of Abimelech; for the few who knew Abimelech and who remembered him noticed the great resemblance between mother and son...."[11] Aspects of Estehar that have no import for Abimelech's development (i.e. the nature of the relationship between her and Gideon) find no expression in the novella. As soon as she gives birth to Abimelech, Estehar is whisked off the stage through the convenient literary convention of death at childbirth.

Yet, Estehar survives in Abimelech's imagination and dreams. She serves, in fact, as the main cause of Abimelech's murder of his brothers. In one of his dreams, Abimelech sees death riding on a black horse and holding a golden sword. On closer scrutiny, Abimelech recognizes the face of death as the face of his late mother. In his dream Abimelech sees her tossing the sword into the house of Gideon at Ophra. He interprets this act as a symbolic instruction to destroy Gideon's household. While the Biblical tale implies that Abimelech's murder of his brothers stems from a lust for power, the modern author intimates that Abimelech's acts are expressions of filial commitment. In consonance with Freudian theories about the mother's indelible impact on her child's future conduct, Estehar becomes the ultimate cause for Abimelech's savagery.

Estehar's unruliness is reincarnated in her son's anarchistic theology that ignores the traditional, moralistic definition of good and evil. The priest who anoints Abimelech as ruler proclaims that he is God's chosen, because God prefers the extreme evil personality to the insipid one. (p. 25) What appears in Estehar as primitive and destructive is transformed in her son into mysterious and paradoxically redemptive powers.

The image of Estehar, the beloved mother who leads her son to his spiritual victories, is counterbalanced by her evil double, who uses her physical resemblance to Estehar as a weapon against Abimelech. This false woman appears in the latter's dreams and lures him into the dangerous underworld of the flesh. (p. 45) The conflict between the demon-mother and the angel-mother dramatizes the hero's psychomachia. This symbolic bifurcation is not intended to characterize either woman, but rather, in the tradition of nineteenth-century, European romantic fiction, to clarify the aspirations and fears of the male hero. Abimelech's fluctuation between the false and the true maternal images is presented as the essential dynamic of his life and the ultimate cause of his death.

According to the Biblical story, Abimelech is struck down by a woman during his siege of the city of Thebez: "And a certain woman threw an upper millstone upon Abimelech's head, and crushed his skull." (Judges 9:53) In Biblical terms, this humiliating ending at the hands of a woman implies God's punishment. The modern version of the story, however, turns this humiliating end into a tragic and heroic one. It indicates that Abimelech drew dangerously close to the walls of the city, because he was captivated by the face of a girl with a strong resemblance to his mother: "...for his soul went out to the girl who was watching him from the top of the tower, and whose face was like the face of his mother. But was it, he asked himself, his real mother, or the false mother, who in his dreams had already lured him time and again to the devil's house?" (p. 94) Abimelech's hesitancy proved to be fatal, for at that moment the girl who appears to embody the false mother throws at him "something dark and round." This explanation of the strange mistake committed by Abimelech anchors the cause of his death in his Achilles' heel, his obsessive love for his mother.

Sadeh succeeds in transforming one of the Bible's most infamous villains into an heroic character. The ruthless, power-hungry ruler becomes, in the modern version, an idealist, a lovable eccentric, and an uncompromising, albeit unconventional, believer in God. Yet, the female characters remain opaque and essentially secondary to the male character, like their Biblical counterparts. Abimelech's mother is not treated in the Bible as an autonomous character, but as a nameless ancillary agent, whose significance for the story clearly derives from her procreative role and maternal link to the male hero.[12] Estehar, in the modern version, is essentially a secondary character; her main function consists of explaining Abimelech's behavior. Her metamorphosis into the symbol of truth, as opposed to the symbol of falsehood, serves to illuminate the erratic actions of the male hero. Similarly, the woman of Thebez receives little attention in the original story, but she emerges from it as an heroic figure. In the modern story, this achievement is denied her. Here, the woman of Thebez represents the image of the false woman, the treacherous female, who, by her beauty and beguiling appearance, brings about the death of an heroic man.[13]

The androcentric perspective of the modern story precludes a serious development of the mother figure. The story's male-centered perspective leaves unanswered potentially intriguing questions about Abimelech's mother. It would be interesting to reconstruct the character of Abimelech's mother as one who is forced to witness her son's ruthlessness and to endure shame or pride at her son's exploits. The original character of the nameless woman of Thebez is also intriguing. One wonders, for example, what motivates her to kill Abimelech. This question remains unanswered both in the Biblical and in the modern text.

Although the modern writers considered in this essay dedicate far more narrative space to their Biblical women, and some of them create female figures not mentioned in the original story, they do not shed much light on the motivations and inner lives of the women they create. Most of the Biblical women characterized in the above works are judged in relation to the male hero, whether as wife (Bathsheba), daughter (Pitdah), or mother (Estehar). When they fail the hero, they emerge as negative types (Bathsheba). When they do not emerge as negative types, they serve as foils enhancing the heroic stature of the male character. The relentless focus on the male hero serves to deny the female character – already a secondary character in the original tale – a chance to develop into a believable character, which might encourage a reader's identification with her. The characterization of Biblical women in much current Israeli fiction perpetuates the androcentric perspective which underlies the original representations. While humanizing male villains (Abimelech), deepening secondary characters (Uriah), or enhancing the tragic stature of male heroes (David, Jephtah) in the Bible, contemporary Israeli prose writers often fail to show a similar interest in, and concern for, female Biblical characters. While marginal Biblical women, like Abimelech's mother, continue to be used as auxiliary characters or foils for the male, characters, like Bathsheba, and heroic characters, like Jephtah's daughter, are demeaned. The treatment of Biblical women reflects a wider tendency in Israeli narrative fiction to marginalize and stereotype female characters, a tendency that is especially noticeable in male authored books.[14] The specific reasons for this tendency, the precise extent to which it deviates from previous tendencies to idealize women, the difference between poetry and narrative fiction regarding presentations of Biblical women in Israeli literature, and most important, the differences between male and female authored works on the subject are issues that lie beyond the scope of the present study. What can be concluded thus far is that the effort of (male) contemporary Israeli authors to humanize or deepen the characterization of Biblical characters is more successful when the latter are male. Female Biblical characters appear to be more central than their original counterparts. Yet, in the final analysis, they function mainly as foils for the male heroes – foils that emerge as far more pernicious than the peripheral female characters of the Hebrew Bible.

Notes

1 This is a substantially revised version of a paper I delivered at the annual convention of the Modern Language Association of America (Los Angeles, 1982), entitled "Images of Biblical Women in Contemporary Israeli Fiction." I would like to thank Elizabeth Abel and Stuart Lasine for their helpful comments. They have no part in the shortcomings of this essay. Thanks are due to the editorial assistance of Noel Wolf.

2 For an overview of the treatment of Biblical women in the Midrash and in modern Hebrew literature see *Women of the Bible* [*Nashim batanakh*], (Ed., Israel Zmora), (Tel Aviv: Mahbarot lesifrut, 1964). The main deficiencies in this anthology are that it fails to explain its selective principles and does not include bibliographical sources.

[3] A detailed analysis of the ideological functions of the major female role-models in the biblical narrative is offered in my book, ***Sexual Politics in the Biblical Narrative: Toward a Critical-Feminist Hermeneutics of the Hebrew*** sity Press, 1981), pp. 133-238.

[4] This and all the following quotations from the Hebrew Bible are from the Revised Standard Version.

[5] Adultery involving a married woman was a crime of the first magnitude under Israelite law (Lev. 20:10; Ex. 20:14). As Phyllis Bird points out, however: "The issue was not simply one of extramarital sex... . The issue was one of property and authority. Adultery was a violation of the fundamental and exclusive right of a man to the sexuality of his wife." See "Images of Women in the Old Testament," in Rosemary R. Ruether (Ed.), *Religion and Sexism* (New York: Simon and Schuster, 1974), pp. 41-88. The quotation is from page 51.

[6] *The Poor Man's Lamb* [*Kivsat harash*], (Tel Aviv: Sifriat Poalim, 1956). References to the book will be included in the text. This and all other quotations from the modern Hebrew works are my own translations.

[7] Abigail, Nabal's wife, who later becomes David's wife, also suffers from a reductive treatment in the modern story. Whereas she emerges from I Samuel 25 as a respectable woman capable of placating an angry ruler and of countering the effects of a short-sighted husband, Shamir's version stresses her sexual appeal, presenting her "colorful dress" and "big made-up eyes" as the devices through which she wins David's heart. (p. 189)

[8] See Phyllis Trible's Analysis of Judges 11 in *Texts of Terror: Literary-Feminist Readings of Biblical Narratives* (Philadelphia: Fortress Press, 1984), pp. 93-118. The positive depiction of Jephtah's daughter, however, serves the interests of a patriarchal ideology. For a detailed discussion of this point, see my essay, "Submission, Silence, Sacrifice: The Story of Jephtah's Daughter," in Lynda Boose and Betty S. Flowers (Eds.), *Fathers and Daughters* (The Johns Hopkins University Press, forthcoming).

[9] "On this Evil Earth," ("Al ha'adama hara'a hazot," included in the updated version of *The Lands of the Jackal* [*Artsot hatan*]), (Tel Aviv: Am Oved, 1976), p. 198. All following references to this story will appear in the text.

[10] The older female characters in Oz's story are stereotyped as sexual objects or nymphomaniacs. Pitdah, Jephtah's daughter, is a wild, sensuous, and hedonistic witch; Nehusha, Jephtah's stepmother, is a frustrated, jealous, and anemic *grande dame*; and Pitdah's mother is a licentious concubine, one of Jephtah's numerous conquests.

[11] *The Death of Abimelech and his Ascent to Heaven in his Mother's Arms (Mot avimelech va'aliyato hashamaima bizro'ot imo)*, (Jerusalem and Tel Aviv: Schocken, 1969), p. 10. All references to his work appear in the text.

[12] This seems to be characteristic of the literary representation of most biblical mothers. See my article, "The Literary Presentation of Mothers and Sexual Politics in the Bible," in Adela Yarbro Collins (Ed.), ***Feminist Perspectives on Biblical Scholarship***, (Chico: Scholars Press, 1985), pp. 117-136.

[13] Sadeh's characterization of other women in his story is rather hostile. Habakkuk's wife is the unfaithful bitch, driving her husband to despair. The woman who seduces Jephet is the adulterous wife of an Egyptian officer. Pabi is a beautiful girl who tries to seduce Abimelech and, having failed, commits suicide. Illicit sex and violent death seem to figure in the lives of all the female characters in the story.

[14] See my forthcoming book: *Sex, Ideology, and Fiction: The Presentation of Women in Israeli Fiction, 1948-1980* (to be published by University of New York Press).

Jonah in the Belly of the Whale: The Iconography of a Passage Rite

Tsili Dolève-Gandelman
and
Claude Gandelman

Jonah and Christian Iconography

Since the beginning of Christianity, Jonah has been an omnipresent theme in religious iconography, because Jonah, the Hebrew prophet, is a prefiguration or prototype of Jesus Christ. In the *Bible des Pauvres* (see appendix, fig. 1), Jonah is depicted on the right panel of the tryptich illustration. Joseph in his pit is on the left panel. Both are pre-figures of Jesus, who is being entombed in the middle image. Jonah, who is about to enter the mouth of the whale (in the lower right-hand corner of the image), is seen as parallel to Jesus, here being lowered into his tomb. Similarly, in the Portable Altar from Stavelot,[1] Jonah, being swallowed by the fish, and Samson, carrying away the doors of Gaza, are depicted parallel to the death and resurrection of Jesus. The association of Jonah with Jesus stems from the New Testament. It is Jesus himself, as recorded in Luke 11:29 and Matthew 12:39-40, who refers to "the sign of the prophet Jonah": "As Jonah was three days and three nights in the whale's belly, so shall the Son of Man be three days and three nights in the heart of the earth."

Another reason Jonah is seen as a prefiguration of Christ concerns Christian commentaries of certain apocalyptic passages in Job (39:20 and 41:4, 5, 10, 11, 22), where the "jaws of Satan," that is, of Hell, are equated with the jaws of the Leviathan. God speaks to Job and asks: "Wilt thou catch the monster with thy hook? Who shall penetrate between its jaws? Who shall open the doors of its snout?..." For the Christian commentators, of course, the answer is Jesus.

As Jonah was in the belly of the whale three days, Jesus descended into Hell and remained there for three days. Saint Gregory, Odon of Cluny, and Bruno of Asti visualize Jesus actually descending, like Jonah, into the mouth of the Leviathan, the embodiment of Hell, and breaking its jaw open with his hook; that is, the Cross (fig. 2).

What is remarkable is that many of the Christian illustrators seem to have known the interpretations of Jonah given by the Jewish Midrashim and Aggadot.[2] There is, for instance, a Midrash in which it is said that the intense heat in the body of the whale made the hair of the prophet fall out;[3] accordingly, he is depicted hairless, coming out of the mouth of the whale in the Spanish *Rippoll Bible* (fig. 3) and in the *Armenbibel of Vienna* or "Codex Vindobonensis" of 1198 (fig. 4). More astonishing yet, in the *Rippoll Bible*, Jonah is depicted (having eventually recovered his hair) as ascending into the hand of God (upper right hand corner of the picture). This is a clear allusion to another Midrash, namely that Jonah was permitted to enter paradise *alive.*[4] Not only is the prophet "descending into his tomb" like Jesus, but he is also ascending alive ("resurrected") into heaven. We shall return to this very important Midrash later. In the meantime, a word must be said concerning anti-Semitic aspects of some illustrations.

Though many of the Christian illustrators seem to have been well acquainted with Jewish Midrashim and Aggadot, certain artists seem to have given an anti-Jewish twist to pictures depicting the boat episode in the Jonah story. Thus, in the *Bible des Pauvres* (see fig. 1), the three men of the crew who throw Jonah overboard wear the conical hats which were typical of the Jews during the period. The crew also have beards, clearly a sign of Jewish identity. Similarly, in the *Salzburger Armenbibel*, in the scene depicting the casting away of Jonah, the Jews wearing conical hats are throwing Jonah overboard (fig. 5). In both cases, that Jonah does not have a beard and does not wear the Jewish hat seems to indicate that he is seen as non-Jewish by the artists.

There is no doubt that for such artists Jonah was a prefiguration of Jesus, not only because of his "descending into Hell" and being resurrected thereafter, but also because he had been "cast into the sea by the Jews" – a meaning which, of course, is imparted visually by the pictures to the naive audiences who decifer them. Interestingly, this anti-Semitic twist does not seem to exist in artists who knew the Midrashic and Aggadic interpretations and represented Jonah as "hairless" (as far as we have been able to ascertain after examining dozens of pictures). Could this mean that some of the artists were Jews or possibly "New Christians?"

Psychoanalytic Interpretations of the Story

After giving this brief account of Christian interpretations, we move on to 20th-century psychoanalytic interpretations of the Jonah story. The chief exponent of such interpretations is Otto Rank. For him, what is decisive in the causal chain which constitutes human existence is not the "Oedipus complex," the relation to the father, but the "trauma of birth."[5] According to him, all human phantasms and fantasies (and, for Rank, myths and religious writings are such fantasies) are the result of the continued efforts which man makes in order to overcome the original "trauma of birth" by re-enacting it in symbolic form. Religion, but also art, achieves such a "re-enacting." In other words, according to Rank, the aim of the individual and of all humanity is the "fictitious" return into the pre-nirvana that was the womb of the mother.

Such a view can be reconciled with Christian interpretations. In certain Christian "myths," God is provided with a uterus. Thus, in the writings of one of the Church Fathers, Petavius, one reads: "... The Son is begotten of the Father from the uterus: although in God there is no uterus, moreover nothing physical, yet in him there is a real creation, a real birth, which is shown even in the word 'uterus.' "[6]

Indeed, the Church itself, both as an institution and as an architectural locus, is often seen in Patristic literature, as well as in many Christian writings throughout the Middle Ages, as "the womb which contains the body of Christ."[7] This is meant not only in the sense that the Church is a "spiritual entity" metaphorically enclosing Christ, but also as a temple made of stones which is actually a "womb made of stones."

Here, incidentally, architectural language provides a link with the Jonah story. Is not this "architectural womb" of the Church called a *nef*, a "nave," that is, the body of a ship? Thus, the Jonah story can be described in terms of Jonah's passing from the "belly of a nave" of a ship to the "belly of the sea" and thence to the "belly of the big fish." Jonah's "pilgrim's progress" is a succession of "being swallowed alive" by various maws until he reaches the final "nave" of paradise. This leads to the idea of the "circularity of being swallowed/swallowing" which can be found in some of the major religions.

Being Swallowed/Swallowing

We would like to suggest here that Christian religion might be described in terms of a circular structure uniting the "swallower" and the "swallowed." Man is already inside the "womb of God" when spewed into Creation – the world – by a human womb, and man returns to the nirvana of pre-birth which is also the nirvana of pre-creation after death. But, in Christianity, between "being spewed out" and the final "being swallowed into," the transformation takes place in reverse order. Christian religion also provides believers with the possibility of "swallowing their swallower" symbolically. This is done through the sacrament of the eucharist, in which the faithful literally "swallow" the body of Christ (*hoc est corpus meum*).

This is one way of reaching the *union mystique*, the being at one with the All, a union which is not only described by a neo-Platonist like Plotinus in the *Enneads*, but also in the Indian *Upanishads*: "Just as when a man is embraced by the beloved, he has no consciousness of that which is outside and inside, so also the mind which is engulfed by the primal self has no consciousness of that which is outside or inside."[8] The Indian metaphor, of course, is sexual and not "oral," as is the case with the Jonah myth or the Christian "eucharist." Yet, the idea is similar; it is that of the interpenetration of man and God.

Furthermore, this circular structure of "being swallowed/swallowing" is also present in the Christian description of the eucharistic meal, as a meal in which a *fish* is eaten in common by the apostles. This certainly relates to the Jewish Midrashim in which paradise is conceived as a banquet in which the sages eat the body of the Leviathan.[9] In the specific Christian context, "fish" stands for "Christ"; indeed, the Greek name for "fish," ICHTYS (IχΘγΣ), is an anagram of CHRIST.[10] But Jonah was swallowed by a "big fish!" Thus, it can be said that another reason which accounts for the fact that Jonah is a prototype of Jesus is his "host"-like quality. He was swallowed by the fish, just as Jesus lets himself be swallowed by his own (fellow) creatures.

The Temple as Whale

The architectonical church, too, manifests this circularity. As already mentioned, the church as a building is a "womb containing the body of Christ." But it is a "womb" which also "swallows" the body of the believer, at least during the moment of the cult or of prayer. The believer, too, is a "swallower" and absorbs physically – if symbolically – the body which "contains him."

We would like to dwell for a moment on the idea of the temple as a womb, be it a church, a *beit-knesset*, or even the *beit-hamikdash*. To the best of our knowledge, the symbol of the Church-womb exists only in the literature of the Christian Church. We do not know of any church which *actually* has the shape of a womb or even the shape of a real human body, although it is true that the plan of the church, which is usually a cross, has *symbolically* the shape of Christ's body on the cross.

Outside the Western realm there are numerous examples of temples which *actually* have the form of bodies, human or otherwise (although not of whales' bodies). Such is the case with many Central American Mayan temples, which often have the shape of a wide-open, all-engulfing maw. Entering the temple on the top of the main pyramid at Uxmal (Mexico) is tantamount to *entering the body* of the God Chac (fig. 6). This is also true of most of the other Chac temples in the region. (The Anthropological Museum of Mexico City contains an exact reproduction of such an anthropomorphic Mayan temple).

Similarly, in the realm of Buddhism there are numerous temples in the shape of Buddha. The faithful "enter" the body of their god. We reproduce here the picture of a "God-maw" on the wall of a Bangkok temple (fig. 7).

What about Jonah's "fish" or "whale?" Is it not the zoomorphic representation of a temple? Actually, one of the Midrashim interprets it in this sense: "At the creation of the world, God made a fish intended to harbor Jonah. He was so large that the prophet was as comfortable inside of him *as in a spacious synagogue*. The eyes of the fish served Jonah as windows, and, besides, there was a diamond, which shone as brilliantly as the sun at midday so that Jonah could see all things in the sea down to its very bottom."[11]

We might add that what we have here is not only a prefiguration of the story of Jesus, but also of Jules Verne's Nautilus. Certain Medieval artists seem to have known this Midrash or similar ones. For instance, the Greek artist who illuminated the so-called *Psalter of Mount Athos* depicts Jonah comfortably seated inside the belly of the whale (fig. 8). He is seen as though by transparency, and a red light (in the original color of the manuscript) seems to emanate from his body as though the idea of the "big diamond" had been transferred to Jonah himself. However it may be, the "synagogue-whale" of the Midrash is the Jewish equivalent of the Central American or Far-Eastern temples as anthropomorphic or zoomorphic beings, as the architectural-anthropomorphic "body of the soul."

The Journey "in the Belly of the Whale" as a Passage Rite

The anthropological concept of *rites de passage* or passage rites also throws some light on the Jonah story. Passage rite, a much used notion in the field of anthropology, was defined by Arnold Van Gennep in his famous book by the same title.[12] He described passage rites as those rituals which accompany every change of place, state, social position, and age. While the contents of specific rituals may differ from one to the other, they nevertheless all have the same triadic structure. The first sequence in the triad consists of "separation rites" concerning the world one leaves. For instance, in the initiation rites of puberty, the world of boyhood and the society of children are left behind by the initiate. The *median sequence*, which is of primary interest here, was labeled by Van Gennep *rites de marge* or *rites liminaires* and marks the *passage itself.*[13] It is in this sense that we shall consider the Jonah story as a "liminal" story. The *third* sequence is that of the "aggregation rites" by which the new world is incorporated, for instance, the social world of men and adults by the initiated boy.

While the passage of time is symbolically "woven" into the very structure of passage rites by the succession of the three sequences just mentioned, Van Gennep showed that a *passage in space* also takes place in the liminal phase of the passage rites.[14] We shall therefore also explore Jonah's adventure from this perspective.

In a classic article, "Betwixt and Between: Liminality Period," Victor Turner described the symbolism attached to the liminal *persona.* The essential feature of the person who passes through passage rites is that of dying (in respect to the old world) and being reborn (in respect to the new). This is a double process which takes place simultaneously during the liminal phase and explains the fact that the metamorphosis or transformation occuring during the passage ritual is cloaked in ambiguity and paradox. In the liminal phase of the Ndembu initiation rites, for instance, the neophytes are said to be "neither living nor dead from one aspect and both living and dead from another."[16] Yet, for Turner, liminality is not only a situation of ambiguity and paradox, but also of creativity and invention. It corresponds to the open-endedness in biological evolution.[17] Another anthropologist, Terence Turner, also insisted that paradox and ambiguity are characteristic of the liminal phase of passage rites. For him, this is due to the fact that in the classification of everyday life, dominated by what one might call "secular logic," the liminality and transformations occuring in the passage rites cannot be accommodated. For instance, in everyday life where secular logic is dominant, the social status of a boy and that of an adult are two mutually exclusive categories. On the contrary, the passage rites provide a higher logical matrix through which those two social categories are no longer exclusive but complementary. This ritualistic or sacred logic is, nevertheless, expressed in what seems to be paradoxical and ambiguous language from the "secular logic" point of view.[18]

Material passage (*le passage matériel*), the actual passage through space, may be expressed in ritual by the procession of participants, by their passing through porticos, standing under canopies, etc. Nicole Belmont, a French anthropologist, has recently analyzed the traditional marriage procession in Europe from this perspective.[19] Victor Turner, in the course of his field work among the Ndembu, remarked on the frequent use of tunnels during the liminal phase (tunnels which are tombs and wombs at the same time).

Whereas passage rites call for a symbolic passage in space, the reverse situation can also happen: the passage in space calls for a ritual act and is marked by porticos, by a cross set up at a crossroads, by the *mezuza* in traditional Jewish homes. The person who passes through a portico is in a liminal situation, as is the man who sets out on a voyage (the portico, incidentally, may represent the voyage itself). From this derives the special status of the stranger, the *voyageur*, in traditional societies. Spatial passage and liminality are connected. Let us observe once more that for Van Gennep the marking of passage in space is not only a symbol, but also a concrete reality.[20] Through her analysis of European folk costumes, Nicole Belmont arrived at the conclusion that the material passage so important for Van Gennep is conceived *after the anatomic reality of birth*, the very first passage carried out by any living being.[21] Here, Belmont, though working with different data and from a different perspective, supported the analysis made by Otto Rank concerning the trauma of birth.

From the outset, the Jonah story tells us about a liminal situation. Jonah himself, who as the Midrash says "entered the world of the dead alive," is portrayed as a liminal figure. Yet, not only the episode in the fish, but the entire structure of the Jonah adventure revolves around the idea of passage in space, so characteristic of passage rites and especially of the liminal phase of these rites. Indeed, the very words of God to Jonah at the beginning of his adventure call on him to set out for a journey: "Koom lekh..." ("Arise, go to Nineveh.") The plot develops following Jonah's reaction to the order, a reaction which, indeed, is a spatial motion, but *in the opposite direction* to that commanded by the Lord. By taking this course, Jonah has put himself into a *liminal situation*. The liminality of his spatial motion is emphasized even more by the voyage on the sea, since the sea, symbolically and mythonomically, refers to the arch-model of *passage matériel*: the parturition process and birth.[22]

The passage in space continues, but this time *in depth*. Jonah is no longer progressing horizontally on the surface of the sea but is cast overboard into the *depths* of the sea in order to prevent the shipwreck of the boat. Jonah finds himself in the belly of the fish, the tomb and the womb, in the typical liminal position described by Victor Turner. He is also in total and invisible seclusion, another characteristic of the liminal phase.[23]

The entrails of the whale in the depth of the sea ("I went to the bottom of the mountains" [2:6]) is the climax of the vertical, spatial passage. From this point, there can only be progress in the backward direction. As in a film in reverse, after being swallowed Jonah is spewed out. After he moves again in horizontal space, God speaks to him for the second time. This time, Jonah accepts the mission and resumes his itinerary in horizontal space: he finally goes to Nineveh, as was demanded of him in the first place. But, Nineveh itself is a liminal city, since it reveals open-endedness, the possibility of transformation (V. Turner). When Jonah's prophecy is not fulfilled, he leaves the city and sits on the east side of the city. He makes a booth and sits under it in the shade. (5:3) Jonah has settled down and sits down. Through this action, we are aware that he is saved from his previous liminal position. Yet, the spatial passage in its most liminal aspect, the passage *on a vertical axis*, continues. This is made manifest by the episode of the growth and sudden dying of the gourd. This last episode indicates the end of passage and the integration into the new world.

Let us observe that the Midrash itself considers Jonah a liminal figure from beginning to end. It is the Midrash which tells that Jonah entered the world of the dead alive,[24] and that he lost his hair in the entrails of the whale, a typical occurrence in separation rites.[25] In addition to the continued passage through space – horizontal and vertical (during the period of three days inside the fish) – Jonah's story implicitly contains another characteristic of the paradoxical liminal phase of passage rites. We have already mentioned that the symbolism of the liminal period is often embedded in paradox and that the logic of this period is set apart from the logic of everyday life. Whereas the passage in space functions as a sort of frame story indicating the liminality of Jonah's adventures, it is the discrepancy between Jonah's secular logic and divine or sacred logic which constitutes the semantic core of the story. Whereas Jonah's logic is "closed," linear logic, where the future is determined by the past, divine logic is "open." In it, the future can be prophesied but *not determined* (witness the prophecy concerning the destruction of Nineveh which is not realized). This "open-endedness," as we have seen, is one of the main features of liminality.

One might say that Jonah, in his clinging to secular logic, is (paradoxically) the contrary of the liminal *persona*. But Jonah's life story is ultimately the story of divine intervention which forced him to live the paradox characteristic of liminality. One might contend that Jonah never reached the final "aggregation" stage and remained a "living/dead." This permanent liminality of the prophet would explain why, according to the Midrash, he was allowed to enter paradise alive. Even this paradise, in certain Midrashim, is seen as the continuation of a liminal stage. Derekh Erez tells us: "The statement that Jonah was permitted to enter paradise alive is understood in the sense that he awaits there the end of time to start on his Messianic mission. The Messiah, the son of David, likewise entered Paradise alive and awaits there 'his time.' "[26]

In Judaism, the fact that the Jonah story is read aloud on Yom Kippur – this very liminal day in the year – also testifies to the liminal character of the story. In Christian iconography, at least one picture shows the liminality of the whale episode: a relief in the church of Sion in Switzerland. In it, Jonah is shown holding in his hand the ear of a large mask, much larger than himself, a mask which can reasonably be interpreted as his *persona*, in the Latin sense of the word (fig. 9). According to an art historian: "*L'homme (Jonah) ressort de la gueule bras levèes, affranchi de la mort par la naissance à une vie nouvelle. Il tient à la main l'oreille du masque qui lui a comuniquè sa vie et dont il est solidaire à jamais*."[27] This mask is his *persona*, of which he had to divest himself in order to emerge "aggregated" into a new life.

We would like to conclude by tentatively extending the concept of liminality to churches and temples in general, that is, by extending it to the psychology of everyday religious life. The whale stage in the Jonah story seems to us to be the sign of the liminality stage all truly religious people go through on a day-to-day basis. It is the sign of the daily entering of the synagogue, the church, the temple, when the faithful *literally* "enter the fish" and remain there in a state which is "neither life nor death" – until they finally recuperate their social consciousness, their *persona*, in order to "aggregate" themselves, momentarily, into "normal" life.

Notes

[1] Reproduced in Emile Mâle, *Religious Art in France in the 12th Century* (Princeton: Princeton University Press, 1978), p. 165.

[2] Classic studies concerning the influence of Jewish Midrashim and Aggadot on Christian Literature are, for instance, Louis Ginzberg, *Die Haggada bei den Kirchenvätern und in der apokryphischen Literatur* (Berlin: S. Calvary, 1900), or Benzion Kellerman, *Der Midrash zum I. Buche Samuelis u. seine Spuren bei Kirchenvätern* (Frankfurt a. Main: J. Kauffman, 1896).

[3] Louis Ginzberg, *The Legends of the Jews* (Philadelphia: The Jewish Publication Society of America, 1967), Vol. IV, p. 252. n. 36.

[4] Ginzberg, *ibid*, p. 253 and n. 38.

[5] See Otto Rank, *The Trauma of Birth* (New York: Robert Brunner, 1952).

[6] Rank, p. 123, n. 1. Quote from Petavius, *De Trinitate*, V/7, 4.

[7] See, for instance, Leonard Barker, *Nature's Work of Art* (New Haven and London: Yale University Press, 1975) pp. 69-71, 135.

[8] Quoted by Rank, *ibid.*, p. 176.

[9] Louis Ginzberg, I, 27; IV, 249; V, 43, 44, 48.

[10] Cf. F. Dölger, *Das Fisch-Symbol in frühchristlichen Zeiten als Kürzung der Namen Jesu* (Münster: 1928).

[11] L. Ginzberg, *ibid.*, Vol. IV, p. 249.

[12] A. Van Gennep, *Les Rites de Passage* (Paris: A. et J. Picard, 1981). English edition, *The Rites of Passage* (London: Routledge and Kegan Paul, 1960).

[13] N. Belmont, in her *Les Signes de la Naissance* (Paris: Plon, 1971), expressed a somewhat similar view.

[14] Van Gennep, *Les Rites de Passage*, p. 275-6.

[15] V. Turner, *The Forest of Symbols* (Ithaca and London: Cornell University Press, 1967), pp. 93-111.

[16] V. Turner, pp. 96-97.

[17] V. Turner, *Dramas, Fields, and Metaphors: Symbolic Action in Human Society* (Ithaca: Cornell University Press, 1974).

[18] Cf. Terence Turner, "Transformation, Hierarchy and Transcendence: A Reformulation of Van Gennep's Model of the Structure of the *Rites de Passage*," in F.S. Moore and B. Myertoff (Eds.), *Secular Ritual* (Amsterdam/Assen: Van Corcum, 1977).

[19] N. Belmont, "Les cortèges de mariage," *Annales* 33 (2), 150-55.

[20] Van Gennep, p. 275.

[21] N. Belmont, "La Notion de Rite de Passage," Colloquium on "The Rites of Passage Today," Neuchâtel. Forthcoming in the Acts of the Colloquium.

[22] Belmont, in *Les Signes de la Naissance*, shows that the ocean is the place of a second birth in certain ceremonies and in the case of imperfect birth.

[23] V. Turner, *Dramas, Fields, and Metaphors*, p. 95.

[24] Ginzberg, IV, p. 253 and n. 38.

[25] Van Gennep, p. 238.

[26] See Ginzberg, IV, p. 147. Quoted from *Derekh Erez* (2:1).

[27] See de Champeaux and Dom Sebastian Sterckx, *Introduction au Monde des Symboles* (Paris, Zodiaque, 1972), commentary to Fig. 135.

Acknowledgement

The authors wish to thank the Commission for Basic Research of the Israel Academy of the Sciences, whose research grant made this study possible.

Fig. 1: Bible des Pauvres: "La mise au Tombeau"

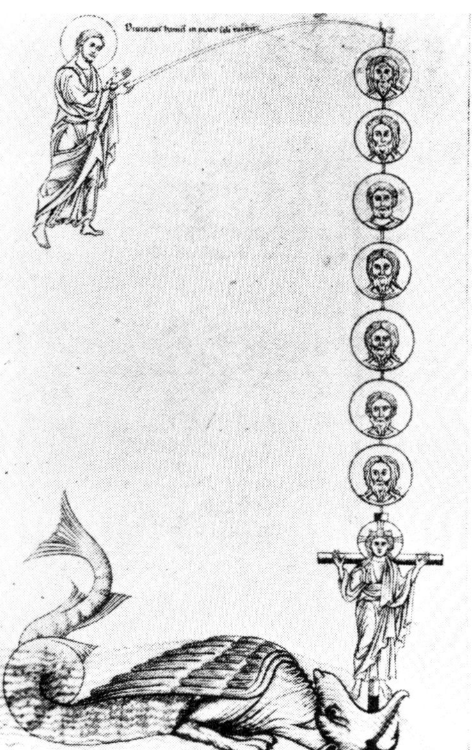

Fig. 2: Hortus Deliciarum: "The capture of Leviathan"

Fig. 3: Rippoll Bible: "The bis-fish episode and final ascension of Jonah to Heaven

Fig. 4: The Vienna Armenbibel: "Jonah comes hairless out of the fish: a parallel to the Resurrection"

Fig. 5: The Salzburger Armenbibel: "The casting out of Jonah"

Fig. 6: Entrance to the high pyramid at Uxmal, Mexico

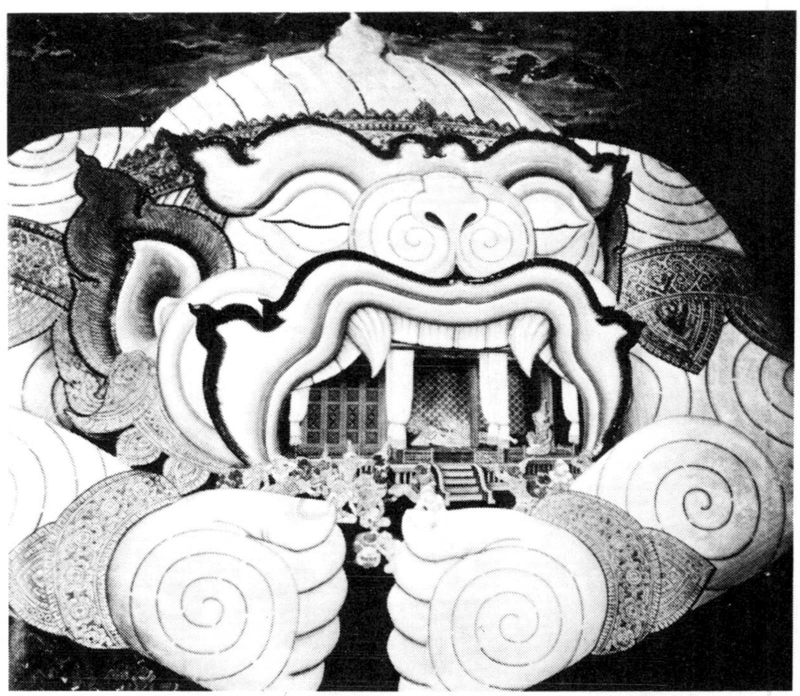

Fig. 7: Representation of an anthropomorphic temple: fresco in the Pagoda of the Emerald Buddha, Bangkok

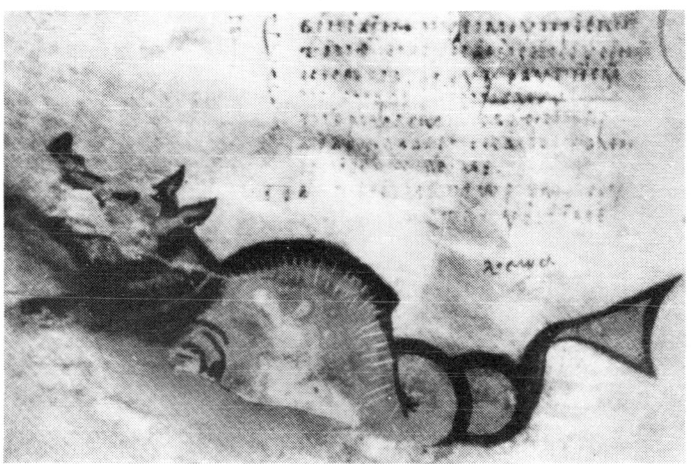

Fig. 8: Psalter of Mount Athos: "Jonah in the belly of the Fish"

Fig. 9: Capital of the Valère Cathedral at Sion, Switzerland: "Jonah coming out of the fish and holding the Mask"

Israel Salanter and the *Musar* Movement

Levi Shalit

I

Like the Baal Shem Tov, spiritual mentor of the Hassidic movement, so too Israel Salanter, founder of the *Musar* (ethical) movement, used to stroll about communing with the Divine. In the course of his solitary meditations, at one with nature in the forests surrounding Salant, he sought to attain a union with the Creator of the universe and to fathom the meaning of divine creation. Just as the Baal Shem Tov did not find full satisfaction solely in learning Torah, so Rabbi Israel Salanter was not satisfied merely with "dry" faith. He felt that faith must be supplemented by reason. God must be grasped by the intellect as well as by the heart, by logic as well as by the will to believe. Rabbi Salanter taught that a system of ethics does not by itself make a person pious, but it helps toward piety by pointing out the path to dutiful living. A person must ask himself: "What is my duty, my responsibility as a human being? What am I required to do, using as my guide my own reason, imperfect and inadequate though it be?" In contrast to Hassidic importunities to God, *Musar* came upon the scene with importunities to the self. In contrast to the slogan of the men of Enlightenment – "Know the World!" – Rabbi Salanter propounded the slogan as in the Temple of Delphi: "Know thyself!"

Hermann Cohen said: "Of what value is the question – 'What is?' – if it is not followed by both the question and the answer – 'What ought to be?' " The answer of the adherents of *Musar* was: "Man ought to become more noble, more moral." In Hermann Cohen's opinion, the problem of logic was nature, while the problem of ethics was man. *Musar* preferred the word God to the word nature. It recognized that human logic had limitations and could not fathom the ways of God. However, the feeling for what is good, for what is proper ethical behaviour, was dictated by a moral seismograph within us. Man must refine this seismograph which registered every deviation from right. He must battle against such deviations, he must war against his evil impulses, he must concentrate on good deeds. He will be serving God in this way, because human morality is the highest expression of the divine will. The natural tendency of men is to gravitate downwards. Yet, he can achieve moral greatness, by working deliberately towards it. While Hassidism held that even in impurity there was a spark of holiness which must be sought out and retained, *Musar* undertook to wrestle uncompromisingly with the evil tendencies in man which accompanied him from birth. While Hassidism emphasised man's good intentions, *Musar* held that good intentions were not enough. They must be embodied in good deeds. A human being must constantly labor to purify himself, not in order to bring the divine presence down to earth, but rather in order to raise himself to ever higher heights, in order that he might attain what was definitely within his reach. While Hassidism plunged into mystic depths in an effort to fathom the mysteries of God's world, *Musar*, to a large extent, bypassed God's eternally inscrutable ways and centered its attention on man, the living individual who is impelled by longings and instincts, good traits and bad ones.

The Messianic idea, which occupied the Jewish imagination throughout the millennia of Jewish dispersion and which was central to all previous movements, played no role whatsoever in *Musar*. The founder of this movement and his successors did study the Zohar and other Cabbalistic texts. They longed for the land of Israel and believed in a coming Jewish redemption. Rabbi Joseph Zundel Salanter, whom Rabbi Israel Salanter regarded as his teacher, left for the land of Israel in 1838, while under the influence of his own teacher, Rabbi Haim of Volozhin, then famed as a lover of Zion. Among Rabbi Israel Salanter's pupils there were several who settled in the Holy Land and founded study houses there. As a movement, however, *Musar* did not stress the will to national redemption. *Musar* did not emphasize the effect of a person's good deeds upon the course of God's world and upon the fate of the Jewish people. *Musar* was more interested in the moral life of the individual self. A moral society, it held, must start with the individual as a morally responsible person. Society was the sum of such individuals. Whereas

Hassidism based itself on the social fraternity, the brotherhood of believing Hassidim, *Musar* was based on the individual. It taught that even if there were no other persons and no society, but only the self alone in the entire world, the self would still have to behave as a moral being.

It has been claimed that *Musar* stressed the *mitzvot*, the Jewish precepts governing human relationships. This is not precise. *Musar* stressed the self and individual responsibility. As a corrolary, there naturally followed man's responsibility to his fellow-men, to his people, to humanity as a whole. A truly moral society would arise as a union of moral individuals. Since *Musar* grew out of synagogue worship and Talmud study, it also preserved and even strengthened the religious enclosures of Jewishness, the *mitzvot* that regulated man's relation to God. It saw no contradiction between the two types of relationships. They were to be seen as two complementary aspects that merged into a unity. The *mitzvot* were laws for moral behaviour that emanated from God, the source of morality. Torah was the moral code which could be grasped by the reasoning mind of man. This approach was consistent with Jewish teaching of all preceding eras, from the Pharisees to the Gaon of Vilna.

Hassidism revived ancient ideas, but it poured them into new vessels. As Rabbi Nachman of Bratslav explained: "I meet with opposition because I travel on a new road where nobody else before me travelled." *Musar* tried to clarify the essence of old ideas in the original vessels, retaining their patina and aroma. It was not a revolutionary movement. Its newness resided in its intensity and sharper coloring.

II

Many of Rabbi Israel Salanter's teachings and rules of behaviour coincide with those of the ethical writers of Central Europe who arose in the thirteenth century in the Jewish communities of Ratisbon, Speyer, Worms, and Mainz, and whose religious trend was best formulated in the *Sefer Hasidim*, the *Book of the Pious*, composed by Judah Ben Samuel of Ratisbon, known as Judah the Pious. This influence of the medieval moralists of Germany may perhaps explain why Salanter was subconsciously drawn to the Jewish communities of Germany. The *Musar* movement of Lithuania may be seen as a late continuation of these moralists, even though this German-Jewish trend had already faded from the memory of the Eastern European communities. Salanter and his pupils did not mention this medieval tendency and did not study the *Sefer Hasidim*. They rather harked back to sources more remote in time and more distant in space, the works of the great Sephardic scholars.

The earliest of the Sephardic philosophers, who derived from the Torah moral laws and ethical concepts with which to start a special trend in Judaism, was Rabbi Bahya Ben Joseph Ibn Pakuda in eleventh-century Spain. His main work, *Hobot Halebabot (The Duties of the Heart)*, was widely read. It taught that the essence of all piety was a pure heart, that the doing of good for its own sake and in gentle humility was more pleasing to God than fervent prayers and ostentatious piety. Other religious moralists who stressed morality as the most essential teaching of the Torah included Bahya's contemporary, Solomon Ibn Gabirol in the text *Midot Hanefesh (On the Improvement of the Qualities of the Soul)*; Jonah Ben Abraham Gerundi (1189-1263) in the tract *Shaare Teshuba (Gates of Repentence)* and in sermons on the ethics of the Torah; and, far more clearly and systematically, Moses Haim Luzzatto in *Mesillat Yesharim (Path of the Upright)*, published in 1740.

Many fruitful Jewish ideas of the post-exilic centuries arose among prominent Sephardic thinkers, but these ideas lived on mostly in books. Among Ashkenazic Jewry, however, these ideas took root in life and won adherents sometimes in small circles and sometimes in larger ones. Sephardic Jews were less numerous, their communities were not as big, and their philosophers penned their thoughts in a style that would appeal to a select audience of intellectual aristocrats. Non-Jewish philosophers of the Iberian Peninsula and of Italy also directed their teaching and writing to small, elite circles. This was true both of the Islamic thinkers and poets who wrote in Arabic and of the Christian theologians who wrote in Latin. It was even more true of the post-medieval scholars and creative artists throughout the Renaissance. None of them had in mind the masses as their potential audience. Among the Sephardic thinkers there was an additional consideration for their reluctance to take the masses into their confidence, literate though these masses were. The religious speculations of the Sephardim were connected with the desire for Jewish redemption. Their tendency was to strengthen faith in the coming of the Messiah. Such an ideal goal could only be entrusted to the few who were deserving, able, and willing to cherish it. Movements for liberation, national and social, usually begin as conspiracies hatched in secret, often among the intelligentsia. Jews living under Islam or in fanatically Christian lands had to be secretive about their fervent striving for redemption from exile. The authors of the ethical tracts sought to achieve this Messianic redemption, or at least to bring it nearer, by living more ethically, by self-purification, by striving toward moral perfection. Many of them, including Luzzato, were Cabbalists intent on intensifying faith in redemption. The followers of *Musar* in Lithuania studied Luzzato's *Mesillat Yesharim* with great ardor.

Luzzato, who was born in Padua in 1707, and died in Acre in 1746, spent his entire short life immersed in Cabbala. His knowledge of Latin opened up to him areas of secular and scientific learning. He has been called the father of neo-Hebrew literature, both because of his elegant style and the richness of his subject matter, embodied in narratives, dramas, poems, and essays. One of his most beautiful dramas was *Migdal Oz (Tower of Strength)*, written in an allegorical pastoral style and widely imitated later.

Luzzatto is still esteemed for his beautiful poems and poetic dramas, but he regarded his Cabbalistic works as his most important ones. With a *minyan*, ten disciples, he conducted mystic rites designed to hasten the hour of redemption. Falsely accused of continuing the heresies of the pseudo-Messiah Shabbatai Zvi, he suffered persecution, was banished from his native Padua, and wandered about from place to place. It was, therefore, natural for him throughout his life to long for Jewish redemption, a longing that permeated his literary works and was best expressed in his *Mesillat Yesharim*. The purpose of *Mesillat Yesharim* was to outline the path to holiness, to teach how to ascend by various gradations, or portals, from sinful living to absolutely perfect moral conduct.

The final stage would be Jewish ecstacy, as redemption came to the sons of Zion.

This goal was also formulated in another of Luzzatto's ethical tracts, *Derekh Etz Haim*. In its introduction, he quoted the prophecy of Hosea on the ingathering of the children of Judah and of Israel under a single leader and the ascent to the land of their origin. He then hinted quite clearly that he, Moses Haim Luzzatto, regarded himself as the leader capable of bringing about this ingathering and redemption, because "from Moses to Moses there arose none like Moses."

The question may well be asked: "Why was such a book so popular among the so-called "dry" scholars, the Lithuanian *Mitnagdim*, who did not share the author's intense ardor for redemption?" Here, we witness, as so often with fecund ideas, a transformation and reinterpretation of the original idea, when it establishes roots in a new soil and in a later era, under changed circumstances and a different spiritual climate, amidst altered aims and ideals.

The life and character of Luzzatto, his mating of poetry and scholarship, of dream and reality, or morality and rationalistic philosophy, must have made an impact upon Salanter. The latter's bent toward philosophy came to the fore in his efforts to know the writings of Immanuel Kant. Though Kant himself was not acquainted with Jewish thought and showed no interest in it, as Hermann Cohen proved, Jewish intellectuals were among his best disciples and interpreters. They included Moses Mendelssohn, Salomon Maimon, Franz Rosenzweig, Martin Buber, Hermann Cohen, and the Marburg neo-Kantians. Salanter, too, felt Kant's influence. What appealed to him most was Kant's "ethics via logic."

The will to base ethics upon logic had also been evident among earlier Jewish teachers of ethics and among Torah commentators, but these had run into difficulties in trying to give a concrete, rational underpinning for metaphysical beliefs. Even Maimonides found this impossible. Faith could not be equated with reason, since faith operated beyond reason's boundaries. Nevertheless, attempts were always made to bridge the unbridgeable, to bring faith within the realm of reason by means of deductive propositions and logical speculations.

As early as the tenth century, Saadia Gaon in his *Emunot Vedeot (Beliefs and Opinions)* and, somewhat later, Rabbi Bahya in *Hobot Halebabot* held that man's pride would not let him accept his inability to widen the domain of conscious cognition. It was the tendency to evil within man – "yetzer hara" – that tried to stop him from penetrating to truth and from searching it out to its furthest reaches. In other words, man could attain to faith via reason. Similarly, the author of *Mesillat Yesharim* stated that through understanding one attained the awe of God. After quoting Job that "awe of God is wisdom," he added that a person who reflected deeply would come to the conclusion that true piety went hand in hand with understanding.

The goals of Israel Salanter's *Musar* are summed up in the titles of the three principal works of Hermann Cohen: "Logik der reinen Erkenntnis, Ethik des reinen Willens, Aesthetik des reinen Gefühls." For "reine[n] Erkenntnis" (pure understanding), Salanter would have substituted "Godhood."

Salanter's interest in Kant stemmed from intellectual affinity. Emil Benjamin, his biographer and disciple, mentioned that Salanter begged him, when in Memel, to get hold of Kant's *Critique of Pure Reason*, "because I need it urgently"; Salanter resided for many years in Königsberg, Kant's city, and both found their final resting place there.

III

There is a saying: "People who can manage people manage people, who can only manage things." Salanter who was born in 1810, belongs to those rare personalities who create movements. He had all the talents of a manager of people. He could fascinate them, organize them, give them a goal, and show them how to reach up to it. The first requirement for launching a successful movement is to have a charismatic leader who can attract followers and inspire them. Salanter was such a leader. Disciples flocked to him, wherever he settled, and were profoundly influenced by him. Young men – intelligent, talented, poor, dissatisfied, and above all hungry for knowledge –

constituted perfect material with which to forge a new movement. Salanter educated them. He was their friend and gave directions to their lives. He knew which of them to select, which to draw near, and which to keep at a distance. There were times when he kept even his best pupils at at distance, and somehow they then felt closer to him. He possessed pedagogical talents and psychological insight. He recognized the special capabilities of each of his pupils, and he guided them to make use of these capabilities.

His disciples adored him, surrounded him with affection, and tried to imitate him. Twelve stood out among them. They were Isaac Blaser, Simcha Zissel Ziv, Naphtali Amsterdam, Zvi Finkel, Eliezer Shulewitz, Eliezer Gordon, Zvi Levitan, Jacob Joseph, Joshua Heller, Moshe Isaac Darshan, Alexander Moshe Lapidot, and Shneur Zalman Hishowitz. All later occupied influential positions. They, too, were excellent organizers and were imbued with the missionary zeal needed by initiators of movements. They became the principal emissaries who disseminated the doctrines of *Musar* and the fame of its inspirer. The first seven of the aforementioned twelve disciples founded *yeshivot* and devoted their lives to educate young students. The other five were writers and orators, among the best of their generation. Soon they too found themselves surrounded by pupils who worshipped them. Among the original twelve, the outstanding educator was Rabbi Simcha Zissel Ziv in Kelem. A generation later, there were still several rabbis who had come, to some extent, under Salanter's direct influence. They included such famed scholars as Rabbi Joseph Leib Bloch, who headed the Teltz Yeshiva; Rabbi Issar Zalman Meltzer and Rabbi Moshe Mordecai Epstein, both of whom headed the Slobodka Yeshiva; Rabbi Joseph Yoizel Hurwitz, the founder and head of the Novarodiker *yeshivot*, which branched off from Salanter's mainstream; Rabbi Naphtali Trop, who headed the Radin Yeshiva; and Rabbi Aaron Bakst, who was active at first in Lomzhe and later in Shavel. These and other disciples of Salanter, who were either his own pupils or the pupils of his pupils, succeeded in a relatively short time to found and consolidate famed *yeshivot*, unparalleled since the Babylonian academies of more than a thousand years earlier. They followed in the footsteps of Salanter. *They taught Musar*. Theirs was the glorious climax of Torah learning in

Eastern Europe. Today's great *yeshivot* in Israel and the diaspora are, in general, continuations of that era.

IV

Opposing wills were merged in Rabbi Israel Salanter. Antithetical forces found a synthesis. On the one hand, his profound, poetic nature sought stillness and seclusion. On the other hand, he was attracted to large cities, communal activities, the tumult of crowds, and the excitement of talk. These contradictions surfaced in his own teaching and among his disciples. In the *yeshivot, Musar* was studied in semi-darkness during twilight hours, in solitude and silent meditation, encouraging introspection to cleanse the mind and purify the heart. At the same time, there were also among the *Musarniks* personalities of passionate temperament, fanatical in their opinions, vigorous in their expressions – resolute characters who did not slink away from the alarm and commotion of the world's highways. Encouraged by their mentor, they set out on these highways. They occupied rabbinical pulpits in large communities beyond the Pale, including St. Petersburg, Helsingfors, Minsk, Moscow, and even New York.

In creating a movement, it is helpful if disciples have a vocabulary of their own – words, phrases, and gestures that take on special meaning, or behaviour patterns that confer uniqueness upon the group and that hold it together. *Musar* created such a vocabulary of new words or old words with new meaning. When young men gathered to study *Musar* together, they were called a *havura* or *vaad* (group). The lectures of their leader were designated as *shmuesn* (chats). *Bourse* was the expression used when members moved about, exchanging their "currencies": profits and losses in good deeds and moral achievements.

A movement is also held together by songs and melodies, sometimes even more solidly than by the ideas and principles with which it started. *Musar* was studied with its own intonation, a sing-song as melancholy as the Lithuanian landscape, a special kind of melody that filled the heart with subtle yearning.

New movements often want to appeal to the sentimental feelings of women. Salanter, the born leader, did not overlook this possibility. In a letter of 1849 addressed to the Vilna community, he suggested that *Musar* groups should gather on Sabbaths and study the improvement of morals, emphasizing man's good inclinations and rebuking his evil ones. He then added that the leaders of these study hours should talk quietly, avoiding harsh threats, and should also teach women ethical behaviour. This inclusion of women was at the time a great innovation.

Salanter was not a writer and he did not want to be one. This, too, is characteristic of many creators of movements. They are often reluctant to record their thoughts in books and thus give them a stamp of permanency, before they have ripened completely. They feel that it is far better to wait for thoughts to be tested by life's experiences and to let later successors record them and give them permanent form. During his lifetime Salanter penned only two essays for his weekly journal *Hitbona*, five leaflets, an *Epistle* on *Musar*, and a few select sayings. His letters to his students are brief and leave room for interpretation.

Salanter was perpetually on the move, wandering from town to town. This is a common trait of innovators, who want to bring their ideas to the people and who have the talent to organize movements. Restlessness drives such energetic missionary leaders to seek followers and to unleash the creative forces fermenting in them. Salanter did not tarry long with his disciples in the Lithuanian *yeshivot* which he built up as nests of *Musar*. He wandered on to Memel, Königsberg, Berlin, Frankfurt, and Paris. He wanted to establish centers of *Musar* in communities in which Jewishness was weak and declining. However, there may also have been a psychological reason for his peregrinations, for his running away from his familiar environment. His was a restless personality, such as is not uncommon among powerful characters.

Salanter did not reveal himself entirely even to his closest students. There was always a corner of his soul into which he would not let any of them peer. His pupil, Rabbi Simcha Zissel Ziv, wrote in a letter: "He is always remaining mysterious and enigmatic, and that's why only very, very few know what very, very little of him is known."

Salanter's contemporaries were often astonished at his strange behaviour and unanticipated actions. This same person, who was so meticulous in carrying out every detail of the religious requirements, stood up in the Vilna synagogue on Yom Kippur, the day of fasting, and ate in the presence of the entire congregation. A plague was raging in the town. Lives had to be saved. Salanter acted in accordance with a religious injunction – that the saving of lives must be given precedence, even if this involves breaking the fast on the holiest day of the year. However, he was not the officially designated rabbi of Vilna. He did not bear responsibility for the community. It was not proper for an individual to do such a thing on his own, since there were constituted authorities. They were able to make such decisions for the Jews of a town, when an emergency occured. Nevertheless, Salanter dared to act on his own. No wonder that his sensational abrogation of the fast aroused consternation and met with the disapproval of rabbis and ordinary people. Yet, this very deed was acclaimed enthusiastically by men of Enlightenment, who saw in Salanter an ally, a liberal, a progressive leader who eased religious proscriptions. They were ready to nominate him to head their projected academy. When Salanter learned of this plan, he left Vilna. The rumours that spread his pronouncements and behaviour linked him with social and cultural reforms, which jeopardized accepted traditions. He is said to have opposed vigorously the communal leaders of Salant, when these helped the "Khapers," official military recruiters, to seize the child of a poor widow and impress him into army service, in order to fill the doubled quota imposed upon Jews by Czar Nicholas I and thereby to save a child of their own from such service. Salanter refused to pray together with leaders who perpetrated this crime.

Salanter sent his pupils into shops to inspect the scales and to make sure that the weights and measures were accurate. He constantly inveighed against the sin of deceiving customers. He encouraged Jewish youngsters to learn the languages of their non-Jewish neighbors and to learn a handicraft. In his later years, he conceived the idea of having the Talmud translated into French. He was refined in his manners and conduct. He dressed immaculately. The *Maskilim,* therefore, wrote about him with great respect. For example, Nahum

Sokolow extolled him. Rabbi Israel Salanter, however, was less interested in social reform and cultural change than in the moral improvements of individuals in accordance with the Torah.

V

Musar was not systematized. It did not develop into a separate sect. While there were revolutionary sparks in the *Musar* movement, these never kindled a conflagration, because *Musar* lacked the national impulse, the Messianic longing, the fervent striving for redemption, which characterized post-exilic Jewish movements. Because of this lack, Musar could not penetrate to the masses. The emphasis on personal betterment could influence select individuals, but was not needed by the humiliated and the impoverished, the insulted and the injured, the suffering Jews enduring the hardships of their protracted exile. Contemplating Salanter's era from the vantage point of later experiences and the Holocaust, we may wonder whether a movement for a moral elite was really needed by Jews enduring political oppression, social degradation, and legal discrimination. Such an elite was an artificial creation and not a natural evolution. Therefore, *Musar* was only moderately successful. Salanter's social and ethical doctrines, his aesthetic, philosophic, and secular innovations stemmed from his own struggles to attain clarity. *Musar*'s principal achievement, the founding of *yeshivot*, arose from the need of the time and milieu. With its call to live in accordance with the laws of the Torah, *Musar* brought light, warmth, and fresh air into humble Jewish homes. It did not improve the Jewish condition in Lithuania, but it did bring spiritual nobility to its adherents and disciples.

Musar began quietly and calmly, in consonance with the quiet, calm landscape through which the Nieman flows. Along the banks of this river, near Kovno, the first *havura* of students came together. Salanter sat in his lonely garret, surrounded by a few pupils, each immersed in his own thoughts, each engaged in taking stock of his own moral character, each striving to ennoble himself with more refined virtues.

As *Musar* began, so it continued in its own unsensational growth. It never became a mass movement like Hassidism. Its philosophy dictated that it remain an elite fraternity. Hassidism came with an appeal to the masses and brought them joy and comfort. *Musar* sought out the individual. Hassidism proclaimed that even a crowded tavern could serve as a house of God. For the *Musarniks*, a synagogue was already too loud. Its small anteroom was quieter, a garret more so and better suited for introspection, for communion with one's soul.

Salanter once said he loved the smaller deed of goodness, provided that the deed was beautiful. Such a saying sufficed to erect a barrier to keep the masses at a distance. One had to have a certain personality to be a beginner in *Musar*. An idea based on idealistic rationalism could not penetrate to the common folk, even though *Musar* had some folk elements. The teachers of *Musar* dressed modestly, unassumingly, like other ordinary Jews. Despite their apparent asceticism, they did become involved in communal affairs. Salanter wanted to publish a dictionary of the Talmud in Yiddish in order to make it more easily accessible to the less learned. His urging that the Talmud be translated into French stemmed from his desire to further non-Jewish understanding of Jews. He edited a Hebrew weekly, *Tvuna*. He agitated for productive, physical labor. The *Musarniks* he inspired separated themselves temporarily from the world, in order to return to it purified as a result of their silent introversion. They were not hermits. They did not seek to escape from reality. They rather contemplated reality as might a wise, compassionate person, who stands upon a balcony and looks out upon a noisy street. They lived simply and their admiration for God's wonderful creation was unlimited. They did not retreat from the world, but only from worldliness. They did not yearn for material luxuries. They were satisfied with little, because they held, like Goethe, that pleasures debase.

With the passage of time and with changes in environmental conditions, movements tend to develop along lines not envisaged by the founders. Within its limited circles, *Musar* too branched off in directions far removed from the mainstream in which Salanter's thought had flowed. *Musar* groups arose that carried rejection of worldliness to a fanatical extreme. They engaged in self-deprecation and asceticism. Instead of being satisfied with modest, unostentatious living, they practiced self-castigation. Instead of merely avoiding to strive for honor, they went out of their way to suppress their feeling for honor; they provoked humiliations (thereby really emphasizing their own superiority). Instead of elevating themselves to a pure, noble life in society, they united in ascetic fellowships that negated society and repudiated secular interests. In Lithuania, however, the movement remained largely faithful to the directions outlined by Salanter and it repudiated fanatical aberrations.

Musar was a limited movement. It did not really expand much, remaining mostly within the closed orbit of the borders of Lithuania. It did not generate an extensive literature as did Hassidism, which has to its credit voluminous, magnificent works. Later came the destruction that wiped out the centers of *Musar*, which had been nurtured by four generations of fervent adherents. The pupils of the Kelem Musar school went singing to their common death, still believing in the triumph of justice, light, and goodness. *Musar* arose out of the deepest moral wellsprings of Judaism. It was a genuine Jewish-Lithuanian movement, the only Torah movement indigenous to the character of the so-called "Litvak."

Contributors

Jeffrey B. Berlin, Office of Admissions, Philadelphia College of Textiles and Science, Philadelphia, PA 19144

Jonathan Boyarin, 141 E. 3rd St. Apt. 3D, New York, NY 10009

Harold Fisch, Institute for Literary Research, Bar-Ilan University, Ramat Gan 52100

Noam Flinker, Dept. of Foreign Literatures & Linguistics, Ben-Gurion University, Beersheva 84105

Esther Fuchs, Dept. of Oriental Studies, University of Arizona, Tucson, AZ 85721

Tsili Dolève-Gandelman and Claude Gandelman, French Dept., University of Haifa, Mt. Carmel, Haifa 31999

Mark H. Gelber, Dept. of Foreign Literatures & Linguistics, Ben-Gurion University, Beersheva 84105

Milton Hindus, 24 Stiles Terrace, Newton Centre, MA 02159

Jacob Kabakoff, 40 Winslow Rd., White Plains, NY 10606

Lothar Kahn, Dept. of Modern Languages, Central Connecticut State University, New Britain, CT 06050

Ludwig W. Kahn, 9 Atherstone Rd., Scarsdale, NY 10583

Nancy A. Kaiser, German Dept., University of Wisconsin-Madison, Madison, WI 53706

Dovid Katz, Oxford Center for Postgraduate Hebrew Studies, Oxford, 0X1 3LW

Richard H. Lawson, 8816 Jackie Dr., San Diego, CA 92119

Joseph Lowin, 20 Sands Point Rd., Monsey, NY 10952

Stéphane Moses, German Dept., Hebrew University-Mt. Scopus, Jerusalem 91905

Zelda Kahan Newman, Rehov Hechalutz 38, Beersheva 84215

Dinnah Pladott, English Department, University of Tel Aviv, Ramat Aviv 69978

Jeffrey L. Sammons, German Dept., Box 18-A Yale Station, New Haven, CT 06520

Gershon Shaked, Dept. of Hebrew Literature, Hebrew University-Mt. Scopus, Jerusalem 91905

Levi Shalit, African Jewish Newspaper, P.O.B. 6169, Johannesburg 2000

Efraim Shmueli, Rehov Bialik 16, Haifa 34407

Harry Zohn, German Dept., Brandeis University, Waltham, MA 02254

Tabula Gratulatoria

Samuel Abrahamsen
New York

Julius Axelrod
Rockville

Murray Baumgarten
Santa Cruz

Benjamin Bender
Brooklyn

Anne & Jeffrey Berlin
Philadelphia

Abe Bernstein
Livingston

Laszlo Biro
Brooklyn

Thomas E. Bird
Little Neck

Bernhardt Blumenthal
Philadelphia

Dani Brecher
Jerusalem

Gisela Brude-Firnau
Waterloo

Saul & Sybil Cherniak –
in memory of Alter Cherniak
Winnipeg

Naomi M. Coval-Apel
Glen Cove

Horst S. Daemmrich
Philadelphia

Helmut Dinse
Varel

Rabbi Reuven & Hilary Drucker
Southfield

Louis Dubb
Port Elizabeth

Mattityahu Elat
Beersheva

Yehuda Elberg
Montreal

Esther N. Elstun
Fairfax

Sol Feinman
Teaneck

Ralph Flax
Southbury

Noam Flinker
Beersheva

Nathan J. Friedman
San Francisco

Esther Fuchs
Tucson

David S. Galton
New York

Samuel Gartner
Bronx

Jody & Mark Gelber
Beersheva/Omer

Rabbi Leonard & Gladys Gewirtz
Wilmington

Sol Gittleman
Medford

Samuel H. Givelber
Beachwood

Yosef Gordon
Middletown

Dr. & Mrs. Oscar Green
New York

Anna Grossman
North Miami Beach

Nathan Grossman
Brooklyn

Klaus Haberkamm
Münster

Martha Liptzin Hauptman
Lexington

Claude Hill
Rutgers

Milton Hindus
Newton Centre

Rivka Horwitz
Beersheva

Herbert Hubert
Evanston

Stella & Jack Jagoda
New York

Morris S. & Bernice Jacobs
Oakland

Alice L. Kahler
Princeton

Ludwig W. Kahn
Scarsdale

Nancy A. Kaiser
Madison

Lotte Kohler
New York

Morris Laub
Berkeley

Richard H. Lawson
San Diego

Hyman Lebowitz
Bayonne

Marvin & Elisabeth Levy
Philadelphia

William C. Levy
New York

Otto M. Lilien
Rehovot

Erwin Lindenfeld
North Syracuse

Leopold Lippman
Teaneck

Mollie Liptzin
Riverdale

Myron B. Liptzin
Chapel Hill

Rav & Mrs. Israel Loewenstein
Rechavia

Dr. Joshua & Yelva Lynfield
Cedarhurst

Kurt L. Maschler
London

Percy Matenko
Brooklyn

Stanley Meisler
Paris

Alexander E. Messer
Oneonta

Mr. & Mrs. Herbert Millman
Rye

Rosalyn & Louis Morgenbesser
Bayside

Howard Needler
New Haven

Mr. & Mrs. Sol Patsiner
Bronx

Benjamin Phelosof
Rochester

Arthur Pillersdorf
Aberdeen

Donald A. Prater
Gingins

Mrs. Oskar K. Rabinowicz
Scarsdale

Henry H.H. Remak
Bloomington

Ernst Rose
New York

Joseph & Doris Rosen
Plainview

David & Dorothy Rothbart
Pittsburgh

Eli Rotschild
Tel Aviv

Eli Sagan
New York

Ismar Schorsch
New York

Ida C. Selavan
Cincinnati

Saul Shapiro
Montreal

Chaim Shoham
Haifa

Franz & Stefanie Sischka
Leinfelden-Echterdingen

Ron Sitton
Jerusalem

Gil Sitton
Jerusalem

Shira Sitton
Jerusalem

Samuel L. Sobel
Bronx

Joseph Soffen
Philadelphia

Manfred Stassen
Bad Godesberg/New York

S.L. Sumberg
New York

Nathan Süsskind
Elmhurst

Samuel Schneider
New York

Helmut Scholz
Stuttgart

Dr. & Mrs. Solomon Schwartz
Berwyn

Joseph P. Strelka
Albany

Pearl Thomas
Rancho Palos Verdes

Judith & Ron Tierney
Bethany

Ilan Troen
Sde Boker

Daniel Walden
University Park

Irving & Fran Waltman
West Hartford

Isidore Warshawsky
Cleveland

Seymour S. Weiner
Amherst

Michael Weingarten
New York

Freed Weininger
Tel Aviv

David Weiss
Montreal

Walter Wertheimer
Andover

Israel Wiener
Southfield

Mel B. Yoken
New Bedford

Helen D. Zank
West Palm Beach

Edmund (Pennant) Zaslow
Bayside

Harry Zohn
West Newton

* * *

Alumni Association of City College
New York

Austrian Embassy
Tel Aviv

Bar-Ilan University
Ramat-Gan

Ben-Gurion University of the Negev
Beersheva

Bibliothek der Kirchlichen Hochschule
Wuppertal-Barmen

Central Connecticut State University
New Britain

Germania Judaica
Köln

Jewish National and University Library
Jerusalem

Kibbutz Gezer
Emek Ha-ayalon

Library of the American Jewish Committee
Jerusalem

National Yiddish Book Center
Amherst

Oberlin College Library
Oberlin

Rodef Shalom Congregation
Pittsburgh

Rutgers University
Dept. of Germanic Languages and Literatures

State University of New York
Buffalo

Universitätsbibliothek
Freiburg i. Br.

University of Arizona Library
Tucson

University of London
Institute of Germanic Studies

Yale University Germanic Seminar
New Haven

Yivo Institute for Jewish Research
New York

Zentralbibliothek
Zürich